T0235392

Communications
in Computer and Information Science 579

Commenced Publication in 2007
Founding and Former Series Editors:
Alfredo Cuzzocrea, Dominik Ślęzak, and Xiaokang Yang

More information about this series at http://www.springer.com/series/7899

Markus Helfert · Karl-Heinz Krempels
Cornel Klein · Brian Donnellan
Oleg Gusikhin (Eds.)

Smart Cities, Green Technologies, and Intelligent Transport Systems

4th International Conference, SMARTGREENS 2015
and 1st International Conference VEHITS 2015
Lisbon, Portugal, May 20–22, 2015
Revised Selected Papers

 Springer

Editors

Markus Helfert
School of Computing
Dublin City University
Dublin
Ireland

Karl-Heinz Krempels
RWTH Aachen University
Aachen
Germany

Cornel Klein
Siemens Corporate Technology
Munich, Bayern
Germany

Brian Donnellan
Maynooth University
Maynooth, Kildare
Ireland

Oleg Gusikhin
Ford Research and Engineering
Detroit, MI
USA

ISSN 1865-0929   ISSN 1865-0937 (electronic)
Communications in Computer and Information Science
ISBN 978-3-319-27752-3   ISBN 978-3-319-27753-0 (eBook)
DOI 10.1007/978-3-319-27753-0

Library of Congress Control Number: 2015957093

Printed on acid-free paper

This Springer imprint is published by SpringerNature
The registered company is Springer International Publishing AG Switzerland

Preface

This book includes extended and revised versions of a set of selected papers from SMARTGREENS 2015 (4th International Conference on Smart Cities and Green ICT Systems) and VEHITS 2015 (First International Conference on Vehicle Technology and Intelligent Transport Systems), held in Lisbon, Portugal, during May 20–22, 2015, sponsored by the Institute for Systems and Technologies of Information, Control and Communication (INSTICC). The SMARTGREENS and VEHITS conferences were held in cooperation with the Lisbon City Council, INTELI and Lisboa E-Nova, Turismo de Lisboa, and CEIIA. Moreover, SMARTGREENS was also technically co-sponsored by IEEE PES – IEEE Power and Energy Society—and held in cooperation with the Association for Computing Machinery – SIGCAS, IEEE Technical Area in Green Computing, GCC – IEEE Technical SubCommittee on Green Communications and Computing, Friends of the Supergrid, and NESUS – Network for Sustainable Ultrascale Computing.

We hope that this book, which includes topics such as "Smart Cities," "Energy-Aware Systems and Technologies," "Sustainable Computing and Communications," and "Sustainable Transportation and Smart Mobility," will interest a global audience of engineers, scientists, and business people working in areas related to the research topics of SMARTGREENS and VEHITS.

SMARTGREENS 2015 received 73 paper submissions from all continents. From these, 15 papers were selected and presented as full papers (30' oral presentation), leading to a full-paper acceptance ratio of about 21 %.

VEHITS 2015 received 27 paper submissions from 17 countries in all continents. From these, three papers were selected and presented as full papers (30' oral presentation), leading to a full-paper acceptance ratio of about 11 %.

The papers included in this book were selected from those with the best reviews, also taking into account the quality of their presentation at both conferences, as assessed by the session chairs. We hope that you find these papers interesting, and we trust they will represent a helpful reference for all those who need to address any of the aforementioned research areas.

We wish to thank all those who supported and helped to organize both conferences. On behalf of the conference Organizing Committee, we would like to thank the authors, whose work mostly contributed to a very successful conference, and the members of the Program Committee, whose expertise and diligence were instrumental in ensuring the quality of the final contributions. We also wish to thank all the members of the Organizing Committee, whose work and commitment was invaluable. Last but not least, we would like to thank Springer for their collaboration in getting this book to print.

September 2015

Markus Helfert
Karl-Heinz Krempels
Cornel Klein
Brian Donnellan
Oleg Gusikhin

Organization

SMARTGREENS Conference Co-chairs

Markus Helfert	Dublin City University, Ireland
Karl-Heinz Krempels	RWTH Aachen University, Germany

SMARTGREENS Program Co-chairs

Cornel Klein	Siemens AG, Germany
Brian Donnellan	National University of Ireland, Maynooth, Ireland

SMARTGREENS Program Committee

Javier M. Aguiar	Universidad de Valladolid, Spain
Jorge Barbosa	FEUP, Portugal
Siegfried Benkner	University of Vienna, Austria
Dumitru Burdescu	University of Craiova, Romania
Rodrigo Calheiros	The University of Melbourne, Australia
Blanca Caminero	Universidad de Castilla-La Mancha, Spain
Olivier Camp	MODESTE/ESEO, France
Davide Careglio	Universitat Politècnica de Catalunya, Spain
Jian-Jia Chen	Karlsruhe Institute of Technology, Germany
Yeh-Ching Chung	National Tsing Hua University, Taiwan
Bruno Ciciani	University of Rome La Sapienza, Italy
Calin Ciufudean	Stefan cel Mare University, Romania
José Cordeiro	E.S.T. Setúbal, I.P.S, Portugal
Georges Da Costa	IRIT, Paul Sabatier University, France
Amélie Coulbaut-Lazzarini	Université Versailles Saint Quentin en Yvelines, France
Brian Donnellan	National University of Ireland, Maynooth, Ireland
Erik Elmroth	Umeå University and Elastisys AB, Sweden
Vincent Freeh	North Carolina State University, USA
Rong Ge	Marquette University, USA
Hamid Gharavi	National Institute of Standards and Technology, USA
Muhammad Hasan	Texas A&M University, USA
Peer Hasselmeyer	NEC Europe Ltd., Germany
Nikos Hatziargyriou	National Technical University, Greece
Ligang He	University of Warwick, UK
Seongsoo Hong	Seoul National University, Republic of Korea
Filip Idzikowski	Poznan University of Technology, Poland
Pertti Järventausta	Tampere University of Technology, Finland
Yingtao Jiang	University of Nevada las Vegas, USA

Stamatis Karnouskos	SAP, Germany
Mohammed G. Khatib	NEC Laboratories America, USA
Seong-Cheol Kim	Seoul National University, Republic of Korea
W.L. Kling	TU Eindhoven, The Netherlands
Mani Krishna	University of Massachusetts Amherst, USA
Craig Lee	The Aerospace Corporation, USA
Marco Listanti	University of Rome La Sapienza, Italy
Shaobo Liu	Marvell Semiconductor, INC, USA
Thomas Ludwig	University of Hamburg, Germany
Jukka Manner	Aalto University, Finland
Ningfang Mi	Northeastern University, USA
Toan Nguyen	Inria, France
Andreas Pfeiffer	Hubject GmbH - joint venture of BMW Group, Bosch, Daimler, EnBW, RWE and Siemens, Germany
Vitor Pires	Escola Superior de Tecnologia de Setúbal - IPS, Portugal
Pierluigi Plebani	Politecnico Di Milano, Italy
Radu Prodan	University of Innsbruck, Austria
Milan Prodanovic	Instituto Imdea Energía, Spain
Gang Quan	Florida International University, USA
Eva González Romera	University of Extremadura, Spain
Enrique Romero-Cadaval	University of Extremadura, Spain
Bo Sheng	University of Massachusetts Boston, USA
Norvald Stol	NTNU, Norway
Ryszard Strzelecki	Gdynia Maritime University, Poland
Dan Keun Sung	Korea Advanced Institute of Science and Technology, Republic of Korea
Afshin Tafazzoli	Abengoa, Spain
Paolo Tenti	University of Padova, Italy
Dimitrios Tsoumakos	Ionian University, Greece
Jorge Vasconcelos	NEWES, New Energy Solutions, Portugal
Shengquan Wang	University of Michigan-Dearborn, USA
Alex Weddell	University of Southampton, UK
Igor Wojnicki	AGH University of Science and Technology, Poland
Yinlong Xu	University of Science and Technology of China, China
Qi Yu	Rochester Institute of Technology, USA
Chau Yuen	Singapore University of Technology and Design, Singapore
Rongliang Zhou	HP Labs, Palo Alto, USA
Yayun Zhou	Siemens AG, Germany
Sotirios Ziavras	New Jersey Institute of Technology, USA

SMARTGREENS Additional Reviewers

Jiri Dokulil	University of Vienna, Austria
Onur Ergin	Technical University of Berlin, Germany
Thomas Menzel	TKN TU Berlin, Germany

SMARTGREENS Invited Speakers

Álvaro Oliveira	Alfamicro, Portugal
Paolo Traverso	Center for Information Technology - IRST (FBK-ICT), Italy
Rudolf Giffinger	Vienna University of Technology, Austria
Andrés Monzón	Universidad Politecnica de Madrid, Spain
Alberto Broggi	VisLab - Università di Parma, Italy

VEHITS Conference Chair

Oleg Gusikhin	Ford Research and Advanced Engineering, USA

VEHITS Program Chair

Markus Helfert	Dublin City University, Ireland

VEHITS Program Committee

Mohamed Benbouzid	University of Brest, France
Sandford Bessler	Research Telecommunications Centre (ftw.), Austria
Ghulam H. Bham	University of Alaska, USA
Brian Caulfield	Trinity College Dublin, Ireland
Federico Cheli	Politecnico di Milano, Italy
Gihwan Cho	Chonbuk University, Republic of Korea
Seibum Choi	Korea Advanced Institute of Science and Technology, Republic of Korea
Tiago Lopes Farias	Universidade Tecnica de Lisboa, Portugal
Lino Figueiredo	ISEP - Instituto Superior de Engenharia do Porto, Portugal
Fernando García	Intelligent Systems Lab., Universidad Carlos III, Spain
Luigi Glielmo	Università del Sannio in Benevento, Italy
Kayhan Gulez	Yildiz Technical University, Turkey
Oleg Gusikhin	Ford Research and Advanced Engineering, USA
Kingsley E. Haynes	George Mason University, USA
Yoichi Hori	University of Tokyo, Japan
Toshiyuki Inagaki	University of Tsukuba, Japan
Xiangjie Kong	Dalian University of Technology, China
Milan Krbálek	Czech Technical University, Czech Republic
Wei Liu	Ecole Polytechnique Fédérale de Lausanne, Switzerland
Gabriel Lodewijks	Delft University of Technology, The Netherlands
Reinhard Mahnke	University of Rostock, Germany
Lyudmila Mihaylova	University of Sheffield, UK

Marta Molinas	Norwegian University of Science and Technology, Norway
Pedro Moura	Institute of Systems and Robotics - University of Coimbra, Portugal
Katsuhiro Nishinari	University of Tokyo, Japan
Carolina Osorio	Massachusetts Institute of Technology, USA
Markos Papageorgiou	Technical University of Crete, Greece
Brian Park	University of Virginia, USA
Jin Peng	Tsinghua University, China
Claudio Roncoli	Technical University of Crete, Greece
Carla Silva	Instituto Superior Técnico, Portugal
Uwe Stilla	Technische Universität München, Germany
Wencong Su	University of Michigan-Dearborn, USA
Tomer Toledo	Technion - Israel Institute of Technology, Israel
Esko Turunen	Tampere University of Technology, Finland
Peter Vortisch	Karlsruhe Institute of Technology, Germany
Peng Zhang	Shangai University, China
Hengbing Zhao	UC Davis, USA

VEHITS Invited Speakers

Karsten Berns	University of Kaiserslautern, Germany
Cornel Klein	Siemens AG, Germany
António Pascoal	Instituto Superior Técnico, Portugal
Alberto Broggi	VisLab - Università di Parma, Italy

Contents

Vehicle Technology and Intelligent Transport Systems

Invited Papers

Smart City Concepts: Chances and Risks of Energy Efficient Urban Development

Rudolf Giffinger[✉]

Centre of Regional Science, Department of Spatial Planning, TU Wien, Vienna, Austria
rudolf.giffinger@tuwien.ac.at

Abstract. On the background of globalisation and climate change discussions about urban development are increasingly concentrating on economic performance and positioning as well as issues of social polarization and environmental conditions. As such trends are in particular affecting urban development attention is focusing on the question how cities might meet challenges of improved quality of life, energy efficiency and sustainable development, but also of improved urban competitiveness in an interregional and even global context.

Due to these trends and challenges the idea of a Smart City concept emerged and has been widely discussed. However, looking on this discussion (and respective strategic efforts) one can easily detect the different understandings which are more or less directly related to the question 'How can cities use and implement technical innovations in the urban fabric?'.

Facing these trends this paper will deal with following questions: Which meaning do innovations have in the different Smart City approaches? What are the impacts of different understandings? Why does the place based understanding of Smart City strengthen a sustainable development?.

Dealing with these questions the contribution gives an overview about the understanding of the Smart City idea and the differences existing across specific approaches. Then, chances and risks regarding energy efficient urban developments are worked out. Finally, the contribution will conclude with specific suggestions of a place based understanding of Smart City initiatives from the point of view of strategic planning.

Keywords: Smart city · Place based understanding · Urban innovation · Integrative approach

1 Introduction

Growing world population and increasingly globalized economic activities are accompanied by a strong growth of energy consumption. These trends are provoking emissions and environmental problems and quality of life is endangered in many countries and regions. In front of these trends there is a comprehensive discussion on how to meet respective challenges and on how to foster sustainability on global, national and local level [1]. Despite intensive discussions and specific political agreements since 25 years manifold recent problematic trends demonstrate the relative weak effective efforts

© Springer International Publishing Switzerland 2015
M. Helfert et al. (Eds.): Smartgreens 2015 and Vehits 2015, CCIS 579, pp. 3–16, 2015.
DOI: 10.1007/978-3-319-27753-0_1

strengthening the sustainable development and trying to meet economic, social and environmental challenges. Nowadays, the discussion of sustainable urban development underpins in particular that we should understand sustainability in the local socioeconomic and environmental context and as a process in a forward looking way. Above all, the social consensus in terms of freedom, equality and social inclusion in strategic activities on community level and the choice options for future generations are emphasized [2, 3].

Since some years it has become obvious that processes of urbanisation are strongly linked with problematic challenges of energy production and consumption and – as a consequence – of emissions of greenhouse gases (GHG) across many countries. Hence, cities and urban agglomerations where more than 50 % of world population is living are coming into the main focus of strategic discussion [4]. As the majority of world energy consumption is concentrated in urban agglomerations, not surprisingly, cities are regarded as main drivers of economic development on the one side but also as crucial drivers of emissions combined with environmental problems on the other side [5]. Along with these facts new technology resp. technical innovations are discussed as crucial factors for transforming energy provision towards renewable energy sources and in particular for improving energy efficiency in urban development. Besides the European Strategy 2020 but also national strategies and local strategies cities are aiming to provide better living conditions and enabling 'a better life' for citizens through the implementation of information and communication technologies (ICT) and other forms of technical innovations. Along with this discussion the term 'Smart City' has become rather prominent.

Following questions have to be dealt with: Which meaning do innovations have in the different Smart City approaches? What are the impacts of different understandings? Why does the place based understanding of Smart City strengthen a sustainable development?

This contribution will show that a place based understanding of the Smart City is a precondition for urban energy efficiency supporting its sustainable development. Doing so, the contribution first introduces into the general impact of urbanisation on emissions and thus shows the importance of cities as actors in these efforts for 'a better life'. Then, it discusses specific approaches of Smart City and outlines the differences between a technical and data driven understanding against a place based understanding. Along with this discussion it is elaborated why the idea of technical innovations as problem solving instrument has to be replaced by the concept of Smart City initiatives which produce urban innovations as outcomes of social learning processes. Hence, it outlines that different to technical innovation a more comprehensive understanding of innovation in the urban context is needed.

2   Energy Efficient Development as a Challenge for Cities

The world supply of energy (TPES – total primary energy supply) is increasing since some decades. In 2012 supply of 13.371 Mtoe (million tonnes) is more than 200 % of supply from 1973, the year of the first oil crises [6]. The enormous increase is not continuous but dependent on global economic development: Energy supply is slightly decreasing along with economic and financial crises in the early 1980ies as well as in the years 2007 to 2010. In comparison of groups of countries, the strongest absolute increase of TPES took place in China and other Asian countries as well as in the OECD-countries whereby the share on global supply of the latter group of countries is decreasing.

The relation between economic wealth (GDP in terms of PPP$ inflation-adjusted per capita) and intensity of CO_2 – emissions (CO_2 kg per year related to the country's respective economic performance) provides in comparison of countries the following evidence for the year 2008 [7]: First, there is a relative strong relation between economic wealth and the intensity of CO_2 – emissions. Countries with increased level of economic wealth are able to keep intensity of emissions comparatively low. Second, outliers of this relation are countries like China, Russia or India as well as some Eastern European countries. They indicate relative high intensity of CO_2 – emissions although economic wealth is not as high as in other countries. Third, the absolute amount of CO_2 – emissions (in 1000 tonnes per year) is a result of the country's size but also of the technical standards of respective national economic activities. China, USA, India and Russia show largest amount of yearly CO_2 – emissions.

Obviously, in countries of Western, Southern and Central Europe, USA and Canada as well as some few urban states in Asia environmental regulations as wells as corresponding technical innovations had improved remarkably so that economic wealth is already combined with low intensities of CO_2 – emissions. Economic wealth is more or less decoupled from increase of emission intensity because of relative high environmental norms and more energy efficient economic activities based on relative new technologies.

For the year 2008 Fig. 1 [8] convincingly demonstrates the strong relation between the intensity of urbanisation (urban population in % of total) and the level of economic wealth (income per person: GDP per capita; GDP in PPP $). Most of the countries are characterized through the trend that the increased urbanisation is combined with increased economic wealth levels. However, a small group of countries from different world regions (outliers) show relative to the level of wealth a very low urbanisation level. Furthermore, another small group of countries indicates, relative to the level of wealth, a very high urbanisation level. Besides, this trend is related with the intensity of CO_2 – emissions (size of bubbles indicates CO_2 kg per year related to the country's respective economic performance) in different ways: Within Europe economically well advanced countries (smaller bubbles in white colour) show a relative small intensity of emissions whereas for instance Uzbekistan, Turkmenistan, Kazakhstan and Ukraine (bigger bubbles in white colour) show relative high intensities. Evidently, oil producing and exporting countries like Qatar, Bahrain or Saudi Arabia (bubbles with dots) show a very high intensity of emissions despite their high level of income and urbanisation.

Correspondingly, there may be some intrinsic logic that higher levels of urbanisation and of economic wealth will support less energy intensive economic activities and CO_2 – emissions. Nevertheless some countries show very deviant positions on the way to a more

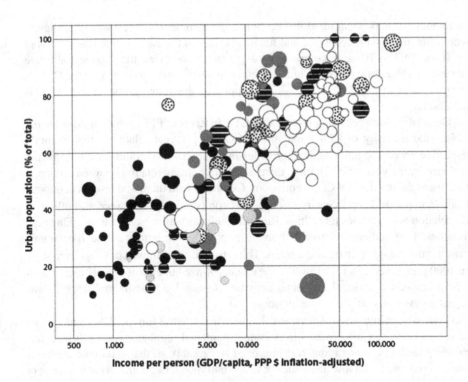

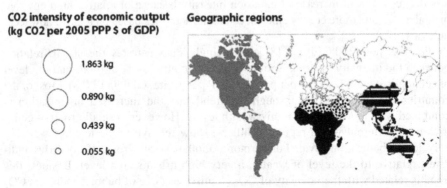

Fig. 1. Urbanisation, economic wealth and CO_2 - emissions intensity. Source: [8].

sustainable development because of national traditional cultures and specific political priorities. These different perspectives of global and national trends already allow two conclusions:

1. In a comparative view many countries with advanced economic wealth show relative low intensity of CO_2 emissions related to its economic performance despite some outliers. Hence, advanced modern economic activities have a positive impact on the

respective national level of emission intensity. But the total amount of CO_2 – emissions is still driven by the size of a country in terms of population or economic performance.

2. Urbanisation combined with economic wealth is a global trend. Countries with higher degrees of urban population show higher levels in economic wealth. Within this trend it is in particular very obvious that cities in more advanced countries (economically, urbanized) show relative low intensity in CO_2 – emissions.

Despite these positive global trends in the intensity of emissions and its relation to urbanisation it is a matter of fact that environmental problems are becoming stronger in front of strongly increasing total amount of CO_2 – emissions. On the background of globalisation and despite technical innovation, higher economic wealth and growth of population and economies are the most relevant driving forces of increasing emissions and in a wider perspective of climate change [9].

To conclude, from an analytical point of view cities are gaining specific importance: Since 2007 more than 50 % of global population lives in urbanized areas. The ongoing process of urbanisation will lead to approximately 66 % of world population dwelling in urbanized areas in 2050 and ask for adequate services and welfare in order to fulfil their own and their collective needs [4]. The process of urbanisation will not take place in the same intensity across all continents [10]. In particular cities in Asia, Africa and Latin America are experiencing a fast growth so that mega-cities have to tackle problems of housing, sanitation as well as of energy and water supply [11–13]. Due to strong social polarisation these problems are mostly concentrated in informal settlements and slums which in addition show specific risks of vulnerability in front of climate change. From a functional point of view this strong process of urbanisation asks for technical innovations in front of increasing demand of energy and corresponding emissions in different fields of urban development (for instance, the housing sector and transportation sector) in which urban quality of life and provision of urban services is increasingly put at risk. Thus, technical innovations and ICT are becoming crucial elements of a city's competitiveness and attraction [5, 14]. They provide more efficient use of infrastructure capacities and modern conditions of communication and mobility.

Thus, cities are drivers of energy consumption but also potential objects and actors tackling specific challenges of energy consumption and improving quality of life. Accordingly, the Europe 2020 strategy defined by the European Commission regards the cities not only as the motors of urban development but also as the enablers to reach the general goals: 20 % reduction of greenhouse gas emissions; 20 % increase of renewable energy consumption and 20 % reduction of energy consumption and as a long term target 80–95 % reduced CO_2 – emissions until 2050. As in particular the target of emissions reduction has become a big challenge since some years the idea of 'Smart City' is discussed intensively [15, 16].

3   Energy Efficiency in Smart Cities

In a recent publication Dameri and Rosenthal-Sabroux [17, p. 2] write in the introduction that *"Today smart city is in the mood, not only in academic or scientific researches, but especially in public government choices and projects."* In fact, the discussion of understanding what is meant by Smart City gained on intensity since some years. In a strict techno-deterministic view the core idea goes back to the emergence of the ICT sector and the increasing possibilities to use information for delivering specific private or public services and steering urban trends. But this has changed over time.

Without giving a full overview of definitions one comprehensive definition comes from Caragliu et al. [18, p. 70] characterizing a city as smart *"... when investments in human and social capital and traditional (transport) and modern (ICT) communication infrastructure fuel sustainable economic growth and a high quality of life, with a wise management of natural resources, through participatory governance."* However, the ongoing discussion of its meaning for urban development is based on rather heterogeneous interests because stakeholders involved have a wide range of different academic and/or professional backgrounds. Facing this fact, Cocchia [19] concludes that innovation and technology are playing a central role improving quality of life. Moreover, the core of the definition is dependent on the specific academic or societal background (research, economy, administration, and politics). Nam and Pardo [20] elaborate its understanding in three dimensions: 'technology' with its mediated services supports the use of infrastructure in a more efficient way; 'people' well educated for strengthening human infrastructure and collective decision making; 'institutions' as pro-active part in combination with the citizens' engagement. Hence, the 'Smart City' should be regarded as the combination of all relevant dimensions. Nam and Pardo [20, p. 288] conclude *"Leading a smart city initiative requires a comprehensive understanding of the complexities and interconnections among social and technical factors of services and physical environments in a city."* And herewith underpin the socio-technical systemic understanding of becoming smart.

Even though the term Smart City is introduced and used in a programmatic way since some years, there is no common understanding but probably some convergence observable in recent discussion. For instance, DG Internal Policies emphasizes in 2014 that Smart City initiatives are multi-stakeholder partnerships addressing problems of common interest with the support of ICT whereby initiatives should tackle challenges in one or more key fields [21]. Key fields are defined in the same way as Giffinger et al. already did in 2007.

Anyhow, all these different definitions emphasize the importance of ICT or of technology and technical innovations. But they do not explicitly discuss how to support a smart and energy efficient urban development. A more precise discussion of corresponding approaches is necessary. In this discussion we understand energy efficiency based on the definition used in the PLEEC-Project from a sustainable perspective: *"Energy efficiency means the use of less energy to provide the same services considering aspects of economic, social and ecologic sustainability and the life-cycle of materials"* [22, p. 5].

According to Giffinger and Lü [23] three different types of approaches are to be distinguished considering the meaning and implementation of ICT and technology in urban development:

- Leydesdorff and Deakin [24] concentrate on the more general question how to support technical-economic innovations. Based on the triple-helix approach they combine the three basic elements 'industry', 'university' and 'government' in the multiple-helix approach with three relevant processes and regulations enabling the collaboration between the three elements and their actors. This approach implicitly assumes that through the interplay of academic, scientific and political efforts technical innovations will have an impact on energy efficiency given that relevant things are invented and corresponding markets are established. Hence, this is a technology driven understanding in which technical innovations will be successful at corresponding markets.

- Batty et al. [25] emphasize the role of ICT in form of integrated data sets and social media as new conditions for research and decision support. They will make investment decisions more effective through better modelling in the transport and logistic sector or improve the use of existing capacities of transport infrastructure. Hence, they reduce their Smart City understanding to a merely data driven and ICT based understanding. They discuss energy efficiency of smart development in particular for the transportation/logistic sector and the mobility sector but not for the housing sector which in many cities shows highest potentials for energy savings or of increased efficiency regarding thermal refurbishment, heating and cooling.
- Giffinger et al. underpin the necessity of a learning based understanding of Smart City [23, 26]. They acknowledge that an evidence based analysis and discussion should identify most relevant assets and deficits which characterize a city. This identification should guarantee a most effective process detecting relevant innovation potentials and support stakeholders' decisions or planning strategies defining (technical) efforts improving energy efficiency in certain fields of urban development. Of course, this approach defined as a stakeholder led process does not allow searching analytically for optimal solution. But the learning process and decision finding within relevant communities should strengthen the sustainability of energy efficient innovations into certain key fields of urban development.

Basically, technical innovations or data driven approaches have specific advantages as described above. They support Smart City processes which are enforcing efficiency through technical innovations or identifying best technical solutions according to certain goals through data driven analytical research efforts. However, these approaches have to cope with specific deficits: The city is reduced to a merely technical product determined by dominant economic interests. In front of varying local conditions general technical solutions are provoking the risks of being ineffective when it is socially not accepted or it enforces unintended impacts: for instance, rebound effects. Such rebound effects denominating the impacts of cost reductions through technical innovations may lead to an increase of consumption (of same or other goods and services) and increase energy consumption in total [27]. Of course, one may argue that these effects are the driving force for economic wealth. But due to the fact of permanently increasing energy consumption and emissions we have to ask for the decoupling of improving quality of life through technical innovations from energy consumption and emissions. Hence, the strengthening of energy efficiency according to the definition above is therefore asking for an integrative approach which is able to introduce not only technical innovations but predominantly to aim at a more energy efficient urban development through effective learning processes aiming at the change of mobility patterns and life styles.

The PLEEC project tries to bring forward this idea of energy efficient urban development [28]. It is based on the assumption that technology, structures (in form of built structures but also of governance structures) and behavior of citizens built the three components which influence energy demand/consumption and emissions of cities. Hence, in this project in collaboration with six medium sized partner cities (Eskilstuna, Sweden; Jyväskylä and Turku, Finland; Tartu, Estonia; Stoke-On-Trent, England; Santiago de Compostela, Spain) the main fields of energy efficient urban development with respective domains had been identified through two web-based rounds of surveys (Fig. 2). The result shows five key fields with a respective number of most important domains.

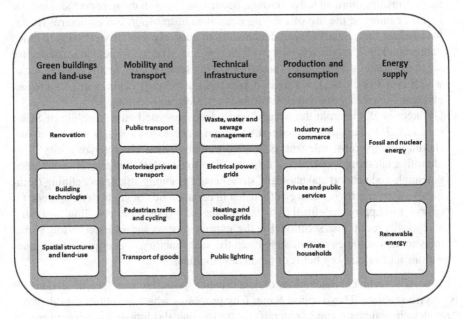

Fig. 2. Key fields and domains in PLEEC – project. Source: [28].

Based on this classification the potentials for a more energy efficient development had been identified in form of an energy Smart City profile by local stakeholders of their home city. The results in Fig. 3 show the assessments of recent status of energy efficient standards and the potentials for improvement in each domain. For instance, the result of the City of Tartu, Estonia, clearly shows discrepancies which can be explained as urban innovation potentials for which smart solutions have to be elaborated. In a next step local stakeholder forums and strategic planning discussion have to identify which kind of projects will be most effective. According to the integrative understanding, the main aim is not only to identify place based technical innovations, but also a combination with corresponding regulations and marketing activities for smart communities creating a more sustainable development.

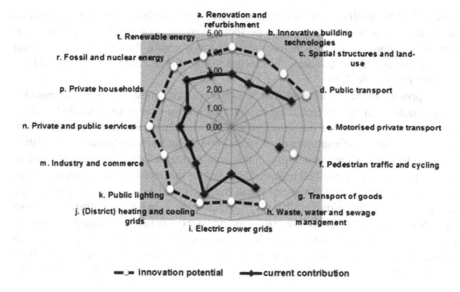

Fig. 3. Energy efficiency potential by urban domains of City of Tartu in 2013/14. Source: [28].

As experiences in PLEEC-project show a place based approach is necessary because cities dispose about very different experiences and problems of energy efficient development. The profile of specific innovation potentials is strongly varying across cities [22]. Hence, the wide range of potential technical innovations always has to be adapted in combination with corresponding regulations due to local structural and socio-economic conditions. According to an adaptive governance understanding this strategic planning approach tries to transform technical innovations into urban innovations [29]. What this means in the context of policy, decision support of stakeholders as well as planning and research activities will be examined in the next chapter.

4 Urban Innovation as Core Element of Smart City Initiatives

In front of different understandings in the Smart City discussion it is now intended to visualize its place based understanding.

Basically, the city can be structured into key fields of urban development whereby each key field is defined by a group of domains in which energy efficiency could potentially be improved. For instance, the comprehensive classification elaborated in the PLEEC-project (see Fig. 2) could be used for this purpose.

Traditionally, activities of urban research and planning are concentrating on certain key fields and respective domains whereas knowledge about single domains was based on specific and mostly separated statistical sources. Since some years, the ICT-driven development allows the use of integrated (big) data bases and the use of social media information in real time as core element of decision making [25]. Hence, a predominantly technical and data driven understanding of the Smart City enforces an urban development which is based on more powerful technical systems and large investments more or less neglecting local needs and preconditions but always combined with risks of rebound and lock-in effects. In this perspective governance efforts and urban development are dominated by economic interests transforming the city into a technical product. The question dominates 'How technical innovations could be implemented and used for a better life?' [5].

In opposite, in the place based understanding the main questions to be answered are 'Why should we need new technologies and what kind of innovation is needed?' which are very often not answered in a sufficient way. Hence, central questions to be dealt with are 'What are the most important challenges?' and 'Which kind of Smart City initiative is most effective?'. Correspondingly, in this view certain information and communication technologies are first of all regarded as a tool for the decision finding process. This tool has to enable the monitoring of urban trends as well as the modelling of certain impacts of Smart City initiatives. It delivers quantitative or qualitative information about the performance within and between domains as assets or deficits of urban development. Thus, it has to improve evidence within a learning and decision finding process. Of course, this information has to be assessed as a more or less important challenge in front of a city's need for a sustainable and in particular energy efficient development (Fig. 4).

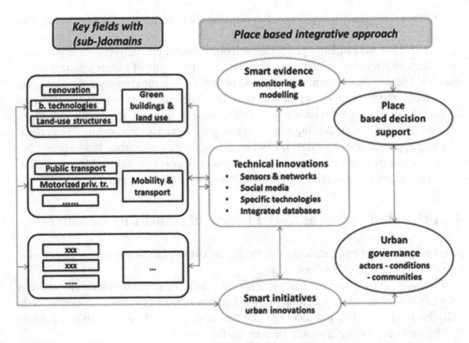

Fig. 4. ICT in a place based Smart City approach. Source: own elaboration; strongly modified from [25, p. 508].

Smart City initiatives, finally, have to meet those challenges in a problem oriented integrative and socially inclusive way. Thus, they need a strategic discussion in which integrative multifaceted solutions, such as urban innovations, are elaborated in a corresponding participatory setting considering the different stakeholders and actors involved. This means that Smart City initiatives always have to combine technical issues with the establishment of smart communities. Corresponding governance efforts have to create such communities which integrate different interests (from above and below, producer and customer) and which support energy efficient solutions. Smart City initiatives are not defined exclusively as technical (silo-) solutions and its management for implementation. But a place based Smart City initiative has to enable urban innovations as a transition process. This process is characterized by the interplay of technical innovations and adaptive governance efforts enabling smart communities in a corresponding social learning process.

5   Perspectives

In the introduction it is demonstrated that cities have become crucial actors tackling environmental problems through energy consumption and CO_2 - emissions. On a global level, the urbanisation process gives rise to the question how one can make urban development more energy efficient. Consequently, cities are asked to become active. The Smart City discussion reflects this development but shows at the same time that there exist completely different understandings of how to do it.

According to the technical and data driven understanding the city becomes an urban digitalized machine in which infrastructure systems are claimed to be used in a more efficient way. But at the same time the city is reduced to a technical object dominated by economic interests neglecting local and social conditions. This gives rise to the expectation of its problematic effectiveness and its missing impacts on sustainable development as local people are not involved in decision finding processes. The risk of ineffective investments becomes obvious: Citizens are reduced to customers who are asked to behave in a solely consumptive but not energy aware way. Hence, rebound effects will emerge. Complex technical solutions usually ask for public or private investments. Thus the risk of lock-in effects increase the more expensive such investments are.

Against this understanding a place based approach is proposed. Basically, this understanding responds to the ICT based data driven understanding but modifies it as learning and evidence based process in which technical innovations are replaced by integrative urban innovations as core elements of urban policies. Through this understanding not the technical innovation comes into the core of discussion but the Smart City initiative understood as an urban innovation which considers the increase of energy efficiency as a transition process. It combines ICT-based innovations with specific governance regulations which allow learning processes of involved stakeholders. A smart initiative as an urban innovation is therefore realized by the empowerment of an effective problem solving community on the adequate spatial level. Good examples are urban initiatives in which all relevant stakeholders are involved organizing new forms of mobility or waste management or internet based financing and (crowed) sourcing of the production of renewable energy.

The advantages of this place based approach become very obvious: The urban innovation gives rise to the expectation that lock-in effects and rebound effects are less dominant because of the strong involvement of relevant groups of stakeholders in bottom-up and problem solving learning processes. Due to the learning process solutions should even support sustainable urban development so far that learning processes and the creation of smart communities are becoming a driving force of social inclusion.

Of course, bottom-up and learning processes need time. Hence, decision finding and corresponding Smart City initiatives usually do not allow fast solutions. This disadvantage will presumably become more important the more complex technical solutions are and the more conflicts between stakeholders at the beginning of this process exist. However, the increase of energy consumption and of CO_2 – emissions in many countries and regions ask for more effective (and faster) solutions.

In this context, cities as political bodies and actors become very important to tackle this problem and bring forward smart initiatives: On the one hand cities with their political power and their administrative organisation predominantly define which information can be produced and will be provided to the public. A well-structured monitoring of urban trends and structural conditions are the base for evidence based discussions and learning processes. It will support the elaboration of initiatives as well as the detection of its short, medium and long termed impacts. Due to more integrated data bases research conditions will be improved supporting the decision finding. Besides, cities as public actors in this process should empower certain initiatives and collaborate in such processes due to some prior objectives on the city level (top-down). The political and strategic enabling of urban innovations has to become one of the major objectives of urban policy. Hence, a clear political commitment supporting sustainable energy efficient urban development is crucial.

References

1. Wheeler, S.: Planning sustainable and livable cities. In: LeGates, R., Stout, F. (eds.) The City Reader. Urban Reader Series, 4th edn. Routledge, London (1998)
2. Marcuse, P.: Sustainability is not enough. Environ. Urbanisation **10**(2), 103–111 (1998)
3. Vos, R.: Perspective designing sustainability: a conceptual orientation. J. Chem. Technol. Biotechnol. **82**, 334–339 (2007)
4. UN: World Urbanisation Prospects: The 2014 Revision, Highlights. UN, New York (2014)
5. Acatech – Deutsche Akademie der Technikwissenschaften (Hrsg.): Smart Cities - Deutsche Hochtechnologie für die Stadt der Zukunft, Nr. 10. Springer, Berlin (2012)
6. IEA – International Energy Agency (2015). http://www.iea.org/publications/freepublications/publication/KeyWorld2014.pdf. Accessed 17 August 2015
7. Gapminder 1 (2015). http://www.gapminder.org/world/#$majorMode=chart$is; shi=t;ly=2003;lb=f;il=t;fs=11;al=30;stl=t;st=t;nsl=t;se=t$wst;tts=C$ts; sp=5.592903225 80644;ti=2008$zpv;v=0$inc_x;mmid=XCOORDS;iid=phAwcNAVuyj1jiMAkmq1iMg; by= ind$inc_y;mmid=YCOORDS; iid=0AkBd6lyS3EmpdEVUcEJVRzlFWWRR cjhveGlrQzd wdUE;by=ind$inc_s;uniValue=8.21;iid=16USvgw1H-rXCK0 ZMmDkyMPd1FXQNpjCj6H CMIn-fmFQ; by=ind$inc_c; uniValue=255; gid=CATID0; by=grp$map_x;scale=log; dataMin=2121;dataMax=199760$map_y;scale=lin; dataMin=-0.1096;dataMax=3.353$map_s; sma=49;smi=2.65$cd;bd=0$inds=. Accessed 17 August 2015

8. Gapminder 2 (2015). http://www.gapminder.org/world/#$majorMode=chart$is; shi=t; ly=2003; lb=f; il=t; fs=11; al=30; stl=t; st=t; nsl=t; se=t$wst; tts=C$ts; sp=5.59290322580644; ti=2008$zpv; v=0$inc_x; mmid=XCOORDS; iid=phAwcNAVuyj1jiMAkmq1iMg; by=ind$inc_y; mmid=YCOORDS; iid=phAwcNAVuyj0-LE4StzCsEw; by=ind$inc_s; uniValue=8.21; iid=0AkBd6lyS3EmpdEVUcEJVRzlFWWRRcjhveGlrQzdwdUE; by=ind$inc_c; uniValue=255; gid=CATID0; by=grp$map_x; scale=log; dataMin=423; dataMax=276046$ map_y; scale=lin; dataMin=-1.9465; dataMax=102$map_s; sma=49; smi=2.65$cd; bd=0$inds=. Accessed 18 August 2015

9. IPCC (2014). http://www.de-ipcc.de/de/200.php. Accessed 20 August 2015

10. Giffinger, R.: Smart city – Stadtentwicklung im Spannungsfeld technologischer und integrativer Anforderungen. In: Blaas, W., Bröthaler, J., Getzner, M., Gutheil-Knopp-Kirchwald, G. (Hrg.) Perspektiven der staatlichen Aufgabenerfüllung. Verlag Österreich, Wien (2014)

11. UN-Habitat: The State of Latin American and Caribbean Cities. United Nations, Kenya (2012a)

12. UN-Habitat: The State of China's Cities 2012/2013. United Nations, China (2012b)

13. UN-Habita: The State of African Cities 2014. United Nations, Kenya (2014)

14. Begg, I.: Cities and competitiveness. Urban Stud. **36**(5–6), 795–810 (1999)

15. European Commission (2010): EUROPE 2020. A European strategy for smart, sustainable and inclusive growth. Brussels

16. Dammann, S. Smart cities and communities perspective of DG energy – C2. Paper presented at FORUM, Stoke-on-Trent, 6 November 2013

17. Dameri, P.D., Rosenthal-Sabroux, C.: Smart city and value creation. In: Dameri, R.P., Rosenthal-Sabroux, C. (eds.) Smart City – How to Create Public and Economic Value with High Technology in Urban Space, pp. 1–12. Springer, New York (2014)

18. Caragliu, A., Del Bo, C., Nijkamp, P.: Smart cities in Europe. J. Urban Technol. **18**(2), 65–82 (2011)

19. Cocchia, A.: Smart and digital city: a systematic literature review. In: Dameri, R.P., Rosenthal-Sabroux, C. (eds.) Smart City – How to Create Public and Economic Value with High Technology in Urban Space, pp. 13–44. Springer, Heidelberg (2014)

20. Nam, T., Pardo, T.: Conceptualizing smart city with dimensions of technology, people, and institutions. In: The Proceedings of the 12th Annual International Conference on Digital Government Research, June 2011

21. DG Internal Policies: Mapping smart cities in the EU (2014). http://www.europarl.europa.eu/RegData/etudes/etudes/join/2014/507480/IPOL-ITRE_ET(2014)507480_EN.pdf. Accessed 10 September 2015

22. PLEEC-Project, Profiles: PLEEC-project, profiles (2014). http://www.pleecproject.eu/results/documents/viewdownload/130-work-package-2/413-energy-smart-city-profiles-of-partner-cities-d2-3.html. Accessed 24 August 2015

23. Giffinger, R., Lü, H.: The smart city perspective: a necessary change from technical to urban innovations. E-book-series (2015). http://www.fondazionefeltrinelli.it/pubblicazioni/. Accessed 7 July 2015

24. Leydesdorff, L., Deakin, M.: The triple-helix model of smart cities: a neo evolutionary perspective. J. Urban Technol. **18**(2), 53–63 (2011)

25. Batty, M., Axhausen, K.W., Giannotti, F., Pozdnoukhov, A., Bazzani, A., Wachowicz, M., Ouzounis, G., Portugali, Y.: Smart cities of the future. Eur. J. Phys. Spec. Topics **214**, 481–518 (2012)

26. Giffinger, R. et al. (2007) Smart cities – ranking of European medium-sized cities. http://www.smart-cities.eu/download/smart_cities_final_report.pdf. Accessed 24 January 2015
27. Herring, H., Roy, R.: Technological innovation, energy efficient design and the rebound effect. Technovation **27**, 194–203 (2007)
28. PLEEC-Project (2014). http://www.pleecproject.eu/. Accessed 24 August 2015
29. Diamantini, D., Borrelli, N.: Theoretical questions for analysing contemporary city. Fondazione Giangiacomo Feltrinelli: e-book – series (2014). http://www.fondazionefeltrinelli.it/pubblicazioni/. Accessed 10 September 2015

Smart Cities Concept and Challenges: Bases for the Assessment of Smart City Projects

Andres Monzon[✉]

Transport Research Centre, Universidad Politécnica of Madrid,
Prof. Aranguren s/n, Madrid, Spain
andres.monzon@upm.es

Abstract. ASCIMER (Assessing Smart Cities in the Mediterranean Region) is a project developed by the Universidad Politecnica of Madrid (UPM) for the EIBURS call on "Smart City Development: Applying European and International Experience to the Mediterranean Region".

Nowadays, many initiatives aimed at analysing the conception process, deployment methods or outcomes of the -referred as- Smart City projects are being developed in multiple fields. Since its conception, the Smart City notion has evolved from the execution of specific projects to the implementation of global strategies to tackle wider city challenges. ASCIMER´s project takes as a departure point that any kind of Smart City assessment should give response to the real challenges that cities of the 21st century are facing. It provides a comprehensive overview of the available possibilities and relates them to the specific city challenges.

A selection of Smart City initiatives will be presented in order to establish relations between the identified city challenges and real Smart Projects designed to solve them. As a result of the project, a Projects Guide has been developed as a tool for the implementation of Smart City projects that efficiently respond to complex and diverse urban challenges without compromising their sustainable development and while improving the quality of life of their citizens.

Keywords: Smart city projects · Challenges · Assessment · Mediterranean region

1 Introduction

Cities are the main poles of human and economic activity. They hold the potential to create synergies allowing great development opportunities to their inhabitants. However, they also generate a wide range of problems that can be difficult to tackle as they grow in size and complexity. Cities are also the places where inequalities are stronger and, if they are not properly managed, their negative effects can surpass the positive ones.

This paper presents the first year outcomes of ASCIMER project, developed under my coordination by a team formed by Fiamma Perez, Victoria Fernandez-Anez and Guillermo Velazquez and with the collaboration of Andrea Torregrosa and Javier Dorao.

M. Helfert et al. (Eds.): Smartgreens 2015 and Vehits 2015, CCIS 579, pp. 17–31, 2015.
DOI: 10.1007/978-3-319-27753-0_2

Urban areas need to manage their development, supporting economic competitiveness, while enhancing social cohesion, environmental sustainability and an increased quality of life of their citizens.

With the development of new technological innovations -mainly ICTs- the concept of the "Smart City" emerges as a means to achieve more efficient and sustainable cities.

Since its conception, the Smart City notion has evolved from the execution of specific projects to the implementation of global strategies to tackle wider city challenges. Thus, it is necessary to get a comprehensive overview of the available possibilities and relate them to the specific city challenges.

2   ASCIMER Project

ASCIMER (Assessing Smart Cities in the Mediterranean Region) is a three-year research project developed by the Universidad Politecnica of Madrid (UPM) for the EIBURS call on "Smart City Development: Applying European and International Experience to the Mediterranean Region".

Nowadays, many initiatives aimed at analysing the conception process, deployment methods or outcomes of the -referred as- Smart City projects are being developed in multiple fields. However, there is a lack of standardized metrics and methodologies to help to assess, prioritize, finance, implement, manage and replicate this kind of projects.

The overall goal of the ASCIMER project is to develop a comprehensive framework to help public and private stakeholders to make informed decisions about Smart City investment strategies and to build skills for evaluation and prioritization of this kind of projects, including solving difficulties regarding deployment and transferability.

To sum up, the goals of the project, along its three years of duration are:

– To define the Smart City concept and to understand how it can contribute to achieve urban development priorities.
– To develop a methodology to assess and prioritize Smart City projects.
– To develop guidelines of implementation and management Smart City Projects.
– To characterize Mediterranean City Challenges and to develop a transferability strategy of Smart City projects. This objective will be part of the other three above.

Here, some of the outputs of the first year of research are presented. The objective of this first Work Package of research was the development of the Smart City concept and the identification of the main urban development priorities with a special focus on the Mediterranean area. Besides some Smart City initiatives have been analysed and summarized in a Projects Guide.

The information has been collected through website search, field visits and a two-day workshop where experts from different fields and countries have been gathered to talk about the experiences they have been involved in, both in the academic and professional world. During the workshop, examples from both northern and southern Mediterranean cities were explained and discussed giving the opportunity to understand the current socioeconomic reality of the cities and what are the different challenges they are facing. By gathering all these experts and different points of view, the workshop enabled the research team to acquire a global knowledge of the present and future of the Smart Cities (Fig. 1).

Fig. 1. ASCIMER project development.

3 Smart City Concept

Despite there is some kind of consensus that the label Smart City represents innovation in city management, its services and infrastructures, a common definition of the term has not yet been stated. There is a wide variety of definitions of what a Smart City could be. However, two trends can be clearly distinguished in relation with what are the main aspects that Smart Cities must take into consideration [4].

On the one hand there is a set of definitions that put emphasis just on one urban aspect (technological, ecological, etc.) leaving apart the rest of the circumstances involved in a city. This group of mono-topic descriptions are misunderstanding that the final goal of a Smart City is to provide a new approach to urban management in which all aspects are treated with the interconnection that takes place in the real life of the city. Improving just one part of an urban ecosystem does not imply that the problems of the whole are being solved.

On the other hand there are some authors that emphasize how the main difference of the Smart City concept is the interconnection of all the urban aspects. The tangled problems between urbanization are infrastructural, social and institutional at the same time and this intertwining is reflected in the Smart City concept. From the definitions, it can be noticed that infrastructures are a central piece of the Smart City and that technology is the enabler that makes it possible, but it is the combination, connection and integration of all systems what becomes fundamental for a city being truly smart [8]. From these definitions it can be inferred that the Smart City concept implies a comprehensive approach to city management and development. These definitions show a balance of the technological, economic and social factors involved in an urban ecosystem. The definitions reflect a holistic approach to the urban problems taking advantage of the new technologies so that the urban model and the relationships among the stakeholders can be redefined [1–3, 6, 8, 9].

3.1 ASCIMER´S Working Definition

The first step of the project was to develop a Smart City definition that will act as a guideline for the selection of projects in this field and the development of the assessment methodology. Thus, the main issues that a Smart City must take into account have been defined.

The main innovations coming from the Smart City concept are the rise of a user-centric approach that considers urban issues from the perspective of the citizen's needs, the engagement of citizens in the city functioning, or a truly holistic approach to urban challenges that becomes essential for Smart Strategies.

This last innovative factor explains why the Smart City is a concept that surpasses earlier maybe similar ones that usually miss the holistic approach, focusing only on improving either human, technological or environmental factors.

ICT-based solutions are the key element that differentiates and confers potential to the Smart City, however simply deploying expensive technologies in the city is a misunderstanding of the concept.

The development of Smart Strategies must be run on the basis of a multi-stakeholder municipally-based partnership. Bottom-up approaches ought to be allowed to coexist with the more traditional top-down ones. Also Smart City solutions must apply inclusive approaches.

As seen, the definition of a Smart City is a very broad concept that has technology as a basic aspect, coupled with social and human capital development.

Regarding all the analysed aspects that are key to define a Smart City, the ASCIMER's Working definition has been developed:

"A Smart City is an integrated system in which human and social capital interact, using technology-based solutions. It aims to efficiently achieve sustainable and resilient development and a high quality of life on the basis of a multistakeholder, municipality based partnership."

4 Smart City Challenges

As cities continue booming tirelessly, their challenges need to be carefully thought through so that population growth, economic development and social progress walk on the same path. Although most of global GDP is produced in cities, not everything happening within these agglomerations implies positive externalities. Cities are also the places where inequalities are stronger and, if they are not properly managed, the negative effects can surpass the positive ones. The Smart City model can lead to a better city planning and management and thus, to the achievement of a sustainable model of urban growth.

In ASCIMER's first year of work, challenges have been identified and classified in different dimensions in order to facilitate next steps of the project. Analysing the urban environment, research works deal with a different number of fields to frame the city. We have identified in the reviewed literature that they can all be allocated within six main City Dimensions: Governance, Economy, Mobility, Environment, People and Living [5].

They represent the specific aspects of a city upon which Smart Initiatives impact to achieve the expected goals of a Smart City strategy (sustainability, efficiency and high quality of life). Technology itself is not considered an action field, but an enabler that improves the efficiency of the projects.

Within each of the Dimensions different City Challenges have been identified both for the northern Mediterranean cities, and for the southern and eastern Mediterranean ones. The cities considered in this paper as belonging to the North Mediterranean Region are those located in countries of the European Union. The countries in the South and East Mediterranean region that have been considered in the study are: Morocco, Algeria, Tunisia, Lybia, Egypt, Jordan, Israel, Lebanon, Syria and Turkey.

Twenty nine Challenges have been identified in total for the northern ones. Among those, twenty related to just one Dimension. And nine multi-Dimension challenges.

For the southern cities twenty Challenges have been identified, eleven of them concerning just one city dimension while the other nine correspond to two or more.

4.1   City Challenges in European Cities

Nowadays cities have many different fields to work on so that they can become better places for living. Demographic changes and the financial crisis have brought to light the urgency of facing these city challenges. But it is not only a matter of the challenges that cities must face today, but the future problems of cities must be taken into account in an integrated way, as proposed in the document of the European Commission "Cities of Tomorrow". Decisions in urban planning and management have long term consequences. Although following this holistic approach, all these challenges can be classified in relation to the Smart City action fields, as shown in Table 1.

Table 1. City challenges in European cities.

Governance	Economy	Mobility	Environment	People	Living
Flexible governance	Unemployment	Sustainable mobility	Energy saving	Unemployment	Affordable housing
Shrinking cities	Shrinking cities	Inclusive mobility	Shrinking cities	Social cohesion	Social cohesion
Territorial cohesion	Economic decline	Multimodal transport system	Holistic approach to environmental and energy issues	Poverty	Health problems
Combination of formal and informal government	Territorial cohesion	Urban ecosystems under pressure	Urban ecosystems under pressure	Ageing population	Emergency management
	Mono-sectoral economy	Traffic congestion	Climate change effects	S.diversity as source of innovation	Urban sprawl
	Sust. local economies	Non-car mobility	Urban sprawl	Cyber Security	Safety and Security
	Social diversity as source of innovation	ICT infrastructure deficit			Cyber Security
	ICT infrast. deficit				

The main challenges that cities face in the Smart Governance action field are related with the urgent need for a change of government model.

Governance models will face the challenge of making themselves more flexible allowing to combine their top-down policies with bottom-up initiatives and also with informality. Demographic changes and territorial cohesion are the other two main challenges to face.

Challenges in the Smart Economy action field are related to the productive structure of the city. After the economic crisis, urban regions have understood the convenience of not focusing their productive model on just one economic sector. Enhancing the creation of a multi-sectoral economy would make cities more resilient to economic downturns, exploiting the unique conditions of each urban agglomeration within a certain region and interconnecting their productive networks can improve this resistance.

Achieving a sustainable, inclusive and efficient mobility system for goods and people is the overall challenge to be dealt with in the Smart Mobility action field. Implementing a multimodal public transport system, fostering alternatives to the car-based mobility and making public transport reachable and available to all citizens are the three main axes that will allow reducing congestion and pollution in cities and improving connectivity.

In the Smart Environment action field different challenges related with the built and natural environment can be found. On one hand there is the need of reducing land consumption for the extension of our cities. Avoiding urban sprawl and looking for more dense and liveable cities will enhance a mix of uses and the concentration of population, reducing the use of the car. On the other hand, the reduction of energy consumption, pollution and CO_2 emissions is a growing ecological demand for achieving a sustainable development. Improving social cohesion and quality of life are the main challenges to face in the Smart People action field. An enriching community life is the final goal, and to achieve so, it is necessary to take initiatives to solve the high levels of unemployment in cities; as well as using the demographic movements and mix of population as an opportunity for innovation, taking into consideration all citizens independently of their age, gender, culture or social condition. The main challenges in this field are related with the supply of housing, health conditions, and crime rate situation. These three aspects, together with the social cohesion of the population are the main issues that set difference for a city to be able to talk about having a good quality of life.

4.2 South and East Mediterranean Challenges

As stated in the UN-Habitat report "The state of African cities 2014" [9] demographic pressures, rapid urbanization and environmental changes are producing more negative urban externalities than positive ones in the majority of the south Mediterranean cities. These cities are growing rapidly in population but their development model is far away from a sustainable one. Due to their less developed situation, in comparison with the north Mediterranean cities, the challenges that these cities face are much more oriented towards fulfilling a basic services provision to their inhabitants.

The South Mediterranean territory is highly urbanized, more than a half of its population lives in cities, but the development models that have been followed have an important influence of past European ones that did not take into account the particularities of the south Mediterranean society. Development models for these urban areas should be revised in order to include the specific requirements of their societies, such as the informality as a way of urban development, the awareness of the lack of certain basic services or the particular conditions of the Government models.

The main challenges of the South Mediterranean cities are related with the scarcity of resources, such as fresh water or food supply. This challenge will become greater as the effects of the climate change continue. Severe droughts are expected to increase during the following years, and so will do the urgency for water supply and the diminishing of the agriculture production. Besides, the high infrastructure deficit that these countries have, with their mobility, water and energy networks in bad conditions result in the small amount of resources available not being as optimized as they could be. Improving the deployment of the supply networks is as important as rising the efficiency of the existing ones, so that the loss in the distribution of the basic utilities is reduced to a minimum.

Table 2. South & East-Mediterranean city challenges.

Governance	Economy	Mobility	Environment	People	Living
Low urban institutional capacities	High infrastructures deficit	Lack of public transport	Scarcity of resources	Urban poverty and inequality	Slum proliferation
Instability in governance	Shortage in access to technology	High infrastructures deficit	Water scarcity	Shortage in access to technology	Urban violence and insecurity
Gap between government and governed	Economy weaknesses and lack of competitiveness	Pollution	Climate change effects	Specific problems of urban youth	Rapid growth and Urban sprawl
Unbalanced geographical development	Specific problems of urban youth	Rapid growth	Pollution	Threats to cultural identity	Deficit of social services
Deficit of social services	Limited urban based industries		Rapid growth and Urban sprawl	Low educational level	Threats to cultural identity
	Unbalanced geographical development				Urban poverty and inequality

Poverty and urban insecurity are the other major challenges in this field. Living conditions in the South Mediterranean cities are less attractive than in the north Mediterranean ones, what in turn has effects on the loss of capacity to attract new businesses and talent. Government instability, in some cases high levels of violence and corruption and a high level of social and spatial polarization are common issues in the south Mediterranean areas. Improving these social and living conditions establishes the foundations for building a better urban future.

Finally, one big drawback that a Smart City initiative in a southern Mediterranean city should carefully take into account is the smaller penetration of smartphones or ICT technology have on its population, comparing it to European countries. Due to the high levels of poverty, not a vast majority of the population living in these cities has access to the necessary technology to make certain Smart City initiatives available to all the citizens. Furthermore, there are also a great number of people who are technology-illiterate. Hence, making available and affordable the necessary technology and fostering educative programs so that the citizens will have knowledge and access to the needed ICT, will be another challenge to have in mind when planning a new initiative (Table 2).

4.3 Relation Between Challenges in European and in South and East Mediterranean Cities

The different Challenges in North and South interrelate, unfolding as cities progress in development and service provision to their inhabitants. When talking about Smart Cities or Smart City projects in the south Mediterranean areas it is necessary to take into account the differences between these cities and the north Mediterranean ones. A Smart City project should not follow the same strategies in one or another urban area because the challenges, starting conditions, available resources and citizens' willingness can be completely different (Fig. 2).

Becoming Smart in much of the south Mediterranean cities means providing some basic services they lack of. Furthermore, when facing these basic services provision it is necessary to look to the failures and needed improvements of the northern Mediterranean cities system. The South Mediterranean cities challenges may be more basic than the northern ones, but the transferability of the projects among cities should be useful for avoiding making the same mistakes twice. For example, many south Mediterranean cities have the necessity of dealing with the provision of an efficient public transport system, or others may be in a more basic stage and they just need to provide a public transport system. But when looking for solutions for the public transport, they should not just think about solving that specific problem but also on giving solutions to the transport system problems that will come afterwards, if they were to follow the same path as the Northern Mediterranean cities, such as the sustainability of the system, the non-car mobility, the inclusiveness of the transport system and the possibility of an effective multi-modal network.

All the relations have been summarized in one global graph that shows ASCI-MER's perspective on city issues. In this diagram the possible links among the southern Mediterranean cities challenges and the general city challenges have been suggested, so that when solving one of the southern challenges, solutions will take into account the other ones. The tangled challenges justify the need of a holistic approach in future cities, to correctly address important citizen's needs.

This developed framework is used to give structure to the Projects Guide.

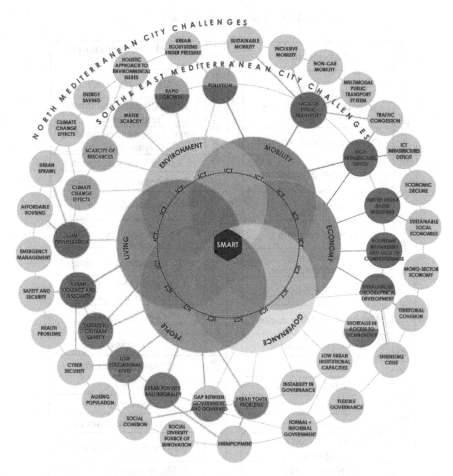

Fig. 2. Relations between Smart City Dimensions, South & East Mediterranean Challenges and general City Challenges.

5 Analysis of Smart City Projects

Different Smart City Projects have been analysed following the outputs of the previous study about the Smart City concept and the challenges cities must face. The analysis has been divided in two phases; firstly a conceptual framework has been developed in order to be used as an orientation through the possibilities of development of Smart City projects in the different dimensions already explained. Secondly, a deep description of a selected group of projects and cities specifying: what kind of Smart City Action the project belongs to and which are the related city dimensions that it comprises; what kind of city challenges they are trying to solve; and background information of the city where the project has been implemented. Besides, a brief explanation of the project itself has been developed including, when possible, the development rate and scale of the project; how it is financed; its key innovation features and its main impacts.

Table 3. Smart City project actions

Smart Governance		Smart Environment	
Smart Governance	Participation	Smart Environment	Network and environmental monitoring
Smart Governance	Transparency and information accessibility	Smart Environment	Energy efficiency
Smart Governance	Transparency and information accessibility	Smart Environment	Urban planning and urban refurbishment
Smart Governance	Public and Social Services	Smart Environment	Smart buildings and building renovation
Smart Governance	Multi-level governance	Smart Environment	Resources management
Smart Governance	Multi-level governance	Smart Environment	Environmental protection
E Smart Economy	Innovation	Smart People	Digital education
E Smart Economy	Entrepreneurship	Smart People	Creativity
E Smart Economy	Local & Global interconnectedness	Smart People	ICT - Enabled working
E Smart Economy	Productivity	Smart People	Community building and urban life management
E Smart Economy	Flexibility of labor market	Smart People	Inclusive society
Smart Mobility	Traffic management	Smart Living	Tourism
Smart Mobility	Public Transport	Smart Living	Culture and leisure
Smart Mobility	ICT Infrastructure	Smart Living	Healthcare
Smart Mobility	Logistics	Smart Living	Security
Smart Mobility	Accessibility	Smart Living	Technology accessibility
Smart Mobility	Clean, non-motorised options	Smart Living	Welfare & Social inclusion
Smart Mobility	Multimodality	Smart Living	Public spaces management

The evolution of the concept of Smart City leads from specific projects to global city strategies through which it is possible to address city challenges at different levels (national, regional, international). Thus, it has been observed that it is necessary develop a strategy within city framework to articulate projects in different dimensions in order to achieve a holistic and comprehensive vision. Consequently, besides the analysis of isolated actions, some outstanding Mediterranean Strategies have been also identified and analysed. City balance in the 6 dimensions is crucial for the good performance. Without a global strategy, a city is in danger to perform some acupunctural projects that lead it to become imbalanced and thus, to the impacts of these projects being drastically reduced

All this information is gathered in a Projects Guide yet to be published. However, in this paper, only the outputs of the conceptual framework and the analysis of independent projects will be presented.

5.1 Smart City Project Actions

Once the concept of Smart City and the main challenges are defined, a systematic approach to the possibilities of action of the Smart City projects has been developed.

The Smart City concept has changed from the execution of specific projects to the implementation of global strategies to tackle city challenges. Thus, it is necessary to get a comprehensive overview of the possibilities and to relate them to the city challenges. As a common point to all of them, the key factor of the Smart City projects has been identified to be the use of ICT.

According to these criteria, project actions have been defined as seen in Table 3. The different Project Actions have been described and put into relation with the various city challenges identified in Part 1.

In a second step, Smart Projects that are being developed in cities have been grouped in the different dimensions. Smart City strategies comprehend a combination of these sub actions. Smart City Project Actions are also composed by more concrete subactions, that are further interwoven. The aim of this second phase is to widen the panel of possibilities of action and to present an approach that is closer to implementation.

Paying special attention to the environmental dimension, it stablishes the relations of the existing city with its territorial support, both natural and built. The relations of the city with its natural environment constitute the departure point for project actions that affect climate, biodiversity, resources (energy, water, etc.) and monitoring. The built environment is present in the project actions related to urban planning and building, either renewal or new construction. The challenges addressed in this dimension intertwine these two dimensions from the point of view of citizens.

5.2 Projects Guide

The Projects Guide is an information tool for cities that want to take advantage of the ICTs and solve their challenges through Smart City Projects.

The guide links city challenges with a wide range of Smart City projects designed to solve them. It is a tool for developing Smart Cities that efficiently respond to complex and diverse urban challenges without compromising their sustainable development and while improving the quality of life of their citizens.

This Projects Guide provides a series of matrices which serve as a tool for decision-making. These matrices relate city challenges with the specific actions designed to tackle them. Therefore, once specific city problems are identified, the guide provides information about the possible actions to take, as well as specific examples of on-going Smart City Projects that can respond to these challenges are this way localized.

The Guide is structured by Smart City Dimensions, with an initial map that shows the name and the location of the projects already found during the research.

Then a matrix shows how these projects are linked to both European and South-East Mediterranean challenges in each of the fields: Economy, Governance, Environment, Mobility, People and Living. Besides it also specifies to what kind of Smart City Action the project belongs and which are the related city dimensions that it comprises.

Table 4. Environmental Smart City projects and challenges. Part 1.

		Smart City Project Actions			
		SEn1. Network and environmental monitoring	SEn2. Energy efficiency		SEn3. Urban planning and urban refurbishment
European City Challenges	Energy saving				
	Shrinking cities				
	Holistic approach to environmental and energy issues				
	Pollution				
	Urban sprawl				
South & East-Mediterranean City Challenges	Scarcity of resources				
	Water scarcity				
	Climate change effect				
	Pollution and congestion				
	Very rapid urbanization				
	Unbalanced geographical development				
		PEn1a. Air Quality Monitoring Network. Amman, Jordan, Country	PEn2a. Watt et Moi. Lyon, France	PEn2b. Smart Grid. Malta.	PEn3a. Lyon Smart Community. Lyon, France
		PEn1b. Smart Water Metering. Kalgoorlie-Boulder, Australia	PEn2c. Renewable Energy & Energy efficiency law. Jordan		PEn3b. CASA neighbourhood, Casablanca, Morocco
		Smart City Projects			

The matrix that relates Environmental challenges with Projects and Projects actions in this fields shows a variety of connections. It comprehends 6 Project actions, each of them linked to at least 2 projects. Some of these types of project present a wider focus, being able to address almost every challenge in both North and South and East-Mediterranean regions. This is the case of Environmental protection projects (Table 5), that are related to most future city challenges. However, more specific projects, like the ones related to energy efficiency (Table 4), are not tackling so many challenges, but are fundamental to cities as urban agglomerations consume over 75 % of the world energy production [7].

Table 5. Environmental Smart City projects and challenges. Part 2.

		Smart City Project Actions		
		SEn4. Smart buildings and building renovation	SEn5. Resources management	SEn6. Environmental protection
European City Challenges	Energy saving			
	Shrinking cities			
	Holistic approach to environmental and energy issues			
	Pollution			
	Urban sprawl			
South & East-Mediterranean City Challenges	Scarcity of resources			
	Water scarcity			
	Climate change effect			
	Pollution and congestion			
	Very rapid urbanization			
	Unbalanced geographical development			
		PEn4a. Cityfied Project. Several, Several.	PEn5a. Jerusalem and Netanya water utilities, Israel	Pen5c. Recover Lost Water Revenue. Olds, Canada	PEn6a. Forest Fire detection. Valencia, Spain.
		PEn4b. Smart CoDe. Several, Several	PEn5b. LifeEWAS. Several, Several	PEn5b. Irriguest life. Victoria-Gasteiz, Spain	
		Smart City Projects		

Regarding the challenges, some of them must be tackled in a holistic approach and have the possibility to be addressed through many different projects like for example pollution and congestion or climate change effect, as cities generate 80 % of greenhouse gases emissions [7]. And of course, this holistic approach is properly a challenge, being necessary to address it through the combination of all the possible projects integrated through global city strategies.

It is important to highlight that every kind of project action is able to address challenges in the different areas of the region. The matrix includes both challenges of the North and South and East. Mediterranean region as the ASCIMER approach understands that the challenges of cities of the North can become future challenges for the cities in the South if they do not take them into account in this stage of their development.

Selected projects offer a variety of options, approaches and different impacts and results trying to cover the variety of issues that can be included in each of the identified project actions. Even if they can present different development degrees, projects of both the North and South and East-Mediterranean regions have been selected as examples, combining different approaches.

Therefore, a tool has been developed in which by selecting the main challenges that a particular city must face, it is possible to get as a result types of projects and specific examples that will help project designers and decision-makers to develop strategies to face present and future problems in the city.

Addressing environmental challenges should be combined with projects in other fields like economy, governance, mobility, people and living in order to develop Smart City Strategies to provide a comprehensive response to the needs of the city. The tool has therefore been developed in each of these different dimensions.

Thus, being part of the Smart City Strategy has been identified as a key element for a City Project to become Smart. For this reason, some of the most outstanding Mediterranean Smart City Strategies are presented to. This part of the guide will also be expanded through the complete ASCIMER project execution.

Finally the last section of the guide includes a preliminary study (already presented in the ASCIMER First Workshop in July 2014) on Smart Cities in the South Mediterranean Region. This short study aims at establishing the context for the development of Smart City actions in the region and also at describing common implementation problems as well as the main types of projects already implemented.

6 Conclusions

During this first year, ASCIMER project has been focused in the development of a conceptual framework for an assessment methodology for Smart City projects in the Mediterranean region. Understanding and classifying the action fields and existing Smart City projects have been the main outputs of the project this year.

Being a complex and multifaceted concept, several types of projects have been defined under this umbrella and thus it becomes necessary to select the main characteristics that a Smart city project must have. Smart city projects must be multidimensional and integrate the different action fields of the city, interacting with human and social capital. Technological solutions must be understood as the tool to achieve the smart city goals and to tackle the challenges cities must face. The main objectives of Smart City projects must be to solve urban problems in an efficient way to improve sustainability of the city and quality of life of its inhabitants. From the governance point of view, projects must be framed in a multi-stakeholder, municipally based partnership in order to provide complex and effective solutions.

Smart city projects main requirement must be addressing the real challenges that cities will face in the future. This is the first step that an assessment methodology must take into account. When analysing the Mediterranean region, it is key to understand the different challenges that cities in the European context and in the South and East-Mediterranean region must face and in which way they are related. Challenges that European cities are facing today can become future challenges in the south if their present ones are not addressed including this vision. Smart city projects must tackle the problems of today's cities while also looking to the potential problems cities will face in the coming decades.

Assessment Methodologies are necessary for evaluating the real impact of Smart projects. Classifying existing solutions and projects is a main step for setting the aspects that a methodology must evaluate. These aspects must be related to the previously defined challenges, understanding in which way they provide a solution to the problems of the city. Providing examples in each of the fields, related to these Project Actions and challenges, results in a tool to develop solutions to city problems with a multidimensional and comprehensive approach.

Taking the findings about city challenges and project analysis of this first year, an assessment methodology will be developed in order to evaluate Smart City projects in the South and East Mediterranean Region. The development of indicators adapted to the main characteristics, projects and challenges of the cities of the Mediterranean region and the definition of the relation between them to develop a correct methodology will be the main goal of ASCIMER during the following year.

References

1. Batty, M. et al.: Smart Cities of the future. UCL Working Paper Series, Paper 188. (2012) ISSN 1467-1298
2. Caragliu, A., del Bo, C., Nijkamp, P.: Smart cities in Europe. In: 3rd Central European Conference in Regional Science– CERS, (2009)
3. Correia, L.M.: Smart cities applications and requirements, White Paper. Net!Works European Technology Platform (2011)
4. EU, Cities of tomorrow. Challenges, visions, ways forward. In: European Commission, Directorate General for Regional Policy (2011)
5. Giffinger, R. et al.: Smart Cities: Ranking of European Medium-Sized Cities. Centre of Regional Science (SRF), Vienna University of Technology, Vienna, Austria (2007)
6. Harrison, C., et al.: Foundations for Smarter Cities. IBM J. Res. Develop. **54**(4), 350–365 (2010)
7. Lazaroiu, G.C., Roscia, M.: Definition methodology for the smart cities model. Energy **47**, 326–332 (2012)
8. Nam, T., Pardo, T.A.: Conceptualizing smart city with dimensions of technology, people, and institutions. In: The Proceedings of the 12th Annual International Conference on Digital Government Research (2011)
9. UN-Habitat The State Of African Cities 2014. Re-imagining sustainable urban transitions. United Nations Human Settlements Programme (2014)

Constructing Human Smart Cities

Álvaro de Oliveira[(⊠)], Margarida Campolargo, and Maria Martins

Alfamicro Lda., Alameda da Guia 192A, 2750-168 Cascais, Portugal
{alvaro.oliveira,margarida.campolargo,
maria.martins}@alfamicro.pt

Abstract. This paper argues that current technology-driven implementations of Smart Cities, although being an important step in the right direction, fall short in exploiting the most important human dimension of cities. In a Human Smart City, people rather than technology are the true actors of the urban "smartness". The creation of a participatory innovation ecosystem in which, citizens and communities interact with public authorities and knowledge developers, in a collaborative mode, exploiting the power of co-designed user centered innovation services, is the driving force. The authors argue that the city challenges are more effectively addressed at the scale of neighbourhood and they provide cases and experiences that demonstrate the viability, importance and impact of this model.

1 Introduction

Due to the progressive urbanization of our societies, it is becoming increasingly difficult for the city authorities to be able to provide suitable services to address citizens' needs. Cities face new challenges every day to create prosperity and ensure good quality of life to its citizens in a World increasingly adopting advanced communication infrastructures and ICT.

Cities are progressively adopting Information and Communication Technologies (ICT) to ensure that its critical infrastructures and utilities are managed more efficiently.

Although the "smartness" of a city cannot be limited to the advanced processes put in place to ensure monitoring, interaction and processing of data collected by ICT infrastructures, and this regardless of the strategic importance of such aspect. Cities are smart when they take full advantage the human capital of its citizens, create innovation ecosystems where the new dynamics of wealth and jobs creation takes place and promote new forms of participatory governance. In short, when they become Human Smart Cities.

2 Urban Innovation Process

Over half of the human population lives in cities today and this figure is estimated to evolve to 70 % in 2050 [1]. Issues such as demographic shifts, health, security, sustainable housing, transportation, energy and environment affect primarily cities and are perceived by citizens as key factors for their quality of life.

M. Helfert et al. (Eds.): Smartgreens 2015 and Vehits 2015, CCIS 579, pp. 32–49, 2015.
DOI: 10.1007/978-3-319-27753-0_3

City administration has therefore to play a strategic and foundational role in the conceptualisation, development and implementation of adequate responses to local or global societal challenges they face today. This is particularly challenging in a context of crisis and mistrust between citizens and Public Administrations.

The Human Smart City model drives and supports the City transformation through the industrialisation and commercialisation of a new generation of local government services, in Europe and worldwide.

In a nutshell, Human Smart City services can be defined as new and innovative "ad hoc" services developed by local government in collaboration with the citizens and other stakeholders, to tackle "wicked" societal problems – or problems the solution of which requires a great number of people to change their mind-sets and behaviours. The main goal of the Human Smart City concept implementation is to create the conditions to improve the quality of life of the citizens leading to well-being and happiness.

Examples of wicked problems come from areas of interest (and legal competence) of local governments, such as waste recycling, water and energy savings, collective mobility, public safety, health and social care. The essence of such problems is threefold:

- It's impossible to start by a clear and univocal problem definition, which depends on the solution framework and the different perspectives of involved stakeholders;
- The constraints the problem is subject to and the resources needed to solve it are changing over time;
- There is no "right" or "optimal" solution and the problem can never be definitively solved.

Most of the areas of interest cited overlap the fields of intervention for Smart City governments. In fact, the conventional wisdom seems to imply that by making wide recourse to the technical "smartness" of sensors, meters, and ICT infrastructures, it would become easier to cope with those wicked problems in a satisfactory manner. By contrast, the Human Smart Cities approach balances technology deployments with "softer" features such as social dialogue, collective vision building, people empowerment and government to citizens (G2C) interaction in physical (as well as virtual) community settings.

ICT infrastructures enabled by the Internet of Things (ability to address and interact with physical objects) and Cloud (computing on demand) solutions promote a better management of critical infrastructures but also offer a yet unexploited potential for new personalised services (e.g. apps based on Open data) and novel types of dialogue between Administrations and citizens, namely though social networks (Such as the Listening and Talking to the Streets approach [2]).

Changes are happening very fast and at a significant scale in cities. Both citizens and Public Authorities are engaging in new approaches to face and adjust to these transformations.

The landing point would then be the design, development, and validation of new urban services by the application of citizen-centric and participatory methods. A claim for democracy, innovation and participation is becoming increasingly pressing, establishing the need to listen and talk to the streets and ultimately change the governance paradigm. These challenges call for a transformation in the way we all work, live, play, and build our future, which in turn places a special burden on those holding the responsibility to govern such processes with an optimum usage of the public resources available. This governance transformation in the Human Smart Cities comes in many forms and should be carefully fostered with the help of new digital technologies that can help the creation of an Innovation City lab as a co-design instrument for the city transformation; the development of services to citizens; new public procurement instruments. PPIs (Public Procurement of innovation), PCPs (Pre-Commercial Procurement) and PPPs (Public Private Partnership); Improvement of the participatory democracy -"Listening and talking to the streets" as well as Security and Privacy by- Design. As a result of the implementation of the Human Smart Cities vision, the government implements and supports a Sustainable Urban Innovation ecosystem (Urban Living Lab), where the virtual communities are encouraged to migrate to the physical environment to meet together and to discover their common Wishes, Interests and Needs (WIN Methodology), co-designing and co-creating new solutions.

Such new approaches are being addressed in innovative projects (such as Peripheria, CitySDK, Citadel or MyNeighbourhood) in which new governance models are experimented, engaging and empowering citizen in the co-creation process of novel city services. In doing so, these experiments and projects contribute to the materialization of the concept of Human Smart City, building upon the need to address the global changes at the citizen level.

Human Smart Cities use technologies as an enabler to connect and engage government and citizens, aiming to rebuild, recreate and motivate urban communities by stimulating and supporting their collaboration activities, leading to a joint increase of social wellbeing.

3 The Path Towards Human Smart Cities

With the arrival of new technologies and the growth of cities, societies have experienced a big change that is reflected in new urban issues. With the new technological trends that are emerging such as Big data, Open data and ubiquitous communications, all leading to a digital society, new ways of living and sharing knowledge are occurring. This transition towards a digital society is having a significant impact in the whole society.

Although the quality of life improved across many dimensions with the evolution of technology, the social cohesiveness of the small groups does not seem to have equally benefited. It is still weak and diluted and cities have lost the strength of inter-personal social interaction that used to make people feel more connected to each other. However, from a social point of view, citizens seem to be in a great need of a sense of belonging and identity, looking for further social inclusion and social integration.

3.1 From Smart Cities to Human Smart Cities

The Smart City concept has been deployed through city-wide sophisticated ICT infrastructures capable of sensing what is happening in a city - parked cars, traffic jams, hospital beds available, energy consumption, water or air quality, temperature, etc.

Using Internet of Things (IoT) all relevant data is collected providing an integrated overview of all city processes. The intensive use of models and data analytics, processed most likely in computing clouds, completes the understanding of the city as a machine and allows for acting in the real word as to adapt it to new circumstances. Cars can be directed to the available parking places, avoid congested zones, ambulances can be redirected, unnecessary consumption of energy can be rationalized, citizens can be warned regarding environmental conditions, etc.)

As just described and often implemented in practice, this Smart City vision exploits a very technology-driven approach to understand and influence the way a city operates.

This is possible as many of the underlying technology systems are technically mature and can effectively bring significant advantages in the management of city services.

The ability to collect and process significant amounts of data also fosters an integrated vision at the base of the Smart City model, highlighting the need to open departmental silos and understand the city's dynamics and the importance of a cross-sector perspective.

A fully developed Smart City schema applies a similar logic to all the functional elements of a city – transportation networks, energy distribution, waste management, air and water quality monitoring – to allow for an integrated control of the city systems, especially when such systems are linked with the different departments of a city administration.

In addition, combining information provided by sensor networks with smartphone apps (specially viable when open access to public data is implemented) allows the personalisation of city services as to fit the needs of a specific citizen according to his position, profile, and patterns of behaviour.

The WIN methodology (Wishes, Interests and Needs developed in Peripheria project [3]) is being adopted in our projects and is published online and in a printed book [4]. This fundamental tool supports the process of citizens engagement and motivation for their collaboration in co-design and co-creation of civic solutions.

But the challenges are bigger and call for a more radical social transformation, affecting the way we all work, live, play, and build our future, which in turn places a special burden on those holding the responsibility to govern such processes with an optimum usage of the public resources available [3].

The concept of Smart Cities evolves to value further the provision of a smart environment for smart living of people, with smart governance and economies, favouring innovation and the exploitation of all human capital available. Cities can only be smart if they exploit data analytics with the purpose of ensuring "smartness", not only in terms of the automation of routine functions, but also in understanding, monitoring, analysing and planning the city, improving the quality of life of its citizens and building a trusted governance model engaging and empowering the citizens in the co-creation of solution for collective social challenges.

In a context of financial crisis, severe limitations have been induced in invested resources in infrastructure and, in some cases, in the provision of urban basic services; this seems to have created a new social consciousness that is currently arising. Citizens are calling for a more effective representation and listening of urban constituencies, overcoming an eroded trust between them and the authorities. In reality, the explosion of mass participation based on Social Networks confirms a "demand from the streets" that are calling for openness, transparency and trust in the governance and political system [5].

The described scenario justifies the need to evolve the concept of Smart Cities by refocusing it again on citizens, their needs and an open collaboration with public authorities.

The Human Smart City concept is built on emergent, sustainable models for urban living, working and governance enabled by Future Internet infrastructures and services. At the core of the vision is the human perspective, as gained through the application of citizen-centric and participatory approaches to the co-design, development, and production of Smart City services that balance the technical "smartness" of sensors, meters, and infrastructures with softer features such as clarity of vision, citizen empowerment, social interaction in physical urban settings, and public-citizens partnership.

The Human Smart City approach is gaining increasing support from city governments across Europe as well as the Smart City research community, as it more effectively addresses key challenges such as low-carbon strategies, the urban environment, sustainable mobility, and social inclusion through a more balanced, holistic approach to technology.

The Human Smart City concept appears as an improvement of the Smart City, focusing on creating a healthier and happier environment for citizens.

In the Human Smart City, the city government implements and supports an ecosystem of urban innovation (Urban Living Lab [6]), which applies co-design and co-production of social and technological innovation services and processes, in order to solve real problems (Fig. 1).

Fig. 1. City governance transformation.

The government agrees to be engaged and involved in citizens' initiatives on the basis of an open, transparent and reliable relationship. In this ecosystem, information technologies are used to solve social problems and address economic and environmental issues, focusing on the welfare and happiness of the citizens [7].

3.2   Human Smart Cities Concept

The Human Smart City concept aims at developing a citizen-driven, smart, all-inclusive and sustainable environment, with a new governance framework in which citizens and government engage in listening and talking to each other. The engagement of citizens in the idea generation is essential to build a trust environment in which community and governance co-design solutions. If citizens are actively collaborating with the city administration it increases their ability to contribute to address urban and social key issues that become a common concern. The big challenge is not to install the infrastructure or adopt new technologies but to involve the public sphere in the civic life.

It is important to point out that the implementation of the Human Smart City concept can be made through the use of frugal technology and does not always require sophisticated and complex infrastructures. This fact is relevant essentially in what concerns the scalability of the solution. Simple and creative solutions can emerge from the local communities which allows, for example big cities to extend their strategies and include broad metropolitan areas, or small cities to integrate new strategies. This is an important advantage, for the city administration, that enables the creation of humanly smart services without having to make significant investments.

Another significant advantage of this concept, from the governance point of view, is the fact that the co-design and co-production of solutions takes out the "burden" of the city administration processes that become lighter and more transparent.

In order to become Human Smart Cities, cities administrations need to build trust with the community and test the collaboration and participation of the citizens. To do so it is important to identify the different needs of the community by establishing contact with the citizens. Most of the time the city administration only gets feedback from a small number of citizens, thus it is important to put in place strategies to "listen and talk" to all the groups of citizens.

4   The Human Smart Cities Approach in Practice

Human Smart Cities are focused on the quality of life, well-being and happiness of citizens. The Human Smart City uses an ICT infrastructure to collect, process, store and analyse large communities of data sets (open data) that encourages developers to develop applications (Apps) that are solutions for existing problems or challenges of the cities. A successful example of the implementation of the Human Smart Cities approach is the MyNeighbourhood (MyN) project. To illustrate the impact of the Human Smart Cities concept in practice we refer to the results of the MyN project as deployed and experimented in real settings in Lisbon, Milan, Aalborg and Birmingham.

The MyNeighbourhood project can be seen as a relevant test bed and proof of concept in the implementation of a Human Smart Cities vision and methodologies. The project is based on the premise that neighbourhoods represent a heretofore untapped, yet powerful, catalyst for human smart city change. MyNeighbourhood aims at transforming the city governance by engaging citizens in an open, transparent and trusted dialog, enhancing and easing the interaction with the city administration: this makes it easier for citizens and business to transmit priorities and needs to city administration, reduces the need for time consuming face-to-face interactions with city administration and removes the burden of bureaucratic processes by facilitating greater neighbour-to-neighbour exchanges.

4.1 MyNeighbourhood Project

MyNeighbourhood project [8], is part of the European Commission ICT PSP Programme in the field of Smart Cities, aims at recreating and strengthening the social ties and interactions within the neighbourhood [9].

MyNeighbourhood aims at recreating and strengthening the social ties and interactions within the neighbourhood (theme presented in Dynamic Neighbourhoods), experimenting with new concepts of a smartness in cities that focuses on people and their well-being rather than just on ICT infrastructures and dashboards.

The project exploits the paradoxical assumption that the same ICT trends that have – in conjunction with other urban trends - helped to erode the citizens' connection to urban neighbourhoods and communities also have the potential to help reinvigorating them. The MyNeighbourhood project promotes qualitative and innovative solutions and the identification of a set of opportunities that will not only influence the neighbourhood but the surrounding ecosystem of the city.

The MyNeighbourhood solution integrates new digital technologies and methodologies, such as social gaming principles (gamification), with the Living Lab methodology to help creating and strengthening existing ties and resolve communal issues in the real life of the neighbourhood. It uses gamification techniques to encourage people to get involved with their own neighbourhoods and engage their family and friends to do the same. The solution is rooted in an open *MyNeighbourhood* Platform that combines the data and functionality of existing "City Transformation Apps" with new tools that connect people locally, both on and offline. It uses gamification techniques to encourage people to get involved with their own neighbourhoods and engage their family and friends to do the same. Building upon the six recognized levels of social innovation (the six levels, from *"The Open Book of Social Innovation"*, are: 1. Prompts, inspirations and diagnoses; 2. Proposals and ideas; 3. Prototyping and pilots; 4. Sustaining; 5. Scaling and diffusion; 6. Systemic change.) [10], the MyNeighbourhood Living Lab approach is using new technologies and ontologies to develop local innovation environments that help to rebuild, empower and scale neighbourhoods value in a manner that reconnects people, recreate communities and, ultimately, makes cities smarter.

The MyN project is based in seven key components (MyN Consortium, 2015):

- Creative citizens and communities: Individuals and groups of people who collaboratively solve problems and creatively self-organize to cooperatively invent, enhance and manage innovative solutions for new ways of living in the City.
- Collaborative enterprises: Entrepreneurial initiatives of production and service that enhance new models of locally-based activities, having direct relationships with users and consumers who, in this case, become co-producers.

- Participative institutions: Parts of larger institutions that operate at the local scale, on locally defined projects and with an extensive participation of interested people. These institutions are open to citizens not only in the sense that they are able to capture people's Wishes, Interests and Needs; they are also able to be engaged by the citizens and transform collaboration with them into a cooperative work.
- Collaborative services: Services where the end users are actively involved and assume the role of service co-designers and co-producers based on peer-to-peer and collaborative relationships, which leads to both new technical solutions to user needs and better social relations among the people who collaborate.
- Design thinking theory and practice:
    - A highly dynamic process that adopts co-design, co-creation and consensus building methodologies and leads to the generation of new prototypes, mock-ups, design games, models, sketches and other materials, devices and artefacts;
    - A set of creative and proactive activities, where the designer also plays the roles of mediator (between different interests) and facilitator (of other participants' ideas and initiatives), in addition to his/her specific skills and knowledge.
- Scaling up: The process of consolidation, replication, and integration of small scale and/or local inventions or working prototypes within larger programmes, product/service systems or infrastructures.
- Socio-digital innovation: The result of combination of ICT with social innovation models, tools, practices and communities.

The MyNeighbourhood project builds a socio-technical system whereby existing communities can interact in a synergic way, in order to: Strengthen and widen a sense of belonging from a single community to the neighbourhood; Assure mutual interdependency characterized by a multiplicity of urban dimensions (social, economic, environmental...); Redirect the singularisation mechanism that is typical of contemporary urban societies towards a highly connected one [11].

In fact, individuals are nowadays more and more focussed on personal utility and satisfaction, which demolishes the relevance of common, social, collective values (social capital) able to develop reciprocity and solidarity mechanisms, which we consider at the base of the neighbourhood's life and conception.

The solution deployment in MyNeighbourhood is based upon three key phases:

- Phase I: Rebuilding Neighbourhoods;
- Phase II: Empowering Neighbourhoods;
- Phase III: Scaling up Neighbourhood Value.

The first phase is characterized by the use the Living Lab methodology to deploy and promote a MyNeighbourhood website that builds upon and improves existing City Information Apps by enabling local residents to connect with each other and share resources – user data such as time, assets & knowledge, ICT tools/apps - to improve their own neighbourhoods. The work with pilot cities aims at 'kick starting' the site in the targeted subject areas: health, environment, participation, transport. One of the goals of this phase is to embed a gamification layer in the MyNeighbourhood site that

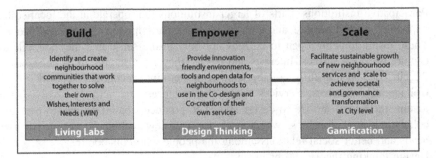

Fig. 2. Human Smart Cities Methodologies.

motivates users to keep returning to the site, do more for their neighbourhood and engage their friends to set up a new MyNeighbourhood site in their own neighbourhood (Fig. 2).

In a second phase, Empowering Neighbourhoods, the MyNeighbourhood portal is used to feed a resident query or need into a 'Neighbourhood Advisor System'. The aim is to establish a database that will understand the request and map it against potential outcomes – ranging from a relevant existing app through to direct contact with others in the neighbourhood who can help or potential crowdsourcing options to create new solutions. In this phase it is important to include a feedback loop into each solution to draw the user back into gamification.

The third phase, Scaling Neighbourhood Value, aims at ensuring that the MyNeighbourhood Platform offers a quick and easy one-stop portal for people to add local content, ideas applications and needs about their own neighbourhood – thereby facilitating a viral effect. The goal is to make ideas and apps widely and openly available – whether newly created or already existing – through on- and offline channels and tactics such as developer competitions and to aggregate and navigate needs at the neighbourhood, city and EU level to provide scalable intelligence at all three of these levels.

The government and public administration is challenged by the need to improve the quality of the services provided to the citizens. This is a big challenge, because it clashes with the inertia of bureaucratic structures and requires higher flexibility of the structure and a positive attitude towards innovation. It is important to include all the actors of the cities (and therefore of the neighbourhood) in the co-creation of consistent and coherent solutions, by stimulating citizens' creativity. This process needs to be supported by proper tools that support the various phases of implementation, from the early ideas for service scenarios and for a service structure. Therefore a handbook was created to provide tools, developed by designers or adapted from other disciplines. In order to create this handbook two activities suggestive and supportive examples of existing engagement tools and approaches used in living lab environments as well as co-design methods were collected. Forty seven cases have been collected, analysed and synthetically described in a table while twenty of them have been described in detail in dedicated cards as in the figure below.

Following the work carried out on the cases, coherent guidelines have been developed for citizens and municipalities as main actors of the pilots' work in MyNeighbourhood Project (Fig. 3).

Fig. 3. Detailed case description card.

The Methodology and tools used in the MyNeighbourhood project were created and shared amongst the pilot teams in order to facilitate the field work. The project pilots participants identified how their services can be gamified on the MyN Platform, thus expressing ideas of how the services could not only use the MyN Platform, but what capabilities can be supported to engage citizens to use the platform, using ideas from gamification. The co-design handbook general structure was also presented to the Pilot teams and represented the basis of the field work carried out in the project. The co-design work preceding the implementation and testing work, has been divided into two main phases: the context analysis phase and Service Design phase [12]. The context analysis phase consisted in the identification of the stakeholders, the existing projects and all the factors that are considered to have influence in the social context and in the solution creation. The field work consisted of interviews, guerrilla

Fig. 4. Citizen Engagement and community activities within the MyNeighbourhood-My City Project.

observation and post-it sessions that created a link favouring the listening and the talking amongst the main actors, including citizens, professionals, experts and volunteers.

The data collection during this phase resulted in the identification of WINs of the citizens and also the needs of the local associations and the municipalities (Fig. 4).

During the co-design phase the data collected in the previous phase was used to co-create solutions and services to address the neighbourhood needs. Several workshops and meetings were held to share ideas and co-design services together with the local stakeholders and citizens. Some tools, such as Blueprints, Stakeholder maps and Journey maps, were used to facilitate the interaction and to progress quicker and obtain results.

During the implementation phase of the project the solutions are being applied to each pilot, in order to observe how the proposed concepts and their implementation fits to the real needs and how people are using products, services and technologies proposed as a result of the co-design process. The aim of this phase was to provide useful feedback from the users that could be used to optimize the services and the Platform.

The three stage methodology instantiation pathway for the implementation phase includes the plan, implementation and reporting.

In stage 1 the representatives of the four participant Cities, supported by the respective innovation ecosystem (Universities and technical developers), have been requested to prepare a Service Implementation Plan. In stage 2 the pilot implementation was worked by each pilot team and the detailed operation was discussed and shared between all partners in the collaborative workgroup set up for that purpose: that is the co-designed implementation processes converging to a common model. In stage 3 the pilots teams reported their individual experiences learning from each other and co-creating a common methodology. This involved weekly virtual meetings and face-to-face meetings every 2 months.

4.2 MyNeighbourhood Pilots

The four city pilots have different issues and specific characteristics: the work developed in the Marvila (Lisbon) [13] neighbourhood, came up with services more oriented to the social inclusion and local economy issues; in Ladyhood (Birmingham) the challenges addressed were mostly related to transportation and mobility; in Quarto Oggiaro (Milan) the needs identification revealed issues related to maintenance of public areas and elderly people social integration; in Nørresundbyv (Aalborg) the solutions created concerned health care and social inclusion of people with disabilities [14].

The choice of these four places enabled the creation of a set of different solutions that can be replicable in other neighbourhoods: Aalborg has 3 services: Voluntary Help; Accessible City; Cultural Assistance; Birmingham has 2 services: Women on Wheels; Travel Buddies; Lisbon has 2 families of services: Ó Vizinho; Made in Marvila; Milan has 2 services: Quarto Food Club; Quarto Gardening.

Each family of services may include many services, typically dozens and being open to expand to others services of the same sort.

4.3 MyNeighbourhood Platform

The MyN platform is the technical solution that meets the goals and services envisioned from the MyNeighbourhood Vision and Concept and from the work done in the living labs and co-design activities within the pilots. It helps to recreate a lost sense of neighbourhood that is rooted in the local place, were people share the same interests and needs. As such, the Platform intends to provide the means of identifying, searching and managing the needs of the individuals within the context of the neighbourhood. This also entails the sharing of knowledge and expertise across the neighbourhood.

The MyN is an open source platform combining web technologies, existing products, social networks, semantic technology and gamification to ensure the engagement of the citizen and the effective response to their wishes interests and needs. Its architecture takes into consideration the bottom-up design process derived from the co-design activities, enhancing the human focus. The design of the platform is based on user-centered methods, and includes a set of tools and principles that will be reflected in the system and in the user interface.

In the product discovery phase, which was the base of the creation of the Platform architecture, product solutions were envisioned from the business intentions and the project vision, but the product discovery was not focused only on the solution. This activity led the stakeholders to spend time understanding more than just what to build: the solution context, business and product strategy, customer segments, product usages, regulatory constraints, legacy product and architecture, users and user goals and how the product will touch the lives of the users.

The Platform is available on the web (www.my-n.eu) and provides, among many functionalities, the features of creating communities within each neighbourhood, creating blogs and discussion, promoting challenges, exchanging products and services in the "Neighbourhood Market Square" as well as georeferencing POIs (Points of interest), such as restaurants, bars, local important places, bus stops, gardens, in the "Neighbourhood places" which also allows the insertion of comments, accessibility rate, photos and other information that the user can add.

To support the project phases (identified above), a number of core features and generic/specific enablers have been identified and co-designed as relevant components of the MyN platform. These features have been implemented and tested in the pilots and new neighbourhoods that joined the MyN Platform. The demonstrated benefits of the MyN Platform for its users include:

- A trustful environment for interaction and cooperation;
- A new sense of belonging to one's own neighbourhood;
- Connectivity with other users and through the platform;
- Awareness and perception of being part of the community;
- Consciousness and sharing of the neighbourhood essence.

Taken together, these benefits form an integral part of the MyN platform's value proposition. At the end of the MyN project, the following vision statement was formulated, which is taken as starting point for the MyN project: MyN enables Smart City Governments to successfully engage their constituents in the co-design and co-production of frugal services, locally based but prone to scaling up, through an alternance of real life activities and online, gamified interactions and collaborations on a dedicated ICT platform, which enhances the sense of belonging to a neighbourhood and exploits citizen intelligence for performance monitoring and continuous improvement of public policy action (Fig. 5).

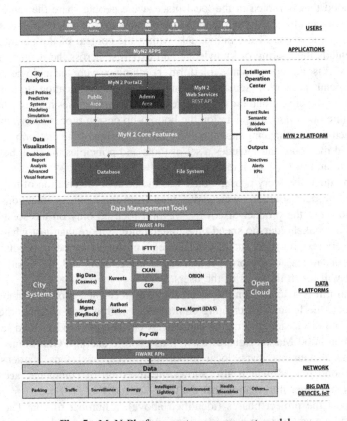

Fig. 5. MyN Platform system component model.

From this statement, six main components emerge as a result of the final vision of the MyN project. As a starting point for the MyN project we can consider the following components to develop:

- Sense of Neighbourhood: The first original trait of the MyN platform is that of being at the same time, supportive of social network-like relationships and of their precise localisation – or association with a specific, cultural and social, space – that is identified with an urban neighbourhood. One of the project's initial value propositions has been exactly to exploit the creation of ICT-supported communities of interest to fill in the gaps in Social Capital engendered by the urbanisation and "metropolisation" processes. Thanks to the WINs – Wishes, Interests and Needs – parable, we did not only manage to involve volunteers in not-for-profit activities, but also established neighbourhood level links to fight against poverty, social exclusion, and create opportunities for growth and jobs in peripheral or secluded environments that are normally considered problem areas of our Cities.

- Off/Online Alternance: MyN has proposed and actuated a new interplay between the Cyber and the City space. Individual participation and collective engagement are grounded on place attachment and the WINs of most active citizens from the local community. When successfully operated, as shown in the MyN Pilots, MyN adoption enhances place identity as well as the sense of belonging to a neighbourhood. However, differently from social networks, MyN points at a problem-solving dimension that is neither fully virtual (this is not the "Facebook of the Neighbourhood") nor totally grounded in the real world (as many problems dealt with in the MyN pilots have emerged on the platform, or at least could not be solved without making recourse to it).

- Co-Design/Co-production of Frugal Services: The micro scale solutions found to those problems are part of a broader conception of public service that is:

  - Co-designed with and co-produced by the people
  - Tackling societal challenges, meaning problems that are notoriously exceeding the capacity of local governments alone to solve them
  - Frugal in nature, meaning that the cost of service design/production is dramatically reduced by the active involvement/engagement of local people.

- Citizen Intelligence: All this activism does not only lead to notable results in terms of supplementing local government actions towards service delivery. It also provides invaluable tools to policy makers and public agencies willing to monitor, interpret and even predict the evolution of the "public opinion" (or local community orientation and propensity) towards the best match of quality/quantity/costs/benefits of neighbourhood-level service systems. The MyN platform comprises ad hoc ICT tools to collect information and provide useful representations in support of decision-making at three main levels:

  - All active neighbourhoods in a City platform;
  - Each individual neighbourhood;
  - Each community (group) page within the neighbourhoods.

- Scaling Up Potential: The scalability of the MyN platform has been confirmed during the project in many respects, from its easiness to scale out (to other neighbourhoods) to its propensity to being taken up (to the broader City level), both internally and externally to the pilots. Based on this preliminary evidence, it can be argued that City Neighbourhoods – rather than Urban or Social Networks – should be in focus of policy action to increase the impact and sustainability of service innovation in Smart Cities.
- Gamification: This has been identified since the early project stages as a key concept in engaging people and is also recognised as a key tool of the Living Labs approach to facilitate user take-up and loyalty in adoption of online services. A well-defined and clear methodology has been defined to support the use of gamification in the MyN platform, consisting of three main parts:
  - Setting the context,
  - Gamification tools (cards), and a process to conduct the gamification, and
  - The crowning of the best "gamified" idea.

The gamification methodology has been developed based on prior experience, current practice and theory and has been refined over the course of the project, to become an important component of the MyN platform and of the way activities/services are built, managed and scaled up over it.

5 Human Smart Cities Network

The MyNeighbourhood project and other projects such as Periphèria [4] support the view that Human Smart Cities are a viable concept with a clear impact on the citizen's perception of the "smartness" of his city.

5.1 Human Smart Cities in Europe

The Human Smart Cities Network, builds a network of cities committed to facilitating the development of effective Smart City strategies and its uptake across a range of cultural, geographical, and infrastructural contexts. Its main objectives are to:

- Allow cities to learn from each other, accelerating the process of social and urban innovation;
- Promote knowledge sharing between cities;
- Promote regular events so that knowledge sharing is potentiated;
- Create a dynamic platform that includes a database of case studies.

The Human Smart Cities Network will allow member-cities to:

- Gain international visibility and collaboration;
- Contribute to the Human Smart Cities policy-making;
- Share Knowledge;
- Access updated news on funding programs and other initiatives;

- Access to the Human Smart City Toolkit, including methodologies, tools, best practices and use cases;
- Access to a task force that aims to build bridges across the Globe.
- In Europe, the Human Smart Cities Manifesto was signed in Rome, on the 29th of May of 2013. Today this Network integrates more than 100 cities.
- Closely related to the Human Smart Cities Network concept is the Open & Agile Smart Cities (OASC) initiative. Signed by 31 cities from Finland, Denmark, Belgium, Portugal, Italy, Spain and Brazil, the OASC initiative aims at adopting common standards for interchange of data and hence will kickstart the use of open platforms and standards such as FIWARE/MyN; this is expected to foster the development of Smart City applications and solutions that can contribute to the emergence of Human Smart Cities.

These commitments marks a milestone in the development of Smart Cities, boosting the transformation of cities into engines of growth and well-being through innovation (Fig. 6).

Fig. 6. Human Smart Cities European Network.

5.2   Human Smart Cities in Brazil

The Human Smart Cities concept has been strongly disseminated in Brazil, raising awareness of Local Authorities and Universities, as well as other stakeholders such as State Governments. This benefited from the wide spread knowledge in Brazil of the innovation activities based on Living Lab methodologies done in Europe, not just by the Association ENOLL but also by companies such as Alfamicro.

In Brazil, open innovation strategies were adopted in Manaus already in 2007 and today spread throughout the Brazilian territory with the support of a Living Lab Network which addresses technical and social innovation domains. It is in the perspective of social innovation that the urban Living Lab has been promoted to transform the City Governance and the creation of wealth and jobs (Fig. 7).

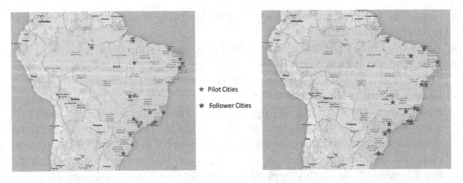

Fig. 7. Human Smart Cities network in Brazil and Brazilian Institute of Smart Cities.

Brazil is particularly interested in the Human Smart City concept to accelerate the process of "listening and talking to the streets", that means, accelerate the adoption of forms of e-participation and open collaboration which are expected to open the way to create common spaces where e.g. the antagonist cultures of the favelas and well off areas of the Cities may converge.

The efforts of coordination in Brazil culminated recently with the creation of the Brazilian Network of Human Smart Cities in partnership with the Forum of Brazilian Municipalities (Science technology and innovation domain).

References

1. United Nations: World Urbanization Prospects, The 2007 Revision. United Nations, New York (2008)
2. Oliveira, A.: MyNeihbourhood Vision. Human Smart Cities Conference, the future of cities today, Lisbon, 13th March 2014
3. Oliveira, A.: The Human Smart Cities Vision. Human Smart Cities Conference, Forum PA, Rome, 29th May 2013
4. Jesse, M., Oliveira, A.: The Human Smart Cities Cookbook, Milan (2013). http://peripheria. eu/library
5. Fernandes, E., de Freitas Roseno, R.: Protesta Brasil – Das Redes sociais às Manifestações de Rua. Prata Editora, São Paulo (2013)
6. Oliveira, A.: The European Network of Living Labs as the platform for Smart Cities & Future Internet, Ghent, 14th December 2010
7. Oliveira, A.: Human Smart Cities: an ecosystem of neighbourhood platforms and Urban Living Labs. Citisense - Innovation from within. Smart City Expo World Congress, Barcelona, 18th November 2013
8. MyNeighbourhood Project (2013). http://my-neighbourhood.eu/. (cited May 30, 2014)
9. Murray, R., Caulier Grice, J., Mulgan, G.: The Open Book of Social Innovation. The Young Foundation/ NESTA, UK (2010)
10. Weissbourd R., Bodini, R.: Dynamic Neighbourhoods. New Tools for Community and Economic Development. Living Cities / RW Ventures, LLC, (S.l.) (2009)
11. Meroni, A.: Creative Communities. Polidesign Press, Milan (2007)

12. Rizzo, F.: Strategie di co-design, teorie, metodi e strumenti per progettare con gli utenti. Franco Angeli, Milan (2009)
13. MyNeighbourhood Project: MyNeighbourhood in Mouraria, pilot video, November 2013. http://vimeo.com/75226308
14. MyNeighbourhood Project. Project video, March 2014. http://my-neighbourhood.eu/myn-project-video

An Open Platform for Children's Independent Mobility

Matteo Gerosa[✉], Annapaola Marconi, Marco Pistore, and Paolo Traverso

Fondazione Bruno Kessler, Via Sommarive, 18, Trento, Italy
{gerosa,marconi,pistore,traverso}@fbk.eu

Abstract. Children's independent mobility is a perfect example of a smart community, where proactive citizens participation and new form of collaboration between citizens and city managers are fundamental to solve daily problems in the city. This application domain, intersecting several areas of a smart city, from sustainable mobility to health and education, is at the same time very relevant from a societal perspective and very challenging from an ICT perspective, since it requires a combination of socio-psychological theories and practices and of advanced ICT techniques and tools. In this paper we illustrate the problem, analyzing on-going initiatives, lessons learnt and potential role of ICT solutions, and propose a solution, the CLIMB Platform, that will be experimented within the city of Trento.

1 Introduction

The idea of smart cities has mainly developed along a technology-centric vision, based on broadband communication networks, smart objects and Internet of things, open public, private, and personal data, electronic and mobile services, and so on. More recently, the vision of a smart community has moved the emphasis towards the people living in the territory and towards the different communities of citizens sharing common goals, interests, and problems. Key elements of a smart community are the proactive participation of citizens to the public life and the related decision-making processes, and the capability to establish new forms of collaboration between citizens and city managers to solve the daily problem of the life in the city.

We believe that it is the mix of new technologies and of citizen engagement that can offer the best opportunities to address the societal challenges and to improve the quality of life in the city. In this paper, we illustrate this concept through a project on children's independent mobility (for short, CLIMB), which we have just started in collaboration with the municipality of Trento.

Children's independent mobility is a paradigmatic example for us, under several points of view. First, it is a specific but important societal problem. Being independent and active road users is indeed fundamental for children's and adolescents' physical, social, cognitive and emotional development. Yet, in recent decades there has been an increase in the number of parents placing restrictions on - and thereby limiting - the independent mobility of their children,

M. Helfert et al. (Eds.): Smartgreens 2015 and Vehits 2015, CCIS 579, pp. 50–71, 2016.
DOI: 10.1007/978-3-319-27753-0_4

in particular for what concerns their journeys to school. Our aim in CLIMB is to enhance independent and active mobility of children aged 6 to 10 by changing the awareness and attitude of parents and society in general and by making the daily journey to school a safe, fun, and social experience.

Second, children's independent mobility intersects several key areas for smart cities, such as sustainable mobility, health and well being, school and education, and citizen participation. CLIMB has hence the potential of planting the seed of a new approach that can then grow and spread in all these areas. Also, CLIMB engages a large part of the community, including families, schools (e.g., teachers), neighborhood (e.g., shop owners), civic servants (e.g., urban police), and volunteers (e.g., elderly people helping children in crossing roads).

Third, the solutions we want to pilot for children's independent mobility requires a combination of socio-psychological theories and practices and of ICT tools. Indeed, proper technology is fundamental to support the whole community in the ideation, management and daily operation of children mobility initiatives and solutions. For this reason, in CLIMB we adopt a technological platform that: (i) enables collecting information and knowledge by integrating and correlating heterogeneous data sources (e.g., open, crowd, sensor data), and thus providing an up-to-date and consistent view on all conditions affecting children's mobility; (ii) supports the whole community (parents, teachers, children, volunteers) in the ideation, management and daily operation of grassroots children mobility initiatives and services; and (iii) makes use of personalized and intuitive tools, mobile solutions, gamification techniques, and virtual/real incentives to increase awareness and promote behavioral changes.

In this paper, we illustrate the vision, problem and solution fostered by CLIMB. In particular, in Sect. 2 we analyze the current situation of children's mobility around Europe, the initiatives set up in recent years by Trento municipality and the key problems they are facing, and the role and potential impact of advanced ICT solutions in addressing these problems. Section 3 presents the CLIMB Platform in details and shows its applicability through a children's independent mobility scenario. Section 4 highlights the innovation aspects of the proposed solution and compares it with other state of the art approaches and initiatives. Finally, in Sect. 5 we discuss future works and conclusions.

2 The Problem

2.1 Children's Independent and Sustainable Mobility

Being an independent and active road user has been proven to be fundamental for the physical, social, cognitive and emotional development of children and adolescents [1-6].

Nevertheless, in recent decades there has been an increase in the number of parents placing restrictions on - and thereby limiting - the independent mobility of their children [2,7-11] and the expression "back-seat generation" is sadly becoming well known in international debates. The reasons why parents choose to drive their children to school vary. For some cases it is due to lack of traffic safety measures for children as pedestrians or cyclists [7]. For others it is related to practical considerations [12,13], convenience and time saving [14], since driving the children to school makes it easier to manage the daily family juggle. Some parents also believe that a "good parent" is one who drives the children all the way to the school [13,15]. Considering that children's mobility accounts for approximately 20 % of the total daily travelling population in the EU (EU, 2002) and that chauffeuring children accounts for a large proportion of cars on the road, the vicious cycle of chauffeuring parents endangering non-chauffeured children is clear [8] and its impact in terms of road traffic and carbon emissions in EU cities is substantial.

Several European countries are carrying out development work designed to *improve the safety of school routes* and reduce the need for car travel to school and leisure activities. However, as stated above, safety concerns is only one amongst other factors preventing independent travel: the main obstacle to children's independent mobility is parents' perception and their *lack of awareness* of the problem [12–15]. Hence, innovative and often costly programmes introduced by cities to increase traffic safety are liable to fail if not combined with initiatives aimed at *changing parents' attitudes and at increasing citizens' awareness* towards this problem [16]. There is the need of accompanying "traditional" campaigns with virtual campaigns, hence amplifying their effects (in terms of parents' awareness, community participation, and behavioural changes), both in dimensional terms (capability to engage a larger community) and in temporal terms (capability to ensure a durable engagement that lasts also after the end of the traditional campaign).

At the same time, plenty of grassroots and participatory initiatives are being launched at a local level providing bottom-up solutions supporting children's freedom of movement (e.g., walking buses, children bike-trains, volunteers at crosswalks, ride-sharing among parents, etc.). However, most of these initiatives struggle to scale up and often do not survive long after their bootstrapping. This is mainly due to their *fragmentation and isolation, lack of reliability, convenience and flexibility of the offered mobility services*, especially if compared to the use of private cars. If the aim is to deliver "smart children mobility services" to citizens, these services cannot be operated each by itself, but should become part of an *integrated mobility solution*, that supports service users (parents, children) and providers (teachers, drivers, traffic aids and volunteers) in their daily operation and management of the different mobility services.

2.2 City of Trento: On-going Initiatives, Lessons Learnt and Needs

Trento is a medium Italian city (ca. 116.000 people) characterized by a modern service sector as well as by a quite consolidated innovation eco-system comprised of a University, several research centres and many innovative companies and start-ups. Despite its small size, the city is spread out and has several neighborhood communities. Typically, each of these neighborhoods has one primary school that serves the whole neighborhood.

Trento has extensive experience in the area of children's mobility. The most important initiative is called "A Piedi Sicuri" (Safe by foot): a project coordinated by the Trento City council to increase the independent mobility of children. The project focuses on making children go to school, alone or accompanied, without using private cars and focusing instead on sustainable transport, such as by foot, bike or bus. The goal of this project is not only to reduce car traffic but also to give children the chance to feel autonomous and responsible outside of their homes. In addition to the city of Trento and to the schools, the project involves also the local traffic cops that are involved in teaching children how to move safely when on foot or by bike during specially designed school lessons.

"A Piedi Sicuri" currently includes the following initiatives and services:

- "Pedibus" or walking bus, currently involving 52 volunteers. The walking bus is self-organized and operated by parents who volunteer to guide groups of children from home to schools following a pre-defined schedule and itinerary. The Trento municipality offers insurance to the volunteer parents and reflective vests (for volunteers) and hats (for the kids).
- "A scuola senz'auto" (To school without car) is a yearly contest between classes and schools that compete on the percentage of children that travel in a sustainable way (bike, bus and by foot) from home to school. The last initiative was held on 13th of February 2015 and involved 8 schools, 14 classes and 1556 children. The average rate of sustainable mobility was 79 % and many classes were able to achieve 100 % of sustainable mobility for a single day.
- "Scuolabus" (School bus): the province of Trento organizes a school bus service in addition to the city bus. School buses cover a wide area and are used to reach the schools, mainly in the neighborhoods, by children living more than 1 Km away from school.
- "Nonni vigili" (Grandparents as traffic cops): the municipality of Trento employs 27 elderly people (from 60 to 75 years) that watch children at the school entrance and exit, and stop cars and provide secure pedestrian crossings. This service is renewed each year and applicants need to attend an 8-hours course on security to better guarantee the safety of the children and of themselves. Each "Grandparent" patrols a specific area/street and traffic cops supervise the service.

Over an 11-year period, this project engaged 24 primary schools, of which 12 are currently actively involved for a total of 2000 children. Results of this initiative are very encouraging: after several experiments, with a significant effort spent in the engagement of children, parents and teachers, independent mobility of children increased in all schools involved of percentages between 8 and 25 %.

The main issue of the "A Piedi Sicuri" project is sustainability. After the first phase of implementation of "A Piedi Sicuri" in a school, it is difficult to keep the school engaged in the following years. Until now promotions has focused on informing parents about the existence of the initiatives, however, despite the considerable effort dedicated by the municipality, this has not been sufficient to guarantee their wide and continuous adoption.

The municipality of Trento is seeking an integrated solution that offers all stakeholders an environment where they can access information and services, provide their own information and collectively manage the already existing children mobility services (i.e. top-down services such as school buses, crosswalks' volunteers, as well as bottom-up initiatives such as walking buses, groups of children walking/cycling to school, ride-sharing among parents) together with new ones, to improve independent mobility of children.

2.3   Role and Potential Impact of ICT Solutions

Recent technological advances in ICT, such as the Internet of Services, the Internet of Things, distributed social networks, and knowledge co-creation networks, represent a possible way to overcome the problems described in previous Sections. In particular, we identified four main obstacle that these advanced ICT solution may help to overcome.

Lack in Convenience and Flexibility of the Offered Mobility Services. ICT solutions can support the collective management of the different mobility services, making them more convenient, addressing the needs of all the key players (i.e., school, parents, drivers, volunteers and children) and enabling their active participation and collaboration in the service organization, provisioning and operation (service co-operation). ICT solution can also offer a swift management of emergencies (e.g. when a parent is sick and will not be able to manage the walking bus the following morning) with automatic or semi-automatic systems to self-organize the service (e.g. automatic notification to the following parent volunteer until one gives his/her availability). This will make the mobility services more robust, flexible and convenient.

Lack of Awareness and Information. By leveraging on the network-effect (networks of people, knowledge and things), ICT can greatly help to derive a comprehensive and up-to-date picture of the current situation of children's mobility in the neighborhood. For example, the information from these networks (e.g., traffic sensors, people mobile phones, cameras, social networks) can be integrated in a map that shows to parents and other stakeholder both real-time and historic data on traffic, accidents, walking bus paths etc. This smart-map of the neighborhood, combined with the use of ICT social networks, is an invaluable tool for parents to connect with each other and exchange information. This will create a comprehensive framework that allow parents to connect with their peers, investigate all the possible solutions to their needs and take informed decisions.

Fragmentation and Isolation of Initiatives. ICT tools can promote the identification and design of novel "grassroots" initiatives and solutions. This is obtained by promoting the engagement of the different actors in the community, both horizontally (different roles: parents, city officers, teachers, volunteers, etc.)

and vertically (people with different capabilities, skills, availabilities, etc.), in the identification, definition and deployment of novel initiatives related to children's independent mobility. ICT tools will not only enable to search for initiatives and join them, but also to propose new initiatives, to rate and comment them and to find the resources to fund them when needed. This system, along with the information sharing tools mentioned above, will greatly help in reducing fragmentation and isolation as it will collect all initiatives and make them available to the whole community.

Parent's Attitude Towards the Problem. ICT tools will help improving parents' awareness towards the problem, their safety perception, knowledge about existing alternatives and thus their attitude towards independent and active mobility. In addition to the information-sharing tools mentioned above, ICT tools can be used for the definition and operation of games that involve the whole community. These games promote participation and virtuous behaviors through virtual and real incentives. In addition to changing parent's attitude, this gamification approach will also amplify the effects and duration of children's independent mobility campaigns and increase their sustainability in time.

3 Proposed Approach and Solution

In this paper we propose an Open Platform for Children's Independent Mobility (CLIMB Platform) that harnesses the collaborative power of ICT networks (networks of people, of knowledge, of services, of things) and combines it with sociopsychological theories and practices (from here on referred as "non-ICT tools") in order to (1) support the whole community in the operation and management

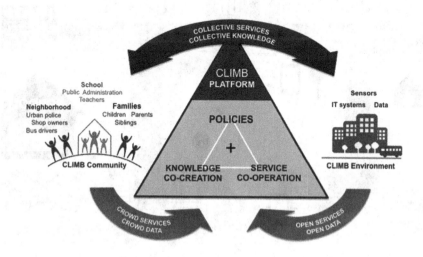

Fig. 1. CLIMB concept at a Glance.

of children's mobility initiatives and services and (2) improve the effectiveness of these initiatives by raising parents awareness towards the problem and by promoting virtuous and active behaviors.

As can be seen from Fig. 1, CLIMB Platform is driven by a set of policies, taking into account all stakeholders' requirements and needs and combines advanced ICT and non-ICT techniques and tools to: (i) exploit the crowd/open services and data available in the neighbourhood; (ii) enable knowledge co-creation and service co-operation for the CLIMB community and (iii) make use of knowledge sharing and gamification techniques in order to increase collective awareness and promote behavioral changes.

3.1   Scenario: A Day in CLIMBVille

In the following we describe a scenario that presents a day in the hypothetical village of CLIMBville (see also Fig. 4), that decided to adopt the CLIMB Platform. The scenario presents events and facts happening in the real world, as well as in the digital world (Fig. 2).

It is Monday morning in CLIMBville and the whole neighbourhood wakes up, ready for a new school week. *Meanwhile in the digital world, unnoticed sensors are idling, waiting for activity. They report their operation on a regular basis, harvest energy during daytime and can be updated remotely.*

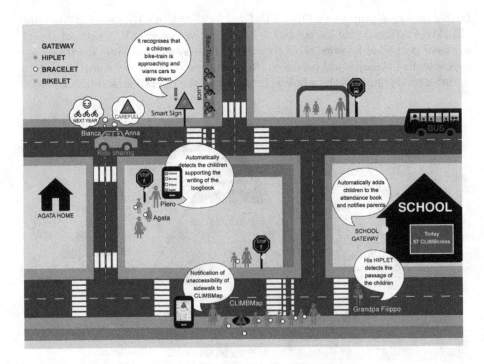

Fig. 2. A typical day in CLIMBVille.

Agata (6 years old) lives less than one km from the school and has a walking bus stop just outside her home. She is having breakfast with her family, when her father, Piero, gets a notification on his smartphone: a volunteer is urgently needed for today's walking bus ride! He accesses the parents' CLIMB chat and after a few messages he understands he is the only one that can save today's ride; he confirms his availability via the walking-bus-app. Agata is very happy: thanks to her father, her class just gained another 20 CLIMBcoins! *CLIMB Platform reacts to the unavailability of a volunteer by starting the collective service for volunteer substitution. A notification is sent to all subs volunteers and the call-for-substitution function is activated on their walking-bus-app. During the execution the data received by the sensors are collected and aggregated to have an up-to-date view of the current operational context and all relevant information on service execution are stored by CLIMB Platform. The Platform is notified about Piero's offering as substitute and assigns additional CLIMBcoins to his team.*

Anna lives 7 km from CLIMBville, but her children (Marco, 6 years old and Bianca, 8 years old) attend the school there. Thanks to the CLIMB Map, Anna found out that there are two other children (Chiara, 7 years old and Luca, 8 years old) who live near them and attend the same school. Through the ride-sharing-app she organised a car-pooling with the other parents to take the children to the nearest school bus stop. Today, as every other Monday, it is her turn. She knows, as notified by the Ride-Sharing App, that Chiara is sick today and she does not need to pick her up. *The CLIMB Platform presents parents, through an interactive digital map, personalised information about community members and available mobility services around them. Displayed data are always anonymised, unless explicitly authorised by the members that can define "trust circles". CLIMB Platform coordinates the distributed and collective operation of the ride-sharing service, handling, in this specific case, the notification of a child not attending a ride.*

When Anna approaches CLIMBville, a smart sign on the street recognises that a children bike-train is approaching and warns her to slow down. While children pass by on their bikes, Bianca thinks she is looking forward to ride to school with her friends: another year and she will finally make it! Anna is not worried: she knows that Luca and other schoolmates will be part of the same bike train. Moreover, the data presented by the CLIMB Portal show that Bianca, for what concerns mobility autonomy, has made incredible progress in the last year. *A set of bikelets is moving, attached to children bikes. Other associated wireless devices (e.g. smart sign on the street) get a message when they are near. This could be a warning message through the feedback mechanism of the bracelet.*

Meanwhile, Piero is waiting for the children at the walking bus stop. From the walking-bus-app he can see the names of the children that are expected at each stop; as children reach the meeting point, Piero immediately sees the information in the walking-bus-app that supports him in the writing of the walking bus logbook. *Children have wearable bracelets that sense they are moving and become active for duty. A wireless signal is sent around that can be picked up by any other receiving sensor and form an instant network at anytime, anywhere (i.e. a lamppost at the stop in this case). A walking bus assembles through the activation of the hiplet and associated smartphone. The hiplet and bracelets form an instant network and the number of members and their associated unique numbers are communicated through the hiplet to the smartphone. The walking-bus-app watches while active if the number of associated bracelets is correct. Any deviation will be noticed and could be escalated to the walking-bus leader for him to take action. Information about the walking-bus ride is sent to the Platform and events are captured and properly handled.*

On the way to school the children notice that the sidewalk is partially not accessible due to some work in progress. Thanks to the CLIMB Platform, they immediately report it, adding a safety notification on the map. *The digital interactive map allows to crowd-source traffic and safety information. In this case, the unavailability of the sidewalk becomes part of the CLIMB collective knowledge and, besides being useful information for the whole community, might trigger recovery actions (e.g. the school decides to temporarily change the route for the walking bus).*

Grandpa Filippo, like every day, presides the walking cross in front of the pharmacy supporting children crossing the street on their way to school. When the children's bike-train and the walking buses pass by, his smart bracelet detects the passage of the children, monitoring another step of their journey. It is impressive to find out that in a year grandpa Filippo has helped more than 40.000 children cross the street! *A gateway near the schoolyard and/or side walk detects that Filippo is available. Filippo's hiplet and the children' bracelets that cross the street will associate and the data is transferred and stored for further processing.*

Once they reach the school, the children see the CLIMBcoins earned today by their class, as well as their own contributions, on the terminal at the entrance. The children are automatically added to the attendance book by the system. Parents receive a notification on their smartphone that their children arrived safely at school. *The gateway(s) at the school will detect the bracelets that are in the school; the information is used to update the attendance book and notify the parents. The game status, which is constantly updated during the children's journeys, is shown on the terminal.*

Silvia recently moved to CLIMBville. Today she is visiting the school with her 7 year old daughter Viola that will attend the second grade from next week. The teacher opens the CLIMB digital map and shows to Silvia the various transport possibilities for her little girl; Silvia receives the login credentials; tonight from home Silvia will be able to evaluate the different transport possibilities, the services used by Viola's schoolmates, read reviews from the other parents and register her child to the most appropriate service; the teacher also gives her the CLIMB leaflet and invites her to the next CLIMB workshop organised by the school.

3.2   CLIMB Platform: Conceptual Architecture

The instantiation of a software platform within a specific application domain and its subsequent adoption by an existing community of end-users needs to be conceived as a problem characterized by three key aspects: *the technical, formal and informal aspects* [17]. The technical aspect concerns the technologies and tools to be introduced in the platform; the formal aspect refers to policies and everything that is regulated by rules and laws; the informal aspect represents the cultural aspects that shape how people perceive the problem, relate to each other and to technology.

The proposed CLIMB Platform (see Fig. 3) covers these three aspects by properly combining ICT and non-ICT tools (technical aspect) whose design and development is driven by a set of policies and guidelines characterizing children's mobility regulations, procedures and best practices (formal aspect), as well as end-users needs, motivations, values and beliefs (informal aspect). At the same time, the use of the ICT and non-ICT tools offered by CLIMB Platform allow exerting an influence on the formal and informal aspects (e.g. community awareness, parents' attitudes toward the problem, children's mobility behaviors, adoption of best-practices in children's mobility procedures and policies) by acting on four key areas of intervention: *knowledge co-creation, service co-operation, knowledge sharing and behavioral change.*

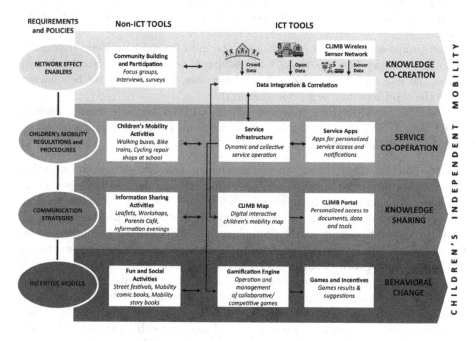

Fig. 3. CLIMB platform conceptual architecture.

In the next Sections we present in details the four solution layers, corresponding to areas of intervention, and the respective ICT and non-ICT tools.

3.3 Knowledge Co-creation

The aim of this layer is to leverage the network-effect (networks of people, knowledge and things) to derive a comprehensive and up-to-date picture of the current situation of children's mobility in the neighborhood. CLIMB Platform exploits the dynamics of networks to reach a critical mass of end-users and to maximize the network-effect impact in terms of collective knowledge creation.

Non-ICT tools consist in activities aimed at building a community of end-users and increasing their participation (e.g. focus groups, interviews).

Regarding the ICT tools, their aim is to collect, integrate and correlate multi-provider and multi-technology data sources from the domain of children's mobility and beyond (e.g., mobility, traffic and safety data; static and real time data; crowd-sensed and crowd-sourced data). They provide the ability to complement already available children mobility data with situational awareness, context sensitivity and real-time information. Data sources include:

- Static data such as street networks available for cars or bikes (e.g., Open-StreetMap data), children mobility transportation routes, schedules etc.
- Real time data provided by the traffic management centres,
- Environmental data such as weather information, pollution data, traffic data etc.,
- User profile and personal preferences to be used for modelling end-user data,
- Social networks, here we do not address virtual networks (e.g., Facebook) but also the real social networks such as classmates, friends that can be relevant for the child mobility (e.g., ride sharing),
- Real-time tracking data collected by the CLIMB wireless sensor network (CLIMB WSN) from wearables and sensors on children, volunteers, bikes, and other smart objects in the neighbourhood.

The CLIMB WSN, based on self-organising and low-energy consumption network solution, constitutes of heterogeneous and autonomous devices such as wearables (i.e., bracelets, hiplets and bikelets), sensors and gateways (devices aggregating, complementing and sending data collected from sensors).

Data integration and correlation plays a key role in the Knowledge co-Creation layer since it allows to aggregate the data collected through the network of things, the network of services and the network of people and transform it into the CLIMB collective knowledge. In particular, the Data Integration and Correlation component pre-processes the heterogeneous raw data and establishes a unique interface that can be accessed and queried by the other CLIMB components to obtain consistent, up-to-date and aggregated information. The data is organised around individuals, groups and locations. This allows the different functionalities to access and obtain meaningful and context-aware data. The person-driven data correlation and organisation also allows for maximum flexibility in privacy settings, allowing for distinction per person, per service, and even per setting / context (real-time).

These components build on top of the experience gathered in project IES Cities [18] about the collection, integration and usage of open data, sensor data and crowdsourced data and use Cloud-computing solutions both for data storage and for data correlation and pre-processing. Moreover, the collected data, properly anonymised and cleaned from sensitive information, are made available as Open Data on the CLIMB Portal (see Knowledge Sharing layer).

3.4   Service Co-operation

The aim of this layer is to provide a set of tools supporting the whole community (parents, teachers, children, volunteers and traffic aids) in their daily collective operation and management of children's mobility services. The functioning of this layer is strictly related to the existing services and initiatives and in particular to the requirements, procedures and regulations for the set-up, operation and management of children's mobility services.

Non-ICT tools comprise the realisation of children mobility activities (e.g. walking buses, bike trains, guarded crosswalks and cycling repair shops at school) whose operation is supported by advanced ICT tools for service co-operation.

In particular, the Service Infrastructure component, aims at provisioning service-oriented techniques and tools supporting the definition, operation and management of distributed, dynamic, and collective children mobility services. The key challenges to be addressed concern (i) the heterogeneity of the services involved (from software services to IoT services provided by smart devices), (ii) the dynamicity of the environment in which they operate (services join/leave the system, change their behaviour, there might be changes in user requirements), (iii) the collective nature of the mobility services to be provisioned, since their operation requires the interaction and collaboration of different entities (IT systems, devices and humans), each having their own requirements and needs.

To better clarify these challenges, in Fig. 4 we present an overview of the different component services in CLIMB, restricting the scope of the system to a subset of the possible children mobility services (i.e., walking bus, bike train, ride-sharing).

If we consider the part of the system related to the walking bus, we notice that the management of this service requires to handle the registration of children, parents and volunteers and their access to the system (User Profile Management component), the training of volunteers (Volunteer Management component), the organization of routes (WSB Manager component) taking into account the needs of families but also route safety (e.g., presence of sidewalks, traffic situation, guarded crosswalks). The daily operation of the service requires to handle the confirmation of children attendance and of volunteers availability for each route (Route Manager), the compilation of attendance books, tracking of children and volunteer position (WSN Manager), as well as managing possible exceptions and changes (e.g. find a substitute for a volunteer, change the route due to roadworks, suspend the route due to weather conditions). Some of this components are in common with the bike train and ride sharing (e.g. Route Manager, Volunteer Management, User Profile Management) this allows not only to avoid replication, but also to enable synergies and collaboration among the different services (e.g., exploit the ride-sharing service to cover a WSB route in case of bad weather).

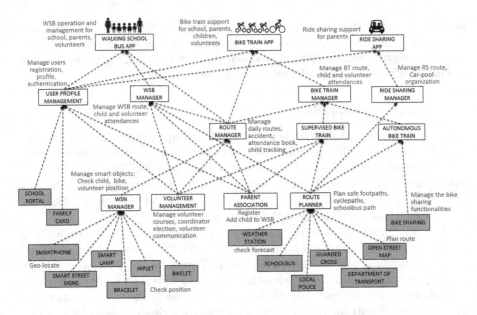

Fig. 4. Service co-Operation: a partial view on CLIMB services.

A first characteristic of the system that clearly emerges from this example, is the variety and *heterogeneity of services* that the platform needs to cope with: from domain-specific functionalities related to mobility (e.g., management of walking bus and bike train routes, support for compilation of attendance books) to general-purpose ones (e.g., user profile and access management, user tracking); from back-end functionalities (in grey in the Figure) that requires interacting with third party systems and devices (e.g. retrieving cycle lines and foot path and traffic/safety street information, interacting with smart objects and sensors) to front-end ones (e.g., mobile and Web Apps to be accessed by parents, volunteers and teachers).

Moreover, the Service co-Operation layer needs to deal with the *dynamicity* of the scenario, both in terms of the variability of the actors and services involved, and of the context changes affecting its operation. In particular, the system should be *open and extensible*, which means that new services (e.g., a new bike-sharing service or a new tracking device), as well as changes in existing services (e.g., changes in parents authorization procedure, changes in volunteer recruiting procedure, changes in any third party system) should be easily managed and require minimum maintenance.

This is made particularly challenging by the collective nature of the mobility services to be provisioned, since their operation requires the interaction and collaboration of different autonomous actors (school, parents and volunteers associations, mobility and transport departments, local police), and thus results in a *high degree of connection and interdependencies* among the different system components (as shown in Fig. 4).

To cope with these challenges, the CLIMB Service Infrastructure is built on top of well-established solutions. In particular, it exploits the Smart Campus Open Service Platform [19] that supports the development, deployment and distribution of new applications on top of Open services. Similarly to Open-data, Open-services can be accessed and re-used to produce value-added services, enabling a collaborative and efficient delivery of high quality end-user applications. Open services can implement domain-specific functionalities (e.g., mobility-related services) or general-purpose ones (e.g., for access management, or interaction with existing social networks); they can model back-end functionalities (e.g. retrieving all the available walking bus routes for a certain city area) or front-end ones (e.g. visualisation of routes on a map); they can be core services that wrap existing third parties' systems, or value-added services developed through the platform and released as Open services.

The solution offered by the Open Service Platform will be extended with advanced techniques and tools for dynamic and incremental service composition [20–23] developed within the ALLOW Ensemble project [24]. These techniques allow modelling each Open service in terms of the functionalities it provides and of the conditions under which the functionality can be used (e.g. context/situation-related properties). At the same time, it allows to define a partial specification of the implementation logic of each Open service, that are then automatically linked to (one or a composition of) functionalities provided by other Open services. This results in a dynamic hierarchical network of Open services, that, thanks to automatic composition and dynamic re-configuration features, allows to effectively cope with changes that are typical of distributed collective systems [25, 26].

The Service co-Operation layer includes also a set of web and mobile Service Apps, providing a personalised access to mobility service users (parents, children) and providers (school, drivers, traffic aids and parents), supporting them in the different activities of the daily co-operation of the services (e.g. registration/booking of mobility services, notifications of service updates/cancelation, offering/requesting rides, setting-up/joining children bike trains or walking buses).

3.5   Knowledge Sharing

This layer aims at effectively sharing the knowledge obtained through the Knowledge co-Creation layer with all the key players in the neighborhood and to facilitate parents and community awareness.

Concerning the non-ICT tools, aimed at setting up an efficient communication strategy, they include information sharing events (e.g. workshops, parent cafés and information evenings) and material distribution (e.g. leaflets).

ICT tools comprise a CLIMB Portal, allowing access to all relevant children's independent mobility documents and news and a CLIMB Map that presents, through a digital interactive map, personalized views on the children's independent mobility situation in the neighborhood (e.g. available mobility services with routes, timetables, usage statistics, safety and traffic situations and recommended safe routes).

The CLIMB Portal is a key tool for the exchange of knowledge on children's independent mobility. In particular, the portal allow accessing all relevant children's independent mobility data, documents and news, comprises site-specific and general dissemination sections, and supports personalised views for registered users (parents, teachers, volunteers, city managers, other stakeholders, researchers and experts in the field). The CLIMB Portal will embed participation tools (e.g., forum, chats and polls) to collect essential data from parents, teachers and other interested parties about mobility initiatives, events and services, allowing them to use the platform as a spokesman for their suggestions and concerns regarding children's independent mobility.

The CLIMB Map aims at presenting, through a digital interactive map, personalised intuitive views to the different end-users (school, city council, parents, children and citizens) on the children's mobility situation in the neighbourhood, in terms of available mobility services (e.g., walking bus, bike trains, school buses routes and schedules) and their value (community feedback, usage statistics and child mobility), as well as safety and traffic information (e.g. guarded crosswalk, sidewalks, bike lanes, traffic and carbon emission level for specific street/time of day), available sensors, etc. The CLIMB Map will include also crowd-sourcing functionalities, allowing end-users to enhance CLIMB collective knowledge by adding mobility, traffic and safety information about their neighbourhood. The CLIMB Map will be developed extending and customising the Smart Mobility Cockpit developed within the STREETLIFE Project [27].

3.6 Behavioral Change

The aim of this layer is to deliver a set of techniques and tools to promote and encourage behavioral change.

A key problem of "traditional" children mobility initiatives is their sustainability and the durability of their effects following their completion. CLIMB Platform offers the possibility of accompanying the "traditional" campaigns with virtual campaigns, hence amplifying their effects (in terms of parents' awareness, community participation, and behavioural changes), both in dimensional terms (capability to engage a larger community) and in temporal terms (capability to ensure a durable engagement that lasts also after the end of the traditional campaign).

Non-ICT tools are devoted to the organization and operation of Fun and Social Activities (e.g. street festivals, mobility comic books), as well as collaborative and competitive games that involve the whole community and, through virtual and real incentives, promote participation, awareness and behavioral change.

In recent years, gamification, as the use of game design elements in non-game contexts [28], has been successfully applied to plenty of systems and apps from many sectors. Both practical experiences from the market and studies from the literature, confirm that gamification can be very useful in increasing citizens' participation and awareness, as well as in promoting virtuous behaviors [29–34].

Although gamification seems very promising in terms of engagement and behavioral change, its realization for a given context is still complex and expensive. Most solutions are tightly coupled to the specific business logic they wish to gamify, which hinders both evolution and reuse. For these reasons, in the last few years research has begun to focus on gamification platforms and tool sets that can help making the design and development of gamification applications easier, faster and cheaper. This is particularly important if, as in the CLIMB project, *the system to be gamified is an entire neighborhood within a Smart City*, with its variety of ICT systems, applications and services.

The main aim of the ICT tools in the Behavioral Change layer is to facilitate the definition, deployment and operation of games which incentivize players to adopt virtuous behaviors in their daily children's mobility choices and actively participate in the operation and governance of children's mobility services.

The Gamification Engine allows to define/customize the dynamics of the game, in terms of the activities contributing to the game (from passive activities automatically detected through sensors, to more active ones performed by the user through CLIMB apps and tools), the type of incentives (e.g., badges, leader-boards and real awards/gifts) and the respective levels/points to get the incentive. The engine will support both competitive and cooperative game formats, thus driving both individual and collective progress. Moreover, the Gamification Engine is responsible for all the activities supporting game execution such as detecting events from logs and real-time data and from end-user service activities, and updating and communicating user gaming profiles.

The solution is built on top of a gamification framework developed within the STREETLIFE project [27], which has been already successfully exploited for the definition and operation of on-the-field games promoting sustainable and green mobility behaviors [35]. The engine will be extended to cope with CLIMB-specific requirements and needs, in particular concerning collaborative games and domain-specific incentive models.

The Games and Incentives component comprises a set of end-user tools that allow inspection of personal and collective progress in the game and suggestions about virtuous mobility behaviors.

4 Related Works

The paradigm of "openness" is transforming the way innovation was traditionally conceptualized. Innovation is no longer created in a closed lab or in R&D departments; it is co-created by different stakeholders who share the knowledge, risk and benefits of the innovation [17]. The Open data movement is gaining popularity worldwide, thanks to the rise of the Internet and to the launch of Open-data government initiatives (e.g., EU Open Data Portal, Data.gov). Additionally, crowd-sourced data has been proven to be very effective for improving and maintaining Open data and their combined effect is widely exploited for distributed knowledge creation (see for instance EU CAPS projects DECAR-BONET, D-CENT, CATALYST and WIKIRATE).

Similarly, the increasing uptake of web services, Service-Oriented Architecture and Future Internet technologies created an ideal ground for Open-services. An Open-service is an elementary Web service with a well-defined API that allows a third party (citizen, or another government entity) to access, aggregate and orchestrate different Open-services to deliver new more complex and value added services. Organisations like Mashery [36], Apigee [37] and 3Scale [38] are building on these trends to provide platforms for the management of Open-services. For instance, ProgrammableWeb [39] now has more than 10,000 API in its directory.

Existing platforms are still far from being able of fully exploit the potential of Open services. This is mainly due to the fact that Open services, although "physically" loosely coupled, strongly depend on one another for their operation. Existing platforms have very limited support for change (such as changes in the behaviour or interface of a service, changes in the environment in which the services operate, new service entering the system, changes in composite service requirements) and their operation regarding each service in isolation without considering the inherent dynamic nature of Open Services [40]. Adaptation of service-based systems is a key investigation topic in the Service-Oriented community and several approaches have been proposed to overcome this problem [41]. However, most of them suffer from crucial limitations that, at least for the moment, confine them to blue sky research, not exploitable in "real-world" applications [42–46].

The CLIMB platform is built on Open source technologies, adopts as driving design concepts interoperability and compatibility with mainstream technology trajectories, and includes many components that are designed to be replicated and customized following ever changing requirements.

Leveraged on the earlier work in projects such as Smart Campus [19], ALLOW and ALLOW Ensembles [20,21,26,47,48], CLIMB Platform will contribute with an Open Services co-Operation Infrastructure that supports the development, deployment and distribution of new collective services on top of Open services and Open data and that includes advanced features for dynamic and incremental service composition and re-configuration, allowing to effectively deal with changes occurring at different levels in the system (e.g. entrance and exit of services, change in provided functionalities, change in requirements). This solution will not only advance the state-of-the-art in the Service Oriented and Future Internet communities, but will also introduce an new "openness" and participatory factor to these communities, hence enabling new scenarios based on service co-Operation for distributed bottom-up approaches exploiting the network effect.

Another innovative aspect of the proposed platform concerns the use of gamification and participation techniques within an highly distributed and complex system.

Gamification, that is, "the use of game design elements in non-game contexts" [28], is a socio–technical element that is injected nowadays in many ICT systems and which can be strategic to increase participation and engagement, as well as in promoting sustainable behaviours, such as environmentally–friendly, ethical, social or healthy habit [29]. The key idea is to motivate people to make certain decisions, or carry out certain tasks that are important in order to reach valuable objectives, even when they are somehow unattractive, by turning them into fun and rewarding actions.

For instance, thanks to gamification, it is possible either to drastically reduce the traffic congestion [49] or, by coupling gamification and crowdsourcing, to involve citizens in sharing information about city parking and to distribute their usage of them in an optimised way [30]. Gamification is also useful for motivating people to regular take part in some form of physical activity [29,31,32]. In the energy field, gamification has been successfully employed to achieve a decrease in energy consumption and to avoid wasting energy [33,34].

Despite the potential of gamification methods and techniques in many domains, its general applicability is in practice still difficult, time-consuming and expensive. Technically speaking, that entails a long and often costly process of analysis, design, development and validation. It also requires extensive re–engineering of pre-existing ICT systems for the injection of the desired gamification features. In most cases, gamification is applied from scratch in a one-shot manner for a very specific system, that is, the game is designed and developed for a unique system producing non-reusable, nor generic, nor flexible solutions.

A possible solution to this problem is the adoption of a gamification engine: a system that allows the gamification of an application by use of ready-to-use gamification tools. There are many commercial engines (e.g. Gamify, Badgeville, Bunchball, BigDoor, Youtopia) and a few free or open source solutions (e.g. UserInfuser, Mozilla Open Badges). Unfortunately, they all have some important limitations. The most important of these are (i) support of a limited number of gamification concepts and (ii) strict-coupling between the gamification domain and the application domain. The first point is considered a problem since the tool is not expressive enough to design a significant variety of gamification scenarios. The second one is more complex and critical since it underlines the situation where the engines do not support strong decoupling between the game domain and the domain of the application that has to be gamified. In fact, current engines require redefining, inside the engine, the application domain in order to apply the supported gamification concepts. This makes the gamification process very expensive and time consuming, even in the case of a simple game on top of a single ICT-system (e.g. Web site or mobile app).

In the CLIMB Platform this becomes even more complex since the game is not about promoting the use of a single ICT system operated by a single provider; rather, we the aim is to *gamify an entire neighbourhood*, with its sensors and services provisioned to citizens via heterogeneous ICT systems that belong to multiple entities (from private companies to the city administration). To this extent, we propose an open-source service-based gamification engine that goes beyond the state-of-the-art since it is extensible, both with respect to the domain elements that are part of the game (e.g. existing ICT systems) and regarding the game concepts, since additional concepts can be added to the gamification framework through plugins and it is generic, in the sense that it is applicable to a variety of application domains.

A first prototype version of the engine has been developed within the STREETLIFE EU Project [27] and has been evaluated through an on-the-filed experiment in Rovereto (one of STREETLIFE project pilots, a town 20 Km south of Trento) with a game that aims at promoting green mobility solutions [35]. The gamification engine will be extended to support collaborative games, teams of players, and personalized missions.

5   Conclusion

Children's independent mobility is an important societal problem where advanced ICT solutions can make a difference supporting the community in the ideation, management and daily operation of children's mobility initiatives.

In this paper we presented an Open ICT platform, the CLIMB Platform, that (i) enables knowledge co-creation by integrating and correlating heterogeneous data sources (i.e., open, crowd-sourced, and sensors data) for an up-to-date and consistent collective knowledge of the children mobility situation in the neighbourhood, (ii) enable service co-operation, supporting the whole community (parents, teachers, children, volunteers) in the ideation, management and daily operation of grassroots children mobility initiatives and services, and (iii) make use of knowledge sharing personalized and intuitive tools, gamification techniques, and virtual/real incentives to increase awareness and promote behavioural changes.

The definition and implementation of the platform is driven by a set of policies and guidelines that take into account all stakeholders' requirements and needs. The effectiveness of the solution will be proven through an in depth evaluation in the city of Trento involving existing communities of end-users.

Acknowledgements. This work is partially funded by the European Commission through FP7 EU SMARTCITIES project STREETLIFE (Grant Agreement 608991), FP7 EU-FET project ALLOW Ensembles (Grant Agreement 600792), and FP7 EU CIP ICT-PSP project IES Cities (Grant Agreement 325097).

We would like to thank Elisabeth Füssl and Ralf Risser (FACTUM), Roland van Straten and Lex van Gijsel (DEVLAB), and Dr Sonja Forward and her team (VTI) for their support in understanding children's independent mobility problem and shaping the CLIMB Platform idea. Special thanks to the City of Trento and its administration for their invaluable help and support.

References

1. Beunderman, J.: People make play: the impact of staffed play provision on children, families and communities. A research report by Demos for Play England National Children's Bureau, London (2010)
2. Daschütz, P.: Flächenbedarf, freizeitmobilität und aktionsraum von kindern und jugendlichen in der stadt. Dissertation, TU Wien (2006)
3. Giuliani, M.V., Alparone, F., Mayer, S.: Children's appropriation of urban space. In: Urban Childhood Conference (1997)

4. Kolotkin, R.L., Meter, K., Williams, G.R.: Quality of life and obesity. Obesity Rev. **2**, 219–229 (2001)
5. Munroe, R.L., Munroe, R.H.: Effect of environmental experience on spatial ability in an east african society. J. Soc. Psychol. **83**, 15–22 (1971)
6. Brown, T., Summerbell, C.: Systematic review of school-based interventions that focus on changing dietary intake and physical activity levels to prevent childhood obesity. An update to the obesity guidance produced by the National Institute for Health and Clinical Excellence (2008)
7. Björklid, P.: Parental restrictions and children's independent mobility. In: IAPS (2002)
8. Hillman, M., Adams, J., Whitelegg, J.: One False Move.. A Study of Children's Independent Mobility. Policy Studies Institute, London (1990)
9. Hillman, M.: Children, Transport and the Quality of Life. Policy Studies Institute, London (1993)
10. O'Brien, M., Jones, D., Sloan, D., Ristin, M.: Children's independent spatial mobility in the urban public realm. Childhood **7**(3), 257–277 (2000)
11. Rissotto, A., Tonucci, F.: Freedom of movement and environmental knowledge in elementary school children. J. Environ. Psychol. **22**, 65–77 (2002)
12. Fotel, T., Thomsen, T.: The surveillance of children's mobility. Surveill. Soc. **1**(4), 535–554 (2004)
13. SKL: Why do parents drive their children to school. SKL rapport (2012)
14. McDonald, N.C., Aalborg, A.: Why parents drive children to school: implications for safe routes to school programs. J. Am. Plan. Assoc. **75**(3), 331–342 (2009)
15. Dowling, R.: Cultures of mothering and car use in suburban sydney: a preliminary investigation. Geoforum **31**(3), 345–353 (2000)
16. Spencer, C., Blades, M.: Children at risk: are we understimating their general environmental competence whilst overstimating their performance? In: Garling, T., Valsiner, J. (eds.) Children within Environments, pp. 39–49. Plenum Press, New York (1985)
17. Arniani, M., Badii, A., Liddo, A.D., Georgi, S., Passani, A., Piccolo, L.S.G., Teli, M.: Collective awareness platform for sustainability and social innovation: An introduction (2014)
18. IES CITIES: Internet-Enabled Services for the Cities across Europe. (FP7 EU Project). http://iescities.eu
19. (Smart Campus Platform). http://www.smartcampuslab.it/
20. Bucchiarone, A., Marconi, A., Mezzina, C.A., Pistore, M., Raik, H.: On-the-fly adaptation of dynamic service-based systems: incrementality, reduction and reuse. In: International Conference on Web Services ICWS, pp. 146–161 (2013)
21. Bucchiarone, A., Marconi, A., Pistore, M., Raik, H.: Dynamic adaptation of fragment-based and context-aware business processes. In: Proceedings of the of ICWS 2012, pp. 33–41 (2012)
22. Raik, H., Bucchiarone, A., Khurshid, N., Marconi, A., Pistore, M.: Astro-captevo: Dynamic context-aware adaptation for service-based systems. In: Proceedings of SERVICES 2012, pp. 385–392 (2012)
23. Sirbu, A., Marconi, A., Pistore, M., Eberle, H., Leymann, F., Unger, T.: Dynamic composition of pervasive process fragments. In: 2011 IEEE International Conference on Web Services (ICWS), pp. 73–80. IEEE (2011)
24. ALLOW Ensembles. (FP7 EU Project). http://www.allow-ensembles.eu

25. Bucchiarone, A., Cappiello, C., Di Nitto, E., Kazhamiakin, R., Mazza, V., Pistore, M.: Design for adaptation of service-based applications: main issues and requirements. In: Dan, A., Gittler, F., Toumani, F. (eds.) ICSOC/ServiceWave 2009. LNCS, vol. 6275, pp. 467–476. Springer, Heidelberg (2010)
26. Bucchiarone, A., Marconi, A., Pistore, M., Traverso, P., Bertoli, P., Kazhamiakin, R.: Domain objects for continuous context-aware adaptation of service-based systems. In: IEEE 20th International Conference on Web Services (ICWS), 2013, pp. 571–578. IEEE (2013)
27. STREETLIFE: Steering Towards Perceptive Mobility of the Future. (FP7 EU Project). http://www.streetlife-project.eu
28. Deterding, S., Dixon, D., Khaled, R., Nacke, L.: From game design elements to gamefulness: defining "Gamification". In: Proceedings of the 15th International Academic MindTrek Conference: Envisioning Future Media Environments. MindTrek 2011, pp. 9–15. ACM (2011)
29. Bielik, P., Tomlein, M., Krátky, P., Mitrík, v., Barla, M., Bieliková, M.: Move2Play: an innovative approach to encouraging people to be more physically active. In: Proceedings of the 2nd ACM SIGHIT International Health Informatics Symposium, IHI 2012, pp. 61–70. ACM (2012)
30. Hoh, B., Yan, T., Ganesan, D., Tracton, K., Iwuchukwu, T., Lee, J.: TruCentive: a game-theoretic incentive platform for trustworthy mobile crowdsourcing parking services. In: 2012 15th International IEEE Conference on Intelligent Transportation Systems (ITSC) (2012)
31. Walsh, G., Golbeck, J.: StepCity: a preliminary investigation of a personal informatics-based social game on behavior change. In: CHI 2014 Extended Abstracts on Human Factors in Computing Systems, CHI EA 2014, pp. 2371–2376. ACM (2014)
32. Bartley, J., Forsyth, J., Pendse, P., Xin, D., Brown, G., Hagseth, P., Agrawal, A., Goldberg, D., Hammond, T.: World of workout: a contextual mobile rpg to encourage long term fitness. In: Proceedings of the Second ACM SIGSPATIAL International Workshop on the Use of GIS in Public Health, HealthGIS 2013, pp. 60–67. ACM (2013)
33. Shiraishi, M., Washio, Y., Takayama, C., Lehdonvirta, V., Kimura, H., Nakajima, T.: Using individual, social and economic persuasion techniques to reduce co2 emissions in a family setting. In: Proceedings of the 4th International Conference on Persuasive Technology. Persuasive 2009, pp. 13:1–13:8. ACM (2009)
34. Cowley, B., Moutinho, J., Bateman, C., Oliveira, A.: Learning principles and interaction design for 'Green My Place': A Massively Multiplayer Serious Game. Entertainment Comput. **2**, 103–113 (2011)
35. Kazhamiakin, R., Marconi, A., Perillo, M., Pistore, M., Valetto, G., Piras, L., Avesani, F., Perri, N.: Using gamification to incentivize sustainable urban mobility. In: Proceedings of IEEE International Conference on Smart Cities, ISC2 (2015)
36. (MASHERY). http://www.mashery.com
37. (APIGEE). http://apigee.com/about/
38. (3SCALE). http://www.3scale.net/
39. (ProgrammableWeb). http://www.programmableweb.com
40. Pistore, M., Traverso, P., Paolucci, M., Wagner, M.: From software services to a future internet of services. In: Future Internet Assembly, pp. 183–192 (2009)
41. Bartalos, P., Bielikova, M.: Automatic dynamic web service composition: a survey and problem formalization. Comput. Inf. **30**(4), 793–827 (2011)

42. Cubo, J., Pimentel, E.: DAMASCo: a framework for the automatic composition of component-based and service-oriented architectures. In: Crnkovic, I., Gruhn, V., Book, M. (eds.) ECSA 2011. LNCS, vol. 6903, pp. 388–404. Springer, Heidelberg (2011)

43. Goser, K., Jurisch, M., Acker, H., Kreher, U., Lauer, M., Rinderle, S., Reichert, M., Dadam, P.: Next-generation process management with adept2. In: BPM Demos (2007)

44. Greenwood, D.P.A.: Goal-oriented autonomic business process modeling and execution: engineering change management demonstration. In: Dumas, M., Reichert, M., Shan, M.-C. (eds.) BPM 2008. LNCS, vol. 5240, pp. 390–393. Springer, Heidelberg (2008)

45. Peltz, C.: Web services orchestration and choreography. IEEE Comput. **36**(10), 43–52 (2003)

46. Hull, R., Damaggio, E., Masellis, R.D., Fournier, F., Gupta, M., Heath, F.T., Hobson, S., Linehan, M.H., Maradugu, S., Nigam, A., Sukaviriya, P.N., Vaculín, R.: Business artifacts with guard-stage-milestone lifecycles: managing artifact interactions with conditions and events. In: DEBS (2011)

47. Bertoli, P., Pistore, M., Traverso, P.: Automated composition of web services via planning in asynchronous domains. Artif. Intell. **174**, 316–361 (2010)

48. Marconi, A., Pistore, M., Traverso, P.: Automated Composition of Web Services: the ASTRO Approach. IEEE Data Eng. Bull. **31**, 23–26 (2008)

49. Merugu, D., Prabhakar, B., Rama, N.: An incentive mechanism for decongesting the roads: a pilot program in bangalore. In: Proceedings of ACM NetEcon Workshop (2009)

Smart Cities and Green ICT Systems

Architectures and Requirements
for the Development of Smart Cities:
A Literature Study

Christiana Kyriazopoulou[✉]

University of Macedonia, Thessaloniki, Greece
christikir@gmail.com

Abstract. In a changing world, the increased urbanization of modern cities makes the development of smart cities necessary. The basic purpose of smart cities is to improve citizens' quality of living as well as to contribute to the financial, social and political progress, the creation of new and more advanced services and the sustainability of the city. The achievement of this goal is feasible through the implementation of architectures and platforms that can incorporate together the various components of the city and make them interact in an effective way. Also, in order to achieve the satisfaction of the specific needs of the city, the system, and by extension the integrated technologies and architectures, has to fulfill a minimum set of requirements. In this paper, we discuss the key architectures that have already been proposed in the literature in order to find the most appropriate ones to be applied to the development of smart cities, and the basic and most common requirements that these architectures aim to satisfy.

Keywords: Smart cities · Platforms · Technologies · Architectures · Internet of Things · Architectural Layers · Service-oriented architecture · Event-driven architecture · Requirements

1 Introduction

Several definitions have been published over the years about the term "Smart City". One of the most widely accepted is that by IBM (2010) that assumes smart city as "the use of information and communication technology to sense, analyze and integrate the key information of core systems in running cities". According to Caragliu et al. (2011) "a city is smart when investments in human and social capital and traditional (transport) and modern (ICT) communication infrastructure fuel sustainable economic growth and a high quality of life, with a wise management of natural resources, through participatory governance". Smart city is also considered to have a strong relationship with digital city. Cocchia (2014) referred that digital city is a subcategory of smart city, because both of them include Information and Communication Technologies (ICT). The main difference is that smart city intends to improve citizens' standard of living through the development of the economy, the social and political progress, the provision of new services and the protection of the environment. Moreover, Su et al. (2011) stated that smart city generates from digital city when it is combined with IoT (IoT).

© Springer International Publishing Switzerland 2015
M. Helfert et al. (Eds.): Smartgreens 2015 and Vehits 2015, CCIS 579, pp. 75–103, 2015.
DOI: 10.1007/978-3-319-27753-0_5

The need for a smart city arises due to urbanization of modern cities and the necessity to solve various daily problems that affect citizens' lives. The technological progress gives us the opportunity not only to manage these problems but also create services and facilities in order to improve people's quality of living. The main sectors that a smart city aims to improve are smart economy, smart people, smart governance, smart mobility, smart environment and smart living (Giffinger et al., 2007). In order to manage these sectors and design useful applications, smart city exploits all the available resources, monitors conditions and collects information through sensors and critical infrastructure. Then, it analyzes and processes them through the use of ICT so as to offer citizens the expectable satisfaction.

To complete successfully the above procedure, system's designers must also take into account the particular needs of the city. In that direction, it is mandatory to establish the main requirements that should be fulfilled by the system and the chosen architecture. The term "Requirement" is used to define an official declaration of some functionality that aims to achieve the existing or the upcoming needs of the city. So, the satisfaction of a minimum set of requirements is thought to be an important aspect when developing a smart city since they intend to accomplish social, economic and business needs that are related to ICT technologies.

The purpose of this paper is to discuss the basic architectures and requirements that have been proposed over the years and specify the ones that are more useful in building smart cities. Section 2, in its first part, presents some of the selected architectures and technologies that should be integrated in a smart city as we find them in the literature, while the second part includes the discussion about their usability and implementation. In Sect. 3, we cite some of the most outstanding works that stated a set of requirements in order to support the various smart cities systems. Then we list, categorize and discuss the basic requirements of these works presenting a table assigning the architectures to the requirements that they aim to fulfill. The last Sect. 4 shows the concluding results and suggestions for future work and research.

2 Architectures

Below we quote several architectures and their including platforms and technologies. Although the literature contains many surveys and suggestions about the architectures that participate in the design and operation of a smart city, there is not yet a standard one that integrates all the functionalities. Furthermore, the greatest number of these architectures is based on a theoretical approach and non in a practical one with real implementation. In this section, we present some of the proposed architectures giving emphasis in the most common platforms that we meet a lot in the literature. We have recognized six perspectives of architectures - the perspective of Architectural Layers, Service Oriented Architecture, Event Driven Architecture, IoT, Combined Architectures and finally the new perspective of Internet of Everything. In the rest of our paper, we cite the works of different researchers, categorizing them chronologically and respectively to the perspective they belong. Finally, we summarize these works in a table for better understanding.

2.1 Architectures State of the Art

2.1.1 Architectural Layers (Al)

AL provide a framework for developing services and applications in smart cities through their fragmentation into pieces (layers) that can be easily modified and adjusted instead of transforming the whole system. Each layer is physically and logically dissociated from the others. This characteristic is the one that makes the perspective unique and explains its choice and great acceptance by a large number of researchers. In this subsection, we mention some of the most outstanding works that choose to implement this architecture in order to create useful facilities for smart cities.

Initially, Ishida (2000) was one of the first researchers to present a comparative study between the digital cities of America Online, Amsterdam, Helsinki and Kyoto. He recognized three layers in digital cities architecture. The first layer is the information layer which includes all the data from real time sensors and files from the Internet that are combined together through geographical information systems (GIS). The second layer is the interface layer which creates a virtual environment of the cities through 3D spaces and 2D maps. The last layer is the interaction layer where people can communicate with each other through the use of agent systems.

Anthopoulos and Tsoukalas (2006) developed the digital city of Trikala in Greece. Their chosen architecture consisted of five layers. The first and last layers are user layers where we can find all the stakeholders of a smart city including the designers of the services and end users respectively. The second layer is the infrastructure layer which contains the technologies, platforms and networks in order to create and offer the services. The third layer is the information layer which consists of all the necessary data about smart city operation, such as geospatial data and other records. The fourth layer is the service layer which contains all the provided applications of the city and allowed the interaction among citizens and organizations.

Expect from the definition that we mentioned it previously, IBM has also stated the structure of the smart city. According to IBM, the structure is divided in three layers, perception, network and application layer. Perception layer recognizes the device and gathers data via sensors, GPS, RFID and other technologies. Network layer processes those data through components related to the intelligence and communication capabilities of the network. Eventually, application layer examines and evaluates the total amount of data through advanced technologies, such as cloud computing and fuzzy techniques.

Su et al. (2011) focused in the building of a smart city and recognized three stages. The first stage is the manufacture of public infrastructure. The second is the manufacture of public platform, which includes network infrastructure, cloud computing platform and sensor networks. The third stage is the manufacture of application systems, which includes some basic applications like the construction of wireless city, smart home, smart public services and social management, smart transportation, smart medical treatment, smart urban management, green city and smart tourism.

Carretero (2012) developed an architecture named ADAPCITY. It is about a self-adaptive system for smart cities which offers heterogeneous devices the ability to react effectively in environmental changes and adapt their behavior according to the new conditions. Moreover, the system is able to recover immediately and update its operations, even create new ones. The proposed architecture is divided in four layers. The physical layer includes the state and behavior of devices and objects. The grid layer includes the process, storage and communication among the data come from physical layer. The management layer uses statistics, data mining and prediction techniques to manage the processed data from grid layer. Finally, the control layer includes the provided services taking into account users desires and optimization measurements.

Finally, Vilajosana et al. (2013) presented a generic architecture after observing many existing platforms and combining their common features. The capillary network layer in the bottom of the platform includes sensors and actuators for data collection, data warehouses for storage of historical, real-time and metadata, as well as database nodes and security infrastructures for data management and control offering. The service layer has the responsibility to receive the incoming data from capillary network layer and then to process, combine and secure them. It manages different types of data, such as big, open and streaming data and also analytics services. The last layer is the application layer where the data are analyzed and converted into useful information, which is eventually provided to people through predefined interfaces.

2.1.2 Service Oriented Architecture (SOA)

SOA is an approach that aims in collection, communication and interaction between services and in their provision to the users taking into account their needs and requests. The communication between different services in a computer system is implemented through data exchange among them and the ability of each service to act as a whole activity on behalf of another service. Every interaction is considered to be unconstrained since services are unrelated, loosely coupled and self-sufficient. However, according to Sprott and Wilkes from Microsoft (2004), SOA is more than this. In fact, it is a pattern that includes all the necessary practices and frameworks to offer people the right services that fit to their preferences through the interface.

One of the most underlying works was that of Anthopoulos and Fitsilis (2010) who tried to create a common architecture for smart cities called Enterprise Architecture. Their approach is based on SOA and contains information of urban development and service delivery in urban environments. Logical and physical architecture has been combined with the enterprise architecture in order to strengthen the evolution of smart cities. As authors admitted, the case of Trikala failed to meet some of the challenges that cities have to face (such as information sharing and storage, connection and access through broadband networks, simulation of daily life and so on) with the primary architecture, so they developed this one in an attempt to overcome the existing problems.

2.1.3 Event Driven Architecture (EDA)

EDA is a framework that deals with the creation, identification, utilization and response to events. These events are usually uncommon, and related to uncertain changes and asynchronous conditions. The result of the actions that EDA executes, provokes the generation of event notifications (and not of an event), which are actually an effect of change occurrence. A change can be detected by sensors and the outcoming events can be processed by the system. EDA is loosely coupled about the unknown results of a change by the event itself but it is tightly coupled to the semantics of an event.

When the semantic heterogeneity of events is high, it is very difficult to implement that architecture in a smart city (Souleiman et al., 2012). EDA can be also combined with SOA since an event can make a service operative.

Moving in that direction, Filipponi et al. (2010) developed SOFIA project in an attempt to monitor the public city places so as to enhance security and detect emergency cases. This project is based on EDA that permits sensors (and especially wireless sensors networks) to observe unusual events. The main components of the architecture are Semantic Information Brokers (SIB) and Knowledge Processors (KP). All the data about smart places are stored in SIB. In the sequel, KPs receive these data from SIB, have access to them, generate and use notifications for the events described by them. The joint action between SIB and KP, leads to the production of Interoperability Open Platform (IOP), which gives applications the opportunity to gain entry to data and share them.

2.1.4   Internet of Things (IoT)

IoT is a paradigm that combines a large amount of heterogeneous devices, which are connected to the Internet and can identify themselves through IP addresses and protocols. All devices are embedded with sensors and actuators and are usually wireless connected to the network. IoT enables the connectivity and communication between sensors and deploys the incoming information in order to provide applications to the people. Radio-frequency identification (RFID) is considered to be a prerequisite of IoT since it is believed that all things of our daily life could be identifiable with the use of radio tags. Cloud computing, which is actually a different term for Internet, has the duty of sharing computational resources and offering services to devices via the Internet without having hardware equipment to manage applications. These technologies are commonly used together and managed to become an inspiration source for many researchers whose works are related to smart cities.

To begin with Schaffers et al. (2011) who considered smart cities as open access environments that are designed according to users' preferences. In order to create innovative services, the use of Future Internet seems to be important as enabling the development of applications based on IoT. Furthermore, Living Labs played a useful role since they showed the way of organizing and coordinating innovative services and projects. A similar approach was followed by Chochliouros et al. (2013), who explained the concept of Living Labs and the benefits of their implementation in smart city facilities, and also highlighted their contribution in the evolution of Future Internet platforms.

Attwood et al. (2011) developed the framework of Smart City Critical Infrastructure (SCCI) which aimed to protect critical infrastructures from failure or help the system to continue its function if a failure was unavoidable to happen. To achieve that, the use of sensor actuator networks (SAN) was necessary, according to the researchers. SAN connected itself to the IoT so as to collect the data and integrate city components that should use an information aggregation utility. The amount of the collected data is so big, that the system should process them itself without human intervention. Semantic Web undertakes the role to take these data, give them meaning and specify the relationships between them, which are widely known as linked data. Cloud computing in its turn, used the service model of Infrastructure as a Service (IaaS) to access the data and process them in real-time. Based on these technologies, researchers developed the basic elements of SCCI, which are Smart Cities Systems Annotation and

Aggregation Service, Critical Response Reasoning Instance, Critical Response Visualization and Control and finally Sensor Actuator Network Overlay State Management.

Ballon et al. (2011) created a European Platform for Intelligent Cities (EPIC) with the intention to be implemented in all European Cities. Their goal was to evaluate the use of cloud platform, Living Labs and e-Government in a European level and examine the satisfaction of requirements and challenges that a smart city has to face. The EPIC integrates the technologies of cloud computing, IoT and semantic Web. Specifically, EPIC used IBM's Test and Development Cloud so as to facilitate public sector to accept the change and the innovation of the cloud. IoT can enable geospatial positioning and 3D display through the use of sensor and RFID. Finally, the semantic layer of the EPIC includes the Command and Control Lexical Grammar (CCLG) technology to solve the problem of the multiple spoken languages in European countries.

Asimakopoulou and Bessis (2011) focused their research on disaster management using crowd sourcing techniques to create smart buildings. Through crowd sourcing technology, citizens participate in the detection of emergency events using APIs in their phones. The role of citizens is enhanced by sensors and critical infrastructure in cars and buildings that explore their environment too. Other technologies that were proposed by the researchers were grid computing to integrate heterogeneous resources, cloud computing to enable access in these resources and pervasive computing to collect and handle data from devices.

In terms of crowd sourcing, Zhou et al. (2015) developed the RiMEA pedestrian simulator in order to facilitate crowd evacuation in emergency cases and evaluate crowd behavior and reactions under those circumstances. The software architecture of the simulator included a simulation kernel, a graphical user interface and a 3D visualization.

Wang et al. (2012) presented how to use World Wind geographic software developed by NASA to 3D reconstruct a city. It is about an open source platform which allows visualization, simulation and interaction in all smart city sectors. The two main components of this technology are data collection and visual display. Data are collected through IoT, network analysis and web map services. Their visual display is feasible through KMZ files which are grounded on KML patterns.

Ye et al. (2012) discussed the architecture of a Smart Sport information system giving emphasis to the including technologies, such as body sensor networks, IoT, cloud computing and data mining. In more detail, the body sensors have the duty to collect data bout the health and daily routine of athletes. Cloud computing is used as the middleware to allow transfer and management of these data. Data mining and techniques, such as mathematical models and artificial intelligence, are used to process and analyze the data so as to get the necessary information. Last but not least, with the contribution of IoT, that information is converted into useful applications.

Jin et al. (2012) analyzed four network architectures based on the IoT. The first architecture is the Autonomous Network Architecture, where users can access the network with or without Internet connection. The second is the Ubiquitous Network Architecture, where users access the Internet to find the expected information since radio technologies, wireless sensors and vehicular ad hoc networks are integrated to the Internet. The third is the Application Layer Overlay Network Architecture, which is capable of reducing the amount of collected data through the IoT by selecting the more useful ones. The last is the Service Oriented Network Architecture, where researchers presented the example of the IDRA platform, which was developed by E.D. Poorter et al. (2011).

Mitton et al. (2012) examined the combination of cloud with sensors and actuators empowering by the IoT. This approach is named "Sensing and Actuation as a Service (SAaaS)". In their system, a smart city is divided in sites. Each site is considered to be autonomous and contains sensors for information gathering and clients as information consumers. The collected information is stored in the Database Manager of the site from where it can be published to users after their request or can be distributed to the other sites if there is a need. The operation of this system is feasible via implementing the proposed schema and modules architecture, which consists of three elements, Hypervisor, Autonomic Enforcer and Volunteer Cloud Manager. The Hypervisor is used to abstract sensors from single devices or from networks. The Adapter facilitates the communication between the devices. The Autonomic Enforcer is the mediator between the above modules and the SAaaS Cloud, exploiting their resources and converting them into applications using IoT capabilities. The Volunteer Cloud Manager concentrates these resources and applications in the cloud and develops strategies after monitoring the connectivity among the devices.

A similar study was undertaken by Distefano et al. (2013). The researchers kept the basic elements of the above framework and went further by distinguishing two phases. The first phase was SAaaS provisioning system and infrastructure setup and the second was SAaaS application setup.

Suciu et al. (2013) proposed the framework SlapOS, which combined cloud and IoT architectures, as a mean for designing smart cities. According to the researchers, the necessary features of building a smart city are sensor networks and open source cloud platforms. Their framework integrates these technologies and has also the ability to transfer and offer IoT applications through the use of cloud middleware.

Roscia et al. (2013) presented a model for smart cities that was called Intelligent Distributed Autonomous Smart City (IDASC). IDASC involves multi-agent systems and IoT to enable observation, audit and performance of the system. It also integrates ZEUS framework to ensure functionality and communication between the agents.

Samaras et al. (2013) developed SEN2SOC platform to be implemented in the SmartSantander City of Spain. Their aim was to enhance the interaction between sensor and social networks through the use of Natural Language Generation (NLG) system in order to improve citizens and visitors experience in living in a smart city. The architecture of SEN2SOC platform is component-based and includes mobile and web applications (IoT) to facilitate users login, support their navigation in city routes and promote feedback, sensor and social data monitoring to collect data from sensor and social media networks and detect anomalies in the environment, statistical analysis to process the income data and export the results from this action, and interface to allow communication between the components. The NLG system, which is embedded in the platform, has the ability to receive information from sensors and convert it into messages that can be easily understood by humans.

Horng (2014) designed a system for smart parking in order to facilitate citizens in finding parking spaces and help in reducing fuel congestion and air pollution. The architecture is based on an Adaptive Recommendation Mechanism, which includes various technologies in order to allow system's implementation. In more detail, it uses wireless sensor networks so as to search the existence of vehicles near a parking space. Then, an Internal Recommendation Mechanism of the specific place informs the Parking Congestion Cloud Center (PCCC) which with its turn transmits these data to the Cloud Server. Finally, the user receives the desirable information through his/hers mobile device, which in the same time acts as a sensor for the Cloud Server.

Asadi Zanjani et al. (2015) focused on energy management in buildings. Their goal was to develop an interface that could enable citizens to manage their energy consumption and be informed about its emissions and cost, so as to control their living spaces. Each living space was equipped with one or two wireless sensor nodes, while all the electrical devices were equipped with smart plugs. As a result, researchers could measure the temperature, humidity and luminosity of the space as well as the power consumption of devices. A web application dealt with presenting to the user those measurements of sensors and plugs.

Bululukova and Wahl (2015) proposed the integration of smart cities in education taking into account the Smart City Wien Framework Strategy initiatives goals and the Europe 2020 objectives. In their work, they referred to the existing study programs and their implementation plan through the integration of smart cities concepts and the use of ICT technologies and big data.

Iano et al. (2015) also dealt with intelligent education and especially with the use of Internet Broadband Network of Things in order to improve e-inclusion, e-learning and supplementary education. They also implemented the Gigabyte - capable Passive Optical Networks (GPON) technology to facilitate the access in the optical fiber and radio networks of Brazil, improve the speed rate of Internet and offer citizens high connectivity to the smart education environment.

2.1.5   Combined Architectures

Except from the perspectives that we analyzed above and the presentation of the most underlying works that have been already published in the literature, there is also the perspective of combined architectures, which manages to integrate characteristics and technologies of the abovementioned ones. It is a common phenomenon for researchers to mix technologies and platforms in order to create an architecture that can probably be implemented in a smart city. In this section, we cite some of these works distinguishing them in categories.

IoT – AL. Khan and Kiani (2012) presented a cloud-based architecture for improving services offered to citizens. According to the researchers, citizens act as providers of data through the use of their phones, and as consumers of the developing services after processing the collected information. The proposed architecture which is based on a cloud environment is divided in seven layers (five horizontal and two vertical) and contains the context-awareness element. The first layer is the platform integration layer which contains the cloud technology and facilitates the access to all kinds of information. The data acquisition and analysis layer enables data collection and includes the context-awareness element to separate useful data from non-useful ones and synthesizes them together. The thematic layer categorizes data in sections according to their context. The service composition layer specifies the origin of data and contains the context-awareness element to state the workflows among corresponding services. The application service layer enables modeling and visualization of data to create applications that meet end users requirements. The management and integration layer manages the flow of data so as to ensure that only relevance data are shifted from one layer to another. Finally, the security layer certifies the authentication of data and their use from authorized users.

Wang and Zhou (2012) presented an abstract study about the use of cloud with Near Field Communication (NFC) technology in smart cities. NFC is a card embedded in mobile devices, which is based on Internet and RFID. Its role is to promote user confirmation, data transmission, distant payments and public information. The researchers distinguished three layers in cloud architecture of NFC application, which were user information storage layer, device information layer and process layer. Process layer included six other layers, from which researchers chose to discuss in more detail the resource scheduling layer.

Szabó et al. (2013) built a framework using Extensible Messaging and Presence Protocol (XMPP) to collect data from citizens' mobile devices. Their intention was to enhance participatory sensing while creating and operating smart city applications. This knowledge is considered to be real-time big data that are processed by IoT. The first scale of the framework's architecture is based on the publish-subscribe feature of the XMPP, which give users the opportunity to take part in information gathering (publish) and enjoy the updating applications after this action (subscribe). The second scale of the architecture is the analytics component, which is distributed in layers in order to anticipate citizens' mobility. According to the researchers, these layers are streaming, persistence, serialization, caching, mobile data process and users defined functions layers and include platforms and technologies that can facilitate data processing and system's recovery after a failure.

Zhang et al. (2013) examined the use of IoT in the food industry of a smart city. Especially, they focused in the creation of an IoT system, which can observe, control and analyze the food supply chain so as to offer citizens protection of consuming contaminated or polluted products. The logic architecture of IoT is divided in four layers, data collection and management, intelligent processing, graphic representation and self-correction, each of which includes specific algorithms and metrics techniques. The collection of data from sensor is feasible through the Self-adaptive Dynamic Partition Sampling (SDPS) strategy in an attempt to eliminate the portion of sample of products that need to be examined so as to enhance the accuracy of the control. Furthermore, the researchers implemented a tracing algorithm to discover the origin of the pollution and a backtracing algorithm to withdraw polluted products that could not be traced in the supply sequence.

Sánchez et al. (2013) presented the architecture of the SmartSantander city in Spain. Their aim was to find the necessary platforms based on IoT to develop a common context for all smart cities. Their proposed architecture consists of three layers which are IoT device, gateway and server layer. The IoT device layer has the duty to estimate the number of the connected devices to the network and facilitates their heterogeneous nature through the use of mobile phones, RFID and other technologies. The gateway layer allows the communication and connectivity between the devices and the network. The server layer enables the access of users in the system by offering high level scalability and availability to the servers. Except from the layers, the architecture is also divided in four subsystems, each of which provides information about its embedded functionalities and is accessible by specific groups of people. Briefly, these subsystems are Authentication, Authorization and Accounting, Testbed Management, Experimental Support and Application Support subsystem.

Bertoncini (2015) created a framework for improving energy efficiency and reducing carbon footprints. The architecture of the framework is multi-layered and includes energy and resource infrastructure as well as human networks. The embedded platforms are the ICT technologies such as real time sensing and monitoring, intelligent processing and big data on line analytics.

Lilis et al. (2015) developed a system so as to integrate the building automation technologies into smart cities. Their proposed integration architecture was divided in four distinct elements. The first element was the Endpoint Node, which included advanced sensors and actuators, and more specifically the IP enabled solar energy harvesting multifunction environmental sensor and the wireless controlling modules communicating with each other through the power lines. The second element was Network Embedded Electronic, which aimed to data collection and interconnection of the endpoints through the use of IoT, data mining algorithms and local storage of data. The third element was the Centralized Management Server, which was actually a RESTful web server that aimed to facilitate the communication between buildings with smart cities. In this level, the IoT was replaced by the Web of Things (WoT). Finally, the last element included all the web services and applications that had been designed to facilitate the operation of the system.

Anadiotis et al. (2015) presented the BESOS Common Information Model to integrate different energy management systems in smart cities and share information and services between them and other external applications. The infrastructure of BESOS contained a large number of Gateways which had the duty of collecting data from energy management systems and delivering them to the middleware layer. The middleware layer using a data meta model integrated the incoming data and transferred them to the application layer. Finally, the application layer offered useful services to the users and the application developers.

IoT – SOA. Andreini et al. (2011) proposed an architecture infused by the notion of SOA, which combined IoT and geo-localization in order to promote access in smart city services. Researchers emphasized in the term of scalability which could be achieved by using the Distributed Hash Table (DHT) protocol.

Hu and Li (2012) proposed the use of 3S and IoT for the creation and design of a smart city. The 3S technology is associated with geospatial information (RS, GPS, GIS) for accurate positioning, with 3D visualization for city construction, with sensor networks for incessant observation, and with DPGrid and GPU (Graphics Processing Unit) technologies for real time processing of data. IoT is thought to be associated with RFID, barcodes and 2D codes technologies for allowing computational systems identify things of daily life, with sensor web for space monitoring, with SOA for managing geospatial data, and with grid and cloud computing for allowing access to services through the use of Internet and wireless networks.

Klingert et al. (2015) developed the DC4Cities system in order to maximize the share of renewable power sources and eliminate the carbon emissions when operating data centers in smart cities. The technical infrastructure of this system included the technologies of sensor networks, big data, IaaS, PaaS, KPIs, service-oriented applications, Energy Management Authority of Smart City (EMA-SC) to manage the coordination between the smart city and data centre, Energy Adaptive Software Controller (EASC) to plan the use of the resources, Renewable Energy Adaptive Interface to retrieve forecasts about the energy sources and Ideal Power Planner (IPP) to transfer energy forecasts and constrains imposed by EMA into a power plan for a data centre.

IoT - SOA – AL. Xiong et al. (2014) introduced a novel architecture of Data Vitalization (DV) in order to indicate a more effective way of managing the heterogeneous incoming data from sensors. DV architecture, which is divided in cells (master, data and special cells), mainly uses the technologies of SOA and cloud computing. An application of DV is the Smart Service Platform (SSP), which architecture distinguishes into four layers-data gathering and storage layer, supporting layer for DV service, application layer for DV and application Layer for development. Data gathering and storage layer collects and stores data in particular cells, while supporting layer for DV service processes these data. These two layers constitute of the data cell, which is applied by a virtual machine and their framework is the infrastructure as a service (IaaS) cloud computing services type. The other two application layers for DV and development concern both end users and developers, since they offer users the desirable applications, users can react as sensors and collect data from their devices and also developers can exploit APIs and create new services. The implemented technologies are virtual machine manager in the third layer and platform as a service (PaaS) in the latter.

IoT – EDA. Based on the EDA of the SOFIA project, Wan et al. (2012) discussed the implementation of Machine to Machine (M2 M) communications in order to improve smart cities applications. M2 M technology has the ability to facilitate the connection between people, computers and mobile devices, and also sensors and actuators. According to the researchers, in order to maximize the efficiency of the smart city system, M2 M communications need to be combined with Internet, sensors, networks and cloud computing, and further with KPs and SIBs.

Feher et al. (2015) presented a probabilistic approach to solve the problem with parking spaces in smart cities. Their approach consisted of a database containing the parking probabilities, an event database to collect parking data, a prediction service to process them and a mobile client to capture parking events. The technologies that were used to fulfill this procedure were various types of sensors, GPS and mobile applications.

IoT - SOA - AL - EDA. Wenge et al. (2014) proposed an architecture for smart cities from the perspective of data management. Their architecture is divided in six layers – data acquisition, data transmitting, data storage and vitalization, support service, domain service and event-driven application layer. The data acquisition layer gathers the data coming from sensor networks and other sources, like RFID and system on a chip (SoC). The data transmitting layer integrates the technologies of wireless networks and ultra wide band in order to facilitate users with Internet access. The data storage and vitalization layer focuses on clarification, correlation, sustainment, development and storage of data using the Internet of data technology (IoD) that is similar to the IoT, and also cloud computing. The support service layer emphasizes in data management and provision to the users through SOA architecture, cloud platforms, visualization and simulation technologies. The domain service layer concerns every single sector of smart city and tries to integrate them together in order to enhance citizens' experience. Ultimately, the event-driven application layer stresses on citizens requirements and tries to offer them applications that satisfy their needs.

2.1.6   Internet of Everything (IoE)

IoE is a future perspective which is being designed to extend, overcome and substitute the IoT. Cisco defines the IoE for smart cities as the technology that connects people, process, data and things in order to improve the livability of cities and communities. IoE provides not only computing devices but every object (everything) with the capability of high connectivity and intelligence so as to operate various facilities. IoT based its function in the great number of the connected objects. Nevertheless, IoE operates via the deployment of networks that have the ability to transport all the collected and created information by these objects and also facilitates the connection of many more objects even if every object. In other words, IoE flags a new and innovative era when smart objects are connected together and everyone from everywhere and at anytime can have access to them. Cisco clarifies the exact procedure that IoE follows. More specifically, IoE exploits the Internet infrastructure and connection networks, manages in an effective way the incoming information from devices, creates applications that can satisfy citizens' requirements in both public and private sectors and makes networks less complex through the use of APIs. Cisco plans aim to the opening of a global innovation centre for IoE in Barcelona by the mid-2016 like the ones that already exists in Brazil and South Korea and those that under construction in Germany and Canada. The purpose of those centers is to operate as the examples of introducing a common pattern when designing new applications for smart cities that are in the initial stages of creating urban facilities. For the time being there are not published use cases for that perspective.

2.2   Architectures Discussion and Implementation

Above we enumerate many architectures and technologies that have been proposed in the literature in order to find implementation in the smart city system or a smart city sector. In this section, we will discuss them and try to determine the platforms that are useful when designing a smart city.

The AL perspective was one of the first to be applied by researchers if we consider the comparative study of T. Ishida between the digital cities of America Online, Amsterdam, Helsinki and Kyoto in 2000. The implementation of this perspective gave researchers the opportunity to modify features in different layers without having to change the whole system. As we recognized from the previous analysis, each researcher made a different proposal of a set of layers since there was not any specification agreed on the layer formation. Even today there is still not a standard pattern to follow when choosing to implement this architecture. It is remarkable that L. Anthopoulos and I.A. Tsoukalas who developed the digital city of Trikala in 2006, admitted that they failed to meet city's challenges with the existing architecture. The integration of more sophisticated technologies, such as sensors, actuators, GPS, cloud and so on managed to enhance layers' functionality. IBM opened the way with the definition of smart city structure and its including technologies. The contribution of Carretero (2012) was also important since he added the characteristic of self-adaptation while creating the ADAPCITY system. Furthermore, Vilajosana et al. (2013) proposed a generic layer architecture presenting the key platforms and technologies to support smart city applications. This architecture offers lots of benefits in designing a system since it can make it more flexible to changes and each change can affect only one layer and not the others. Furthermore, the separation of the smart city system into layers facilitates the implementation of reusable components, while the component distribution helps the system to be more scalable and reliable. No serious technology restrictions have been noticed while implementing this architecture. The effectiveness of this perspective will be improved, if it is combined with more advanced technologies or even another perspective. This attempt is really valuable when building a smart city since the system can better respond to all challenges and requirements (Table 1).

The SOA perspective takes into account citizens' needs and preferences and tries to provide them with high quality services. These services can communicate and interact with each other while being independent and loosely coupled. Anthopoulos and Fitsilis (2010) used this architecture in order to improve the city system of Trikala and in an attempt to create a common architecture for smart cities. The implementation of this perspective fits very well with the purpose of a smart city which is to offer citizens the right services that satisfy their needs. Service orientation seems to be one of the most useful architectures since its functionality offers a great number of advantages such as flexibility, service re-use, ability to create both new functions and combinations of functions. However, there are still issues to be solved concerning the complexity, performance and cost of the designing system. SOA functionality can be enhanced if it is combined with IoT.

The EDA perspective has the ability to identify an uncommon situation and respond to unusual events. This feature is very expedient in cases of crowd sourcing and monitoring public spaces in smart cities. Filipponi et al. (2010) developed SOFIA project in order to ensure citizens security. A subway station use case, facilitated by SOFIA infrastructure, was implemented to prove the effectiveness of the architecture in detecting abnormal events. However, the basic disadvantage of this perspective is that it can not respond properly when the events are characterized with great heterogeneity (Souleiman et al., 2012). One solution could be the combination with SOA since an event can trigger the operation of a service. Another solution could be a combination with IoT since the existence of sensor networks can enhance the efficiency of EDA.

The IoT perspective is the most common approach used nowadays considering the number of published works in that domain. Internet is also related to sensor networks and cloud computing, technologies that are necessary when collecting, managing and storing information for developing smart city applications. However, some researchers made modifications in the features of these technologies to fulfill the requirements of their systems. For instance, both Mitton et al. (2012) and Distefano et al. (2013) used the approach of Sensing and Actuation as a Service (SAaaS). The first researcher presented the case study of a smart city and the latter the use cases of smart traffic control and smart surveillance systems respectively. Other researchers added extra technologies to the mentioned ones for improving the functionality of their systems. More specifically, Ballon et al. (2011) incorporated the technology of Command and Control Lexical Grammar in EPIC framework which is already implemented in the smart cities of Brussels, Issy-les-Molineaux, Manchester and Tirgu Mures in Romania still studying its implementation results. Furthermore, Samaras et al. (2013) added the technology of Natural Language Generation in SEN2SOC platform and illustrated two significant scenarios including citizens and city authorities. Another group of researchers used these technologies for developing applications for only one smart city sector. For example, Ye et al. (2012) dealt with smart sport applications presenting the cases of smart stadiums, smart shoes, smart athletes and smart fitness. Horng (2014) designed an adaptive mechanism for smart parking, the effectiveness of which was proved via a simulation test. Zhou et al. (2015) developed the RiMEA pedestrian simulator and in order to demonstrate its reliability, they made tests of fourteen scenarios. Wang et al. (2012) dealt with 3D city reconstruction through the use of World Wind software showing three implementation scenarios of Lujiazui city, weather data and subway lines. The general idea that came out of this analysis is that this perspective is really valuable since it can gather data from citizens' devices and external sensors, transfer and process them via the Internet, create applications that fit to citizens needs and finally store these applications in the cloud to eliminate the waste of resources. This architecture is suitable for smart city development considering all of the above-mentioned features and can be implemented alone or combined with another perspective. However, attention is required in terms of privacy of citizens' personal data since they are stored in the internet and are vulnerable in hacking and stealing. It is worthwhile to mention that scientific community tries to extend IoT and enhance its functionality, creating the new IoE.

The combined architectures perspective is possibly the most appropriate for building smart cities since the integration, communication and connectivity between various technologies can help in the creation and easy management of more advanced applications. After a careful study we realized that Internet technologies are the key components to all architectures. Researchers combined them with AL, SOA and EDA. Combining IoT with AL was the primary choice of Szabó et al. (2013) who dealt with participatory sensing presenting three use case applications, concerning crowd sourcing based on public transport, soccer events and university campus all of which are still under development. Also, Zhang et al. (2013) dealt with the use of IoT in food industry and highlighted two cases, one general and one including big data, proving the efficiency of SDPS strategy, tracing and backtracking algorithms. Furthermore, Bertoncini et al. (2015) focused on the energy efficiency and illustrated two implementation cases, the INGRID case, which integrated smart electricity grid with hydrogen mobility infrastructure and the GEYSER case, which emphasized on a smart data centre hub interacting with smart energy grids and telco networks. However, Andreini et al. (2011) preferred to combine IoT with SOA and presented a use case for proving the effectiveness of their proposed architecture. Moreover, Klingert et al. (2015) developed the DC4Cities system and validated it including three trials and different services inside data centers in Barcelona, Trento and Milan. An extraordinary attempt was done by Xiong et al. (2014) who combined IoT with SOA and AL to create a Data Vitalization architecture so as to find a way of better managing the incoming data from sensors presenting the social hotspots sense use case. Equally significant was the work of Wan et al. (2012) who extended the EDA of SOFIA project by adding M2 M communications technology combined with IoT and sensors showing a case study of vehicular networks. Finally, the work of Feher et al. (2015) was also innovative since they proposed a probabilistic approach for smart parking illustrating tests in two different scenarios, the downtown scenario where streets were full of parking cars and the suburb scenario where there were plenty of parking spaces on the streets.

As a matter of fact, the combination of the perspectives can help the smart city system to gain the max of its effectiveness by offering citizens the desirable applications, avoiding failures or recovering immediately in case of one and detecting for abnormal events enhancing citizens' security.

Table 1. Smart City Architectures and Technologies.

Researchers	Research Area	Architectures	Technologies
Ishida (2000)	Digital cities of America, Amsterdam, Helsinki & Kyoto	AL	Sensors, Internet files, GIS, 3D/2D spaces and maps, agent systems
Anthopoulos and Tsoukalas (2006)	Digital city of Trikala	AL	Networks, geospatial data
IBM (2010)	Smart city structure	AL	Sensors, GPS, RFID, networks, cloud computing, fuzzy techniques
Su et al. (2011)	Smart city manufacture	AL	Network infrastructure, cloud, sensors
Carretero (2012)	ADAPCITY	AL	Data mining, statistics, prediction & optimization measurements
Vilajosana et al. (2013)	Generic architecture for smart cities	AL	Sensors, actuators, data warehouses, security infrastructures, interface
Anthopoulos and Fitsilis (2010)	A common architecture – Enterprise Architecture	SOA	Logical and physical architecture, service delivery
Filiponi et al. (2010)	SOFIA Project	EDA	Sensors networks, SIBs, KPs, IOP
Schaffers et al. (2011)	Smart city and the Future Internet	IoT	IoT, Living Labs

(Continued)

Table 1. (*Continued*)

Researchers	Research Area	Architectures	Technologies
Chochliouros et al. (2013)	Living Labs in smart cities	IoT	IoT, Living Labs
Attwood et al. (2011)	Smart City Critical Infrastructures	IoT	IoT, Sensor actuator networks, Semantic Web, IaaS
Ballon et al. (2011)	European Platform for Intelligent Cities	IoT	Test & Development Cloud, Living Labs, Semantic Web, RFID, sensors, CCLG
Asimakopoulou and Bessis (2011)	Disaster Management and smart buildings	IoT	Crowd sourcing, sensors, grid, cloud and pervasive computing
Zhou et al. (2015)	RiMEA Pedestrian Simulator	IoT	Simulation kernel, graphical user interface, 3D visualization
Wang et al. (2012)	World Wind for 3D reconstruction of smart cities	IoT	IoT, networks, web maps, KMZ files
Ye et al. (2012)	Smart Sports	IoT	Body sensor network, cloud, data mining
J. Jin et al. (2012)	Smart City Network Architectures	IoT	IoT
Mitton et al. (2012)	Cloud and sensors in smart cities	IoT	IoT, SAaS
Distefano et al. (2013)	SAaaS in smart cities	IoT	IoT, SAaS
Suciu et al. (2013)	SlapOS	IoT	IoT, open source cloud, sensors
Roscia et al. (2013)	Intelligent Distributed Autonomous Smart Cities	IoT	IoT, multi-agent system, ZEUS framework
Samaras et al. (2013)	SEN2SOC platform	IoT	IoT, Natural Language Generation, sensor and social networks
Horng (2014)	Smart Parking	IoT	IoT, adaptive recommendation mechanism, wireless sensors, cloud
Zanjani et al. (2015)	Energy Book for Buildings	IoT	Wireless sensor nodes, actuators, smart plugs, web applications
Bululukova and Wahl (2015)	Smart city integration in teaching and research	IoT	ICT, big data

(*Continued*)

Table 1. (*Continued*)

Researchers	Research Area	Architectures	Technologies
Iano et al. (2015)	Intelligent education	IoT	Internet broadband network of Things, Gigabyte Passive Optical Networks
Khan and Kiani (2012)	Cloud for citizens services in smart cities	IoT – AL	IoT, cloud, context-awareness component
Wang and Zhou (2012)	Cloud based on NFC in smart cities	IoT – AL	IoT, cloud computing, NFC card, RFID
Szabó et al. (2013)	Participatory sensing	IoT – AL	IoT, XMPP, analytics component
Zhang et al. (2013)	Smart Food Supply Chain	IoT – AL	IoT, sensor networs, SDPS, tracing and backtracing algorithms
Sánchez et al. (2013)	SmartSantander	IoT – AL	IoT
Bertoncini (2015)	Smart city energy efficiency	IoT – AL	Real time sensing/monitoring, intelligent processing, big data analytics
Lilis et al. (2015)	Integrating building automation technologies with smart cities	IoT – AL	IoT, WoT, sensors, actuators, data mining, RESTful web server
Anadiotis et al. (2015)	BESOS Common Information Model	IoT – AL	APIs, energy management systems
Andreini et al. (2011)	Geo-localized services in SC	IoT – SOA	IoT, wireless sensors, SOA, DHT
Hu and Li (2012)	Smart city design	IoT – SOA	3S, GPS, 3D, sensors, DPGrid, GPU, RFID, 2D code, cloud, grid computing
Klingert et al. (2015)	DC4Cities	IoT – SOA	Sensors, big data, IaaS, PaaS, KPIs, service-oriented applications, EMA-SC
Xiong et al. (2014)	Data vitalization in smart cities	IoT – SOA – AL	IoT, SOA, sensor networks, IaaS, PaaS
Wan et al. (2012)	M2 M communications in SC	IoT – EDA	IoT, sensors, actuators, cloud, KPs, SIBs
Feher et al. (2015)	Probabilistic approach to parking	IoT – EDA	IoT, sensors, GPS, mobile client, event database
Wenge et al. (2014)	Smart city architecture from data management perspective	IoT – SOA – EDA – AL	IoT, sensors, RFID, SoC, wireless networks, ultra wide band, IoD, cloud, visualization & simulation technologies

3 Requirements

Requirements play an important role when building a smart city. They are considered to be official and validated declarations of some functionality that aim to fulfill a particular need of the city. As a result, they are measurable and most of the times predefined even before a need arised or discovered. They work toward to satisfy social, economic or business needs and for this purpose are related to ICT technologies either directly or indirectly. Each smart city system has to gratify a minimum number of fundamental requirements in order to be effective and fulfill its mission. The selected architecture to be applied aims to satisfy a set of requirements, the number of which depends on the nature, potentials, and initiatives of the designing system as well as on the different social, financial and environmental characteristics of the cities and the needs of its stakeholders.

Below we cite some of the most outstanding works that stated a set of requirements in order to support the various smart cities systems. Then we list and discuss the basic requirements of these works presenting a table assigning the architectures to the requirements that they aimed to fulfill.

3.1 Requirements Background

To begin with a group of researchers who published in 2011 a survey on behalf of the Net!works European Technology Platform about smart cities applications and requirements giving emphasis on five domains of the city: economic, social and privacy implications; e-government; health, inclusion and assisting living; intelligent transportation systems; smart grids, energy efficiency and environment. As the researchers mentioned, the key technical requirements to provide e-government at the smart city level was standardization and interoperability. At health domain, they addressed the technical requirements of data security, encryption, authorization and authentication, smart devices connectivity and interactivity, power requirements for devices, end user interface, service discovery, scalability and survivability, persistence, interworking, community to community application messaging propagation, auditing and logging, location information sharing, and application service migration. At the domain of transportation systems, they proposed the requirements of security, privacy and authentication, flexible and scalable networks, heterogeneity with different types of sensors, actuators and radio interfaces, exploitation of location information, and real time exchange of data. At the last domain of smart grid and energy efficiency, they presented the requirements of real time and redundant communication, standardization, interoperability, sensor and actuator networks, ICT infrastructure and reliability for adaptation.

Emphasizing on the satisfaction of only one type of requirements was the primary study of Jin et al. (2012) who focused on Quality of Service. They identified four network architectures for smart city applications based on the IoT and presented their performance and effectiveness in order to maintain the Quality of Service guarantees.

In order to permit the implementation of their survey, Samaras et al. (2013) clarified the requirements needed to support their proposed SEN2SOC platform. Initially, they differentiated the requirements into functional and non functional ones, to prioritize them into mandatory, desirable and optional depending on their importance and criticality. Then, they stated the specific categories of requirements, which were sensor data, sensor data statistical analysis, users as sensors, users' recommendations, web applications, alerts, social media analysis, user access to SEN2SOC applications, SEN2SOC architecture, experimentation, and evaluation of SEN2SOC experiment.

Finally, W. M. da Silva et al. (2013), after analyzing lots of researches published in the literature, they presented their own set of requirements from a technological perspective and assigned them to the architectures they studied. Their proposed requirements were objects interoperability, sustainability, real time monitoring, historical data, mobility, availability, privacy, distributed sensing and processing, service composition and integrated urban management, social aspects, and flexibility / extensibility.

3.2   Requirements Analysis

As we can easily recognize from the previous section, there is not yet a common set of requirements officially formulated. Each researcher proposed a set of requirements that was related to the needs of a specific smart city system or a specific sector that was the subject of their survey. Of course this is reasonable since it is very difficult to state a standard set of requirements for all smart cities because every city has different social, cultural, economic, political and business structure. Furthermore, all the requirements were formulated from a technical perspective and did not take into account citizens needs and preferences. In this section, we demonstrate the basic requirements both technical and user centric that must be satisfied when implementing some of the mentioned architectures and technologies as we recognized them during our literature study.

- **Data Collection.** The collection of data is a basic activity for the smart city system in order to maintain its operation. To achieve this goal, the desirable data must be available and most of the times open. The system should have the ability of recognizing and categorizing various types of data, such as big or historical, and also the size of data involved, if they are few or many, since they are continually being modified due to human intervention or environmental changes. Another source for collecting data is through citizens' involvement, who can contribute to this procedure via the use of their smart devices. This requirement can be met through the use of sensors and actuators to capture big and open data, cloud computing to manage the available data, data mining to deal with historical data and crowd sourcing to enhance participatory sensing. It is worthwhile to mention, that every researcher can choose from the previous technologies only those that fulfill better the mission of the smart city system and depend on the type of data it aims to manage.
- **Data Streaming and Processing.** The stream and process of data should both occur in real time. To make this happen, the system should have the ability of having access to the incoming data and being in position of estimating the nature, size, complexity and reliability of the stream. Moreover, data processing should be distributed in order to benefit effectively from the system's infrastructure. This

requirement can be met through the use of networks that can facilitate and deliver the stream and be also distributed.

- **Data Security.** It is of great importance that all the data used by the city should be safe and secure. It is about confidential and critical data that can not be disclosed to all citizens either they are related to city authorities or to a sector like hospitals or citizens' personal and professional data. For this direction, encryption techniques, privacy policies, authentication mechanisms and access control must be established in order to guarantee the nature and distribution of those data.

- **Monitoring.** Monitoring in smart cities happens in real time in order to observe all the components of the city and acquire useful information about them. The main goal of the real time monitoring is to predict and forecast various situations that can affect the city's prosperity. This is feasible through the use of mobile technologies, smart devices, IoT and RFID.

- **Heterogeneity.** A smart city system has to deal with great heterogeneity of the information flows and the devices involved. This requirement can be met through the existence and use of sensors and actuators, as well as with radio tags, user interfaces and control loops in order to overcome in some degree the complexity of the overall system.

- **Adaptation**. A smart city system has to be flexible and adaptive to changes. More specifically, it should be able to react effectively when a change occurs and adapt its behavior according to the new circumstances. Also, it should be able to recover immediately after a change, update its operations and if it is possible to create new and more advanced ones. In order to fulfill this requirement, the system should use sensing mechanisms, prediction techniques and data mining.

- **Sustainability.** The sustainability of the city is related to social, financial, and environmental aspects. Social sustainability refers to the provision of useful and important services to the citizens such as transportation, electricity and telecommunications. Financial sustainability refers to the wealth of the city, inflow of money, businesses operation and attractiveness of investments. Lastly, environmental sustainability refers to the energy efficiency and management of natural resources. In order to satisfy this requirement, the system should use ICT technologies together with big data analysis, financial models, cost management, energy production and pollution measurements.

- **Interoperability.** The interoperability of smart city refers to the cooperation between various devices together, which usually use different kinds of platforms. Nowadays, a great effort is being undertaken to enable connectivity between the devices through the creation of common standards and protocols that can facilitate the collaboration among different operating systems. Moreover, some experts proposed the design of an open architecture that can facilitate information sharing and better integration of devices and applications. In order to meet this requirement, the system should use and exploit all the available sensors, the communications gateways and the IoT.

- **User Satisfaction.** Except from the technical specifications, a smart city should also take into account citizens needs and requests. The system should offer usefulness to all stakeholders through the management of relevant data and the design of a friendly interface. It is important that the system would have the ability of distinguishing the various types of stakeholders and providing each of them with the necessary feedback. In general, users should benefit from the system's use, a fact that would have both social and economic impact.

- **City Oriented.** Orientation to the city requirement means that the system should offer valuable services and applications that would affect the city as a whole and every domain separately. It also aims to strengthen the usability and attractiveness of these services not only for the specific city and its stakeholders, but also for other smart cities. Finally, its purpose is to improve the everyday life of citizens and increase public safety.

3.3 Assigning Requirements to Architectures

In this section we assign the architectures proposed by the researchers with the requirements that each of them aimed to fulfill. For a better understanding, we concentrate them in the table below (Table 2).

3.4 Requirements Discussion

As we can easily realize from the above table, each researcher aimed to satisfy a specific number of requirements and not all of them. This is reasonable if we consider that every city has different social, cultural, economic and business needs and as a result it is difficult to state a common pattern for all smart cities. According to that, each researcher defined his/her own set of requirements that corresponded better to the needs of the analyzed city. Moreover, there were researchers that dealt with only one sector of the city. So, they gave emphasis on a specific set of requirements in order to maintain or improve the operation of the sector. In other words, every architecture was designed to target a particular problem and solve it in an effective manner. The works that aimed to satisfy most of these requirements were that of Filiponi et al. (2010) and Vilajosana et al. (2013).

Some technical requirements such as data collection and data streaming and processing were observed to exist in a great number of the proposed architectures. That is obvious if we take into account that every system in order to perform effectively needs income, flow, transfer and process of relevant information. Especially data stream and process seems to be the primary requirement that every system aims to fulfill according to the results presented in the table. In order to satisfy this requirement, researchers used various technologies to better manage the incoming data.

Moreover, data collection, stream and process, and monitoring were presented to exist together in many researches. That means that the proposed system used to monitor in real time the external and environmental conditions, and also collect and process the available data through critical infrastructure. These three requirements combined together were included in the works of Vilajosana et al. (2013), Filiponi et al. (2010), Attwood et al. (2011), Asimakopoulou and Bessis (2011), Ye et al. (2012), Samaras et al. (2013), Khan and Kiani (2012), Szabó et al. (2013) and Feher et al. (2015).

Data security is considered to be one of the most serious requirements in the extent that it is mandatory for a system to satisfy it. Unfortunately, only two works from those presented focused on the privacy and confidentiality of citizens, and government information. So, only Vilajosana et al. (2013) and Khan and Kiani (2012) realized the necessity of satisfying this requirement. The first authors developed the capillary network layer in their platform which included security infrastructures for data management and control offering and the service layer which had the responsibility to receive the incoming data from capillary network layer and then to process and secure them. The latter authors developed the security layer in their framework which certified the authentication of data and their use from authorized users.

Heterogeneity is referred to the different types of devices used by the citizens during their daily life and the various types of incoming data flow in the system. According to this, IBM (2010) developed the perception layer to recognize the various types of involving devices. Carretero (2012) built a system to provide heterogeneous devices with the ability of reacting effectively to environmental changes. Mitton et al. (2012) and Distefano et al. (2013) used the Adapter element to facilitate the communication between heterogeneous devices. Sánchez et al. (2013) created the IoT device layer to overcome the heterogeneous nature of the devices and help them interact properly via the use of IoT. Finally, Xiong et al. (2014) developed Data Vitalization architecture in order to indicate a more effective way of managing the heterogeneous incoming data from sensors.

Adaptation is related to the ability of the system to react effectively when a change appears and adjust its behavior according to the new conditions. In that direction, Carretero (2012) developed a self-adaptive architecture named ADAPCITY to facilitate the system to adapt its operation and recover when a change occurred, while Attwood et al. (2011) used adaptation mechanisms to control critical infrastructure failures. Horng (2014) created an Adaptive Recommendation Mechanism for improving parking services, while Zhang et al. (2013) proposed a Self-adaptive Dynamic Partition Sampling strategy for protecting citizens from consuming contaminated products.

Sustainability is affiliated with the social, financial and environmental aspects of the city trying to simplify service delivery, reduce cost and manage energy. Six works from those presented dealt with it. Notably, Vilajosana et al. (2013) built a self-sustainable model to bootstrap the smart city market through the use big data flows. Schaffers et al. (2011) dealt with sustainable, open and user-driven innovation frameworks based on Future Internet to improve social cohesion, economic growth and optimization of energy and water usage. Bululukova and Wahl (2015) gave emphasis on integrating sustainable smart cities concepts to academic level to enhance teaching and research, while Iano et al. (2015) used Internet broadband network of Things to promote sustainable computing and communication technologies for being applied to education system of Brazil. Bertoncini (2015) developed an Integrated Sustainable Urban Model to manage urban energy infrastructure to optimize consumption of energy, decrease the exploit of resources and eliminate costs. Lastly, Khan and Kiani (2012) proposed a cloud architecture to facilitate sustainable urban development, socio-economic growth and management of sustainable natural resources.

Interoperability is related to the coordination between different devices together, which are usually based on different types of technologies. In that term, Lilis et al. (2015) proposed the implementation of interoperable technologies and referred to interoperability challenges in order to manage building automation. Ballon et al. (2011)

Table 2. Smart City Architectures and Requirements.

Researchers	Requirements									
	Data collection	Data stream & process	Data security	Monitoring	Heterogeneity	Adaptation	Sustainability	Inter-operability	User satisfaction	City oriented
Ishida	+			+					+	
Anthopoulos & Tsoukalas	+							+	+	+
IBM	+	+			+					
Su et al.	+	+		+				+		+
Carretero	+	+			+	+				+
Vilajosana et al.	+	+	+	+						+
Anthopoulos & Fitsilis		+					+			+
Filiponi et al.	+	+		+	+			+		+
Schaffers et al.		+					+			+
Chochliouros et al.		+						+		+
Attwood et al.	+	+		+		+		+		+
Ballon et al.	+	+								+
Asimakopoulou & Bessis	+	+		+				+		+
Zhou et al.		+		+					+	
Wang et al.	+			+						+
Ye et al.	+	+		+					+	
Jin et al.	+	+								
Mitton et al.	+	+			+			+		
Distefano et al.	+	+			+					

(Continued)

Table 2. (*Continued*)

Researchers	Requirements									
	Data collection	Data stream & process	Data security	Monitoring	Heterogeneity	Adaptation	Sustainability	Inter-operability	User satisfaction	City oriented
Suciu et al.		+						+		
Roscia et al.	+	+		+				+		
Samaras et al.	+	+		+					+	
Horng (2014)		+		+		+			+	+
Zanjani et al.		+		+					+	+
Bululukova & Wahl	+	+					+			+
Iano et al.	+	+					+			+
Khan & Kiani	+	+	+	+			+		+	
Wang & Zhou		+					+		+	
Szabó et al.	+	+		+					+	
Zhang et al.	+	+		+		+				+
Sánchez et al.		+		+	+					+
Bertoncini		+		+			+			+
Lilis et al.	+							+		+
Anadiotis et al.	+	+								
Andreini et al.	+	+						+	+	
Hu & Li	+	+		+				+		
Klingert et al.	+	+								+
Xiong et al.	+	+			+					
Wan et al.		+		+						+
Feher et al.	+	+		+					+	
Wenge et al.	+	+								

presented a cloud platform to be applied by all European smart cities to overcome the interoperability problems of the different spoken languages and the adaptation of new technologies standards and protocols. Hu and Li (2012) emphasized on the use of GIS and IoT as open networks to facilitate objects interoperability. Filiponi et al. (2010) developed the Interoperability Open Platform which allowed different applications domains and sub-systems to interoperate and share data. Suciu et al. (2013) proposed the SlapOS framework in which an interoperable decentralized open source cloud platform for IoT applications was embedded and aimed to enhance existing M2 M and their IoT foundations. Cochliouros et al. (2013) used Living Labs so as to promote interoperability. Anthopoulos and Tsoukalas (2006) dealt with interoperability issues, so that the digital city's of Trikala infrastructure could transact with legacy systems already installed in public and private sector. Su et al. (2011) proposed a construction frame of applications system which aimed to achieve interoperability in the construction of smart urban management sub-system. Roscia et al. (2013) used a graphic user interface to ensure interoperability between systems and heterogeneous agents.

User satisfaction is also an important requirement that many systems aim to satisfy. The main goal for smart cities is to offer to the citizens a great experience and improve their quality of living. To achieve this, they take into account their needs and preferences. As we can see from the table, many works are user centric and try to provide citizens as with advanced services and applications through the use of friendly interfaces. So, for example we have different suggestions from the creation of a smart sports information system to smart parking services.

Orientation to the city is the last requirement from the list of the key ones that a smart city system tries to fulfill. This requirement is related to the services and applications that affect a sector of the city or the whole of it and of course they have an impact to citizens' daily life. In that direction, many works dealt with that requirement and created systems to replace old ones or be completely new like the SmartSantander city of Spain and the Digital city of Trikala or enhance the functionality of sectors like energy efficiency in buildings, control of the food chain for avoiding the consumption of contaminated products, and improvement of the education procedure.

4 Conclusions and Future Work

In this paper we presented and discussed many architectures and requirements that have been proposed in the literature in order to build a smart city system or a smart city component. We cited and analyzed various works that belonged to different perspectives, such as AL, SOA, EDA, IoT and combined architectures and also the embedded technologies of these perspectives. Moreover, we presented and discussed the key requirements that every architecture aims to satisfy. Finally, we summarized these works in two tables, one presenting the perspectives and their integrated technologies and a second assigning architectures to the requirements they tried to fulfill.

Based on the above analysis, we deduce that the perspective of AL was preferred by many researchers even though the chosen layers varied among their works. SOA was also selected to be applied in smart cities since it distinguishes the city in different components which offer all kinds of services to the citizens. Considering the number of published works in the literature, we can easily determine that AL were mostly preferred for implementation than SOA. In the sequel, EDA implementation was only observed to one European project. On the contrary, IoT is the new trend and many recommendations about its implementation have been published until today. Its association with sensor networks and cloud computing amplifies its acceptance and choice by researchers. In recent years there is the tendency to combine IoT with the other perspectives to improve the functionality of smart city system. The most common combination is IoT with AL in which researchers used to add extra technologies to enhance system's capabilities. The combination of IoT with SOA was chosen to facilitate geolocalization matters and offer citizens the right services according to their requests. Finally, the combination of IoT with EDA was selected for improving the functionality of the SOFIA project by adding Internet technologies to the proposed architecture. There were also remarkable attempts that tried to combine together three or even all the abovementioned perspectives to empower the smart city with the advantages that each of them can offer to the citizens.

As far as technical requirements are concerned, data collection, data stream and process, and interoperability are the most common to be fulfilled by the chosen architecture. Also, user and city oriented requirements are taken into account trying to satisfy stakeholders and improve the operation of the city. However, security must be noted since it is mandatory to ensure the safety and privacy of the confidential personal data and information of citizens, institutions and government.

In the future, IoE intends to launch a new era in smart city development. Its purpose is to extend the capabilities of IoT and create a common pattern in designing applications for smart cities that are in the initial stages of building their infrastructure. Even if it is not implemented yet, it is expected to offer lots of capabilities to the citizens. As a matter of fact, IoE seems to be a promising architecture since it aims to totally change the economy, society and our way of living.

References

Caragliu, A., Del Bo, C., Nijkamp, P.: Smart cities in europe. J. Urban Technol. **18**, 65–82 (2011)

Cocchia, A.: Smart and digital city: a systematic literature review. In: Dameri, R.P., Rosenthal-Sabroux, C. (eds.) Smart City, pp 13–43. Springer, New York (2014)

Su, K., Li, J., Fu, H.: Smart city and the applications. In: IEEE International Conference on Electronics, Communications and Control, pp. 1028–1031. (IEEE Xplore) (2011)

Giffinger, R., Fertner, C., Kramar, H., Kalasek, R., Pichler-Milanovic, N., Meijers, E.: Smart Cities: Ranking of European medium-sized cities. Vienna, University of Technology (2007)

Ishida, T.: Understanding digital cities. In: Ishida, T., Isbister, K. (eds.) Digital Cities 1999. LNCS, vol. 1765, pp. 7–17. Springer, Heidelberg (2000)

Anthopoulos, L.G., Tsoukalas, I.A.: The implementation model of a digital city: the case study of the digital city of trikala, Greece: eTrikala. J. e-Gov. **2**(2), 91–109 (2006)

Carretero, J.: ADAPCITY: A Self-adaptive, reliable architecture for heterogeneous devices in Smart Cities. European Commissions-ICT Proposers (2012)

Vilajosana, I., Llosa, J., Martinez, B., Domingo-Prieto, M., Angles, A.: Boot-strapping smart cities through a self-sustainable model based on big data flows. IEEE Commun. Mag. **51**(6), 128–134 (2013)

Anthopoulos, L., Fitsilis, P.: From digital to ubiquitous cities: defining a common architecture for urban development. In: IEEE 6th International Conference on Intelligent Environments, pp. 301–306 (2010)

Filipponi, L., Vitaletti, A., Landi, G., Memeo, V., Laura, G., Pucci, P.: Smart city: an EDA for monitoring public spaces with heterogeneous sensors. In: IEEE 4th International Conference on Sensor Technologies and Applications, pp 281–286 (2010)

Schaffers, H., Komninos, N., Pallot, M., Trousse, B., Nilsson, M., Oliveira, A.: Smart cities and the future internet: towards cooperation frameworks for open innovation. In: Domingue, J., et al. (eds.) Future Internet Assembly. LNCS, vol. 6656, pp. 431–446. Springer, Heidelberg (2011)

Chochliouros, I.P., Spiliopoulou, A.S., Sfakianakis, E., Georgiadou, E., Rethimiotaki, E.: Living labs in smart cities as critical enablers for making real the modern future internet. In: Zee, G. A., Vorst, J.G.G. (eds.) Shell Conference 1988. LNCS, vol. 384, pp. 314–323. Springer, Heidelberg (1989)

Attwood, A., Merabti, M., Fergus, P., Abuelmaatti, O.: SCCIR: Smart cities critical infrastructure response framework. In: IEEE Developments in E-Systems Engineering, pp. 460–464 (2011)

Ballon, P., Glidden, J., Kranas, P., Menychtas, A., Ruston, S., Van Der Graaf, S.: Is there a need for a cloud platform for European Smart Cities? In: eChallenges e-2011 Conference Proceedings Paul Cunningham and Miriam Cunningham (Eds) IIMC International Information Management Corporation (2011)

Asimakopoulou, E., Bessis, N.: Buildings and Crowds: Forming Smart Cities for more effective disaster management. In: IEEE Fifth International Conference on Innovative Mo-bile and Internet Services in Ubiquitous Computing, pp. 229–234 (2011)

Zhou, Y., Klein, W., Mayer, H.G.: Guideline for crowd evacuation simulation – validation for a pedestrian simulator with RiMEA test scenarios. In: Proceedings of the 4th International Conference on Smart Cities and Green ICT Systems (SMARTGREENS-2015), pp. 35–42 (2015)

Wang, R., Jin, L., Xiao, R., Guo, S., Li, S.: 3D Reconstruction and interaction for smart city based on world wind. In: IEEE International Conference on Audio, Language and Image Processing, pp. 953–956 (2012)

Ye, Q., Wang, Z., Qian, J., Gao, S., Sun, Y.: Smart sport-emergence trend of sport information. Int. J. Digital Content Technol. Appl. **6**(11), 336–342 (2012)

Jin, J., Gubbi, J., Luo, T., Palaniswami, M.: Network architecture and QoS issues in the IoT for a smart city. In: IEEE International Symposium on Communications and Information Technologies, pp. 956–961 (2012)

Poorter, E.D., Moerman, I., Demeester, P.: Enabling direct connectivity between heterogeneous objects in the internet of things through a network-service-oriented architecture. EURASIP J. Wireless Commun. Networking (2011)

Mitton, N., Papavasiliou, S., Puliafito, A., Trivedi, K.S.: Combining Cloud and sensors in a smart city environment. EURASIP J. Wirel. Commun. Netw. **2012**, 247 (2012). Springer

Distefano, S., Merlino, G., Puliafito, A.: Exploiting SAaaS in smart city scenarios. In: Huang, D.-S., Bevilacqua, V., Figueroa, J.C., Premaratne, P. (eds.) ICIC 2013. LNCS, vol. 7995, pp. 638–647. Springer, Heidelberg (2013)

Suciu, G., Vulpe, A., Todoran, G., Gropotova, J., Suciu, V.: Cloud computing and IoT for smart city deployments. In: International Conference: CKS - Challenges of the Knowledge Soc, pp. 1409–1416 (2013)

Roscia, M., Longo, M., Lazaroiu, G.C.: Smart City by multi-agent systems. In: IEEE International Conference on Renewable Energy Research and Applications, pp. 371–376. (IEEE Xplore) (2013)

Samaras, C., Vakali, A., Giatsoglou, M., Chatzakou, D., Angelis, L.: Requirements and architecture design principles for a smart city experiment with sensor and social networks integration. In: ACM Proceedings of the 17th Panhellenic Conference on Informatics, pp. 327–334 (2013)

Horng, G.-J.: The adaptive recommendation mechanism for distributed parking ser-vice in Smart City. Wirel. Pers. Commun. **80**, 395–413 (2014)

Asadi Zanjani, N., Lilis, G., Conus, G., Kayal, M.: Energy book for buildings - occupants incorporation in energy efficiency of buildings. In: Proceedings of the 4th International Conference on Smart Cities and Green ICT Systems (SMARTGREENS-2015), pp. 89–94 (2015)

Bululukova, D., Wahl, H.: Towards a sustainable smart cities integration in teaching and research. In: Proceedings of the 4th International Conference on Smart Cities and Green ICT Systems (SMARTGREENS-2015), pp. 101–106 (2015)

Iano, Y., Lima, I.T., Loschi, H.J., Lustosa, T.C., Mesquita, O.S., Moretti, A.: Sustainable computing and communications - internet broadband network of things applied to intelligent education. In: Proceedings of the 4th International Conference on Smart Cities and Green ICT Systems (SMARTGREENS-2015), pp. 350–356 (2015)

Khan, Z., Kiani, S.L.: A Cloud-based architecture for citizen services in Smart Cities. In: IEEE/ACM Fifth International Conference on Utility and Cloud Computing, pp. 315–320 (2012)

Wang, Y., Zhou, Y.: Cloud architecture based on near field communication in the smart city. In: IEEE the 7th International Conference on Computer Science & Education, pp 231–234 (2012)

Szabó, R., Farkas, K., Ispány, M., Benczúr, A.A., Bátfai, N., Jeszenszky, P., Laki, S., Vágner, A., Kollár, L., Sidló, Cs., Besenczi, R., Smajda, M., Kövér, G., Szincsák, T., Kádek, T., Kósa, M., Adamkó, A., Lendák, I., Wiandt, B., Tomás, T., Nagy, A.Z., Fehér, G.: Framework for Smart City applications based on participatory sensing. In: 4th IEEE International Conference on Cognitive Infocommunications, pp. 295–300 (2013)

Zhang, Q., Huang, T., Zhu, Y., Qiu, M.: A case study of sensor data collection and analysis in Smart City: Provenance in Smart Food Supply Chain'. Int. J. Distrib. Sensor Netw. **2013**, 12 (2013). Hindawi Publishing

Sanchez, L., Gutierrez, V., Galache, J.A., Sotres, P., Santana, J.R., Casanueva, J., Munoz, L.: Smartsantander: experimentation and service provision in the smart city. In: IEEE 16th International Symposium at Wireless Personal Multimedia Communications, pp. 1–6 (2013)

Bertoncini, M.: Multi-resource optimized smart management of urban energy infrastructures for improving smart city energy efficiency. In: Proceedings of the 4th International Conference on Smart Cities and Green ICT Systems (SMARTGREENS-2015), pp. 107–114 (2015)

Lilis, G., Conus, G., Asadi, N., Kayal, M.: Integrating building automation technologies with smart cities - an assessment study of past, current and future interoperable technologies. In: Proceedings of the 4th International Conference on Smart Cities and Green ICT Systems (SMARTGREENS-2015), pp. 370–375 (2015)

Anadiotis, G., Hatzoplaki, E., Tsatsakis, K., Tsitsanis, T.: A data model for energy decision support systems for smart cities - the case of BESOS common information model. In: Proceedings of the 4th International Conference on Smart Cities and Green ICT Systems (SMARTGREENS-2015), pp. 51–59 (2015)

Andreini, F., Crisciani, F., Cicconetti, C., Mambrini, R.: A scalable architecture for geo-localized service access in Smart Cities. In: Future Network and Mobile Summit 2011 Conference Proceedings, Paul Cunningham and Miriam Cunningham, IIMC (2011)

Hu, M., Li, C.: Design smart city based on 3S, internet of things, grid computing and cloud computing technology. In: Wang, Y., Zhang, X. (eds.) IOT 2012. CCIS, vol. 312, pp. 466–472. Springer, Heidelberg (2012)

Klingert S., Niedermeier F., Dupont C., Giuliani G., Schulze T., de Meer H.: Renewable energy-aware data centre operations for smart cities - The DC4Cities approach. In: Proceedings of the 4th International Conference on Smart Cities and Green ICT Systems (SMARTGREENS-2015), pp. 26–34 (2015)

Xiong, Z., Zhengand, Y., Li, C.: Data vitalization's perspective towards smart city: a reference model for data service oriented architecture. In: 14th IEEE/ACM International Symposium on Cluster, Cloud,Grid Computing, pp 865–874 (2014)

Wan, J., Li, D., Zou, C., Zhou, K.: M2 M Communications for smart city: an event-based architecture. In: IEEE 12th International Conference on Computer and Information Technology, pp. 895–900 (2012)

Feher G., Andras Lajtha B., Lovasz A.: A probabilistic approach to parking - benefits of routing instead of spotting. In: Proceedings of the 4th International Conference on Smart Cities and Green ICT Systems, pp. 95–100 (2015)

Wenge, R., Zhang, X., Dave, C., Chao, L., Hao, S.: Smart city architecture: a technology guide for implementation and design challenges. IEEE China Commun. Netw. Technol. Appl. 11, 56–69 (2014)

Souleiman, H., O'Riain, S., Curry, E.: Approximate semantic matching of heterogeneous events. In: 6th ACM International Conference on Distributed Event-Based Systems, pp. 252–263. ACM (2012)

Da Silva, W.M., Tomas, G.H.R.P., Dias, K.L., Alvaro, A., Afonso, R.A., Garcia, V.C.: Smart cities software architectures: a survey. In: SAC 2013, pp. 1722-1727. ACM, Coimbra, Portugal, 18-22 March 2013. 978-1-4503-1656-9/13/03

Net!Works European Technology Platform: Smart Cities Applications and Requirements. White paper (2011)

IBM: Smarter thinking for a smarter planet (2010)

Sprott, D., Wilkes, L.: Understanding Service-oriented Architecture. Microsoft (2004). http://msdn.microsoft.com/enus/library/aa480021.aspx

Cisco: Internet of Everything. http://internetofeverything.cisco.com

Cisco: The Internet of Everything for Cities. http://www.cisco.com/web/about/ac79/docs/ps/motm/IoE-Smart-City_PoV.pdf

People in Smart Buildings: Daily Practices in Automated Areas

A. Coulbaut-Lazzarini[1]([✉]) and G. Bailly[2]

[1] UFR des Sciences, Université Versailles Saint-Quentin, Versailles, France
amelie.coulbaut@uvsq.fr
[2] Département de Géographie, Université du Maine, Le Mans, France
guillaume.bailly@univ-lemans.fr

Abstract. Managing the energy needs of buildings is central. This question is deeply linked with people density in urban area which is still increasing. We are at a turning point: reaching the goal of the low carbon transition. As is known, the reduction of this sector's carbon footprint entails the reduction of the carbon dioxide emissions that it produces. Consequently, the search of human and technical solutions in a multi-scale and systemic perspective is a central element of this process. First, we observe uses required by sites managers. Second, we aim to show users' strategies facing automation, both in terms of space occupation and lighting use. Then, we focus on people's involvement and their behavioural change considering the participatory design of services and systems for smart buildings. Finally, we address the power of collective identity, as a quest of good balance between human action and automation.

Keywords: Energy · Daily practices · Behaviour change · Sociology · Geography

1 Introduction

According to World Bank figures for 2014 (http://www.worldbank.org/, 2014), the urban population accounts for 53 % of the total global population. By 2030, almost 60 % of the world's population will live in urban areas (http://www.un.org/en/sustainablefuture/cities.asp, 2014). Veron [1] says that city dwellers will account for over 70 % of the world's population in 2050. The United Nations World Urbanization Prospects has estimated that 79 % of the population in France live in urban settings (http://www.worldbank.org, 2013). In a perspective of durability, as shown by Guermond [2], the phenomenon of population density raises the question of the density's management in territories. Finding good responses entails reflection on the morphologies of cities, their link to hinterlands and the manner to govern these vast areas [3, 4]. One simple solution doesn't exist [5–7]. There is an intense debate between those who defend compactness [8, 9] and those who maintain the idea of a peri-urban area [10–15]. Morphology is a mirror of the urban fabric that can be observed by satellite view [16]. This reflects human beings' habits and their spatial relation with their environment. Human activity depends on the generation of energy resources despite their diminution and their cost [17]. Modification of energy consumption is an

M. Helfert et al. (Eds.): Smartgreens 2015 and Vehits 2015, CCIS 579, pp. 104–127, 2015.
DOI: 10.1007/978-3-319-27753-0_6

important question. As Poinsot [18] has shown, it challenges the pertinence of the multi-scale territorial response in France. Pappalardo [19] shows us that cities are the main places of energy consumption in the building sector, housing and tertiary. She has found that in France the building sector is the most energy intensive sector (23 % of national emissions). Reducing the carbon footprint implies the reduction of CO_2 emission. The Report of the United Nations Conference on Sustainable Development (http://www.uncsd2012.org/ 2012) reaffirms the will to ensure the promotion of an economically, socially and environmentally sustainable future for our planet and for current and future generations. Reaching these goals entails compliance with urban planning measures, particularly their legal regulations and standards (io: In France, Law No. 2010-788 of 12 July 2010 on the national commitment to the environment). Therefore, research on technological innovation can contribute to reduce resource and energy consumption. While many projects have developed technical approaches to generate and maintain energy in the city (Fenix, Rider, and Reflexe), none has enabled a real-time energy monitoring of the entire production chain supply facilities at multiple scales (building and related areas such as districts). Our study is part of a programme with multiple partners that consists of the creation of a technical solution for energy management by building a smart grid demonstrator, which eventually should be broadened to the level of an eco-district. This project involved important firms, leaders in the energy sector, as well as small businesses and academic partners.

Nonetheless, monitoring an energy chain supply is irreducible to a technical approach. If cities are artefacts, they live through human beings' interactions [20–22].

Our project considered these aspects, so we assumed responsibility for the part of the programme work package that concerns the behaviours and daily practices of the people working in the selected buildings.

In this research program what particularly caught our attention was the role of human beings in the heart of that system. Our field study focused on two main sites: two French firms located in the West of Paris. We wondered how a community of actors contributes to the implementation of sustainable and virtuous practices in terms of low-carbon transition. How are roles distributed? What rules govern the interactions in these places? Who makes the rules? What are the effects on the scale of the building and beyond (eco-district)? Is the emergence of good practices effective? Can it be transposed to other locations?

After a brief presentation of our theoretical frameworks and methodologies, this paper will first show the required uses, with dedicated areas, and the place of automation. It will then try to explain the real practices, in terms of space use, lighting use strategies and reactions towards automation. It will further show how involving people, with participatory design of services and systems for smart buildings, can motivate behaviour change. Lastly, this discussion will question the idea of collective identity and the balance automation/human action.

2 Theoretical Framework: A Complex Approach

Ethnology will allow us to create and analyse our observations of actors and his actions in live. This discipline is observation-based and has two dimensions. On the one hand, it is based on facts, details and specificity collection [23], and seeks to "rebuild their form and meaning" [24]. On the other hand, it tries to "bring closer, generate dialogue, and show what is common in this world of differences". Agier [24] and other ethnologists have contributed to the establishment of our field study. Agier has explained:

"The ground is not a thing, it's not a place, nor a social category, an ethnic group or an institution. It is all of this, maybe, as appropriate, but it is firstly a set of personal relationships where "you learn something". "Doing fieldwork", it means establishing personal relationships with people who we do not know in advance, to whom we somewhat break in and enter into their lives. So we must convince them of the validity of our presence, also that they have nothing to lose even if they have little to win, and most of all they have nothing to worry about. Relationships can be harmonious and friendly with some people, conflictive with others." (p.35).

Our approach also conforms to a "geo-cratic practice" [25, 26] that considers actors' behaviours and their interaction as a social production. Through political geography and not simply a geopolitical geography as posited by Rosière [27], conflicts and cooperation are in the heart of the research. This type of research considers the importance of the citizens' perspectives within a democratic approach in which the researcher is at the service of the power of democracy. Our objective is to question people's power and capacity [28] to produce norms and to reach a new kind of spatial justice. Our approach is also conform to the heritage of the French social geography relating and interrogated by Séchet, Veschambre [29]. This geography is a response to social demand, focused on social inequalities, exclusion, human dramas and that examines the social relations of domination.

3 Methodological Aspects: Crossed Social Sciences Methodologies

We studied these elements from a social sciences perspective, that employs methodologies borrowed from sociology, ethnography and social geography. Our data collection is based on semi-structured interviews, questionnaires and ethnographic observations.

This complex methodological approach enables the collection of quantitative survey data and a qualitative discourse analysis. Observations allowed direct access to users' practices and behaviours on site. Thanks to this methodological tool, we can study how much discourses are far from real practices or not.

The surveys were conducted in two buildings that serve as the headquarters of two leading companies in the energy field.

The qualitative analysis is based on twenty-three semi-structured interviews conducted with the users of these buildings. An interview guide was created that included questions about energy use and behaviour in the building. The data collection process started with semi-structured interviews, which were recorded. Interviews were textually transcribed and analysed with Alceste, a text analysis software. This methodology was completed by systematizing key themes and classical content analysis.

Interviews were firstly "groomed", which means formatted to be analysable by our software for text analysis. We then began the analysis through an automated data processing with Alceste. This software cuts the text, making elementary context units (UCE), pieces of text selected and analysed by the software. These UCE are then spread within classes by detecting strong oppositions emerging from the text. Each speech class groups a number of words belonging to a lexical world distant from those of the other speech classes.

As Rouré and Reinert [30] explain, while the speaker converses, s/he goes through his/her successive. These worlds, having their own objects, impose their own type of vocabulary. The statistical study of this vocabulary's distribution must allow us to track down the "mental environments" successively invested by the speaker. Authors precise we can then see in lexical worlds. Alceste software will help us find these lexical worlds.

To make the cross-sorting with which we analyze specific vocabulary of our corpus, we had to choose one element from this corpus, either one word or one variable. The software has a drop-down list of all the words of the corpus in alphabetical order. As such we can cross each word with the whole corpus. Alceste then gives us significant elements, with Khi-2, and with the repeat factor and the category to which the term belongs.

These category-specific keys are adjectives and adverbs, verbs (of action and movement in particular), the demonstrative …

Throughout these keys, we can get information about interviewed people's position (according to Achard, [31]). Three positions are possible [31]: witness, actor or patient. These positions define people's way of living and acting. Alceste software spread the indicators of these positions into speech classes. Witness position is defined by an over-representation of adjectives, adverbs and nouns (sign of a descriptive discourse), and also descriptive elements, spatial elements and no markers of person like personal pronouns. Actor's position is defined on the contrary by an over-representation of verbs, indicating an action or a move in discourse, associated with markers of person. Finally, the patient's position is defined by discursive relation markers, which indicate argument and storytelling and logical and temporal elements.

These elements are our first guide through the analysis.

For the quantitative analysis, we constructed a questionnaire to be asked to all users of the two main buildings of the study. Since managers wanted to know exactly what we could ask to the building users, this step needed negotiation. Moreover, in the first building, the questionnaire was implemented by the communication service of the company, as they didn't want researchers to have access to their employees' email lists. We were only told that it had been sent to 825 persons. The questionnaire was available for one month on each site and we got 264 answers from users. These answers are the basis of our quantitative analysis. We used Modalisa software to help us analyse the data. Modalisa is a software dedicated to surveys quantitative analysis. It allows the finding of indicators such as type of behaviour or elements of freedom appearing from modalities of energy and space use.

Observations were a more complex process. In none of the buildings the higher hierarchy accepted researchers to come and observe their employees. In fact we had to find ways to be there for others reasons. Interviews on site were one of our best pretexts. When several interviews were made on the same day, we had a good reason to move from one place to another inside the building. Sometimes we could spend lunchtime on site. This was also a moment for informal discussion, and sometimes people showed us one part of the building to underline what they had said. Technical visits also served this purpose. As both buildings aspire to be models of energy efficiency, we visited each building at different times and with different guides, feigning that we had not understood certain topics or required additional information regarding some technical aspect. In this manner, we were able to visit all parts of both buildings and observe people's use and behaviour in these spaces.

4 Required Uses: Dedicated Areas, Automation

The buildings we studied are located in the West of Paris region (Fig. 1). They are both located in dense urban areas and are, for their respective zone, quite big buildings.

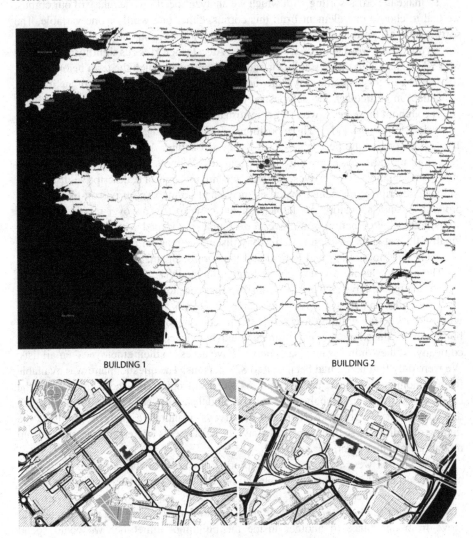

BUILDING 1   BUILDING 2

Fig. 1. Maps of buildings' localisation.

The first building is located in a business district, while the second is in a city centre, with residential buildings, office and mixed-use buildings, shops and a park. With its 7 floors, it is one of the highest buildings of this area. The two buildings are quite different in their conception, and that can have an impact on automation and required uses of space.

The first building was constructed in 1986, with a reinforced concrete structure and a stone façade. It has 9 floors, covers an area of 34 000 square meters and roughly 1000 people are working there. Energy efficiency systems have been implemented in the last ten years, quite twenty years after the building's construction.

The second building was constructed in 2001. It is covered with a double skin consisting of a concrete wall and double-glazed façade. It covers an area of 11 814 square meters and roughly 600 people are working there. It was directly built in a perspective of energy efficiency.

The first element we could clearly observe in these buildings was space allocation. It appears that in the designers' mind, energy efficiency design in tertiary buildings begins by allocating a place to each occupant. The floor plans (Fig. 2) of the buildings studied show how space is divided.

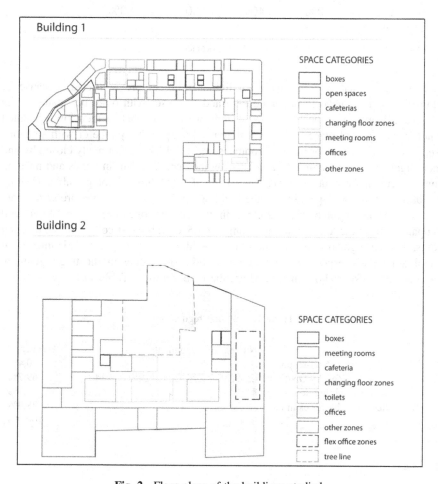

Fig. 2. Floor plans of the buildings studied.

Offices should be the main workplace for each occupant, but we see that other types of places can be used to work, such as meeting rooms or boxes. These places present different type of lighting and heating regulation. Knowing that energy use is different depending on the type of offices or others places people work in, we first asked people what was their type of workplace. As shown by the figure below (Fig. 3), most people work in an open plan configuration.

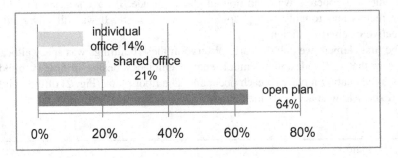

Fig. 3. Workplace.

This means that a space where individual choices are restricted, because of automation and the need to negotiate light and heat uses with other occupants of the open plan. People are expected to stay in their workplace whether their job is adapted or not to that type of place. Whenever they need to speak by phone or with someone else, they can use boxes or meeting rooms, some of which are not really closed by and where light or heating cannot be regulated by the occupant. But in boxes and meeting rooms, occupants can at least get light, even if regulation is not possible. Heating regulation is different depending on the building: in the first one, boxes are semi-open, with no thermal regulation possibility. In the second one, boxes are closed and occupants can set the temperature to a range of 1,5°C warmer or colder. In the meeting rooms, thermal regulation is possible in both buildings. In workplaces, it is interesting to look at people's responses about the possibilities of lighting and heating regulation. These responses show how integrated are the required uses (Table 1).

Table 1. Lighting regulation.

	Number of respondents		Frequency
Non-response	I	1	0,4%
Yes, by ON/OFF		184	69,7%
Yes, by lighting controller	▮	5	1,9%
No (collective light, for example)		74	28,0%
Total	264		100,0%

Lighting and heating regulations' possibilities:

For lighting regulation, most of people say they can turn light on or off if they want. But 28 % say they cannot. It is interesting because 64 % of people work in open-plan offices, where there is one dial for the whole open-plan. And in the other offices (shared by two people or individual), there is also a dial for the office. It means that 28 % of people think that they must conform to required uses and not touching the lighting dial. Or maybe even more, they really think there is no dial, which would be the highest degree of integration of required uses.

In open plan workplaces, people are expected not to modify heating regulation, even if they can. And there is not too much communication about heating regulations, so that people don't touch it. Indeed, many people explained to us they didn't even know where thermostat for their workplace was. Interviewee N°6 explained to us "Some people are not used to touching. You know that you have one thermostat for a whole open-plan. Someone who doesn't speak to colleagues, doesn't even know there is a thermostat." During our observations, someone showed us where the thermostat was for open plan places: in a corner where you clearly don't see it unless you know it is there. There are also established uses towards heating regulation, asking to let automation play and for human not to touch. During the interviews, one person explained that "we mustn't touch it because it will modify building's regulations, it is better not to touch" (interviewee N°2).

Moreover, so as to be sure that thermal regulation will not be too much used, technical staff explained that they limited the real effect of thermal regulation to a range of 1,5°C warmer or colder, even though +3/-3°C is registered on the thermostat. Interviewee N°7, who is a technical staff member, stated at the beginning regulation was more or less 3°C, but now it is more or less 1, 5°C, so influence is less important.

Intelligent planning of energy efficiency are generally thought as technological processes, with a high degree of automation. For example, a light cut is implemented every day at lunchtime, and another in the evening. There are also presence sensors in the cafeterias, in the toilets and in the corridors. But as observed, light in the corridors is always on due to the sensor's timer, and the fact that it takes one person alone cross a corridor for lights to turn on all the way long. Nevertheless, technical analysis shows that energy management systems allow for energy consumption reduction. Cutting off lights in the evening, which also turns off most of the screens like those in the hall and cafeterias seems to be particularly efficient. This automatic system replaces human action, because designers estimated it to be more efficient to ask an automatic system to do the job.

However, people are still asked to turn off the lights when they use meeting rooms, where they also have to turn off video projector. To understand how automation is implemented and how people perceive it, the following figure (Fig. 4) shows the distribution of places depending on automation, in the speeches of interviewees. The software for text analysis distinguished three speech classes with only class 1 and class 2 having significant impact. Since the software works by significant oppositions, class 3 is more common to all respondents and does not vary by types of people. Class 1 essentially groups discourses of people from technical staff. On the contrary, other occupants are linked to class 2. That's why we choose to present here only some results

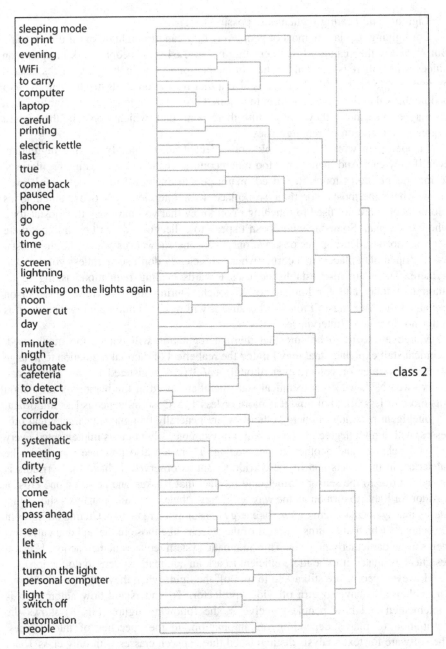

Fig. 4. Ascending hierarchical classification for class 2 of speech.

from this class. The Ascending Hierarchical Classification (AHC) helps to figure local relationships between forms of a same class (Table 2).

Table 2. Heating regulation.

	Number of respondents		Frequency
Non-response	∣ 1		0,4%
Yes, as much as they want	▨ 16		6,1%
Yes, but to a limited extend (+/-3°C for example)	▬▬▬▬▬	117	44,3%
No	▭▭▭▭▭▭	130	49,2%
Total	264		100,0%

This distribution organises most representative words. We can see how terms like "lighting" or "screen" articulate with "switching on the lights again" and are positioned on the same branch as time indicators like "noon", "day", "night", "minute", but also "to go". Actions in connection with lightning are strongly correlated to time notion, which is a key point as well for automation as for people's action. The distribution that the software proposed is particularly relevant for our analysis. It indicates the different places, with on the one hand "corridors" and "cafeterias" related to automated lightning, that are directly connected to terms "to detect" (mainly referred to sensors) and "automate" (which stands for automation). On the other hand, on the lowest branch of the AHC, rooms, and particularly "meeting rooms" are very close to terms like "let", "turn on the light", or even "light" and "switch off". So two types of places appears: those where lightning is mostly or totally automated, and those where "people" (last term of the AHC) can act on, like meeting rooms.

Moreover, at the very bottom of the graph, the two last terms directly connected are "automation" and "people". This reveals how much interfaces between human and technical systems are important and how much the balance between automation and people's action is to question. People's real practices, including reactions towards automation is a first step to do so.

5   Real Practices: Space Use, Lighting Use Strategies and Reactions Towards Automation

Real practices are not necessary in adequacy with previsions of energy uses.

We can imagine that a configuration with many open plan areas can minimize energy use, which was probably what designers intended. However, as we can see on the next figure, this is not convincing.

We notice that light is mostly on. In fact interviews show that as soon as one person needs light, it seems normal for everyone to turn the light on for the whole open plan. The only exception is the open plan where the responsible for the energy saving program behavioural program sits. In this last place, someone explained us that they must be exemplary there, even if it became sometimes really uncomfortable. Elsewhere, another person told us light was most often on and she didn't need it so much. Her strategy was then to ask technical staff to remove half of the bulbs in her part of the

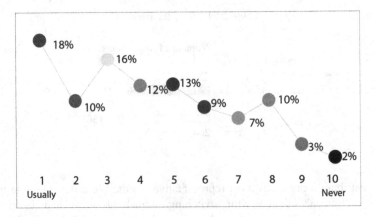

Fig. 5. Light use frequency.

office (Interview n°4): "being close to the window, I asked to remove my lights because I don't need it. But it's true that people next to the corridor needs it" (Fig. 5).

Anywhere, some occupants find solutions to get more comfortable work conditions. These solutions often means diverted space uses. Floor plans (Fig. 6) make it visible.

On these floor plans, it appears people sometimes choose other places than their office to get comfortable work conditions, regarding lighting or heating aspects. There, their strategies are not to fight against automation but to find some ways to make it acceptable. For example, if their office is close to a corridor and light in not enough and they cannot (or don't want to) turn on the light of the whole open-plan, they can go to the cafeteria (Fig. 7). They can sit close to large windows and get light (turning on the dial or simply coming into the cafeteria).

If space uses and lighting and heating uses strategies show occupants' real practices, it is also important to explore their reactions towards automation. Interviewees had some different positions about this subject. These positions range from a will of a total automation to a clear preference for accountability and awareness.

Total Automation: Interview N°2: "in buildings like here, I think the best is to use automation at maximum. To automate because it is difficult to act upon a common building, I think that if anybody can act as he want that can become a problem. It is defeating the very purpose of the optimisation we try to reach. So I think that in a public building we will try to reach the highest level of automation to ensure optimal performance."

Intermediate Position, with a Preference for Automation: Interview n°12: "First is technical aspects and automation. Because changing behaviour... I think bad habits come back and one should make wake-up calls." Interview n°15: "what is good is indeed to implement automation, as for lightning cut offs, which makes things visible. So it is not so bad. Because it is a kind of daily wake-up call. Turning off the light, it turns off. But one should not be dispossessed of some reflexes by saying the system will do anything. It is a fair balance, I think."

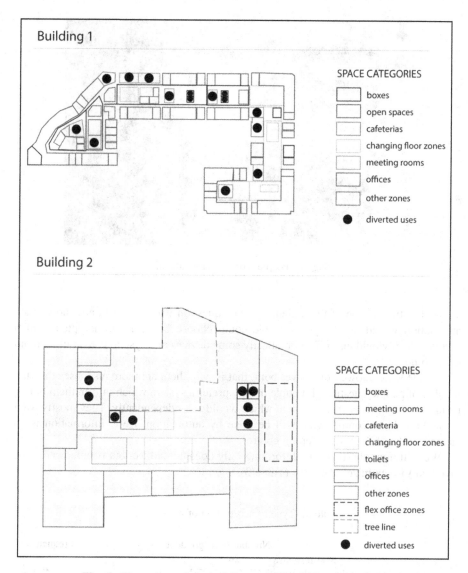

Fig. 6. Floor plans of the building and diverted uses of places.

Intermediate Position, with a Preference for Accountability: Interview n°3: "Accountability would be ideal but as it is hard to obtain a little bit of automation is necessary. Both are needed. Sometimes one should compare practices at home and at work. Automation is sometimes convenient."

Accountability: Interview N°1: "Which is important is much more reaching accountability than automation".

Fig. 7. People working in a cafeteria.

In the straight line of these elements, one question was asked to know how much automation would be accepted. People could choose between the acceptation of a system which would turn off automatically some devices or a system that would remind them to do so.

People were allowed to answer both, that is why there are more responses than the number of people questioned. People mostly prefer a system which inform them but let them free to act rather than a system which would act independently. They mostly want to be able to control what will be done by automation. Here, information is an element to be able to act, keeping control.

We will now question this: Informing only does not suffice, but people need to be involved to maximize efficiency (Table 3).

Table 3. Type of acceptation of automation.

	Number of respondents	Frequency
Non-response	24	
You would accept that a technical system automatically turns off some devices	113	42,8%
You would accept that a technical system reminds you to turn off devices you don't use	177	67,0%
Total/ interrogés	264	

6   Involving People: Participatory Design of Services and Systems for Smart Buildings, Motivating Behaviour Change

Seeing the differences between required uses and real practices, we tried to understand users' attitude towards energy efficiency. Were they interested?

The first question we asked was whether they would accept to get information about energy in their professional environment. We can see the results in the next figure.

Most of people are interested in information about energy and energy efficiency at work. Then we tried to know how they would get information.

Regarding energy efficiency, we observe that 63 % of people questioned would choose the intranet if was possible for them to use an information channel at work. The second choice (which is used by hierarchy) is the diffusion of those information by using screens in different locations such as cafeteria or reception (29, 5 %). We notice this is not the most preferential choice of users.

In "other" choice, people proposed the creation of a dedicated website, email alerts or pop-up windows, or smartphone application. Generally, people would like to have an easy, personal and private access to the information. Ideally they wish to obtain that information when they want (Fig. 8).

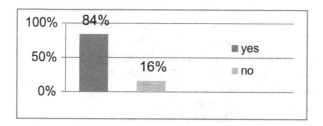

Fig. 8. Willing of information about energy at work.

By the way, users' reactions and perceptions towards information strongly differs depending on communication tools that provide them messages (Table 4).

Table 4. Preferred channel to get information about energy efficiency.

	Number of respondents	Frequency
Non-response	34	
Displayed on a data box that you can place in your office or your workplace	70	26,5%
Displayed on screens in different places (main hall, cafeterias...)	78	29,5%
Displayed on the intranet	166	62,9%
Other	6	2,3%
Total/ questioned	264	

basis of questioned people

There is a significant difference between the use of digital signage screens and classic advertising billboards. The digital signage screens seems to be more attractive for the buildings' occupants. Moreover, time and location need to be taken into account. In fact, digital signage screens are placed in friendliness places during informal periods. In this case, people take the time to watch the information messages and have the possibility to talk to each other. The classic advertising billboards, located in corridors, rooms, are not proper for exchange. Indeed, the corridors are dedicated to passage, usually people don't stay there, and they go fast. They don't stop. So, information is partially taken into account. Rooms are dedicated to work. For that reason people are fully concentrated on their task. Time is precious, consequently, information about energy savings belongs to moments it flew. The inscribable info signs are considered by users as the worst tool used by the company. People have not enough time to read it. The responses about awareness campaign are really interesting to study. It introduce a time notion: the campaign is organized in a short given time. This is thought as a real event. This short time allows people to catch quickly the information. People are not disturbed for a long time. Indeed, the multi-canal information is employed and individuals can choose the method of the message and the preferential location to receive it (Table 5).

Table 5. Communication tools making people tick.

	Number of respondents		Frequency
Non-response	14		
Awareness campaigns		146	55,3%
Scientific books and papers		69	26,1%
Day, breakfasts/events around energy themes		80	30,3%
Info sign		40	15,2%
Postings in the hall/corridors/rooms		98	37,1%
Displayed on screens in different places (main hall, cafeterias...)		142	53,8%
Total/ questioned	264		

Once that was established, we needed to go further, and see what type of message people would get (Fig. 9).

We clearly see that not only people are interested in energy efficiency and want to be actors in the process (item how to save energy), but they also want to know what their firm does: 80 % want to know more about energy saving actions implemented, and around 60 % want to know projects the company is involved in. We can see here collective identity elements.

We also asked people what compensation would they require for their effort in contributing to energy savings. Once again we noticed that most employees are ready to make an effort without a need for compensation, as shown in the next figure.

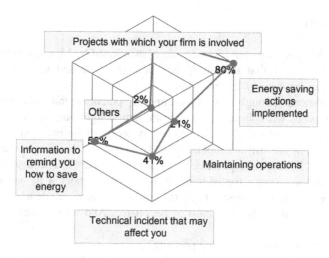

Fig. 9. Type of message users would like to receive.

The first compensation asked is funding for environmental projects. People are not individualistic, they want a better environment for everyone (Fig. 10).

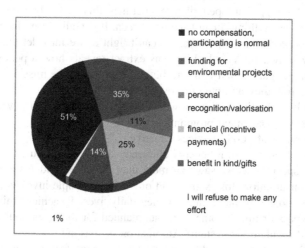

Fig. 10. Compensations for energy savings.

As it can be seen, for an efficient intelligent energy management system to be implemented, there is a real need to inform, co-construct and make users actors of energy efficiency programs and systems. It seems we must not forget that "*Actor doesn't exist out of system defining his freedom and the rationality he can use in his action. But the system only exists by actor who is the only one to build it, make it alive and possibly change it*" [32]. In this perspective, some tools for another type of intelligence could be useful [33, 34].

7 Discussion

Each practice has got a structural framework, as mentioned by Maresca and Dujin [35]. We must thus remind that this study couldn't be transposed to another context, although we can learn many lessons from it.

Several elements strongly modify occupants' practices and behaviour towards energy use: type of workplace, situation from natural light and heating sources and degree of automation of technical devices and systems are the main ones.

Energy sources are still a geopolitical stake even on a building's scale. Among possible actions, lighting is especially important in occupant's discourses. Our quantitative data shows a strong use of lighting, so we can wonder if its use and will of saving really exists. But we must get in mind that 63,6 % of respondent' s workplace is an open plan area, where lighting must be negotiated. And we saw that it maximized light use.

Who makes the rules? Collective pressure?

Groups generally adjust their practices to expressed needs. Therefore, as soon as an individual needs lighting, light is turned on in the whole open plan.

Nevertheless there are specific places exceptions, being collectively invested as exemplarity zones, as shown by our interviews analysis. The following extract clearly states it:

"in fact I think we… we have felt over in… we try to much to reduce consumption and we never light up our open plan. Sometimes this is really annoying for me. Because I don't see anything, I can't see my screen. It is really tiring for me. Since we are in the [awareness program] cradle, we can't fight it, we must let the light off."

As recently shown by Vanolo [36], this extract reveals how a person can accept practices which go against their comfort, but are conform to the mission they accepted to fulfil and the role they accepted or chose to play.

Consequently, valuating actions towards energy efficiency is a key factor for the success of energy management programs.

Is the emergence of good practices effective?

People's involvement toward energy efficiency seem to contribute to a more or less long-lasting perspective, as we saw that more than 50 % respondents are interested in an history of consumption, for example. In order to get people involved, they need to appropriate this subject by anchoring it in their daily lives. To achieve this, maybe they will need to bypass or hijack some elements planned for them, without them [37].

Who should regulate the system? Automation or reason?

Strong differences appear when balancing awareness/automation. Most people believe in behavioural change efficiency for long term effect, but many also think that automation is better for short term outcomes. Others underline the weakening their responsibility brought about by automation, which "does all for me" (interview extract).

This question about the mode of action efficiency, either human or automation, is a key point for buildings energy efficiency understanding [38].

What are the effects on the scale of the building and beyond (eco-district)?

This paper underlines how much human/machine interaction is a big stake to go through urban project in a multi-scale perspective. It is no longer only the point to know how organizing governance with stakeholders able to agree about a common objective. Neither it is to solve the equation of interpersonal contradictions to give meaning to the project.

From a philosophic point of view, there is a deep question of the acceptance and the use of the Reason notion. Can we entrust to independent technology (power of algorithm) the capacity to shape human being's behaviour inside the buildings and beyond (the ecodistricts, the cities)?

Should we preserve our control to trace our destiny based on controversy and imperfect choices?

Two essential questions catch our attention. Firstly, the increase in databases numbers and their exploitation, and the centralizing of individual data, create a colossal ecosystem to exploit. It's progressively invested due to spectacular augmentation of computer's power algorithmic capacities. NBIC convergence is unavoidable [39, 40]. Secondly, should we let the algorithm establish a standard for energetic buildings production? Should we let computers choose the best energetic needs of buildings, based on the exploitation of interconnected databases and composed by many local levels of data collection?

In which case, the occupant would not be an adjustable agent that could devote itself to the task for which it was employed by the company. This is no longer science fiction [41].

In an optimistic perspective, this action research raises the issue of the emergence of a sustainable and stable collective intelligence through space and time [42–45]. In other words, to be an efficient pathway for change, information must be connected to people's involvement towards elements influencing their daily life at work.

Most people believe in eco-district concept's impact on the inhabitants' social relationships. This element is extremely interesting because it shows that a place can be, in people's mind, a source of social relationships change [46, 47]. A collective will of expression appears, reminding that intelligent energy management must favour this belonging feeling [48].

This feeling of belonging to a collective identity [49] not yet constructed or reinforced is essential. Indeed it fixes the common basis to involve buildings occupants in co-construction actions with site managers and other stakeholders. As such these actions will not only be accepted by occupants but also done with enthusiasm.

This element needs to be looked alongside the need of appropriation [50–52] of programs and actions linked to energy efficiency. Occupants need to feel they are actors in their workplace, regardless of whether technical system acceptance and/or practices and behavioural changes are pertinent.

Aside from this researchers have shown that the appropriation of an idea, a program or a technical device permits deeper changes in behaviour and practices. Malhotra and Galetta [53] explained: *"when social influences generate a feeling of internalization and identification on the part of the user, they have a positive influence on the attitude toward the acceptance and use of the new system. The findings also suggest that internalization of the induced behavior by the adopters of new information system plays a stronger role in shaping acceptance and usage behavior than perceived use-*

fulness". In a general way, many recent papers in human and social sciences show the need for people's support [54] in changing their environment. These papers are mainly addressing private housing or public space, but we see that our data about tertiary buildings and professional environment come aligns with these.

These questions feed an interesting debate. How to hybrid natural ecosystems and computing ecosystem to invent or reinvent the cities of the 21st century?

8 Conclusion

In this paper, we have shown what were required uses towards space and energy use, particularly lighting and heating, and the place of automation in the daily lives of users. We then saw that real practices were not necessary alongside required uses. Next, we showed how involving people, with participatory design of services and systems for smart buildings, can motivate behaviour change. Lastly, the discussion brought into the open the different elements at stake for occupants of intelligent buildings, such as the questions of appropriation of a program and the power of collective identity.

On future work, we will try to implement programs that enhance collective intelligence and collective identity in intelligent buildings.

We are convinced that individual capacities are ignored. We will explore that phenomenon at different scales to broaden our field of research. This energy potential based on the emergence of social links run could be in the long a real engine of a true ecological and sociological transition. We will both use social geography and computing. Our goal is to build interfaces. We want to understand the different forms of empowerment mechanisms created by citizen groups, before their political capture.

Placing the modelling in the centre of our field of research is one of our main goal. We consider social interactions as a basis of modelling. Indeed, we will include spatial dimension both using spatial analysis and social geography. To explore that possibility, we will use geographical information system, (through web mapping solutions) at the scale of the building, integrating vertical dimension (the different floors). The beginning of a reflexion about indicators will help us to understand and define the good balance between automation and humans' behaviours (Fig. 11).

Our gradient of interaction is based on two axes of reflexion. Each axe is composed by the association of keywords. Those are considered as nodes in the road of automation. Each node symbolises a step in terms of human/machine interaction. Using this principle can help us to understand the degree of social and spatial acceptance relative to automation. On the one hand, the first axe called 'systechnic' is composed by a series of four terms: acceptance, appropriation, implication, and co-development. On the other hand, the second axe called 'spaces of social species' is composed by the same keywords as shown in the first axe, but in a different order. We could also place the interviewees' attitudes in one of the quarter of our gradient. Moreover this gradient is not static. We integrate the time in the process. Doing this will help us to understand behavioural changes of users facing modifications depending on automation. Each node is a marker. If we consider that an actor clearly rejects automation, we can ask him to determinate this reject using a percentage. As a result, for each keyword node we can

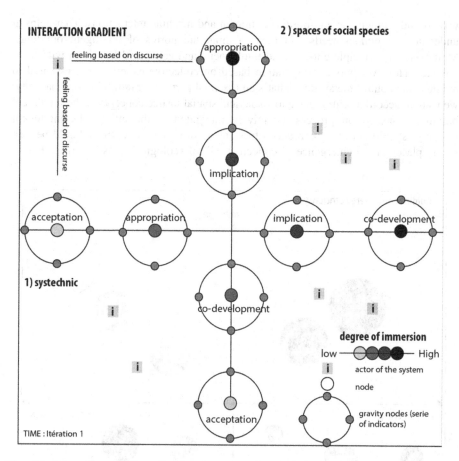

Fig. 11. Interaction gradient for development of technical systems and human beings involvement and social relationships.

place gravity nodes associated to indicators. The aggregation of each gravity nodes will allow us to determine the location of each person in our gradient of interaction.

Furthermore, being focused on the work context is important in that type of study. It allows us to understand barrier effects which could block the process of cooperation. A typology of hierarchical pressure inside buildings and sites could be an interesting field to exploit. Hierarchical pressure could have a real impact in terms of programme based on energy efficiency. That's why a second gradient could be built. It will oppose first competitive and cooperative working climate. Secondly, we could observe the degree of pressure at work, classified by a list of companies, based on interviews.

We will use cross-cutting methodologies both from the social sciences and the computer Science. Indeed, according to different authors of those fields of research, collective strategies are often more effective than individual strategies. This is demonstrated, in many cases in games theory as shown by [55] and also in social science [56, 57]. Using an interdisciplinary approach is from our point of view a good way to find a pragmatic equilibrium in human and machine interactions. That helps at understanding human needs and then to think the norms of intelligent buildings. Moreover, this principle allows us to think social and ecological transition with technologies. However human cooperation based on collective experience is essential to regulate and control the system. That's an essential part of our definition of smart city: we want to accord a central place to social and spatial justice concepts in the intelligent buildings construction process, effectively integrated to the cities. The intelligent buildings should not only be reduced to symbols of green value: they should be also strong places of the emergence of collective will of ecological transition (Fig. 12).

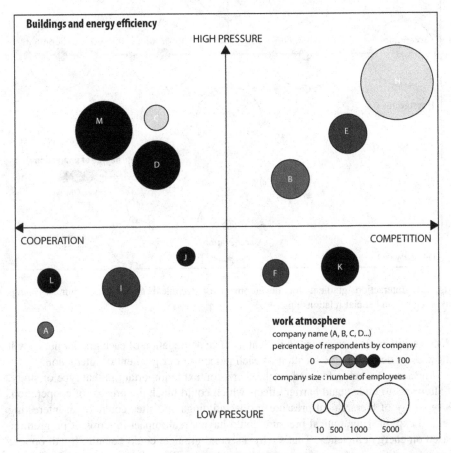

Fig. 12. Hierarchical pressure and type of social interactions.

Acknowledgements. The field study was done as part of a project (EPIT 2.0) funded by BPI France, Région Ile-de-France, Conseil Général de l'Essonne, Conseil Général des Yvelines. We thank all the partners of this project for granting us access to the sites. We also thank Chaire Campus durable, Bouygues Bâtiment IdF - UVSQ for its support.

References

1. Véron, J.: Enjeux économiques, sociaux et environnementaux de l'urbanisation du monde. Mondes En Dév. **142**, 39–52 (2008)
2. Guermond, Y.: Repenser l'urbanisme par le développement durable? Nat. Sci. Sociétés. **14**, 80–83 (2006)
3. Di Méo, G.: La métropolisation Une clé de lecture de l'organisation contemporaine des espaces géographiques. Inf. Géographique **74**, 23–38 (2010)
4. Jouve, B., Lefevre, C.: De la gouvernance urbaine au gouvernement des villes? Rev. Fr. Sci. Polit. **49**, 835–854 (1999)
5. Féré, C.: Villes rêvées, villes durables? Géocarrefour. **85**, 182–184 (2010)
6. Laigle, L.: Les villes durables en Europe: conceptions, enjeux et mise en œuvre. Ann. Mines - Responsab. Environ. **52**, 7–14 (2008)
7. Dubois-Taine, G., Chalas, Y.: La ville émergente., Paris (1997)
8. Dantzig, G.B., Saaty, T.L.: Compact City: Plan for a Liveable Urban Environment. W. H. Freeman and company, San Francisco (1973)
9. Newman, P.W.G., Kenworthy, J.R.: Cities and Automobile Dependence: An International Sourcebook. Gower, Aldershot (1989)
10. Bessy-Pietry, P.: Les formes récentes de la croissance urbaine. Economie et statistique **336**, 35–52 (2000)
11. Castel, J.-C.: Les liens entre l'organisation urbaine et les déplacements. CERTU (2006)
12. Charpentier, S.: Du périurbain au périurbanisme : analyse des (bonnes et mauvaises) pratiques de lutte contre l'étalement urbain dans l'aire urbaine du Mans., Université du Maine (2014)
13. Chauvier, E.: Itinéraires dans la périurbanité « molle »: entre tout-fonctionnel et résistance. Articulo - J. Urban Res. (2012)
14. Hilal, M., Sencébé, Y.: Mobilités quotidiennes et urbanité suburbaine. Espac. Sociétés. **108**, 133–154 (2002)
15. Marry, S.: Densité urbaine et qualité de vie. En quoi la compréhension des représentations de la densité urbaine est-elle prépondérante dans l'analyse et la conception de formes urbaines propices à une certaine qualité de vie? EPE (2009)
16. Demaze, M.T.: Un panorama de la télédétection de l'étalement urbain. Trav. Doc. ESO. pp. 99–124 (2010)
17. Ganguly, A.: Donner une valeur à la biodiversité. Annuels. [Numero_Volume_Chiffre], pp. 123–125 (2009)
18. Poinsot, Y.: La dimension géographique du ménagement des ressources énergétiques renouvelables: le cas français dans son contexte européen. Ann. Géographie. **685**, 287–309 (2012)
19. Villes et enjeux énergétiques: Pappalardo, c. Ann. Mines - Responsab. Environ. **49**, 16–23 (2008)
20. Ballas, D.: What makes a "happy city"? Curr. Res. Cities **32**(Supplement 1), S39–S50 (2013)
21. Mahdavinejad, M., Shamshirband, M., Pilbala, N., Yari, F.: Socio-cultural approach to create an educative city case: Tehran-Iran. World Conf. Des. Arts Educ. (DAE-2012) **51**, 943–947 (2012)
22. Yanarella, E., Levine, R.: Charter of European cities and towns towards sustainability. In: The City as Fulcrum of Global Sustainability. Anthem Press (2011)
23. Servier, J.: Méthode de l'ethnologie. PUF (1993)
24. Agier, M.: La sagesse de l'ethnologue. l'Oeil Neuf, Paris (2004)

25. Bussi, M.: L'espace négocié. Démocratie électorale et développement local (2001)
26. Bussi, M.: Pour une géographie de la démocratie. Espace Polit. Rev. En Ligne Géographie Polit. Géopolitique (2007)
27. Rosière, S.: Géographie politique et géopolitique. Une grammaire de l'espace politique. Ellipses, Paris (2003)
28. Nussbaum, M.: Capabilités: Comment créer les conditions d'un monde plus juste ? Editions Flammarion (2012)
29. Séchet, R., Veschambre, V. (eds.): Penser et faire la géographie sociale: Contribution à une épistémologie de la géographie sociale. Presses universitaires de Rennes, Rennes (2006)
30. Roure, H., Reinert, M.: Analyse d'un entretien à l'aide d'une méthode d'analyse lexicale. JADT **1993**, 418–428 (1993)
31. Achard, P.: La sociologie du langage. PUF, Paris (1993)
32. Crozier, M., Friedberg, E.: L'acteur et le système: Les contraintes de l'action collective. Seuil, Paris (1992)
33. Delvoye, J.-M., Girardot, J.-J.: Les outils d'intelligence territoriale pour les acteurs de terrain à Seraing: entre appropriation des méthodes et acquisition de compétences. HAL (2005)
34. López-Ruiz, V.-R., Alfaro-Navarro, J.-L., Nevado-Peña, D.: Knowledge-city index construction: An intellectual capital perspective. Empir. Approaches Knowl. City Res. **41**, 5560–5572 (2014)
35. Maresca, B., Dujin, A.: La transition énergétique à l'épreuve du mode de vie. Flux. **96**, 10–23 (2014)
36. Vanolo, A.: Smartmentality: The Smart City as Disciplinary Strategy. Urban Stud. **51**, 883–898 (2014)
37. De Certeau, M.: L'invention du quotidien, tome 1 : Arts de faire. Gallimard (1990)
38. De Brito, C.: Le développement durable: nécessité de changer les comportements ou opportunités pour les technologies propres? Ann. Mines - Responsab. Environ. **2**, 19–25 (2008)
39. De Broca, A.: Du vieil Homme au nouveau: trans-humanisme? Défis pour penser l'Homme de demain. Éthique Santé. **9**, 121–126 (2012)
40. Larrieu, P.: Les enjeux éthiques de la neuroamélioration. Médecine Droit. **2014**, 61–65 (2014)
41. Bostrom, N.: Superintelligence: Paths, Dangers. Strategies. Oxford University Press, Oxford (2014)
42. Boisvert, R., Milette, C.: Le développement des communautés au Québec: la part de l'intelligence collective. Santé Publique. **21**, 183–190 (2009)
43. Marek, A., Breuer, C., Devillet, G.: Une démarche participative sur l'intelligence territoriale en vue du redéploiement d'une province. In: Interdisciplinarité dans l'aménagement et développement des territoires, p. 9. INTI-International Network of Territorial Intelligence, Gatineau, Canada (2013)
44. Masselot, C., Galibert, O.: Digital socialization in a Territorial Intelligence case: The Fontaine d'Ouche area in Dijon (Burgundy, France). In: 12th Annual International Conference of Territorial Intelligence "Innovación Social y nuevos modos de gobernanza para la transición socio-ecológica", Espagne November (2013)
45. Viera, J.: Droit de l'Union européenne et démocratie numérique. Clés pour l'éco-citoyenneté. Cah. Numér. **10**, 41–62 (2014)
46. Coutard, O., Levy, J.-P.: Écologies urbaines. Économica-Anthropos, Paris (2010)
47. Emelianoff, C.: Durabilité urbaine, modes de vie et solidarités à long rayon d'action. In: Coutard O., Lévy J.-P., Écologies urbaines, pp. 302–327, Paris (2010)

48. Dureau, F., Lévy, J.-P.: Morphologie urbaine et consommations énergétiques : un éclairage à partir de la recherche française. In: Ecologies urbaines, pp. 84–101. Economica-Anthropos (2010)
49. Castells, M.: L'Ere de l'information, tome 2: Le Pouvoir de l'identité. Fayard, Paris (1999)
50. Boutilier, R.G., Thomson, I.: Modelling and Measuring the Social License to Operate: Fruits of a Dialogue Between Theory and Practice (2001). http://socialicense.com/publications/Modelling%20and%20Measuring%20the%20SLO.pdf
51. Jouet, J.: Retour critique sur la sociologie des usages. Réseaux CENTHermès Sci. Publ. **18**, 487–521 (2000)
52. Raufflet, E.: De l'acceptabilité sociale au développement local résilient. VertigO - Rev. Électronique En Sci. Environ. (2014)
53. Malhotra, Y., Galletta, D.F.: Extending the technology acceptance model to account for social influence: theoretical bases and empirical validation. In: Proceedings of the 32nd Annual Hawaii International Conference on Systems Sciences, HICSS-32, p. 14 (1999)
54. Morel-Brochet, A., Ortar, N.: Les modes d'habiter à l'épreuve de la durabilité. Norois. **2**, 7–12 (2014)
55. AlSkaif, T., Zapata, M.-G., Bellata, B.: A Game Theoretic Approach. In: Helfert, M., Krempels, K.-H., Donnellan, B., Klein, C. (Eds.) Proceedings of the 4th International Conference on Smart Cities and Green ICT Systems, pp. 300–306, Portugal (2015)
56. Parlebas, P.: Sociométrie, réseaux et communication. Presses universitaires de France, Paris (1992)
57. Parlebas, P.: Modélisation du jeu sportif : le système des scores du volley-ball. Mathématiques Sci. Hum. **91**, 57–80 (1985)

Introducing Flexibility into Data Centers for Smart Cities

Sonja Klingert[1]([⊠]), Florian Niedermeier[2], Corentin Dupont[3], Giovanni Giuliani[4],
Thomas Schulze[1], and Hermann de Meer[2]

[1] Software Engineering Group, University of Mannheim, Mannheim, Germany
{klingert,schulze}@informatik.uni-mannheim.de
[2] Computer Networking and Computer Communications Group, University of Passau,
Passau, Germany
{niederme,demeer}@fim.uni-passau.de
[3] Create-Net, Trento, Italy
corentin.dupont@create-net.org
[4] HP Italy Innovation Center, Milan, Italy
giuliani@hp.com

Abstract. In Europe, more and more cities are aiming to become part of the
"smart cities" vision. Smart Cities are based on a plethora of sensor data which
need to be processed in data centres. Therefore data centres play an important
role in making cities smart. However, at the same time they are huge consumers
of electrical energy and thus counteract smart cities' goals of an IT based low
carbon economy. The project DC4Cities takes up the challenge of turning data
centres into flexible energy consumers that to a high degree run on renewable
energy sources. It offers a technical solution for optimizing the share of renewables in data centre energy consumption and supports this by novel contracts and
business models. This paper introduces power management options between data
centres and a smart city which are backed by adaptation strategies within the data
centre. It also presents a set of contracts that complement the technical solution
and a trial evaluation of the approach.

Keywords: Data centre · Energy-aware · Renewable energy source · Smart cities ·
Workload scheduling

1 Introduction

In 1516 Sir Thomas More published his book "Utopia", a vision of a perfect society
which became the blueprint of many future visions for an ideal society. Today, facing
the risk of climate change processes we cannot control, we are again badly in need of
visions. With urbanization progressing, conservative approaches to managing cities are
increasingly facing their limits. To provide its citizens with a high quality of living while
maintaining a sustainable ecosystem, large cities worldwide are trying to evolve into
Smart Cities, getting one step closer to providing the surroundings to a utopian society.
However, this smartness comes at a price: to make truly smart decisions, large amounts
of data have to be collected from throughout the city by sensor networks. These data
have to be consolidated, processed and interpreted before providing useful insights.

© Springer International Publishing Switzerland 2015
M. Helfert et al. (Eds.): Smartgreens 2015 and Vehits 2015, CCIS 579, pp. 128–145, 2015.
DOI: 10.1007/978-3-319-27753-0_7

On the side of electricity supply, a sustainable and eco-friendly power generation will require a much higher fraction of renewable power than is common today. Especially with sources like wind and solar, this may lead to increased volatility in the power grid.

Data centres and their capability to provide large amounts of computing power play a key role in these future Smart Cities: on one hand, they enable processing of big data, which is an important foundation to intelligent decisions. On the other hand, data centres are large consumers of electrical power, so their power supply has to be adapted to support a sustainable and eco-friendly city environment in such a way as to consume primarily renewable power.

Providing the computational power to drive future smart cities at the lowest possible carbon footprint is the vision of the project introduced in this paper: DC4Cities. This paper gives more insight into the DC4Cities research and associated prototype that implements it. Section 2 gives a more detailed overview on the general research idea, Sect. 3 introduces the architecture of the DC4Cities implementation, and Sect. 4 presents first simulation results. Finally, Sect. 5 positions our approach in relation to others' work.

2   General Approach

Operating a DC that is powered by 100 % renewables is not a problem if its energy supply can for example be completely covered by hydro or geothermal sources. To save CO_2 emissions caused by DCs, one might suggest to move DCs to places with exuberant supply of renewables like Norway. Even though large DC owners like Google are considering this as a solution for parts of their DCs, it is not practicable in all scenarios. Some DCs need to be close to users and inside cities for manifold reasons: Companies often see security risks in outsourcing data or other IT services, especially to foreign countries. Network latency is another aspect that makes moving services to distant locations unfeasible (e.g. near real-time stock exchange services). So, if moving DCs to locations with exuberant supply of renewable energy is not an option, DCs need to become more energy aware, energy efficient, and energy adaptive as an alternative in order to increase the percentage of renewables. However, running a DC at high levels of renewable energy sources in a city is a great challenge. A main reason for this is the lack of availability of locally produced renewable energy due to space limitations or environmental constraints.

In order to tackle this problem, DCs need to try to adapt better to the availability of renewable power, minimize their energy consumption for specific tasks in general and adhere to constraints of a higher directive which is managing energy aspects in a smart city – the so called Energy Management Authority – Smart City (EMA-SC). Figure 1 schematically compares the result of a renewable-energy optimized and a non-optimized DC. On the left hand side of Fig. 1, the power demand of a traditional, i.e. non-optimized DC is shown, which clearly does not reflect the generation curve of renewable power. The right hand side of Fig. 1 depicts the energy profile of the same DC after DC4Cities has been applied. Here, the renewable generation and power demand curves are much more aligned, and therefore, the amount of renewable energy used by the DC is much higher. In order to reach this goal, an active coordination between EMA-SC and a DC is mandatory for setting reasonable goals as well as technique for controlling energy adaptation within the DC.

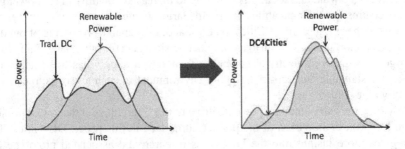

Fig. 1. DC4Cities impact on renewable energy utilization.

The EMA-SC is responsible for the energy coordination within a smart city and the communication with DCs. It monitors the energy consumption and computes the desired power demand both for the smart city as a whole and individual DCs, and it sets certain targets for DCs and other large consumers inside the city. In case some of the targets cannot be reached, it also tries to resolve such conflicts by facilitating the negotiation of objectives with the respective consumers' organizations. In the case of a DC such an escalation could for example lead to workload relocation within a federation of DCs having different energy sources or simply the payment of a fine.

For the DC internal adaptation, two objectives are pursued: on one hand, re-organizing workload (and thus the energy consumption profile) in order to match power demand with the shape of the renewable supply curve, and on the other hand minimizing overall energy consumption in order to reduce cost and emissions.

The DC4Cities energy controller (in the middle of Fig. 2) retrieves forecasts about the energy source mix directly from the providers or indirectly through forecasting models. This is done through the "Renewable Energy Adaptive Interface". For example for local solar panels, we start from weather forecasting data.

This information is processed periodically (e.g. every 15 min) and merged with the power objectives of a DC in order to compute the ideal power plan for the DC (see Sect. 2.1). Inside a DC, this "energy budget" will then be split onto the different services; for each service, a so-called "Energy Adaptive Software Controller" (EASC) uses DC specific monitoring and automation tools to correctly schedule and tune the SW/HW resource usage of this service in line with the directives received by the controller through the "Energy Adaptive DC Operation Interface". The expected result is that the actual power consumption of the whole DC will be considerably closer to the previously computed ideal power plan, thus meeting the DC power objectives received from the Smart City Authority.

2.1 Coordination Between Smart City and Data Centre

Coordination between the smart city and DCs under its energy management scheme is managed by EMA-SC. We assume that the smart city has certain goals, e.g., regarding

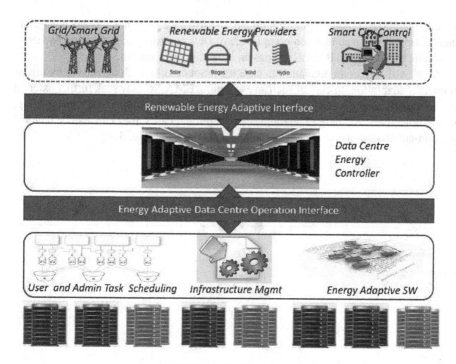

Fig. 2. DC4Cities high-level architecture.

the share of renewable energy in the energy mix of its big consumers or the city-wide total CO_2 emissions. The scope or level of abstraction of these goals may be infeasible for immediate technical enforcement. However, by subdividing the goals into more concrete objectives, the smart city goals can be translated into constraints regarding power/energy usage. Once these constraints are in place and information on future renewable power availability has been obtained, EMA-SC is able to calculate power budgets for the large consumers inside the city. To this end, the DC4Cities software includes a component named *Ideal Power Planner* (IPP). The IPP is responsible for transforming renewable energy forecasts and power/energy usage constraints imposed by EMA into a power plan for a DC. The IPP executes the following steps:

1. Calculate the total amount of renewable power available to the DC from the renewable power availability forecast(s).
2. Using information on the minimum (DCPowerMIN) and maximum (DCPowerMAX) power demand of the DC, scale the values obtained in step 1 so that the difference of the maximum and minimum corresponds to the difference of DCPowerMAX and DCPowerMIN.
3. Shift the result of step 2 so that the minimum aligns with DCPowerMIN
4. Apply any constraints from smart city side, e.g., power and energy constraints

These power plans are then communicated to the DCs, which will follow them as closely as possible. While the basic compliance of power/energy objectives has to be secured via trial runs at configuration time of the software system, everyday changes in energy supply may lead to a non-compliance of DCs regarding objectives set by EMA. To handle this case, DC4Cities includes an escalation mechanism.

A DC will trigger an escalation in case it cannot comply with objectives by means of internal adaptation. In case of such an escalation, EMA-SC may seek further external solutions such as suggesting and supporting a federation with other DCs or updating/adding objectives. As these escalations are exceptional cases, they can also be handled in a non-automated manner between the DC and EMA-SC (Fig. 3).

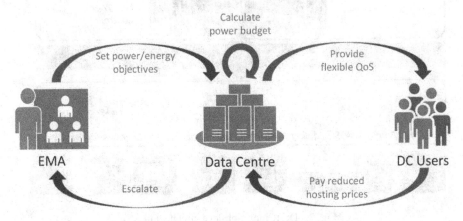

Fig. 3. Communication between EMA, DC and DC users.

Escalation may be triggered manually or automatically in case no DC operation compliant with the IPP can be calculated or if a threshold agreed on in the contract is violated. Depending on the time until the occurrence of the predicted non-compliance, two stages of escalation are envisioned: A 'warning' which marks a possible exceeding of thresholds in the future (e.g., > 6 h), and an 'alarm' (e.g., < 6 h). Possible reactions of EMA-SC depend on the underlying *RenEnergy* contract with the DC (see Sect. 2.3). The following de-escalations are envisioned:

- Tolerating violation of objectives due to unforeseen temporary events, either at DC side or originating from energy side;
- The RenEnergy contract might allow a certain number and frequency of violations;
- Incurring a penalty according to an agreed reward/penalty scheme;
- Changing objectives (temporarily/permanent);
- Setting contingency objectives in order to prevent decrease in goal achievement;
- Offering federation assistance.

Obviously, the occurrence of an escalation depends on the metrics used by the DC4Cities system in order to assess the "fitness" of the DC with respect to its goals. The metrics are, for instance, used to measure the distance between the ideal power plan and the actual power demand of the DC. Based on the distance and a threshold value, escalation events might be determined.

2.2   Energy Adaptation Within a Data Centre

Following the communication with EMA-SC, compliance with set goals needs to be implemented inside the DC. The novelty of DC4Cities is to propose a multi-level API able to allow each level of a modern DC to follow energy directives (see Fig. 4). There are three levels: IaaS, PaaS and individual applications.

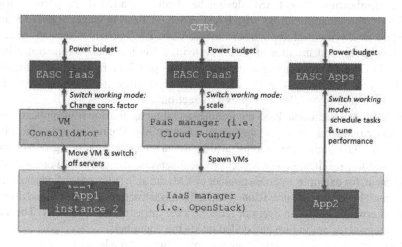

Fig. 4. Components of the DC subsystem.

First, some tasks performed in the DC need to be rescheduled to match the hours of renewable power availability. This scheduling requires detailed knowledge about the applications running in the DC and should therefore be tackled at the level of PaaS, where knowledge of applications running is available. Additionally, the PaaS layer provides a uniform interface to interact with applications and to scale them up and down.

The secondary objective of DC4Cities is to save energy in the DC. Previous projects such as FIT4Green[1] showed that it is most efficient to use the IaaS layer in order to consolidate virtual machines (VMs) on the most efficient servers, and then switch off the unused servers.

Thirdly, specific applications in the DC, like maintenance jobs, need to be controlled. Applications such as virus scan or database compression are ideal candidates because they perform regular tasks that can be rescheduled if needed.

IaaS Optimization. At IaaS level, we adapt key parameters of an existing VM scheduler, such as the consolidation factor. This allows for the VM scheduler to follow energy directives provided by EMA, while respecting the SLA of each VM. For instance, when there is little renewable power available, we increase the consolidation factor. This will cause the migration and consolidation of VMs to a lower number of servers and in a second step a shutdown of unused servers. If there is a

---

[1] http://www.fit4green.eu.

high level of renewable power available, VM scheduler constraints are relaxed, so that VMs will not need to be as densely consolidated. At this level the VMs are "anonymous": there is no knowledge regarding the type of software running inside them nor at what time they might be shut down, since this is at the discretion of the client. A tool such as Plug4Green [9] may be used.

PaaS Optimization. The EASC design has been extended to support Platform-as-a-Service based applications with EASC-PaaS. A PaaS manager allows for automating the deployment of applications inside VMs. PaaS provides services to easily provision, scale, and monitor applications with a limited user/administrator intervention. In EASC-PaaS scaling operation services provided by PaaS infrastructures are employed. Furthermore a PaaS environment is often itself based on an IaaS framework running the VMs (see previous section).

However, in a traditional PaaS environment, scaling up and down an application will not necessarily have a big impact on energy consumption. The reason is that most PaaS architectures have static provisioning: scaling down an application or a group of applications will not result in switching off physical servers. In the Cloud Foundry[2] PaaS environment, for example, a certain number of VMs are able to host so-called application containers. These VMs are provisioned when the infrastructure is installed, and does not change afterwards unless an operator redeploys the infrastructure manually. The applications themselves are in turn embedded inside the containers.

The energy management must then take place in the three layers:

1. Application layer: The EASC will scale up and down the number of containers owned by an application based on the renewable energy availability;
2. PaaS layer: The containers must be consolidated inside the minimum number of VMs, turning off empty VMs;
3. IaaS layer: The VMs must be consolidated on the minimum number of physical servers. The freed-up servers should then be switched off to save energy.

Two new components were developed to address points 2 and 3, and can be seen in Fig. 5 The first, the PaaS consolidator, is able to scale up and down the number of VMs hosting containers in a PaaS environment. The second is the IaaS consolidator, able to consolidate VMs and switch on and off servers according to the demand.

Application Optimization. As a third adaptation strategy, DC4Cities ultimately controls some key applications and processes of a DC. This includes virus scanning, data-base cleaning, but also physical server scheduled maintenance. Indeed, server maintenance is a recurring activity in a DC and it has a significant energetic impact [15].

There are two kinds of applications directly controlled by DC4Cities: task-oriented and service-oriented. In the first case tasks are scheduled and performed by the applications, such as offline video transcoding or web crawling. In some cases, those tasks can be post- or pre-poned. We take advantage of this possibility to schedule tasks at the right moment (obviously compliant with the underlying contract). The DC4Cities

---

[2] http://www.cloudfoundry.org.

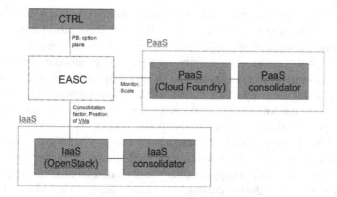

Fig. 5. EASC in a PaaS and IaaS environment.

prototype then monitors the progress of the task and its KPIs. If it is e.g. too late, it will modify its schedule to finish faster.

Service-oriented applications, on the other hand, have a continuous service to perform, such as serving web pages. In this case, we tune the performance of the application within an identified range while respecting the SLA. For example, in the case of a web server, we increase/decrease the number of client threads within the boundaries of the SLA.

Coordination Strategies. The optimization in DC4Cities happens at two stages. First, relatively autonomous application managers (the EASCs) allow for enforcing energy budgets at IaaS, PaaS and individual application levels. Indeed, a situation with fully autonomous energy-aware applications, following the same energy directives, enables an increased usage of renewables. Secondly, DC4Cities offers an additional level of coordination: the prototype communicates with each EASC to retrieve their scheduling options and can then arbitrate between them. This level of coordination is necessary to achieve better results: the energy directives need to be adapted for each EASC, because each underlying application has a different level of flexibility. Furthermore, the execution patterns provided by each application need to be consolidated in a central system in order to make decisions. This would, e.g., avoid the creation of power demand peaks.

The central system should also be able to split the energy budget granted by the EMA between the overlapping systems. Indeed, the energy allocation for the EASC-Apps is overlapping the energy allocation of the EASC-PaaS, because some applications might be operated by PaaS managers. Similarly, the energy allocation for the EASC-PaaS is overlapping the energy allocation of the EASC-IaaS, because VMs created by a scaling command on a PaaS manager are hosted by an IaaS manager.

2.3 Incentives and Monitoring

The previous sections showed a consistent vision on how to integrate DC energy management into a smart city relying heavily on renewable energy from a technical point of view. However, the technical solution needs to be underpinned by an equally consistent economic framework in order to be viable from a business point of view, both for participating DCs and the smart city. Only if the business part of the concept reinforces the technical solution, the DC4Cities vision can become a reality.

As the first goal is not to 'save' energy, i.e. to reduce the amount of energy needed, but rather to rearrange the power profile of a DC in a way that it is aligned to renewable power supply, today's energy tariffs do not lead to a direct power cost reduction. The reason is that – to our knowledge – no energy tariff in Europe rewards the temporal alignment of power demand with renewable power supply.

In Europe energy suppliers, i.e. the actors in the energy system that sell power to the final power consumers, act as price buffer between the power supply with volatile prices and the customer. So even if a supplier offers tariffs based on time-of-use pricing, e.g. lower prices at night than during the day, these tariffs are never as volatile as real time supply cost or prices at the EEX or other stock exchanges. The plethora of "green" energy tariffs offered by most energy suppliers and promising a certain degree (often 100 %) has a different background than the DC4Cities concept: They define "green" by renewable power based on certificates for renewable energy being fed into the power grid anywhere, and thus they regularly level out the volatility of – locally produced – renewable power. The disadvantage of this approach is obviously huge energy losses due to the energy transport over vast distances (e.g. wind or hydro energy from the north of Europe to the south) and the associated voltage transformations.

Some big players, also large DCs, can circumvent energy suppliers and their tariffs and directly buy their energy at the stock exchange. However, even in this case prices do not reflect the volatility of the supply of renewable energy – prices at the stock exchange are an indicator of a temporal scarcity which can derive from various sources, renewable energy supply being just one of them. Here the smart city comes into play as mediator between energy system and DC – in our vision a mediator with pre-defined goals regarding the share of renewable energy at the city's energy mix.

Facing the lack of the right pricing signals from the energy system and ignoring the option of a 'dictator' smart city, the EMA-SC introduced in Sect. 2.1 needs to incentivize DCs to adhere to the DC4Cities scheme. To this end, a two-stage system of contracts retracing the technical communication as shown in Fig. 6 is proposed: The so-called RenEnergy contract between EMA-SC and the DC replaces or amends the regular energy tariff in a way comparable to a technical contract like a SLA between a DC and its customers. Between the DC and their customers regular SLAs are upgraded to GreenSLAs, as suggested in former work of the authors (e.g. [6]).

The 'RenEnergy' contract contains both a model regarding which behaviour shall be rewarded or penalized and how to monitor this behaviour.

The behaviour of the DC is reflected in the timely adaption of the original power demand of the DC as a reaction to the information about the expected renewable power supply power profile as received from the EMA-SC. As shown in Sect. 2.1 an ideal power plan (IPP) is calculated as reference power profile and power plan for the DC. The better the adaptation behaviour, the higher the reward.

There are several approaches to designing a compensation scheme: both reward and penalty components can be either fully fixed, fully variable or contain both fixed and variable parts. Generally, the more rigid the components, the less risk for an EMA-SC;

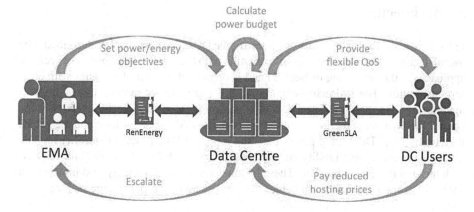

Fig. 6. A system of contracts complementing the technical cooperation.

the more variable, the higher the incentive character can possibly be. A variable compensation is more like a price signal: It depends on the "price elasticity of demand" of the DC energy demand to which degree the DC reacts to the signal. The fixed reward represents the general willingness of the DC to agree to a contract that limits its degree of freedom with regards to power consumption. Then a penalty could further steer its behaviour dynamically.

Recently, the authors conducted a questionnaire in connection with a slightly different compensation scheme among DCs in Europe[3]. The goal was to get information about the willingness of DC managers to adapt their power profile to requirements of the power grid. The result of this questionnaire clearly hints that both options, fixed and variable pricing components, should be offered in a compensation scheme, as the share of DCs who prefer a high fixed and a low variable component is about equal to the one who prefer it the other way round.

In order for the RenEnergy contracts to be implemented, the behaviour of the DC needs to be monitored. The deviation between the IPP and the realized power profile of the DC is the basis for a new metric, DCAdapt, which – simply expressed - denotes the deviation between plan and realization in percentage values. An additional metric developed for this purpose is RenPercent that represents the share of renewable energy consumption of the power profile of a DC. It is the second pillar of RenEnergy contracts. The contract then needs to specify which metric should achieve which values or move within a certain target corridor in order to result in a specified reward.

However, the DC's options to adapt the workload - and with it its power profile - to the IPP are limited due to contracts with its customers laid down in service level agreements, SLAs. Former work by the authors suggested how to turn these into GreenSLAs (e.g. the above mentioned [6]) that reward the customers for collaboration whenever an adaption process in the DC is necessary. These GreenSLAs are implemented in the DC4Cities system through 'green points' that are granted to those customers that permit the DC to shift its workload when required by the IPP.

---

[3] See D2.4 of the All4Green Project (public deliverable) at www.all4green-project.eu.

3   Architecture

In the following, the high-level architecture of the DC4Cities approach is described. The overall technical architecture is in strict relation with the pattern described in the general approach (at the beginning of Sect. 2) and is organized in a set of modules with clear responsibilities. The following diagram (Fig. 7) graphically represents the different modules and interactions. The DC4Cities control system periodically executes three control loops, namely the power planning loop, the EASC control loop and the EASC monitoring loop. During the power planning loop, the D4C process controller module retrieves the energy availability and weather forecasts (cf. Fig. 7 – Step 1) for the next 24 h through the ERDS handler. These include both local and energy grid information about the amount of power available, the sources used, the percentage of renewable energy as well as weather forecasts.

Within the first step of the EASC control loop the D4C process controller module determines the overall data centre power consumption plan, i.e. the maximum power consumption that still satisfies the energy/power objectives set by EMA-SC (cf. Fig. 7 – Step 2). This is done by using the previously gathered information provided by the power planning loop and the data centre power consumption plan calculated in the previous iteration of the EASC control loop (cf. Sect. 2.1). Next, the data centre power plan is split into quotas, each assigned to a specific application/service running in the data centre (cf. Fig. 7 – Step 3 and Sect. 2.2). The split is based on a set of policies, which can be selected and configured by the DC business manager (DCBM) (cf. Fig. 7 – Step 4). These power plan quotas are input to an Energy Aware Software Controller (EASC). Based on this input, an EASC calculates in the second step of the EASC control loop a set of alternative power plan options for the next 24 h that correspond as close as possible to the power plan quotas (cf. Fig. 7 – Step 5) and are sent to the option plan collector (cf. Fig. 7 – Step 6). These power plans are then consolidated into a single data centre power plan, which

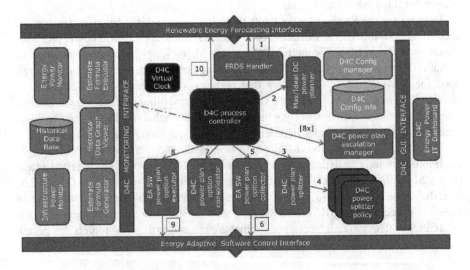

Fig. 7. DC4Cities architecture.

contains the optimal combination of all power plans (cf. Fig. 7 – Step 7). Both the flexibilities expressed in the power plan options and the data centre energy contracts are used to optimize the power consumption plan for the next time window. Subsequently, the global data centre plan is sent together with power/energy goals and possible constraint violations to the Escalation Manager, which calculates short, medium and long-term information that is provided to the CDBM and possibly EMA-SC through the dashboard (cf. Fig. 7 – Step 8). In case an escalation, e.g. a short-term violation of goals, needs to be handled data centre service priorities or goals can be redefined and the process can be repeated (cf. Fig. 7 – Step 8). In case no escalation needs to be managed, the option plan is communicated to the EASC, which enacts the power plan. For that purpose, the EASC will use automation tools to control the SW/HW resources of the service in line with the received plan (Working Mode). Finally, the controller will share the DC power plan with the energy provider, to enable some form of demand/response cooperation.

The EASC Monitoring loop retrieves business performance and power consumption information from the EASC on a regular basis. This data is persisted into the historical database and can be further used for forecasting models.

Besides the external interfaces described in Sect. 2, additional internal interfaces connect the controller to the web presentation of the dashboard (on the right side of Fig. 7) and to the historical database subsystem (left) used to store all monitored data as well as to support predictions using correlation models based on the collected data. The DC Energy/Power and IT Dashboard provides a graphical user interface for DCBM and EMA-SC to monitor and control/configure the high-level energy/business view of the data centre control system. It interacts with the main control modules through a specific internal web service interface, allowing the D4C Dashboard to be implemented as a web application.

For consistency reasons and forecasting, data is exported from the existing monitoring systems of the data centre IT and DCIM systems into the D4C historical data base through the monitoring components. A historical graph viewer supports the dashboard presentation with graphs about the past, actual and forecasted data, as well as showing the savings achieved through the different DC4Cities optimizations, and the positioning of D4C performance with respect to the energy/power goals. The forecasting is implemented by using the forecast/estimations formula generator modules and executors.

For efficient testing all D4C modules refer to a D4C virtual clock. This for instance allows replaying past scenarios in a compressed time window.

The prototype of DC4Cities is implemented in Java and hosted inside a Tomcat Application Server; the external interfaces are defined and supported using JSON/Rest technology.

4   Initial Trial Results

The EU project DC4Cities includes three trials to validate the system using different services inside DCs who have different power providers with various characteristics:

- CSUC and IMI; Barcelona (Spain), powered by Gas Natural; CPU intensive video conversion tasks; federation option
- CN/APSS; Trento (Italy), powered by Italian grid, located with lots of hydro production; report generation tasks for health system

- HP; Milan (Italy), powered both by local photovoltaics (PVs) and the Italian grid; test lab for a Web E-learning platform offering a world-wide service (HP LIFE, an HP Living Progress initiative).

The first trial phase reported consistent results in the three trials; inside this paper we report details about the HP trial that includes both grid and local renewable as energy sources. Additional information about all trials can be found in the deliverable D6.2 of the project[4].

The Energy Ecosystem of the HP trial described in Fig. 8 is very peculiar: inside the Technology Showroom 2 HP Moonshot chassis are hosted in a dedicated rack that is powered, through 2 Intelligent PDUs, directly by the control module of the Inverter connected to a set of locally installed solar panels. On top of the roof 8 PV modules have been installed, 250 W each (1640 mm × 990 mm × 40 mm – approx 1.5 m^2 - oriented to South and with 30 degree inclination), for a total of 2 kW peak. A second line is connected to the internal HP power distribution to power the rack when no energy is produced by the PVs, e.g. at night. Additional meters with data loggers have been used in real-time to measure (and store) the power generated by the PVs, the consumption of the servers, and the exchange with the HP grid (surplus of solar power provided to the grid, or drawn from the grid in case of insufficient solar power).

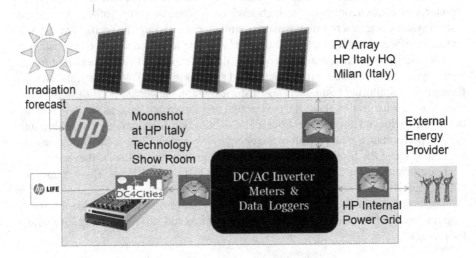

Fig. 8. HP trial power ecosystem.

The test bed realized at *HP Italy Innovation Centre Cloud Lab's* is composed of 2 different HP Moonshots chassis, each one capable of hosting up to 45 cartridges (low

---

[4] D6.2 will be published soon at the project website www.dc4cities.eu.

power servers); current configuration hosts 14 ProLiant Moonshot Server Cartridge[5] in one chassis and 15 Moonshot M300 Servers[6] in another chassis.

There's a central monitoring system, based in Zabbix (open source monitoring tool) collecting all data about the full system from all sources, i.e. application and infrastructure performance and power consumption. The Zabbix server collects all data and stores them inside its internal data base and provides operators with a sophisticated web based GUI to analyze and display real time and historical values.

Energy measurement is performed by a HP hardware component named iLO[7] (Integrated Lights-Out), accessible through the Insight Control software suite, and already referenced in the traditional data centre test bed. iLO offers the ability to read real-time electrical power consumption down to single server level (each single Moonshot cartridges). A specific Zabbix server side agent has been developed to query the chassis iLO and retrieve the actual power consumption of each Moonshot cartridge as well as the full chassis (including fans and network switches), with a monitoring rate of 1 min. Another specific Zabbix server side agent will extract data from the internal meters of the Inverter Control systems and log PV production and the total power consumed by the rack (by difference the power drained from the grid through the backup line will be computed).

HP trial workload is a web application, i.e. a testing lab for a worldwide service offered by HP, i.e. HP Life (http://www-life-global.org). This application needs to be always available to the users, 24×7 as it offers a web based e-learning platform for entrepreneurs spread over the globe. The load testing tool (open source "jmeter[8]") was configured to reproduce the pattern of the real application scenario in a reproducible way.

The M&V methodology has been utilized in this case to define the "profile days" for the trial. An analysis has been performed on PV historical data, by considering for each day peak power, peak power hour, total production, and numbers of sub-peaks of the power curve. The most significant categorization parameters to extract significant day profile candidates pattern turned out to be the total daily production and the number of sub-peaks. At the end 4 day profiles (Day 1, Day 2, Day 3, Day 4) have been selected for the PV production, their energy production patterns are summarized I Fig. 9.

The trial was run twice in two different configurations. The first time with 8 PVs, and results were positive, but during the peak production hours the available power (over 1,5 kW) was way above the HP Moonshot consumption (approx. 500 W), therefore a second configuration was setup to make the trial more challenging, i.e. using only 4PVs, thus having a peak of approx. 750 W local power production during sunny days. Profile Day 1 is the most favourable one from the PV production perspective. In Fig. 10 the local PV power production and the grid RenPercent are represented as filled areas in the background, while the lines represent the baseline power consumption (without DC4Cities) and the actual power using DC4Cities optimizer.

---

[5] **CPU** Intel® Atom™ Processor 2 GHz, **Memory** 8 GB.

[6] **CPU** Intel® Atom™ Processor 2.4 GHz, **Memory** 32 GB.

[7] http://h18013.www1.hp.com/products/servers/management/ilo_table.html?
jumpid=reg_R1002_USEN.

[8] http://jmeter.apache.org/.

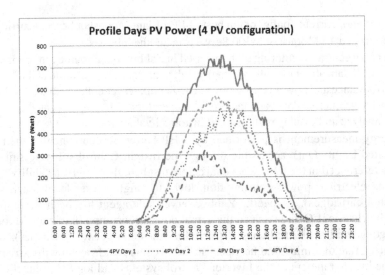

Fig. 9. Profile days power.

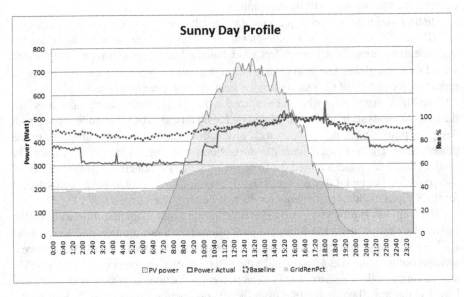

Fig. 10. Day 1 - sunny day profile (4 PVs).

In the next table the metrics measured during the different test runs have been collected, to allow an easy comparison. The first set of rows show the metrics measured with the 4 PVs configuration, in the second part with the 8 PVs configuration. Inside each set at the beginning each single day profile is presented singularly, and then the totals for the 4 days run (Table 1).

Table 1. HP test runs.

PV setting	Day(s)	Baseline RenPercent	DC4Cities RenPercent	RenPercent Delta	RenPercent Delta%
4 PVs config (Max 1KW)	Day 1	64.81%	67.39%	2.58	3.98%
	Day 2	55.69%	58.90%	3.21	5.76%
	Day 3	54.45%	56.74%	2.29	4.20%
	Day 4	45.74%	47.55%	1.81	3.95%
	Trial days	55.17%	57.64%	2.47	4.47%
8 PVs config (Max 2KW)	Day 1	68.20%	70.34%	2.14	3.13%
	Day 2	61.85%	64.68%	2.83	4.57%
	Day 3	58.57%	61.65%	3.08	5.25%
	Day 4	53.99%	57.26%	2.27	6.05%
	Trial days	60.65%	63.52%	2.87	4.73%
	Simulator Apr-Oct	62.40%	65.19%	2.79	4.47%

It's clear that DC4Cities is saving a significant amount of energy (over 13 % reduced consumption) and therefore the efficiency of the whole application (since the total work done is not significantly affected – ranges between +1 % to −2.78 % with respect to SLA) is definitely increasing. The improvement ranges between 12.29 % in the worst day and 16.87 % in the best day for 4 PVs configuration (almost identical data were measured in 8 PVs setting).

5   Related Work

Our work is an amalgamation of three different areas: research about integrating renewable energy into smart city energy supply and distribution, also related to the integration of renewables into the smart grid. The second area is energy-aware operation of DCs via workload control, and the third concerns with energy aware contracts of and with DCs.

Brenna et al. [7] look into energy challenges of smart cities, including how to increase the share of distributed energy sources at the smart city's power consumption; however, the distribution of available power among consumers is not a topic. The same applies to [14] who deal with integrating intermittent energy sources into the smart grid, using demand response. Also here, the notion that power is a limited resource and therefore may require maximum consumption objectives is not analysed. [12] suggest energy budget optimization for households with shiftable and non-shiftable loads by scheduling the shiftable load and buying/selling energy under different information assumptions. Although the value of this work is high for DC4Cities as regarding shiftable load the setting is comparable, the contract option was preferred due to the high reliability of reaction. [16] report experiences regarding demand response with data centres and shifting options similar to the DC4Cities approach, however, this endeavour is restricted to demand response only, not the task to retrace the curve of renewable power supply to the highest degree possible with DC power demand.

In [11], the authors propose GreenSwitch, a model-based approach for scheduling dynamically the workload and selecting the source of energy to use. The authors focus on the trade-offs involved in powering DCs with solar and/or wind energy, and propose an implementation of their solar powered mini DC. [5] model data centre flexibility in the context of demand/response schemes. The authors propose using the models to combine several different DC power adaptation strategies to collectively reach a requested demand/response target power demand. In contrast to these approaches, we propose the possibility to schedule the workload more fine-grained, at application level. In [9], the authors present Plug4Green, an energy aware VM manager with a focus on flexibility and adaptability to new scenarios. Its main capacity is to migrate VMs and manage servers on/off state to save energy while respecting an extensive SLA. Plug4Green is re-used as a IaaS VM manager in the presented work (see Sect. 2.2.1). A similar tool is OpenStack Neat.

Finally, the question of how to incentivize DCs in order to modify their behaviour according to the availability of renewable energy arises: It relates to both, to work in the area of SLA induced workload planning as well as energy aware contracts of DCs with their power providers. There is some research of the authors about how to turn SLAs into GreenSLAs in order to increase the flexibility of the DC, e.g. [6]; and the authors build on this knowledge base to a high degree. Using SLAs as constraints to operate DC services like in [13] helped a lot understanding the problem of job scheduling but fell short of the incentive aspect. Apart from the relation between the DC and its customers, in order to make DCs be interested in following renewable power patterns, they need to have corresponding contracts with their energy service providers. There is a lot of literature on different options how to make any type of customer comply with demand response schemes like in [1, 8]. But regarding the specific also technical challenges of integrating DCs in demand response schemes, again the authors need to refer to their own work, e.g. [2, 4].

6   Conclusions

This paper presented a vision on how to maximize the share of renewable energy sources when operating a DC given the conditions of a smart city aiming at a local low-carbon power supply. It was shown that this is not only technically feasible but that there is also design options for the relation between the DC and the smart city which offer incentives for the DC to participate in the scheme.

However, the approach is obviously dependent on the individual technical infrastructure and the real applications running in the DC as well as on financial and geographical conditions of the smart city where it is located. In order to evaluate the feasibility of the presented approach complementing trials were carried through, which showed that the concept is viable. These trials are only first examples which need to be extended to other DCs with various business models and configurations in order to gain a deeper understanding of the opportunities of the DC4Cities approach.

Acknowledgements. This work was carried out within the European Project DC4Cities (FP7-ICT-2013.6.2).

References

1. Aalami, H., Moghaddam, M.P., Yousefi, G.: Demand response modeling considering interruptible/curtailable loads and capacity market programs. Appl. Energy 87(1), 243–250 (2010). Elsevier

2. Basmadjian, R., Niedermeier, F., Lovasz, G., de Meer, H., Klingert, S.: GreenSDAs leveraging power adaption collaboration between energy provider and data centres. In: Proceedings of 3rd Conference on Sustainable Internet and ICT for Sustainability. IEEE, pp. 1–9 (2013)

3. Beloglazov, A., Buyya, R.: OpenStack Neat: a framework for dynamic and energy-efficient consolidation of virtual machines in openstack clouds. In: Fox, G.C., Walker, D.W. (eds.) Concurrency and Computation: Practice and Experience. Wiley, Hoboken (2014)

4. Berl, A., Klingert, S., Beck, M., de Meer, H.: Integrating data centres into demand-response management: a local case study. In: 39th Conference of Industrial Electronics Society (IECON), pp. 4762–4767. IEEE (2013)

5. Berl, A., Lovász, G., von Tüllenburg, F., de Meer, H.: Modelling power adaption flexibility of data centres for demand-response management. In: Pierson, J.-M., Da Costa, G., Dittmann, L. (eds.) EE-LSDS 2013. LNCS, vol. 8046, pp. 63–66. Springer, Heidelberg (2013)

6. Botero, J.B., Klingert, S., Hesselbach-Serra, X., Falcone, A., Giuliani, G.: GreenSLAs: providing energy consumption flexibility in DCs through energy-aware contracts. In: 2nd International Conference on Smart Grids and Green IT Systems (SMARTGREENS), pp. 119–122. SCITEPRESS (2013)

7. Brenna, M., Falvo, M.C., Foiadelli, F., Martirano, L., Massaro, F., Poli, D., Vaccaro, A.: Challenges in energy systems for the smart-cities of the future. In: Proceedings of 2nd IEEE EnergyCon Conference, pp. 755-762. IEEE (2012)

8. Chao, H.: Demand response in wholesale electricity markets: the choice of customer baseline. J. Regul. Econ. 39, 68–88 (2011). Springer

9. Dupont, C., Hermenier, F., Schulze, T., Basmadjian, R., Somov, A., Giuliani, G.: Plug4Green: a flexible energy aware VM manager to fit data centre particularities. J. AdHoc Netw. 25(1), 505–519 (2015). Special Issue on Energy-Aware Data Centres

10. European Commission: Investing in the Development of Low Carbon Technologies (SET-Plan). COM 519 final (2009)

11. Goiri, I., Katsak, W., Le, K., Nguyen, T., Bianchini, R.: Parasol and greenswitch: managing datacenters powered by renewable energy. SIGARCH Comput. Archit. News 41(1), 51–64 (2013)

12. Liu, Y., Yuen, C., Ul Hassan, N., Huang, S., Yu, R., Xie, S.: Electricity cost minimization for a microgrid with distributed energy resource under different information availability. IEEE Trans. Ind. Electron. 62(4), 1–12 (2014)

13. Sakellarriou, R., Yarmolenko, V.: Job scheduling on the grid: towards SLA-based scheduling. In: Grandinetti, L. (ed.) High Performance Computing and Grids in Action Advance in Parallel Computing, vol. 16, pp. 207–222. IOS, Amsterdam (2009)

14. Sioshansi, F.P. (ed.): Smart Grid: Integrating Renewable, Distributed & Efficient Energy. Elsevier, Philadelphia (2012)

15. Soundararajan, V., Anderson, J.M.: The impact of management operations on the virtualized datacenter. SIGARCH Comput. Archit. News 38(3), 326–337 (2010)

16. Wierman, A., Liu, Z., Liu, I., Mohsenian-Rad, H.: Opportunities and challenges for data center demand response. In: Proceedings of International Green Computing Conference (IGCC), pp.1–10 (2014)

Automatic Validation for Crowd Simulation: Test Suite for a Pedestrian Simulator Based on Different Scenarios

Yayun Zhou[✉], Wolfram Klein, and Hermann Georg Mayer

Siemens AG, Corporate Technology, CT RTC AUC,
Otto-Hahn-Ring 6, 81739 Munich, Germany
{yayun.zhou,wolfram.klein,hermann-georg.mayer}@siemens.com

Abstract. Evacuation simulation and especially the determination of evacuation times is a very complex task. Moreover the prognosis of place and time of critical bottlenecks within the building during the evacuation is critical due to complex building structures and the correct pedestrian behavior. Therefore, an extensive validation and calibration of the simulation algorithms is an indispensable requirement for every simulation tool. An automatic test suite for different scenarios will facilitate this task yielding in proven, automated and reproducible results. The microscopic pedestrian simulator tested in this paper is developed by our group. The tool can be used to guide the crowd evacuation and prepare respond plans for emergent situations as reference to city council and law enforcement agency. It is important that the simulation results reveal the true behavior of pedestrian; for certain precaution actions can be taken in order to guarantee the safety of the crowd.

In this paper, we documented the performance of our simulator tested with all 14 scenarios proposed by the RiMEA (Richtlinie fur Mikroskopische Entfluchtungs-Analysen) guideline. The test results show that our simulator passes all the tests. Moreover, our pedestrian simulator constantly improves its performance by cooperating with construction companies and government departments running on-site tests with first-hand data. Now it covers even emergency scenarios such as fire/smoke and floods.

1 Introduction

Nowadays, more and more people are moving from small villages to big cities forming metropolises worldwide. The increasing population density and limited living space make metropolises top targets for terror attacks and make them vulnerable to natural disasters. A key task for smart city is to make the city safer to its residents. Central stations, skyscrapers and sport stadiums should be designed to reduce risk by removing congestion, reducing crowd density at hot spots, minimizing evacuation times or maximizing throughput. In those cases, a simulation software which simulates the crowd movement, predicts the evacuation time and identifies the possible bottleneck is very helpful to design smart

© Springer International Publishing Switzerland 2015
M. Helfert et al. (Eds.): Smartgreens 2015 and Vehits 2015, CCIS 579, pp. 146–164, 2016.
DOI: 10.1007/978-3-319-27753-0_8

buildings. As for existing non-smart-buildings, the pedestrian simulator can provide insight in evacuation time and aids to prepare respond plans.

Because of its various applications and convincing results, adopting pedestrian flow simulation is becoming a popular topic in designing public transport systems and large infrastructure facilities [5, 9, 11]. There are two major types of models adopted by pedestrian behavior simulation: microscopic models and macroscopic models. The so-called microscopic models simulate the behavior of a single pedestrian while the macroscopic models consider flows of pedestrian entities. The macroscopic models are often used to study large scale behavior and typically use network-based models (e.g. [6]) or fluid dynamics models (e.g. [7]). The microscopic models on the other hand are often interested in local small scale behavior of pedestrian flows. The microscopic models can be further distinguished into force models (e.g. [2]), discrete-choice models (e.g. [1]) and agent-based models (e.g. [14]).

Despite of all the advantages and numerous researches done before, the features mentioned above can only be exploited if the simulation tool fulfills several technical demands: First of all, the simulator should provide results with a well defined accuracy: The simulation results should be investigated and compared with real measurements. For certain cases, the simulation model and parameter should be calibrated in order to achieve better performance. A second critical limitation is the simulation speed, i.e. time needed until a simulation result is available. Moreover, the usability of the software also affects its acceptance. After all, the potential users are most likely to be architects or government officer who are neither familiar with mathematical modeling nor have programing experiences. Therefore, the abstract results should be properly visualized to help users link simulated scenarios to real situations.

Based on these prerequisites, our group developed a pedestrian simulation environment named Crowd Control, which has already been used for several evacuation projects in the field of trains and buildings [3, 10]. In the newly released version of our simulator, more scenario-models such as fire/smoke, and flood are integrated, which allow our simulator to meet various simulation demands. In order to ensure its accuracy after the extension, certain tests must be performed. In this paper, we test our newly released simulator with the test scenarios proposed by the RiMEA guidelines [13] and document the test results. With the user-friendly graphical interface, we are able to create the test scenario by simple mouse-clicks. The test results show that our simulator passes all the tests within short simulation time. Besides, the 2D and 3D visualization kits of our simulator allow us to check the simulation results; a detailed analysis can be done by exporting the results to Excel, e.g.

The remaining of the paper is organized as follows: In Sect. 2 the theoretical background and the simulation model are briefly introduced; In Sect. 3 the software architecture is sketched; In Sect. 4 the test scenarios and test results are documented; In Sect. 6 the performance of the simulator is evaluated and a conclusion is drawn based on the simulation results.

2   Simulation Model

The simulator tested in this paper is developed based on a discrete, microscopic force model. The simulation model is a cellular automaton on a hexagonal grid (Fig. 1). At each time step each cell has a certain state: It is either empty or occupied by a pedestrian or a fixed obstacle. The positions are updated according to a set of rules [10]. In comparison to continuous simulation, a discrete model is much faster and does not suffer from artifacts such as instability factors like non realistic oscillatory behavior. In addition, it is easier to include interactions of the pedestrian with dynamic events like closing or opening gates or catastrophic events like fire spread, since calculations can be restricted to discrete events in time. While macroscopic pedestrian simulation is predominantly focused on producing statistical data (like flows and densities), microscopic simulation can help to identify even the behavior of single pedestrians. Of course one has to be aware that the behavior of a specific single individual can never be anticipated, but the interaction of a larger number of individuals can be emulated by microscopic simulation very well [5].

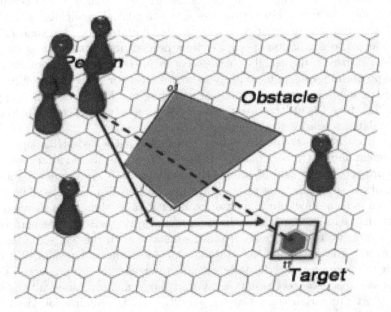

Fig. 1. Schematic sketch of a cellular automaton simulating microscopic pedestrian dynamics.

In the simulation model, each pedestrian is initially assigned with an individual velocity, which is considered as a normally distributed variable, whose average and variance are given parameters. In each time step, pedestrians adjust their speed during the simulation as responses to the change of situation. For instance, a pedestrian slows down his movement when the crowd density is too high (for example congestion). The observation area is divided in hexagon cells and each cell is in a certain state for each time step: It is as mentioned above either empty or occupied and an occupied cell cannot be entered. In every time step a person can move one cell forward or stay at the current cell, but cannot move farther than one cell. The update scheme of the cellular automaton has to guarantee, that pedestrians with a higher speed are allowed to move more often than pedestrians with a lower speed. Thus a slow person might not move at each time step compared to faster moving person. Once the set of persons which are allowed to move is determined, they are updated sequentially. The movement rule is similar to the so-called static floor field cellular automaton [2], in which the movement is determined by a potential f. In the simplest case, the movement rule for a single pedestrian is purely deterministic: Find the unoccupied neighboring cell with the minimal total potential value $f_{total} = f_{navigation}(x; y) + f_{pedestrian}(x; y)$. In this equation, the $f_{pedestrian}(x; y)$ represents the force that the pedestrians repel each other, while the $f_{navigation}(x; y)$ represents the force that the pedestrians are attracted by the target. For more details about the simulation model, please refer to [10].

3   Software Architecture

In this section, we will introduce the architecture of our simulator. Figure 2 shows the main components of the software and its data flow. The software comprises a simulation kernel, a graphical user interface, a tool for statistical evaluation and a 3D visualization. The graphical user interface enables the user to create specific scenarios using tools provided by the software. Besides, the scenarios also can be extracted from architectural drawings [12] or data bases. In addition, it is possible to couple the simulation with third party tools, such as Microsoft Excel, which is very useful for processing results and analyzing data. Furthermore,

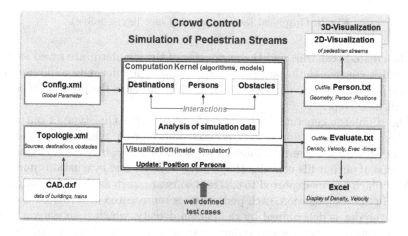

Fig. 2. Software Architecture.

the tool has been calibrated with many real measurements and recently extended by adding more items like fire model, flood model to extend its functionality.

Figure 3 shows the graphical user interface, in which user can create a scenario by adding source, destination, walls, obstacles and staircases. Besides, it provides the user possibilities to create more vivid scenarios by add 3D elements, such as trees. The recent version also allows user to add extra dynamic models such as fire spots to simulate the pedestrian behavior under certain emergency situations. All the objects can be configured by adjusting the parameters. For instance, the user can assign a source (the place where a group of pedestrians are generated) with a pedestrian velocity profile. In this way, sources representing pedestrians with different ages can be generated. In this paper, all the test scenarios are created by this graphical user interface.

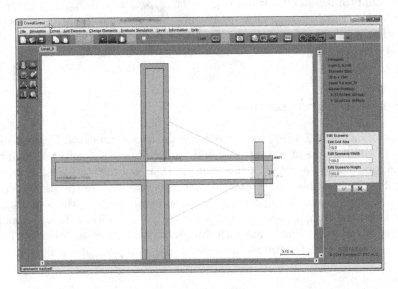

Fig. 3. Graphical User Interface (Color figure online).

The created scenarios and the parameter of the simulator are saved as XML files, which contain the topology and model relevant information. Those input files are passed to the computation kernel, which updates the position of persons for each time step.

The simulator generates two types of output files. One type of output file contains the geometry and person position information, which is used to visualize the crowd movement combined with a 2D or 3D visualization engine. The other type of output file contains the density, velocity and evacuation time information, which can be exported to external software, such as Excel to analyze the results. In 2D visualization, each pedestrian is represented as a colored dot. The color of the dot is determined by the person density, which is shown via a very intuitive coloring scheme green yellow - red for a small, medium or high density. In this way, critical spots can be easily identified by the presence of red color.

The 3D visualization is realized by an interface to the 3D-Game-Engine Irrlicht. The computed output file of the simulation storing the geometry and all persons positions at all time steps is directly taken over by the Irrlicht-Engine. The 3D visualization is capable of displaying stairs, doors, narrow corridors, passages, ramps and pillars. It helps the user interpret and analyze the results directly. Similar to the 2D-visualization, crowds or congestion can be seen and discussed directly by that coloring scheme.

Figure 4 shows an example of a 3D visualization. The user can follow the movement of the persons in a familiar, well known 3D-environment without any delay. The control panel on the right side allows the user to navigate and move in the 3D-Game-Engine to gain a better observation perspective. The zoom functionality enables the user to analyze details of the scenarios. The animation control allows the user to review the simulation or analyze the situation of a specific time. Using menus under the control panel, the user can even identify and walk as one specific person through the scenario. All those functions are developed to increase the usability, which as mentioned in the first section is very crucial for the acceptance of a simulator.

Fig. 4. Example of a 3D Visualization (Color figure online).

4   RiMEA Test Scenarios and Test Results

As mentioned in the first section, a pedestrian simulation tool must fulfill several technical demands and certain guidelines, such as the IMO (International Maritime Organization) [8] guidelines and the RiMEA (Richtlinie für Mikroskopische Entfluchtungs-Analysen) guidelines [13]. According to the Rimea guideline, 14 scenarios should be tested in order to check the performance of a person stream simulator and verify its functionality. The test scenarios in this paper are generated according to the Rimea-Standard V.2.2.1. The test results and their corresponding parameters for the concrete application to the Crowd Control simulation tool from Siemens are documented in this paper. Due to the special grid property of our simulator, in addition to the standard RiMEA tests, the tests are repeated several times in different rotation angle and shifted horizontally and vertically to prove the robustness of the simulator. Besides that, the scenarios are tested with different grid sizes.

There are some important assumptions in the RiMEA guideline. The first assumption is the velocity of person group with different ages on the ground. The velocities are defined in the following Table 1 [15]:

Table 1. Velocities on the ground according to Weidmann.

Person group (Age)	Velocities on the ground (m/s)	
	Minimum	Maximum
under 30	0.58	1.61
30 to 50	1.41	1.54
Over 50	0.68	1.41
Person with limited mobility	0.46	0.76

The second assumption is the velocity of person group with different ages climbing up and down the staircases. The velocities are defined in the following Table 2 [4]:

Table 2. Velocities on the staircase according to Fruin.

Person group (Age)	Velocities on the staricase (m/s)			
	Climbing down		Climbing up	
	Indoor	Outdoor	Indoor	Outdoor
under 30	0.76	0.81	0.55	0.58
30 to 50	0.65	0.78	0.50	0.58
Over 50	0.55	0.59	0.42	0.42
Person with limited mobility	0.42		0.32	

All tests are repeated several times in order to identify the influence of the basic grid to the simulation results. The tests are repeated in the following orders:

- by rotating the topology in different angles
- by shifting the topology vertically
- by shifting the topology horizontally
- by using different grid sizes for the basic hexagonal grid

The first 3 tests are single pedestrian tests. In the first test, it should be proven, that a person with a given velocity ($1.33\,m/s$) runs through a 2 m wide, 40 m long corridor within the given time. The expected time is between 26 to 34 s.

Inaccuracy tolerance of the person position is 0.4 m (body size, 1 s reaction time). Inaccuracy tolerance of velocity is 5 %. In the second test, the person retains the same given velocity as the first test climbing up a staircase. It should be proven, that a person climbs up a 2 m wide, 10 m long (the slope length) stair with a defined velocity in a given time range. In the third test, the person retains the given velocity climbing down a staircase. It should be proven, that a person climbs down a 2 m wide, 10 m long (the slope length) stair with a defined velocity in a given time range. Table 3 shows the test results of the first 3 test scenarios. From the table, we can see that all the results of repeated tests (shift, rotate topology and change grid size) lie in the given time range.

Table 3. Test results of RiMEA test 1–3.

RiMEA test number	Tested time of simulator (s)		Allowed time range (s)	
	Minimum	Maximum	Minimum	Maximum
Test 1	30.27	32.72	26	34
Test 2	11.63	12.89	10.84	14.17
Test 3	8.69	9.25	7.22	9.44

RiMEA test 4 is to check the relationship of a special flow with the person density. The special flow with respect to the person density is given:

$$\Theta_{s,max} = \rho \cdot 1.34 \cdot (1 - e^{-1.913 \cdot (\frac{1}{\rho} - \frac{1}{t \cdot 5.4})}) \qquad (1)$$

In order to realize the test, a ring is generated with internal radius 70 m and external radius 74 m (Fig. 5(a)). 8 person blocks each generates 5000 persons and the persons walk in circles. The ring radius remains constant, but the number of persons increases as time goes by. The test results are plotted in the diagram (Fig. 5(b)). We can see that the test results fit the Weidmann diagram very well.

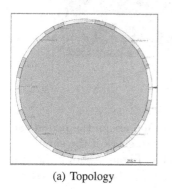

(a) Topology

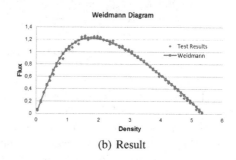

(b) Result

Fig. 5. RiMEA test 4.

RiMEA test 5 is to check the reaction time of each person. In this test, 10 persons stand in an 8 m × 5 m room with a 1 m wide exit in the middle of the 5 m long wall. The reaction time is to be set uniformly distributed in the interval of 10 s and 100 s. We need to verify that each reaction time corresponds to a person. In this test, our simulator generates 10 persons in the interval [10, 100], since the first person is not generated at 10 s, the time interval between two persons reaction time is 90/11. We can compare the reaction time of each person with the expected value $10 + i \cdot d$, where i is the index of the person and d is the time interval between two persons reaction time. The simulation results confirm the conclusion.

In RiMEA test 6, 20 pedestrians walk along a 2 m × 10 m corridor and turn left, go further along a 2 m × 10 m corridor. There should be no person go though the walls. To carry out this test, we set three areas outside the corridor (three rectangular areas: outside top left, outside top right and outside bottom) to check if the number of person in each area equals to zero. We also repeated this test to test the robustness of the simulator and all the tests fulfill the requirement. Figure 6 shows one of these tests.

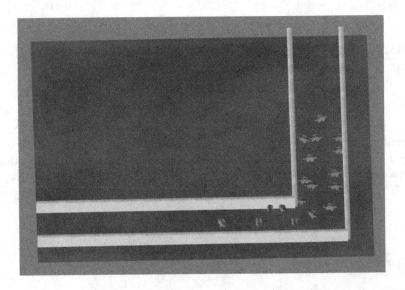

Fig. 6. RiMEA test 6.

In RiMEA test 7, we choose a group of 50 persons and assign the pedestrian velocity according to Table 1 listed above. The task is to check if the simulated velocity corresponds to the velocity listed in the table. Figure 7 shows the test results. From this figure, we can see that the minimal velocity and maximal velocity of each group lie in the given range listed in Table 1.

In RiMEA test 8, a test topology with three floors is given (Fig. 8). Each room contains 4 persons and has a 1 m wide door. This topology is adopted to

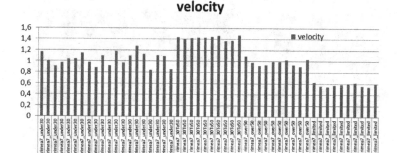

Fig. 7. Result of RiMEA test 7.

1. Floor   2. and 3. Floor

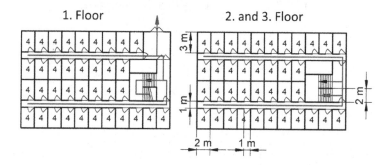

Fig. 8. Topology of RiMEA test 8.

test the influence of parameter in each person on the total evacuation time. If the parameter of each person is changed, the total evacuation time should also change correspondingly. In this test, the persons are assigned with different velocities for each simulation run. We need to check if the evacuation time is within the given tolerance. We also repeat the tests with different topology orientation and location, the evacuation time variation is under the given tolerance.

In RiMEA test 9, 1000 persons with same figure size and no reaction delay are uniformly distributed in a public room with four exits. The topology of the test room is shown in the following picture (Fig. 9). Assume that people in this group are all adults and their velocities are set according to Table 1. In the first test, the time of the last people leaves the room is documented. Then two exits are closed and the test is repeated to check the time of the last people leaves the room again. Then we calculate the ratio of the evacuation time with four doors open and the evacuation time with two doors open. If the ratio lies between 0.4 and 0.6, the simulator passes the test. In our test, the ratio lines between 0.49 and 0.56.

For RiMEA test 10, we construct a test topology (Fig. 10) with a corridor, 12 rooms each with a 0.9 m door are located along the corridor. 23 adults with no reaction delay and defined velocity according to the Table 1 are scattered in

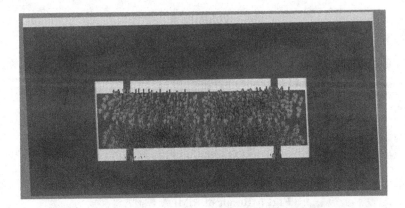

Fig. 9. RiMEA test 9 with 4 doors open.

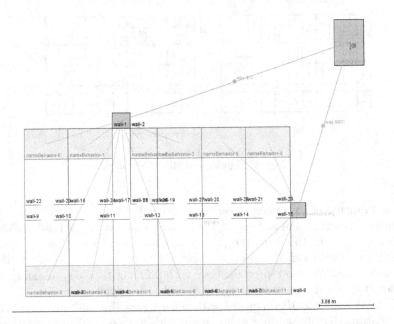

Fig. 10. Test topology for RiMEA test 10.

rooms. The people in room $1, 2, 3, 4, 7, 8, 9$ and 10 are assigned to use the main exit and the remaining people are assigned to use the second exit. The expected result is that the people behave just like the assignment and leave the region using the assigned exit. We set a tripwire in the corridor. The tripwire is located between room 5 and room 11, which separates two exits. If the number of persons who cross this line is 0, it means that persons use the assigned exit to leave the room. In all the tests, no person crosses the tripwire.

RiMEA test 11 is about the choice of emergency route. The test topology is a public room with two exits: exit 1 and exit 2 (Fig. 11). 1000 adults with no reaction delay are gathered on the left side of the room (achieve the maximal person density). The velocities of the people are set according to the Table 1. The people should leave the room through two exits. The expected result is that the people prefer to leave the room through a nearer exit (in this case, exit 1), but if the exit 1 is over-crowded, people should choose the alternative exit (exit 2) to leave the room.

In this test two tripwires are defined to count the number of persons crossing these lines. The number of the persons who cross the tripwire 1 stands for the number of persons who leave the room with exit 1, and the number of the persons who cross the tripwire 2 stands for the number of the persons who leave the room with exit 2. The test criteria is to check the number of persons using exit 1 and exit 2 respectively. The simulator passes the test if two criteria are satisfied:

1. More persons use exit 1 than exit 2;
2. At least 20 % of the persons use exit 2;

In all the repeated tests, the ratio of the persons using the exit 2 lies between 22.6 % and 42.4 %, the simulator passes this test as well.

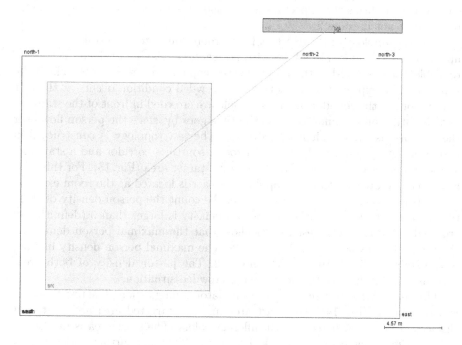

Fig. 11. Test topology for RiMEA test 11.

The test topology of RiMEA test 12 is two rooms connected by a narrow corridor (Fig. 12). 150 adults with no reaction delay are gathered on the left side of room 1 and room 2 has an exit. These 150 people in room should leave the room through exit in room 2. Since the corridor is very narrow, the person

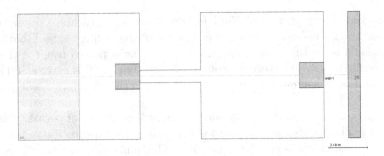

Fig. 12. Test topology for RiMEA test 12.

flow is limited. The expected result is that the crowded condition occurs only in room 1 but not in room 2. For this test, we select two areas (one is in room 1 right before the narrow corridor and the other is in room 2). The person density of these two areas are checked to see where the crowded condition occurs. The simulation results show that the maximal person density in region 2 lies between 1.40 to 1.96, while the average person density in region 1 lies between 3.33 to 4.63, which confirms the expectation that the crowded condition occurs only in room 1 but not in room 2.

The test topology of RiMEA test 13 is a room connected to a staircase toward upstairs by a corridor. 150 adults with no reaction delay and velocity according to Table 2 are gathered in the room. These people leave the room by taking the staircase. The expected result is that the crowded condition occurs at the exit of the room to the corridor. Besides, people are crowded in front of the staircase and the situation becomes worse as the time goes by, since the person flow over the staircase is smaller than the corridor. The test topology is constructed in two levels: at the first level, there is a room, source, a corridor and a staircase; at the second level, there is a staircase and a target area (Fig. 13). For this test, we define two areas in the test topology. Area 1 is located at the room exit and area 2 is located in front of the staircase. We count the person density of these two areas to check if the maximal person density is larger than 3 (definition of crowded situation). The test results show that the maximal person density at the room exit lies between 3.24 and 4.28. The maximal person density in front of the staircase lies between 3.78 and 4.72. The person density of both areas exceeds the threshold of the definition of crowded situation.

The last RiMEA test refers to the simulator configuration. The test topology is shown below (Fig. 14). The start area and the targeted area are located at the second floor and marked with different colors. The start area is marked as red and the targeted area is marked as green. They are further connected by two staircases and a long corridor on the ground floor. The task is to check how a pedestrian chooses his route: he chooses a long route which is on the same floor or a short route though the staircases and the corridor on the ground floor. For different simulators, different choices can be made (short, long, mixed or configurable). Our simulator supports the version "short". That means all persons select the shortest path. In this test, we construct a two levels topology:

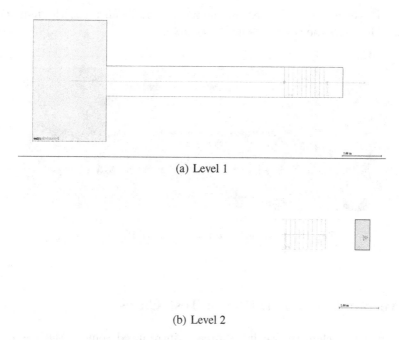

(a) Level 1

(b) Level 2

Fig. 13. Test topology of RiMEA test 13.

Fig. 14. Test topology for RiMEA test 14 (Color figure online).

the first level has two staircases and no other obstacles; the source and target areas are located at the second floor. Besides the staircases to downstairs, there is a corridor connecting these two areas at the same level (Fig. 15). The simulator passes the test if no person crosses the tripwire set in the second floor corridor. The tests are repeated by rotating, shifting the topology as well as changing the cell size to verify the robustness of the simulator. In all tests, the number of persons who cross the tripwire equals to zero.

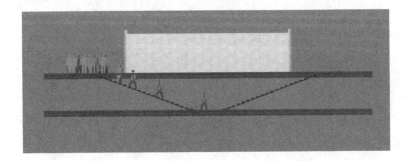

Fig. 15. Constructed topology for RiMEA test 14.

5   Automated Generation of Test Cases

In the previous chapters we have already introduced some variations of the existing, static test scenarios: due the discrete nature of the simulator (equidistant hexagonal grid, Round Robin movements of pedestrians etc.) the scenarios should be tested by applying rigid transforms, i.e. a combination of rotations and shifts. This can already be done with the test environment described above. In a loop around the actual application of the simulation, shifts and rotations are combined to change the alignment of the complete scenario relative to the grid. This significantly improves the relevance of evacuation times and eliminates outliers in the simulation data, which are caused by grid-based aliasing artifacts.

A more extensive testing can be performed if not only the alignment of complete scenarios are changed, but if the elements of the scenarios themselves can be changed between different runs of the simulator (or even during the run). In order to enable such a feature, we decided to implement a domain specific (scripting) language for the definition of simulator elements. The language was implemented with Java and it is based on method chaining. Although this concept should be used carefully, it provides a good readability for end users since it resembles the natural construction process. The following example illustrates the usage of the scripting language for construction tasks:

```
boundary(30, 10);
location("src").polygon(rectangle(p(1, 1), p(9, 9)));
location("dst").polygon(rectangle(p(21, 1), p(29, 9)));
personBlock(10).from("src").to("trg").inTimeSpan(0, 0);
```

Those four lines of code construct a simple, yet working scenario, which is displayed in Fig. 16(a). The scenario consists of a pedestrian source "src" and a

(a) Topology   (b) Result

Fig. 16. Automatically generated scenario.

destination "dst". Then ten persons will be generated at the very beginning of
the simulation time and they will try to reach the destination.

In a similar way, walls and obstacles can be added to the scenario by defining
their geometrical form (Fig. 16(b)):

```
wall("w0").polyline(p(14, 0), p(14, 8));
wall("w1").polyline(p(16, 2), p(16, 10));
```

This forces the pedestrians onto a detour between source and destination, and
hence will increase the evacuation time. Instead of providing fixed coordinates,
the flexibility can be increased by using variables changing their values in loops.

```
for (int y = 0; y <= 8; y += 0.5)
{
basic_scenario();
wall("w0").polyline(p(14, 0), p(14, y));
}
```

Now the length of the first wall is gradually increased for 0.5 units in each run
(Fig. 17), while the rest of the scenario remains static (same elements as before,
constructed in method basic_scenario). By using this simple option of adding
dynamic elements, we now get 16 different scenarios, which will produce an
individual evacuation time. In the same way we can now construct an abundant
variety of test for different sizes of stair cases, different numbers or behaviors
of occupants and so on. Therefore tests will become more realistic since they
will cover a broader variety of options found in reality. In addition, the loops
containing the dynamic changes of the scenario can easily be distributed to be
computed on different CPUs or even in a cloud environment. Moreover, the
results of each test can be checked automatically, e.g. if the evacuation time is
less/greater than a certain threshold value (test passed/failed).

Apart from testing, the domain specific language can also be applied for optimization. Given the situation above one could formulate conditions for an optimal scenario: like keep the size of a stair case as small as possible while minimizing the evacuation time. The former condition influences the costs of a building,
while the latter improves the safety. Clearly their might be often situation where
some parameters can only be optimized at the the cost of weakening another.
We already presented a practical example of such an optimization in [12].

In the following example, the idea is to add a coffee bar to a commercial
building in the center of the lobby. For evaluating the evacuation, 90 occupants

(a) Topology   (b) Result

Fig. 17. Automatically generated scenario.

have been routed through the building to the exit near the coffee bar. We varied
the layout of the coffee bar and compared the evacuation times with the original
layout (no coffee bar). In order to avoid random deviations, we performed 50
simulation runs for each scenario.

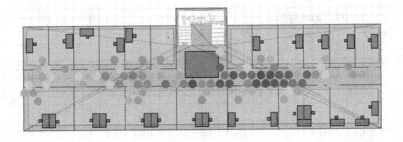

Fig. 18. Modification with a coffee bar of 4 × 3 m.

As one can derive from Fig. 18, some issues regarding the modification can
already be detected visually. In this case, a traffic jam forms in front of the
coffee bar, particularly in the right wing of the building (due to more persons
occupying the right wing). A more detailed analysis can be done by looking at
the following table of results (Table 4).

Table 4. Evaluation of modifications.

Scenario	Size (Bar)	Egress time
A	without	183.4 s
B	2 × 2 m	183.1 s
C	2 × 3 m	182.7 s
D	4 × 2 m	189.4 s
E	4 × 3 m	196.2 s

There is a significant influence on the evacuation time for the last two scenarios D and E compared to the original layout A (Δ_t: 6.0 s and 12.8 s, respectively).
Therefore, the architect would probably not choose one of those layouts. However, the slight differences in the evacuation times of the remaining scenarios B

and C are most probably due to statistical noise ($<1.0\,$s), and therefore can be omitted. So in order to maximize the size of the coffee bar while still providing a safe egress, a good choice would be scenario D.

6   Conclusions

In this paper, all tests listed in the RiMEA guideline are implemented and used to test the Crowd Control Simulator. The tests are repeated by rotating, shifting the topology as well as changing the cell size to verify the robustness of the simulator. The test results show that the simulator passes all the tests, which indicates its reliability and robustness. Apart from the mentioned RiMEA test cases, a new scripting language was introduced to enable automated generation of test scenarios. Simulation results are automatically compared with given result sets by the Java JUnit framework. These test cases are regularly checked after each software update. Selected test cases are checked at each update of the source repository. An automated notification system was installed to remind developers on testing once the status of the repository has changed.

Our simulator offers architectures, city planners, authorities and other potential users a powerful tool to get precise and valuable simulations results, in order to improve the infrastructure planning and the safety of passengers. This new version of the simulator not only allows the user to create a test scenario by using its graphical user interface, but it is also possible to import BIM-IFC files (Building Information Modeling) in order to accelerated the engineering process [12]. With the newly integrated emission model (such as fire, smoke) and flood model, the simulator can calculate an optimal escape route for emergent situation provided that the building is equipped with sensors and detectors. There are enough applications for a robust reliable pedestrian behavior simulation tool like our Crowd Control Simulator. It is highly desirable to complement the RiMEA tests with scenarios based on measured data. However, collecting this data and finding appropriate measures for qualitative assessment of simulation results is still an open field of research. It is also the interests of the authors to collect more test scenarios, on which different models can be tested, compared and calibrated.

References

1. Antonini, G., Bierlaire, M., Weber, M.: Discrete choice models of pedestrian walking behavior. Res. Part B: Methodol. **40**, 667–687 (2006)
2. Burstedde, C., Kaluck, K., Schadschneider, A., Zittartzl, A.: Simulation of pedestrian dynamics using a two dimensional cellular automation. Physica A: Stat. Mech. Appl. **295**, 507–525 (2001)
3. Davidich, M., Köster, G.: Towards automatic and robust adjustment of human behavioral parameters in a pedestrian stream model to measured data. Saf. Sci. **50**, 1253–1260 (2012)

4. Fruin, J.: Pedestrian planning and design. Metropolitan Association of Urban Designers and Environmental Planners (1971). http://books.google.de/books?id=AydSAAAAMAAJ
5. Gilg, A., Klein, W., Mayer, H., Witte, F.: Intelligent crowd control, the various use cases in public mass transit. In: International Conference on Railway Engineering (2014)
6. Hamacher, H., Tjandra, S.A.: Mathematical modelling of evacuation problems: a state of the art. Pedestrian and Evacuation Dynamics (2002)
7. Helbing, D.: A fluid-dynamic model for the movement of pedestrians. Complex Systems 6, 391–415 (1992)
8. IMO: Guidelines of the international maritime organisation imo (2014). http://www.imo.org/Pages/home.aspx
9. Kneidl, A., Hartmann, D., Mayer, H., Borrmann, A.: A holistic multi-scale approach for simulation o pedestrian. In: Proceedings of the 6th International Conference on Pedestrian and Evacuation Dynamics (2012)
10. Köster, G., Hartmann, D., Klein, W.: Microscopic pedestrian simulations: from passenger exchange times to regional evacuation. In: Hu, B., Morasch, K., Pickl, S., Siegle, M. (eds.) Operations Research Proceedings, pp. 571–576. Springer, Heidelberg (2010)
11. Lämmel, G., Rieser, M., Nagel, K.: Large scale microscopic evacuation simulation. In: Klingsch, W.W.F., Rogsch, C., Schadschneider, A., Schreckenberg, M. (eds.) Pedestrian and Evacuation Dynamics, pp. 547–553. Springer, Heidelberg (2008)
12. Mayer, H., Klein, W., Frey, C., Daum, S., Kielar, P., Borrmann, A.: Pedestrian simulation based on bim data. In: 2014 ASHRAE/IBPSA-USA Building Simulation Conference (2014)
13. RiMEA e.V.: Rimea guidline on evacuation scenarios (2009). http://www.rimea.de/fileadmin/files/dok/analyse/Analyse_PedGo_20060609.pdf
14. Ronald, N., Sterling, L., Kirleyr, M.: An agent-based approach to modelling pedestrian behaviour. Int. J. Simul. Syst. Sci. Technol. 8(1), 25–38 (2007)
15. Weidmann, U.: Transporttechnik der fussgänger. Schriftenreihe des Institut für Verkehrsplanung, Transporttechnik, Strassen- und Eisenbahnbau 90 (1992)

A 2DOFvibrational Energy Harvester Exploiting Velocity Amplification: Modeling and Testing

Elisabetta Boco[1](✉), Valeria Nico[1], Declan O'Donoghue[1], Ronan Frizzell[2], Gerard Kelly[2], and Jeff Punch[1]

[1] Stokes Institute, University of Limerick, Limerick, Ireland
{elisabetta.boco,valeria.nico,declan.odonoghue,jeff.punch}@ul.ie
[2] Efficient Energy Transfer (ηET) Department,
Bell Labs, Alcatel-Lucent, Dublin, Ireland
ronan.frizzell@alcatel-lucent.com

Abstract. A two Degree of Freedom (2DOF) velocity-amplified electromagnetic vibrational energy harvester is presented. The device consists of two masses: a smaller mass which oscillates inside a larger one due to two sets of mechanical springs. The larger mass itself oscillates between two sets of springs. This configuration allows the larger mass to transfer momentum to the smaller mass during impact, which significantly amplifies the velocity of the smaller mass. The smaller mass is designed to disconnect from the larger mass, when input vibrations of sufficient magnitude are present. This leads to significant nonlinearities that increases the bandwidth over which the system can harvest energy. By coupling high strength magnets (placed on the larger mass) and a coil (embedded in the smaller mass), an electric current is induced in the coil through the relative motion of the two masses. This paper characterizes the nonlinear response of a 2DOF velocity-amplified electromagnetic energy harvester using a transfer function analysis. Optimization tools are then presented for designing efficient 2DOF vibration energy harvesters for use at various input frequencies and amplitudes. The first of these tools is a theoretical approach for optimizing the electromagnetic damping that is based on linear approximations. The second approach is a nonlinear model of the 2DOF system that takes into account collisions between the masses and the associated transfer of momentum. In all cases experimental results are used to validate the performance of the design tools. Finally, a performance evaluation using the volumetric Figure of Merit is presented and compared with recent literature, showing the favorable relative performance of the 2DOF system.

Keywords: Energy harvesting · Nonlinearity · Multiple degree of freedom · Electromagnetic optimization · Collision modelling

1 Introduction

Nowadays Information and Communication Technology (ICT) is used in almost all fields of everyday life, so that global power demand is constantly increasing,

© Springer International Publishing Switzerland 2015
M. Helfert et al. (Eds.): Smartgreens 2015 and Vehits 2015, CCIS 579, pp. 165–183, 2016.
DOI: 10.1007/978-3-319-27753-0_9

mainly involving a greater number of sensors and micro- or nano-scales device (i.e. wireless sensors networks for temperature or pressure in buildings, industrial plants or in the environment). One prominent example of this is the widespread use of sensors, receivers and data analysis technologies in building a smart city.

A "smart city" is a city in which many aspects of the environment is controlled, in order to have the best service possible to the citizens, using a network of sensors, receivers and data analysis software: as an example, checking the traffic or pollution conditions in order to regulate the public transport service. Such an extensive use of ICT requires that every node of the network can be autonomously powered. Classical batteries are not the best technology to do so, mainly because they are polluting and because they have a very limited lifetime. If sensors are embedded in a structure, replacing their batteries when exhausted, can be impossible. Energy harvesting comes from the necessity to build self-powering devices, that can stay in operation for a very long time. To do this, harvesting aims to extract energy already present in the environment in many forms, such as temperature gradients, vibrations and electromagnetic waves, and use this energy to drive low-power electronic devices.

Vibrations are one of the most appealing kinds of ambient energy: they are always present, at any scale, and their intensity can be very different depending on the surrounding conditions. There are many possible ways to convert vibrational energy to electricity: piezoelectric, electromagnetic or variable capacitors. In this work, the electromagnetic conversion method is used, because it is applicable at many scales and it can produce quite high power densities provided that there is high relative velocity between the magnet and coil [1]. Nonlinear systems are advantageous compared to linear systems since although linear systems have a higher response at resonance, nonlinear systems are more flexible because they do not need to be tuned, i.e. they are naturally able to harvest energy from broad band excitations. In this manner, a single nonlinear device can be used in many different applications and it can be efficient even if the excitation frequency spectrum is not stationary in time, which is a feature of many real vibration profiles [2, 3].

The aim of the work is to describe in detail the operation of 2DOF systems under different loading conditions and to provide methods for analyzing and optimizing their design. The first part of the current paper presents the experimental characterization of a two degree-of-freedom (2DOF) velocity-amplified electromagnetic energy harvester. To exploit nonlinearities, and to provide velocity amplification, an uncoupled 2DOF system is used: a 2DOF harvester can enlarge the energy conversion bandwidth [4–6], but it does not improve the harvesting capability for random excitations as long as the masses are coupled [7]. Moreover, for electromagnetic conversion, the most important feature is high relative velocity between coil and magnets: in order to have velocity amplification through the momentum transfer between two impacting masses, the masses need to be uncoupled. A transfer function analysis is used to describe the observed nonlinearities in detail. Following this, an optimization process for designing the coil of the electromagnetic generator is proposed. This is based on a linear analytical model, which can be used to predict the optimal coil settings for a given volume. Finally, a more complex numerical model is then presented, which is able to represent the nonlinearity of the 2DOF system, and its capability to reproduce the spectrum of the real device is discussed.

2   Transfer Function Characterization

The purpose of this section is to investigate the nonlinear response of a 2DOF vibration energy harvester. In order to do so, the system was tested experimentally under different levels of acceleration and the transfer function is used to highlight nonlinearities in the system response.

2.1   Experimental Setup and Procedure

The system consists of a large mass, where four magnets are orientated in the configurations shown in Fig. 1. The large mass can move between two springs which are attached to the outer housing that serve to transfer energy from the vibrating base into the larger mass itself. A smaller mass, enclosed within the cavity of the larger mass is designed to separate from the larger mass when sufficient excitation is present. This configuration allows the larger mass to impart momentum to the smaller mass during impact, which significantly amplifies the velocity of the smaller mass [8–10]. All impacting surfaces have high quality factor (Q) springs attached to mediate the impacts and efficiently transfer loads.

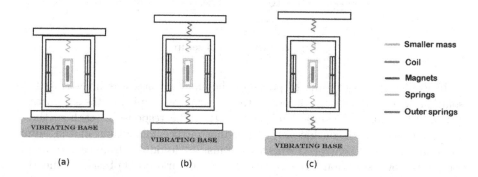

Fig. 1. Schematic of the 2DOF energy harvester. (a) shows Configuration (1), with the outer mass steady. (b) shows Configuration (2), where the movement of the outer mass is constrained by the cap. The springs are always connected to the large mass. (c) shows Configuration (3), with the outer mass free to move.

Following an impact, the final velocity of the smaller mass, v_{2f} is equal to [8]:

$$v_{2f} = \frac{(e+1)m_1 v_{1i} + (m_2 - em_1)v_{2i}}{m_1 + m_2} \tag{1}$$

The volume of the outside mass is $1.29 \cdot 10^2 \, \text{cm}^3$. The closed loop system used to control a LDS V406 permanent magnet shaker from Bruel & Kjaer is shown schematically in Fig. 2. Output signals from the Dactron Comet shaker control system were amplified using a LDS TPO 25 Power Oscillator and used to drive the shaker. The voltage response of the harvester for each coil was measured using LabView through an appropriate data acquisition card. For each coil, data have been acquired using the load resistance which maximized the power output. A high sensitivity ($1.96\,mV/g$) PCB Piezotronic accelerometer was employed to provide feedback to the controller in order to ensure that the correct acceleration levels were applied.

To fully characterize the system, two configurations were tested (see Fig. 1(a) and (b)): (1) motion of the larger mass was prevented and so only the smaller mass was free to oscillate; (2) motion of the smaller mass was free but motion of the larger mass was restricted by the top of the housing which was lowered to ensure the larger mass could not detach from its supporting springs (this meant that spring forces were always active on the larger mass). These configurations allowed different modes of operation of the 2DOF system to be investigated in order to better understand the response of the system.

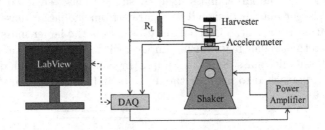

Fig. 2. Experimental setup.

In Configuration (1), the response of the smaller mass was investigated in isolation, while the response of having the larger mass coupled to the supporting springs was examined using Configuration (2). The response of each of these configurations varied considerably depending on the magnitude of the input acceleration, as this controlled whether the masses decoupled from each other or not. Under low excitation levels ($a = 0.2\,g$), Configuration (1) behaved linearly, while system (2) could be considered to be a pair of coupled harmonic oscillators. In addition, there where further nonlinearities due to the electromagnetic conversion.

Under higher levels of excitation ($a = 0.5\,g$), the smaller mass in configuration (1) received sufficient energy to break contact with the larger mass, leading to nonlinearity in the system response. This was caused by the fact that while the smaller mass was detached from larger mass, no elastic spring force acted on it. This means that the effective elastic constant experienced by the system depends on the time that each mass moved freely in the detached configuration. Higher accelerations also allowed such changes in the system's effective elastic constants to affect configuration (2), resulting in the system acting as coupled 2DOF oscillator with a softening nonlinearity.

To verify these empirical observations, the different configurations were tested under increasing and decreasing sine wave frequency sweeps (from 5 to 100 Hz in 260 s) with different amplitudes of accelerations, as presented in Fig. 4, and the voltage output was recorded. Finally, the transfer function was calculated for each configuration as described in the following section.

2.2   Transfer Function Analysis

Let y(t) be the output of our system, and let x(t) be the input. Let X(f) and Y(f) be the Laplace transforms of the input and the output respectively:

$$X(s) = \int_{-\infty}^{+\infty} x(t)e^{-st}dt \qquad (2)$$

$$Y(s) = \int_{-\infty}^{+\infty} y(t)e^{-st}dt \qquad (3)$$

where:

$$s = j\omega \qquad (4)$$

The Laplace transform is equal to the Fourier transform, and represents the frequency behaviour of the system. So, for a linear system, the transfer function is defined as:

$$H(\omega) = \frac{Y(\omega)}{X(\omega)} \qquad (5)$$

When the system is linear, $H(\omega)$ is a well-defined mathematical function, because it has a unique value for each value of ω, whereas for a nonlinear system it depends also on the shape and amplitude of the input signal. This means that the transfer function is not mathematically well defined for nonlinear systems. Nonetheless, transfer function analysis is a very useful method to know whether a system is linear or not for different input signals [11], as deviations from linearity result in distinct variations in the transfer function, as will be discussed in the next section.

2.3   Transfer Function Results

The first method to detect nonlinearities in the device is to compare the resulting spectrum from the transfer function analysis in Fig. 3 to a simple linear response (shown in Fig. 3(a), blue line). A linear response is characterized by a sharp resonant peak that is symmetric about that peak. The left column in Fig. 3 shows that nonlinearity due to the change in the effective stiffness of the springs is evident as the acceleration increases. This is caused by the smaller mass spending more and more time detached from the springs with increasing acceleration which led to a reduction of the resonant frequency of the system due to a decrease in the effective stiffness, an effect that is more pronounced for higher acceleration levels.

The overall shape of the power spectrum varied for the different cases indicating deviation from linear behaviour. For example, at very low acceleration amplitude ($a = 0.05\,g$), in Configuration (1), the behaviour was linear and the resonant peak was sharp and symmetric, as shown in Fig. 3(a), with the blue line. By increasing the acceleration, however, the resonant frequency decreased to lower frequencies, becoming more and more asymmetric but displaying a broader band response (Fig. 3(a), $a = 0.1\,g$ to $a = 0.5\,g$). Very similar responses were seen for Configuration (2) in Fig. 3(b) and (c). The second fingerprint of nonlinearity in the transfer function characterization is the hysteresis phenomenon. When a sine sweep is applied to a linear system, the response is the same regardless of whether the sweep is applied with increasing or decreasing frequencies. In a nonlinear system, however, the behaviour for increasing or decreasing sweeps are different: as already stated, the transfer function is not a mathematically well-defined function for nonlinear systems as it can have two possible values for the same input frequency, one for the increasing sweep and one for the decreasing sweep [3]. The transfer function analysis in Fig. 4(a) shows that at very low acceleration the behaviour under increasing and decreasing sine sweeps was the same, while with increased acceleration hysteresis was evident (Fig. 4(b) and (c)).

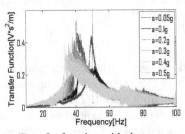

(a) Transfer function with the outer mass steady.

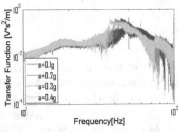

(b) Transfer Function with the outer mass starting to move.

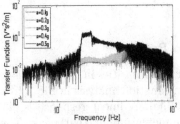

(c) Transfer Function with the outer mass fully compressing the springs.

Fig. 3. (a) Transfer function for Configuration (1) and (b) and (c) for Configuration (2), varying the acceleration (Color figure online).

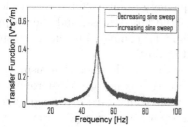

(a) Hysteresis in the almost linear case. The output has been acquired at $a=0.05g$, so the smaller mass cannot detach from the springs

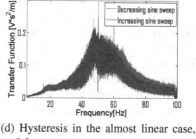

(d) Hysteresis in the almost linear case, $a=0.1g$

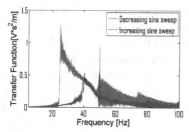

(b) Hysteresis with $a = 0.2g$ acceleration. The acceleration in input is $a = 0.2g$, so that the smaller mass is starting to detach from the springs

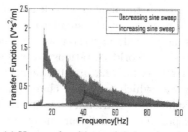

(e) Hysteresis with $a = 0.3g$ acceleration

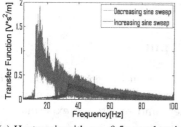

(c) Hysteresis with $a = 0.5g$ acceleration. The acceleration $a = 0.5g$ is enough to let the smaller mass detach from the springs and spend more time decoupled from the larger mass, leading to a decrease in the resonant frequency.

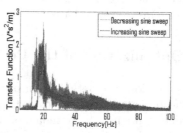

(f) Hysteresis with $a = 0.5g$ acceleration

Fig. 4. Hysteresis for Configuration (1), on the left column and for Configuration (2), on the right column.

The same analysis has also been conducted using configuration (2), in order to investigate the effect of the impacts (Fig. 4(d),(e) and (f)).

The frequency shifting was quite similar when the outer mass started to fully compress the springs (Fig. 4(d) and (e)). Then, the effect of the velocity amplification became dominant, and the frequency response shifted to very low frequency, due to the higher displacement of the larger mass, and the output increased by about an order of magnitude (Fig. 4(f)) compared to the increasing sine sweep for Configuration (1), 0.5 g case (Fig. 3(c)).

The noisy behaviour outside resonance is due to the fact that using the sine sweep method to measure the transfer function is not the most robust to noise [11]. An alternative, more precise method is an analysis through single harmonics excitation. This method is slower than a sine sweep, however, and since the nonlinear effects are very evident despite the noise, it was not considered necessary.

The main problem with linear oscillators as energy harvesters, is that they are only able to harvest energy effectively from a narrow frequency range around their natural resonance. This leads to a serious difficulty when reducing linear oscillator in size as, the smaller the system, the higher the resonance frequency: a millimetre scale harvester would have a natural frequency in the kHz range, whereas real-world vibrations are usually under few thousands of Hz [12,13].

Therefore, high natural frequencies are not compatible with many real-world vibrations, which are often characterized by low frequency, broad spectra and are usually not stationary in time. The analysis conducted here reveals that the response of a nonlinear energy harvester is more suitable for a broad band excitation, and that the scale is not the only factor to determine the frequency response, since the softening effect can also shift the resonance. Finally, there is the possibility also to use the nonlinear response to control the resonance frequency, however how much control is possible would need to be determined on a system-by-system basis.

3   Optimization of the Power Output

In this section, the optimization of the power output is performed, both from the theoretical and the experimental point of view. A linear model is presented, in order to predict the optimal coil parameters and results are experimentally verified.

3.1   Linear Approximation for Optimization

An electromagnetic energy harvester can be described by a system of two coupled equations: the first is the equation of motion of the device, the second is the voltage output. The value of the magnetic flux into the coil acts as the coupling coefficient [14,15]. In this paper, a numerical model is proposed to predict the optimum coil parameters for a given magnetic field. Of particular interest are the wire diameter and number of turns that optimize the voltage and power output of the harvester.

The procedure used in this analysis was to select different wire diameters for a fixed internal radius and coil height, and then to determine the result-ing coil parameters; namely the coil length (l), coil resistance (R_c) and coil inductance (L). The parameters for the different wire diameters were then used to solve the system equations for a single-dof (1DOF) system, as in Configuration (1), in order to determine the optimum wire diameter.

The system of equations to solve is:

$$\begin{cases} M\ddot{z} = -k_{eff}z - \gamma\dot{z} - \frac{BlV}{R_L} - A\sin(\omega t) \\ \dot{V} = \frac{R_L}{L}(Bl\dot{z} - \frac{R_C}{R_L}V - V) \end{cases} \tag{6}$$

where z is the relative displacement between the magnet and coil, M is the inertial mass, γ is the mechanical damping, B is the magnetic field, l is the length of the wire, R_L is the load resistance, L is the inductance, R_C is the coil resistance and V is the induced voltage.

To be able to predict the optimum coil wire diameter, the coil internal radius (r_i), the number of turns (N_{turns}) and the wire diameter itself (d_w) have been fixed in each simulation. From these parameters, it is possible to obtain:

$$N_{turnsh} = \frac{tf}{d} \tag{7}$$

where N_{turnsh} is number of wire turns along the height of the coil, t is the thickness of the coil, f is the fill factor and d is the diameter of the wire:

$$Nturns_{surf} = \frac{N_{turns}f}{N_{turnsh}} \tag{8}$$

where $Nturns_{surf}$ is the number of wire turns along the radial direction.

The outer radius of the coil is dependent on the number of turns and on the wire radius:

$$ro = ri + dNturns_{surf} \tag{9}$$

where ro and ri are respectively the outer and the inner radius of the coil.

The coil length is given by:

$$l = N_{turns}(ro + ri)\pi \tag{10}$$

The coil resistance can be determined from the wire length and resistivity:

$$R_C = \frac{\rho l}{(\pi(D/2)^2)} \tag{11}$$

where R_c is the coil resistance, ρ is the resistivity of the wire and D is the diameter of the coil.

The coil inductance (given in μH) can then be determined from Wheeler's formula [16, 17]:

$$L = 0.02\frac{[(ro + ri)/2]^2 N_{turns}^2}{6(ro + ri)/2 + 9t + 10(ro - ri)} \tag{12}$$

where ro, ri, t are in mm.

The mass of the coil, m_B, is given by:

$$m_B = tf\pi(\frac{ro + ri}{2})^2\rho_m \tag{13}$$

where ρ_m is the mass density (of copper). m_B is an important quantity since the coil is embedded in the mass in this analysis and so contributes to the total inertial mass (M) given by:

$$M = m + m_B \tag{14}$$

where m is the mass of the coil housing.

The system of equations has been solved with the Heun method, to avoid numerical divergence [18]. The device is assumed to be in Configuration (1) from Fig. 1, with the smaller mass always attached to the springs. The power output has been calculated using $R_L = R_C$ (theoretical resistance matching is the optimal condition), and an effective spring constant has been calculated in order to match the mean value of the experimental resonance frequencies using the experimental value of the smaller mass (approximately 20 g, with slight variations for the different coils analyzed).

Figure 5 shows simulation results for three different wire diameters for the 1DOF system with an input acceleration of $a = 0.4\,g$. Plots from different levels of acceleration are not included, because they didn't show any difference in the optimization condition: it is well known that in a linear system, with fixed resonance frequency and mechanical damping, the relative performance of systems with different electrical damping will remain unchanged for different levels of acceleration. The results show that although the smallest wire diameter gives the highest voltage, the power is optimal using the intermediate wire diameter of $170\,\mu m$. The approach can also be extended to the analysis of multi-mass systems.

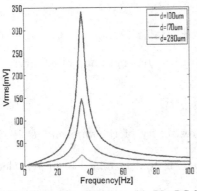

(a) Simulated voltage output with *RL=RC* for the three coils.

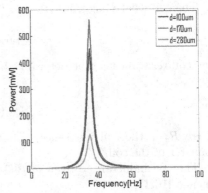

(b) Simulated power output with *RL=RC* for the three coils.

Fig. 5. Simulation results in linear approximation for the transducer only.

In the following section, experimental results are used to verify that the optimum coil wire diameter found through simulation is correct for the actual systems of interest to this paper.

3.2 Experimental Validation of Optimum Coil Wire Diameter

The same experimental setup shown in Fig. 2 was used to generate the results in Fig. 6. Configuration (1) from Fig. 1 was tested. Three different wire diameters were analyzed in order to determine the most reasonable wire to use for winding the coil in terms of voltage and power output. The wire diameters selected were based on the modeling of the previous section and the experimental results serve to verify the model.

Different levels of acceleration ($a = 0.2\,g$, $a = 0.4\,g$, $a = 0.6\,g$) were provided as input to the two configurations of interest in order to verify that the optimal configuration did not change due to the frequency shifting observed in Sect. 2.3. As a first stage, the system was optimized for Configuration (1): the results are shown in Fig. 6. Although the voltage output increases with decreasing wire diameter, the power output shows a maximum for the $170\,\mu m$ diameter, before decreasing again for the lowest wire diameter. This is due to the increasing resistance of the coil itself. The same effect is shown for increasing acceleration amplitude, as evident by comparing Fig. 6(d) and (f). The three coils used had the same volume, but they featured different wire diameters of $100\,\mu m$, $170\,\mu m$ and $280\,\mu m$. Each test was conducted by finding the optimal load resistance for the different coils and then measuring the voltage and power output. At $a = 0.6\,g$ acceleration for Configuration (1), the difference between the power output produced by the different coils reduces. This could be due to the fact that the optimization theory is linear, which means that the system is required to maintain a fixed resonance frequency. This is clearly not true for a nonlinear system: the shifting in the frequency behavior affects parameters such as the impedance of the coil, which is not taken into account in the optimization and will be the aim of future research.

4 System Dynamics

In this section a numerical model of the 2DOF system in Configuration (3) and its experimental validation are presented in order to investigate the nonlinear dynamics of the masses and how this affect the frequency response.

4.1 Numerical Model of the Nonlinear System

A model that can represent the dynamics of the system in Configuration (3) is presented here. It can be seen that the masses are connected to the springs only for a short time while the system is active and, at other times, the masses are free to move and not interact with each other or the housing. The model considers both cases of springs transferring forces between the masses and free motion of

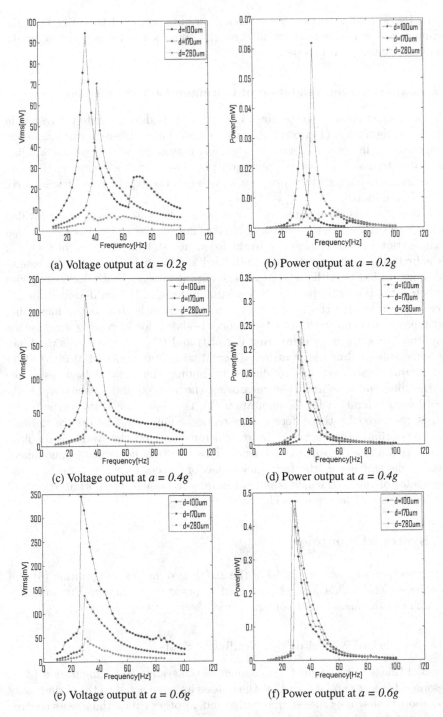

Fig. 6. Simulated voltage and power output comparison at different acceleration levels for Configuration (1).

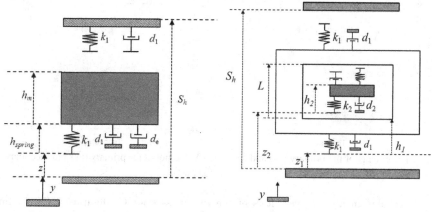

(a) Schematic model for the 1DOF system   (b) Schematic model of the 2DOF system

Fig. 7. Schematics of the systems under examination.

the masses. Due to the complexity of the full system, a simplified model for a 1DOF harvester is presented as an example of the working principle of the full model. The 1DOF model was then extended to fully describe the 2DOF system in Configuration (3) as shown in Fig. 7, where:

- k_1 and k_2 are the elastic constants of the springs;
- d_1 and d_2 are the mechanical damping coefficients;
- d_e is the electromagnetic damping coefficient;
- S_h, h_2, h_m, L are defined in Fig. 7;
- h_{spring} is the free length of the spring;
- z, z_1 and z_2 are the mass displacements;
- y is the excitation displacement.

The 1DOF model has a logic step that checks the position of the mass at each time-step. With reference to Fig. 7(a), the mass can be in one of three different states:

- the mass can come in contact with the bottom spring, which allows load transfer to or from the mass;
- the mass can contact the top spring and transfer load to or from it;
- the mass does not interact with the housing or with the springs.

The equations that represent these three conditions are the following:

$$
\begin{cases}
m_1\ddot{z}_1 = -d_1\dot{z}_1 - k_1(z_1 - h_{spring}) - \alpha V_L - m_1\ddot{y} - m_1 g \\
\qquad\qquad\qquad\qquad\qquad\qquad\qquad\text{for } z_1 < h_{spring} \\
m_1\ddot{z}_1 = -d_1\dot{z}_1 - \alpha V_L - m_1\ddot{y} - m_1 g \\
\qquad\qquad\text{for } z_1 > h_{spring} \text{ and } z_1 + h_m < S_h - h_{spring} \\
m_1\ddot{z}_1 = -d_1\dot{z}_1 - k_1(z_1 + h_m - S_h + h_{spring}) - \alpha V_L - m_1\ddot{y} - m_1 g \\
\qquad\qquad\qquad\qquad\qquad\qquad\text{for } z_1 + h_m > S_h - h_{spring}
\end{cases}
$$

$$\tag{15}$$

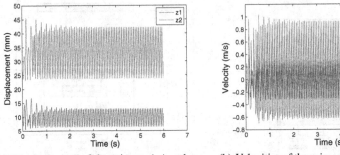

(a) Displacements of the primary (z_1) and secondary (z_2) mass.

(b) Velocities of the primary (v_1) and secondary (v_2) mass.

Fig. 8. Displacements and velocities of the two masses for Configuration (3) for an excitation of $a_{rms} = 0.6\,g$ and 14 Hz (Color figure online).

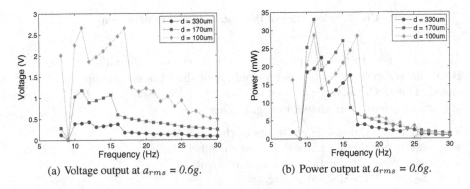

(a) Voltage output at $a_{rms} = 0.6g$.

(b) Power output at $a_{rms} = 0.6g$.

Fig. 9. Simulated power output for the three coils at different levels of acceleration for Configuration (3).

The working principle of the full model for Configuration (3) is based on similar equations to those shown for the 1DOF model in Eq. 15. The model was extended to include all states of the system defined by the different possible positions of the two masses. This system has not been included here as the number of equations involved was high. With reference to the 2DOF model in Fig. 7(b), each mass can have three different states:

- connected to the bottom spring and so transferring load;
- connected to the top spring;
- not in contact, so no spring forces are active on it.

In total there are nine different combinations, and hence nine different dynamic systems, that combine harmonic oscillator and free motion equations, need to be solved and were similar in nature to those presented in Eq. 15. The system was solved using the Runge-Kutta Method and the positions of the masses were checked at each time-step, in order to integrate the correct equations.

Simulations were carried out, using the full 2DOF model, to verify the correct behavior of the model itself. The displacement of the masses and their velocities are shown in Fig. 8 for a sinusoidal excitation of amplitude $a_{rms} = 0.6\,g$ and 14 Hz. It is interesting to note that the model can represent the velocity amplification of the smaller mass due to the impacts with the larger mass. This effect is shown in Fig. 8(b) where it is possible to note that the velocity of the secondary mass (red) is higher that the velocity of primary mass (blue).

The full system of equations for the 2DOF system was solved over a range of frequencies in order to validate the frequency response of the system. Moreover different wire diameters for the coils were tested to verify the consistency of the complete model with the experimental data. Figure 9 shows the predicted trend of the output voltage and power over a range of frequencies at $a_{rms} = 0.6\,g$, for three different wire diameters: $330\,\mu m$, $170\,\mu m$, $100\,\mu m$.

4.2 Experimental Validation of the Model

The same process was repeated for Configuration (3) in Fig. 1, in order to verify if the same trends are observed in a multi-mass system which experiences the velocity amplification effect. In this case, a wire diameter of $d = 330\,\mu m$ was used instead of the $280\,\mu m$ diameter wire. Figure 10 show that the optimal wire diameter is again $170\,\mu m$.

The theoretical results in Fig. 9 are consistent with the experimental data in Fig. 10: the optimal wire diameter is $170\,\mu m$ in both cases. The simulation can also represent the trend of the output signal over a range of frequencies. The softening nonlinearity present in the experimental system in Fig. 10 is evident in Fig. 9, since there are two peaks at 11 Hz and 17 Hz that are lower than the natural resonance frequencies of the two masses. The results also show that at $a = 0.6\,g$ the nonlinearity of the whole system dominates, leading to two large peaks at lower frequencies and the spectrum is wider than for a linear device. The

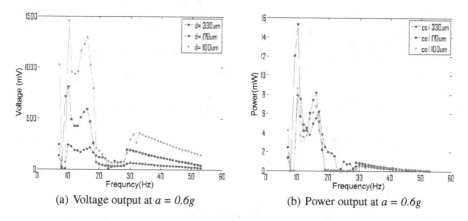

(a) Voltage output at $a = 0.6g$ (b) Power output at $a = 0.6g$

Fig. 10. Experimental voltage and power output for the three coils at different level of accelerations for Configuration (3).

broadening of the resonance peak demonstrates an enhanced energy harvesting capability such that the system responds to a wider band of input frequencies. It is clear from the results that the model is capable of reproducing the dynamics and the frequency response of the system, indicating its utility as a design tool for frequency tuning. Further improvements to the model would involve accounting for the insulation thickness in the coil and a more realistic expression for the magnetic field that takes into account edge effects. These points will be addressed in future work.

5   Comparison with Devices from Recent Literature

The performance of the device has been compared to some recently reported energy harvesters in the literature using the Volumetric Figure of Merit (FoM_v) [19,20], defined in Eq. 16:

$$FoM_v = \frac{Useful Power Output}{\frac{1}{16}Y_0\rho_{Au}Vol^{\frac{4}{3}}\omega^3} \tag{16}$$

The FoM_v represents the ratio between the actual power output and the device and the calculated power output obtained from an harmonic oscillator with the same volume, and the same resonant frequency of the analysed one, built in gold. For the harvester presented in this paper the value of the Figure of Merit is $FoM_v = 0.32$.

The high FoM_v at low frequency demonstrates the effectiveness of velocity amplification in electromagnetic energy harvesting, even though the present

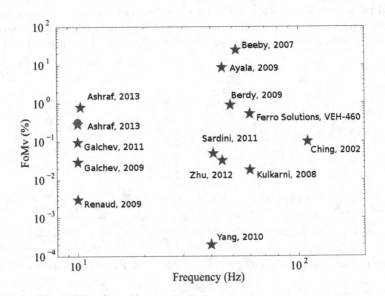

Fig. 11. Comparison between recently published FoM [20–32]. In red, our first prototype (Color figure online).

device is a "proof of concept" of velocity amplification technique in energy harvesting. In order to make the device usable in different contexts (such as human motion, automotive or vibrating machineries energy harvesting) a new scaled down geometry will be addressed.

6 Conclusions

In this paper the response of a 2DOF velocity-amplified electromagnetic energy harvester has been characterized in details. The response of these systems was shown to be complex, which creates the need for the linear and nonlinear modeling techniques described in Sects. 3 and 4 of this paper. These techniques can be used as tools for optimizing the design of 2DOF harvesters, ensuring efficient devices are achieved.

To have a good understanding of the real system behaviour, the first section of the paper analyzed the nonlinearity occurring in the system for different configurations, which highlighted a softening phenomenon. This feature has the effect of shifting the resonance frequencies of the harvester to lower values, and also widening the bandwidth of the response. As a consequence, it is possible to harvest energy from a wider band of frequencies, making it unnecessary to tune the harvester each time the driving frequency changes. The transfer function characterization also clearly demonstrates the gain in the output signal due to velocity amplification (Fig. 11).

In the second part of the paper, an optimization model has been proposed that is capable of predicting the most appropriate coil wire diameter for maximum voltage and/or power. The model employs a linear approximation, and it has been verified through comparison with three sets of measured data from different coils. The experimental tests were carried out using three levels of acceleration, and it was verified that the optimal coil configuration did not change substantially with the frequency shifting that occurs due to the nonlinearity of the system. This linear approximation can be useful as a guideline to optimize the electromagnetic transducer because it doesn't require a large amount of parameters, as is the case with non-linear approach.

In Sect. 4, a theoretical model that reproduces the dynamics of the system in Configuration (3) is developed. The model achieves good agreement with the experimental results since it captures the velocity amplification that is the main feature of the device. The model can be used for choosing the optimal configuration of the geometrical parameters in order to tune the response of the system to the main frequencies of the ambient vibrations.

Finally, it has been shown that the harvester compares well with other devices from the recent literature, despite the prototype used in this study being a "proof-of-concept" device for investigating the velocity-amplification effect in vibration energy harvesters.

Future works will focus on the scaling down of the system, in order to enable future integration on vibrating systems such as bridges or rotating machines.

Acknowledgements. The authors acknowledge the financial support of Science Foundation Ireland under Grant No. 10/CE/I1853 and the Irish Research Council (IRC) for funding under their Enterprise Partnership Scheme (EPS). This work was financially supported by the Industrial Development Agency (IDA) Ireland.

References

1. Waters, R.L., Chisum, B., Jazo, H., Fralick, M.: Development of an electromagnetic transducer for energy harvesting of kinetic energy and its applicability to a mems-scale device. In: Nanopower Forum 2008 (2008)
2. Cottone, F., Vocca, H., Gammaitoni, L.: Nonlinear energy harvesting. Phys. Rev. Lett. **102**, 080601-1–080601-4 (2009). American Physical Society
3. Leadenham, A., Erturk, S.: M-shaped asymmetric nonlinear oscillator for broadband vibration energy harvesting: harmonic balance analysis and experimental validation. J. Sound Vib. **333**(23), 6029–6223 (2014). Elsevier
4. Wu, H., Tang, L., Yang, Y., Soh, C.K.: A novel two-degree-of-freedom piezoelectric energy harvester. J. Intell. Mater. Syst. Struct. **24**(3), 357–368 (2013)
5. Wu, H., Tang, L., Yang, Y., Soh, C.K.: Development of a broadband nonlinear two-degree-of-freedom piezoelectric energy harvester. J. Intell. Mater. Syst. Struct. **25**(14), 1875–1889 (2012). SAGE
6. Jang, S.J., Rustighi, E., Brennan, M.J., Lee, Y.P., Jung, H.J.: Design of a 2dof vibrational energy harvesting device. J. Intell. Mater. Syst. Struct. **22**(5), 443–448 (2011). SAGE
7. Tang, X., Zuo, L.: Vibration energy harvesting from random force and motion excitations. Smart Mater. Struct. **21**, 075025:9 (2012)
8. Cottone, F., Frizzell, R., Goyal, S., Kelly, G., Punch, J.: Enhanced vibrational energy harvester based on velocity amplification. J. Intell. Mater. Syst. Struct. **25**(4), 443–451 (2014). SAGE
9. Nico, V., O'Donoghue, D., Frizzell, R., Kelly, G., Punch, J.: A multiple degree-of-freedom velocity-amplified vibrational energy harvester part b: Modelling. In: ASME 2014 International Conference on Smart Materials, SMASIS, September 2014
10. O'Donoghue, D., Nico, V., Frizzell, R., Kelly, G., Punch, J.: A novel velocity amplified vibrational energy harvester: experimental analysis. In: ASME 2014 International Conference on Smart Materials, SMASIS, September 2014
11. Muller, S., Massarani, P.: Transfer-function measurement with sweeps. J. Audio Eng. Soc. **49**(6), 443–471 (2001). AES
12. Mizuno, M., Chetwynd, D.G.: Investigation of a resonance microgenerator. J. Micromech. Microeng. **13**, 209–216 (2003). Institute of Physics Publishing
13. Rebeiz, G.M., Regehr, W.G., Rutledge, D.B., Savage Jr., L.: Submillimeter-wave antennas on thin membranes. Int. J. Infrared Millimeter Waves **8**(10), 1249–1255 (1987). Springer
14. Bouendeu, E., Greiner, A., Smith, P.J., Korvink, J.G.: Design synthesis of electromagnetic vibration-driven energy generators using a variational formulation. J. Microelectromech. Syst. **20**(2), 466–475 (2011). IEEE
15. Poulin, G., Sarraute, E., Costa, F.: Generation of electrical energy for portable devices: Comparative study of an electromagnetic and a piezoelectric system. Sens. Actuators A Phys. **116**(3), 461–471 (2004). Elsevier
16. Wheeler, H.: Formulas for the skin effect. Proc. I.R.E. **30**(9), 412–424 (1942)

17. Wheeler, H.A.: Simple inductance formulas for radio coils. Proc. I.R.E. **16**(10), 1398–1400 (1928)
18. Grasselli, M., Pelinovsky, D.: Numerical Mathematics. Jones & Bartlett Learning, Burlington (2008)
19. Mitcheson, P.D., Yeatmann, E.M., Rao, G.K., Holmes, A.S., Green, T.C.: Energy harvesting from human and machine motion for wireless electronic devices. Proc. IEEE **96**(9), 1457–1486 (2008). IEEE
20. Ashraf, K., Khir, M.M., Dennis, J.O., Baharudin, Z.: Improved energy harvesting from low frequency vibrations by resonance amplification at multiple frequencies. Sens. Actuators A Phys. **195**, 123–132 (2013). Elsevier
21. Ashraf, K., Khir, M.M., Dennis, J.O., Baharudin, Z.: A wideband, frequency up-converting bounded vibration energy harvester for a low frequency environment. Smart Mater. Struct. **22**(2), 025018 (2013). IOP Publishing
22. Galchev, T.V., Cullagh, J., Peterson, R.L., Najafi, K.: Harvesting traffic-induced vibrations for structural health monitoring of bridges. J. Micromech. Microeng. **21**(10), 104005 (2011). IOP Publishing
23. Galchev, T., Kim, H., Najafi, K.: A parametric frequency increased power generator for scavenging low frequency ambient vibrations. Procedia Chem. **1**(1), 1439–1442 (2009). Elsevier
24. Renaud, M., Fiorini, P., van Schaijk, R., van Hoof, C.: Harvesting energy from the motion of human limbs: the design and analysis of an impact-based piezoelectric generator. Smart Mater. Struct. **18**(3), 035001 (2009). IOP Publishing
25. Beeby, S.P., Torah, R.N., Tudor, M.J., Glynne-Jones, P., O'Donnell, T., Saha, C.R., Roy, S.: A micro electromagnetic generator for vibration energy harvesting. J. Micromech. Microeng. **17**(7), 1257 (2007). IOP Publishing
26. Ayala, I.N., Zhu, D., Tudor, M.J., Beeby, S.P.: Autonomous tunable energy harvester. In: PowerMEMS (2009)
27. Berdy, D.F., Srisungsitthisunti, p., Xu, X., Rhoads, J., Jung, B., Peroulis, D.: Compact low frequency meandered piezoelectric energy harvester. In: PowerMEMS (2009)
28. Ching, N.N., Wong, H.Y., Li, W.J., Leong, P.H., Wen, Z.: A laser-micromachined multi-modal resonating power transducer for wireless sensing systems. Sens. Actuators A Phys. **97**, 685–690 (2002). Elsevier
29. Sardini, E., Serpelloni, M.: An efficient electromagnetic power harvesting device for low-frequency applications. Sens. Actuators A Phys. **172**(2), 475–482 (2011). Elsevier
30. Zhu, D., Beeby, S., Tudor, J., Harris, N.: Vibration energy harvesting using the halbach array. Smart Mater. Struct. **21**(7), 075020 (2012). IOP Publishing
31. Kulkarni, S., Koukharenko, E., Torah, R., Tudor, J., Beeby, S., O'Donnell, T., Roy, S.: Design, fabrication and test of integrated micro-scale vibration-based electromagnetic generator. Sens. Actuators A Phys. **145**, 336–342 (2008). Elsevier
32. Yang, B., Lee, C.: Non-resonant electromagnetic wideband energy harvesting mechanism for low frequency vibrations. Microsyst. Technol. **16**, 961–966 (2010). Springer

Voltage Control in Low Voltage Grids with Distributed Energy Resources: A Droop-Based Approach

António Grilo[1,2(✉)] and Mário Nunes[1,3]

[1] INESC-ID, Lisbon, Portugal
antonio.grilo@inesc-id.pt
[2] Instituto Superior Técnico, Universidade de Lisboa, Lisbon, Portugal
[3] INOV, Lisbon, Portugal
mario.nunes@inov.pt

Abstract. The challenges associated with the integration of Distributed Energy Resources (DERs) in the electrical grid are among the main motivations for the implementation of Smart Grid functionalities. Bi-directionality of power flows leads to a potential imbalance between load and generation, requiring more dynamic voltage control mechanisms. Although the Smart Grid communication capabilities make it possible to implement more optimal centralized voltage control mechanisms, it may be still useful to have backup distributed mechanisms that are able to keep an acceptable operational level even upon communication failure due to equipment malfunction or intentional damage. Based on this need, this paper presents two droop-based voltage control algorithms, which can operate in the absence of a communication infrastructure. A time-division mechanism is used to avoid conflicts between decisions at the local level. The results show that the distributed algorithms are able to acceptably approach the performance of a centralized algorithm.

Keywords: Smart grid · Low voltage distribution · Voltage limit control · Droop-based techniques

1 Introduction

Increasing energy demand and the threat of global warming are leading to the exploitation of additional and cleaner energy sources. A consequence of this trend is the growing penetration of Distributed Energy Resources (DERs), encompassing Distributed Generation (DG) and Distributed Storage (DS). DG installations may now belong to grid consumers, which become prosumers, i.e., both producers and consumers of energy. Photovoltaic (PV) DG in particular had a significant growth in recent years, with incentives given by EU countries like Portugal (see [1]), motivating its adoption and turning it into a business case. The support of bi-directional power flows resulting from DG and DS, as well as the need for loss reduction are leading to deep changes of the power distribution grid, namely in Low Voltage (LV) distribution, pointing in the direction of a more responsive and efficient Smart Grid.

© Springer International Publishing Switzerland 2015
M. Helfert et al. (Eds.): Smartgreens 2015 and Vehits 2015, CCIS 579, pp. 184–198, 2015.
DOI: 10.1007/978-3-319-27753-0_10

Although the introduction of DERs has many advantages, it also brings significant challenges. High DER penetration may lead to local imbalance between energy production and consumption, with consequent instability of voltage levels, adding to the problem of load variability along the day. Violation of voltage operating limits leads to Quality of Power (QoP) degradation, with possible penalty to the DSO. It may also ultimately lead to conductor overheating and equipment failure (including user appliances) if no control procedures are in place. Currently, the usual control procedure is to let the DER generate the maximum contracted power while connected and automatically disconnect it from the grid once the voltage level measured at its grid coupling point becomes too high. Although this solution is simple and only relies on local measurements, it is usually inefficient, since it does not allow for a steady finer grain adaptation. Moreover, it may lead to voltage level instability, since several DERs may needlessly disconnect at the same time, causing a sudden drop in injected power, which can lead to the opposite situation: undervoltage.

This paper presents two droop-based algorithms for control of DG in LV distribution grids, together with a comparative evaluation. The objective of the proposed algorithms is to perform a fine grain adaption of power injected in the LV grid by DERs in order to maximize DG production up to the limit established by the contract between the DG client and the DSO, while keeping the voltage levels within operating limits. All decisions are made locally by the DERs based on local measurements at the coupling points. These algorithms can thus operate in LV distribution grids where a Smart Grid communication network is still not implemented or as a backup mechanism when the communication network is congested or broken.

The performance of the proposed algorithms was compared with the basic connect/disconnect mechanism described above, as well as with a future Smart Grid enabled centralized algorithm. Simulation results show that the performance of the proposed algorithms approaches that of the centralized algorithm, while being significantly better than the basic mechanism.

The rest of the paper is organized as follows: Sect. 2 presents the problem definition, including the abstract grid model; Sect. 3 presents the related work; Sect. 4 describes the proposed voltage regulation algorithms; Sect. 5 presents the comparative performance evaluation based on simulation results; Sect. 6 concludes the paper.

2 Problem Definition

The one-line diagram of a simplified LV grid architecture is depicted in Fig. 1. The Medium Voltage (MV) feeder terminates at the secondary substation (SS), where typically several LV feeders are connected to the LV side of the MV/LV transformer, which imposes the voltage level at the beginning of the LV feeders. This voltage level may be equal to the nominal voltage level (e.g., 230 V) or slightly higher in order to compensate technical losses, e.g., cable impedances, which are also represented in Fig. 1. LV feeders can be single phase or multiple phase.

Notice that this is a simple abstract model, which can be tailored to specific scenarios by assigning electrical elements to phases, impedance values to the loads and configuring the generation capacity of DERs. In this paper, only resistive loads will be included in the analysed scenarios.

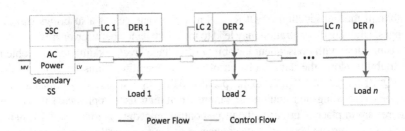

Fig. 1. Example of LV grid architecture.

It is considered that the DSO has established a contract with the DG client, according to which the DSO will buy all the power injected by the DG client, up to a certain limit. The algorithms described in this paper aim to perform a fine grain control of power injected in the LV grid by DERs in order to maximize DG production up to the limit established by the contract. It should be noted that maximizing the DG production entails a voltage increase in case the load is too low. Consequently, the solutions generated by the algorithms must result in voltage values within the operating limits.

The proposed algorithms operate in a single phase of an LV feeder and should be replicated if there are more phases/feeders. Each DER is coupled to a phase of the LV feeder and its injected power may be limited by setpoints issued by a Local Controller (LC). The LC establishes these setpoints based on its local algorithm or based on setpoint commands centrally issued by the Secondary Substation Controller (SSC).

Only active power adaptation is taken into account, since reactive power adaptation is less cost-effective and efficient, requiring the DER or coupler hardware to integrate large capacitor banks in order to have a significant impact on the voltage level – an asset that is not available in every equipment.

3 Related Work

During the last decades, DSOs have employed voltage regulation equipment such as transformer tap-changers, line regulators and shunt capacitors placed at the substations and distribution feeders in order to keep the voltages within the operating limits [2]. This equipment operates correctly in distribution grids without DERs, since they are designed to only compensate the voltage drop along the branch lines. Consequently, it is usually deployed in long branch lines, typical of suburban or rural environments. When DERs are present, the voltage along the grid becomes more unpredictable due to the more complex power flow. It may present values that are higher than the voltage imposed at the head end by the power transformer, and this may happen at any location. Planning for the installation of voltage regulation equipment becomes more difficult.

In [3], the authors analyse the impact of DG installation in the voltage profile of the LV distribution grid. They state that when there is significant DG penetration, the voltage is prone to rise. If the upper operating voltage limit is reached at some DG unit interfaces, the respective individual protections fire, removing those DG units from the grid, i.e., their injected power is reduced to zero. On the other hand, if there is a sudden power reduction due to DG intermittence, the voltage decreases very quickly, which also constitutes a problem. The paper proposes a solution based on the transmission of setpoints to the DG controllers whose output voltage exceeds the operating limits. Transmission of setpoints requires an integrated communication infrastructure of the kind to be found in the future Smart Grid.

Several proposals can be found in the literature on how to calculate the setpoints. In general, the methods are based on measurements of voltage, current and power factor at grid connection points. Based on these measurements, an algorithm calculates the power flow and issues the setpoints until the optimal power values are attained. A very popular method for power flow calculation is Backward/Forward Sweep (BFS). In [4], the authors propose a variant of this method that is suitable for radial topologies, which are typical of LV distribution grids.

In [5], a distributed algorithm is proposed, whereby the transformer tap-changer controller agent mitigates voltage limit violations by issuing permission to willing DG controllers to adapt their active and/or reactive power, or alternatively by adapting the tap-changer. This system also assumes that a Smart Grid communication infrastructure is in place, allowing sensing and control messages to be exchanged between the distributed agents.

Voltage control droop-based techniques were previously proposed in the literature, such as in [6, 7]. The former proposes two techniques for active power control, one using a fixed slope factor, another using location-based slope factors obtained from the voltage sensitivity matrix in order to achieve fairness among DG sites. In [7], the authors propose a multi-objective droop-based optimization scheme, which is also able to control the reactive power and minimize the line losses. Although the proposed techniques are able to effectively control line voltage, they assume that the voltage sensitivity matrix is known, unlike the techniques proposed in this paper. Besides, as far as the authors know, the problem of simultaneous conflictual decisions between DG controllers was not previously addressed.

4 Algorithm Description

Two droop-based algorithms (incremental and linear) were developed, which are based exclusively on local decisions based on voltage and current measurements taken at the DER interface with the grid, being suitable for implementation at LC level. These algorithms periodically sense the voltage level at the DER's interface and adapt the injected power accordingly. They differ in the way they perform this adaptation.

Notice that, if the feeder has more than one LC, each LC independently runs the algorithm. This brings the issue of convergence when different LCs are making interfering decisions. In order to tackle this problem, a time division scheme is proposed. According to this scheme, time is divided into timeslot windows. A timeslot window corresponds to an iteration, i.e., to a decision cycle. The LCs are synchronized to a common clock (e.g., GPS synchronization) and each tries to separate its decision in time by randomly selecting a time slot within the timeslot window in each iteration. The duration of the timeslot is assumed fixed and related with the response time of the DER, which is a specific characteristic of the equipment in use. The general scheme of this time division decision cycle is depicted in Fig. 2 and is the same for the two proposed algorithms. The differences lie on the injected power adaptation decisions taken within the selected time slot.

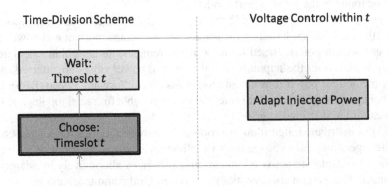

Fig. 2. General time division voltage control scheme.

The following subsections describe how the proposed distributed algorithms running at each LC make their decisions within the respective timeslots, in each iteration. Since these algorithms will be compared with a basic connect/disconnect scheme and a centralized algorithm, a summary of the latter is also presented. From this point onward, when we refer simply to the injected power, this will mean the active power only, as already stated in Sect. 2.

4.1 Incremental Algorithm

In the incremental algorithm, in each iteration t, the LC performs the following steps within its assigned timeslot:

1. Measures the root mean square (RMS) voltage and current at the DER's coupling point, respectively V_{rms}^t, I_{rms}^t (t) and power factor (PF). Then, it calculates an estimate of the power currently being injected:

$$P_G^t = V_{rms}^t \cdot I_{rms}^t \cdot PF \tag{1}$$

2. Adapts the respective maximum allowed injected power (P_{max}) as follows:

$$P_{max}^{t+1} = \begin{cases} \alpha_1 \cdot P_G^t, & V(t) > V_{max} \\ P_G^t, & V(t) = V_{max} \\ min\left[P_{MAX}, \alpha_2 \cdot P_G^t\right], & V(t) < V_{max} \end{cases} \tag{2}$$

where α_1 and α_2 are constants ($0 < \alpha_1 < 1$ and $\alpha_2 > 1$), V_{max} is the high RMS voltage limit and P_{MAX} is the maximum power that the DER is able to inject at that moment into the network (it may correspond to either technical or a contract limit).

4.2 Linear Algorithm

In the linear algorithm, in each iteration t, the LC performs the following steps within its assigned timeslot:

1. Measures V_{rms}^t, I_{rms}^t (t) and PF, and then calculates the P_G^t estimate as in Eq. (1).
2. Performs a test, setting the injected power to $P_{test} = \beta \cdot P_G^t$, with $0 < \beta < 1$. It then measures the resultant RMS voltage V_{rms}^{test} and RMS current I_{rms}^{test}.
3. It adapts P_{max} assuming that the relationship between RMS voltage and RMS current is approximately linear (Ohm's Law), as follows:

$$P_{max}^{t+1} = min\left[P_{MAX}, V_{max} \cdot \left[\begin{array}{c} I_{rms}^t + \\ \left(V_{max} - V_{rms}^t\right) \cdot \\ \left(I_{test} - I_{rms}^t\right) / \left(V_{test} - V_{rms}^t\right) \end{array} \right] \right] \tag{3}$$

It should be noted that, due to the fact that a power change and measurement test is performed in each timeslot, the timeslots in the linear algorithm should be considered twice as long as those in the incremental algorithm.

4.3 Basic Connect/Disconnet Scheme

In the basic connect/disconnect mechanism, which is common in commercial photo-voltaic inverters, the DERs try to inject the maximum power while connected, but will disconnect if the voltage at the coupling point rises beyond V_{max}. In the implementation considered in this paper, in each iteration t, the LC performs the following decision within its assigned timeslot:

$$P_{max}^{t+1} = \begin{cases} 0, V(t) \geq V_{max} \\ \\ P_{MAX}, V(t) < V_{max} \end{cases} \tag{4}$$

4.4 Centralized Algorithm

The centralized algorithm was submitted as patent in [8] and will be the subject of another publication. As such, only a short summary of its operation is provided. The algorithm is meant to run at the SSC. It takes measurements of voltage, current and power factor variation at each one of DER coupling points for different power values injected by the different DERs, from which an impedance matrix is defined that allows the calculation of the currents and voltages at the different DERs for different production values. Based on the referred impedance matrix, a solution for the production of each DER is obtained that optimizes an objective function, subject to a set of restrictions on currents and voltages at the output of each DG. Different objective functions can be defined. In this study, the objective function seeks to optimize the total power injected by the DERs.

5   Simulation Results

The simulation environment is depicted in Fig. 3. It runs in Linux and integrates a Discrete Event Simulator (DES) developed by the authors in C and the *Ngspice* circuit simulator [9]. The DES implements the algorithms, manages dynamic load changes, performs initialization tasks (including *Ngspice* scenario configuration) and performs the global control of the discrete event simulation timeline. In order to update and retrieve the status of the electrical grid, the DES issues appropriate commands to the *Ngspice* process. Dynamic changes, such as changes in the load values, as well as the results of the decision cycles (i.e., changes of injected currents by the DERs, represented by independent current sources in *Ngspice*) are also issued to *Ngspice* in a similar way. The interaction between the two programs is performed through Linux pipes.

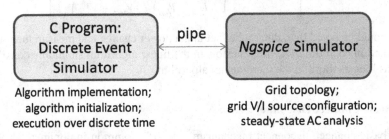

Fig. 3.   Simulation environment integrating the *Ngspice* circuit simulator.

The simulations presented in this paper are divided in two parts: simple single phase scenarios and more complex three-phase scenarios. The single phase scenarios allow the study of the main characteristics of the proposed algorithms, as well as an initial assessment of their performance. The three-phase scenarios allow a more realistic assessment, taking into account possible imbalance of injected power between phases.

The values of the distributed algorithm parameters were constant across all simulations and are listed in Table 1. Three performance metrics were selected:

Table 1.   Parameters of the distributed algorithms.

α_1	0.95
α_2	1.02
β	0.95

- Convergence latency: this is related to the time that it will take to converge to a good enough solution. The convergence criteria require that the achieved voltage values at DER coupling points fall within the operating limits and that the difference between successive values is less than 3 V. The latency is normalized to the length of the timeslot of the incremental algorithm. Latency will not be considered for the centralized algorithm, since in this case it would depend on the performance of the supporting communication technologies, which is out-of-scope in this paper.

- Total DER production: This is the sum of the values of power injected by the DERs.
- Production fairness: since the DSO will buy all the power injected by the DER clients, the latter is interested on maximizing this value. However, compliance with voltage limits may lead to some DERs being forced to reduce their production, which may lead to unfairness, especially if the power setpoints are generated locally. In order to evaluate the fairness of the proposed algorithms, the Jain's fairness index is used.

5.1   Single Phase Scenarios

The single-phase configuration is an instantiation of the topology described in Sect. 1, with four equal resistive loads and four co-located DERs. The DERs are able to inject up to $P_{MAX} = 6$ kW into the grid, which may correspond to either the contracted limit or to a technical limit. The voltage imposed by the SS at the beginning of the LV feeder corresponds to the nominal value $V_{nom} = 230V$. The voltage limits are $V_{max} = 1.1 \times V_{nom} = 253V$ and $V_{min} = 0.9 \times V_{nom} = 207V$. It is considered that the power consumption contract establishes a maximum of 6 kW of consumed power for each load. This means that the lowest acceptable load resistance value is approximately $\frac{(V_{min})^2}{6000} = 7.1\Omega$. Two values were chosen for the line resistances (including neutral resistance): 0.1 Ω and 0.2 Ω, which correspond to two different scenarios: shorter and longer feeder, respectively. Although the longer feeder scenario entails a higher risk of undervoltage in case of heavy load (especially at the most distant client sites), it is valid under the assumption that the coincidence factor estimated by the DSO is low. In the beginning, all DERs are configured to inject 6 kW into the grid.

In the charts that follow, each point corresponds to the average of 10 simulations. The convergence latency, total DER production and fairness as functions of the value of load resistances, are depicted for the short feeder scenario in Figs. 4, 5, and 6, respectively. Four values of load resistance were considered: 20 Ω, 40 Ω, 80 Ω and 160 Ω. Different algorithm configurations are labelled with the name of the algorithm, followed by the number of timeslots that an iteration comprises.

In this scenario, the load is able to sink most of the injected DER power in all configurations. Potential voltage limit violations will only arise for load resistance values of 160 Ω. This is the only place where the basic connect/disconnect scheme will not converge. All other algorithm configurations converge within a single iteration. The differences in latency are thus due to the different iteration lengths. As expected, the highest latency belongs to the linear-2slot configuration, with the linear-1slot latency being the same as that of the incremental-2slot configuration.

Regarding the total DER production, the performance is very similar in all converging settings. As expected, the maximum value is achieved by the centralized algorithm, followed by the incremental and linear algorithms. The lowest performance is presented by the basic connect/disconnect scheme. It should be noted that the incremental and linear algorithm configurations present a trend to gradually reduce the DER production as the value of load resistance increases.

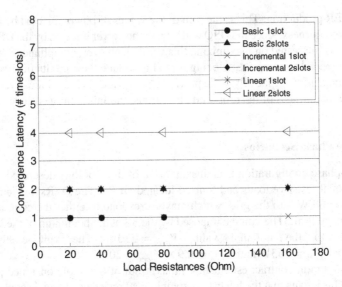

Fig. 4. Single phase scenario: convergence latency with line resistances of 0.1 Ω.

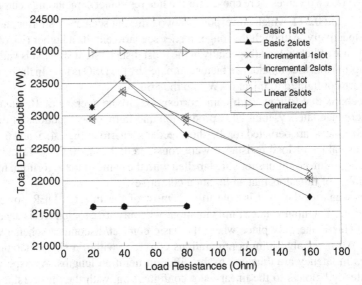

Fig. 5. Single phase scenario: total DER production with line resistances of 0.1 Ω.

The production fairness approaches the maximum of 1.0 in all configurations. Again, a slight reduction is observed for the incremental and linear algorithms, when the load resistance increases beyond 80 Ω.

For the longer feeder scenario, the metrics are depicted in Figs. 7, 8, and 9. This scenario is more challenging, which is illustrated by the fact that the basic connect/disconnect scheme only converges for the lowest value of load resistance (20 Ω). As the load resistance increases, the convergence latency also increases. The linear-1slot

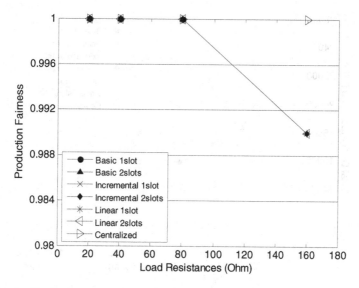

Fig. 6. Single phase scenario: production fairness with line resistances of 0.1 Ω.

configuration only converges for 20 Ω and 40 Ω, where it presents the highest values. This is due to conflictual decisions between different LCs when a single timeslot is used. The latency is lower for the linear-2slot configuration, which is lower than that of incremental-2slots. However, incremental-1slot presents the lowest latency. Total DER production and fairness present very similar curves in all converging configurations, which only slightly depart from the values achieved by the centralized algorithm. Again, production and fairness tend to get worse as the value of load resistance increases.

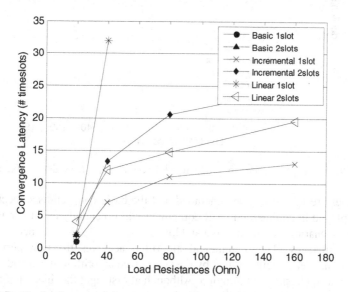

Fig. 7. Single phase scenario: convergence latency with line resistances of 0.2 Ω.

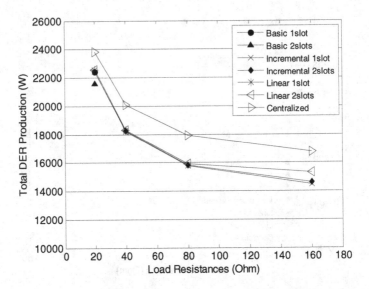

Fig. 8. Single phase scenario: total DER production with line resistances of 0.2 Ω.

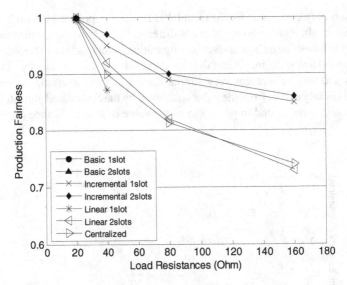

Fig. 9. Single phase scenario: production fairness with line resistances of 0.2 Ω.

From these results, it can be concluded that the basic connect/disconnect scheme widely employed in commercial DER equipment will potentially lead to convergence problems in scenarios with higher line and load resistance, resulting in decreased DER production efficiency. The incremental algorithm achieves the best performance, approaching the ideal solution found by the centralized algorithm. It can and should be employed in a single slot configuration. Although at first sight the linear algorithm has the potential to converge faster, since it allows larger variations of injected power in each iteration, this may lead to more significant conflictual LC decisions when employed in a single timeslot configuration. With two timeslots, while resolving the conflicts, it will be slower than the incremental algorithm using a single timeslot. The latter is more robust to LC decision conflicts, since the LCs performs small state changes in each decision cycle. It must now be verified if these conclusions hold in a more complex scenario.

5.2 Three-Phase Scenario

The algorithms were also tested in the more complex three-phase scenario depicted in Fig. 10. The three phases have a common neutral, which is characterized by the same line resistance values as the phase cables. Consequently, it is expected that changes in one phase will affect the others, hindering the convergence of the droop-based algorithms. The load resistance is in this case fixed as 80 Ohm. In order to test the effect of DER production balance between phases, two different configurations are considered: in the balanced configuration, all DERs in all phases are active, while in the unbalanced configuration DER production is active in one phase only. For each configuration, there are two variants: DER injected power limit of 6 kW and unlimited injected power.

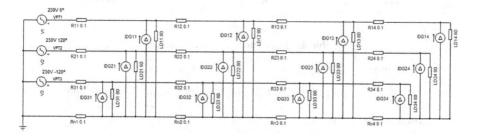

Fig. 10. Three-phase scenario.

Only two distributed algorithms were used in this study: incremental algorithm with 1 timeslot and linear algorithm with 2 timeslots.[1] These were again compared with the centralized algorithm. The convergence latency (when applicable), DER production per phase and fairness results are listed in Tables 2, 3, and 4.

In the three-phase scenario, it is not so clear which algorithm converges faster. It can be seen that the convergence of the linear algorithm significantly improves when the maximum power of the DERs is limited to 6 kW. Curiously, the convergence of the incremental algorithm gets worse. Being able to perform significant changes in the values of injected power in each iteration, the linear algorithm can take advantage of the reduced solution space provided by the injected power limit. On the other hand, the incremental algorithm relies on small changes of the injected power in each iteration, which may take more or less time to converge, depending on the current sensitivity

---

[1] Based on offline experiments, it was concluded that the performance of the incremental algorithm was not improved by an additional timeslot, while the linear algorithm would degrade its performance if configured to use a single timeslot.

Table 2. Three-phase scenario: convergence latency (# timeslots).

Algorithm	Balanced		Unbalanced	
	6k Limit	Unlimited	6k Limit	Unlimited
Incremental	198	149	198	116
Linear	6	396	124	153

Table 3. Three-phase scenario: DER production per phase (W).

Algorithm	Balanced		Unbalanced	
	6k Limit	Unlimited	6k Limit	Unlimited
Incremental	23210	54514	16502	27742
Linear	23286	61390	16772	31010
Centralized	23963	58933	23573	30304

Table 4. Three-phase scenario: fairness.

Algorithm	Balanced		Unbalanced	
	6k Limit	Unlimited	6k Limit	Unlimited
Incremental	1.0	0.34	0.82	0.34
Linear	1.0	0.27	0.78	0.27
Centralized	1.0	0.33	1.0	0.32

matrix. It may also experience additional delay due to oscillations around the final solution when algorithm decisions are overridden by imposing a non-linear limit to the maximum injected power. These shortcomings were not apparent in the simpler single-phase scenarios but became patent in the three-phase scenario. The linear algorithm was better in terms of production optimization in all configurations, approaching the centralized algorithm in the balanced scenario with 6 kW limited injection, or even surpassing it in both unlimited configurations. When the latter happens, there is a fairness penalty.

An interesting observation is that, as expected, a balanced configuration leads to an higher production per phase, even in the case where the injected power is unlimited, i.e., to concentrate all production in a single phase always leads to a lower total DER production in comparison with the case where the DERs are evenly distributed among the several phases. This result applies to all tested algorithms, including the centralized one. The reason for this is that voltage control will impose a limit on the injected power in each coupling point, even if the source could potentially inject more power.

6 Conclusions

This paper has presented two droop-based algorithms that try to maximize DER production in LV distribution grids with DER penetration, while keeping the voltage levels within the operating limits. The incremental algorithm performs small changes of injected active power in each decision cycle, while the linear algorithms changes the injected power based in the assumption of a linear relationship between the injected power and the voltage level at the coupling point.

The proposed algorithms were evaluated and compared with a state-of-the-art connect/disconnect scheme and a centralized algorithm that makes decisions based on knowledge about voltage and current levels at all DER coupling points. Simulation results show that the proposed algorithms approach the optimal solutions obtained by the centralized algorithm, with the incremental algorithm presenting faster convergence in single-phase scenarios, in all configurations. In three-phase scenarios, the linear algorithm usually presented faster convergence and was able to maximize the DER production, remaining closer to the centralized algorithm. It was also observed that balancing the DERs among the three phases, generally leads to more efficient DER production in comparison with unbalanced configurations where DERs are attached to only one phase in detriment of the others.

As future work, the authors plan to study the impact of communication network performance on the centralized voltage control schemes, as well as to define hybrid distributed/centralized algorithms, as well as optimization and dynamic adaptation of the distributed algorithm parameters.

Acknowledgements. This work was supported in part by European Community's Seventh Framework Programme (FP7-SMARTCITIES-2013) under Grant 609132 (http://www.e-balance-project.eu/), in part by national funding from QREN through the "Monitorização e controlo inteligente da rede de Baixa Tensão" (Monitor BT) project and in part by FCT – Fundação para a Ciência e a Tecnologia, with reference UID/CEC/50021/2013.

References

1. DL 153/2014, 20th of October, by which the distributed electricity generation activity is regulated
2. U.S. Department of Energy, 2012. Application of Automated Controls for Voltage a Reactive Power Management
3. Silva, N., Delgado, N., Costa, N., Bernardo A., Carrapatoso, A.: Control architectures to perform voltage regulation on low voltage networks using DG. In: CIRED 2012 Workshop on Integration of Renewables into the Distribution Grid, pp. 1–4. Lisbon (2012). ISBN: 978-1-84919-628-4
4. Krushna, K., Kumar, S.V.: Three-Phase Unbalanced Radial Distribution Load Flow Method. Int. Refereed J. Eng. Sci. (IRJES) 1(1), 39–42 (2012). ISSN (Online) 2319-183X, (Print) 2319-1821
5. Sajadi, A., Sebtahmadi, S., Koniak, M., Biczel, P., Mekhilef, S.: Distributed control scheme for voltage regulation in smart grids. Int. J. Smart Grid Clean Energy (SGCE) 1(1), 53–59 (2012). ISSN (Online) 2373-3594, (Print) 2315-4462

6. Tonkosky, R., Lopes, L., El-Fouly, T.: Coordinated active power curtailment of grid connected PV inverters for overvoltage prevention. IEEE Trans. Sustain. Energy **2**(2), 139–147 (2011)
7. Samadi, A., Shayesteh, E., Eriksson, R., Rawn, B., Soeder, L.: Multi-objective coordinated droop-based voltage regulation in distribution grids with PV systems. Renew. Energy Elsevier **71**(2014), 315–323 (2014)
8. Nunes, M.: Dynamic control method of power injected into the power grid by distributed generators. PCT/2015000040, Patent submitted in July 2015
9. Ngspice circuit simulator. http://ngspice.sourceforge.net/

A Sensitivity Based Approach for Efficient PMU Deployment on Smart Grid

Richard Barella[1], Duc Nguyen[1], Ryan Winter[1], Kuei-Ti Lu[1], Scott Wallace[1], Xinghui Zhao[1]([✉]), and Eduardo Cotilla-Sanchez[2]

[1] School of Engineering and Computer Science, Washington State University,
14204 NE Salmon Creek Avenue, Vancouver, WA 98686, USA
{richard.t.barella,duc.nguyen,ryan.j.winter,kuei-ti.lu,wallaces,
x.zhao}@wsu.edu
[2] School of Electrical Engineering and Computer Science, Oregon State University,
1148 Kelley Engineering Center, Corvallis, OR 97331, USA
ecs@eecs.oregonstate.edu

Abstract. Smart grid technology utilizes phasor measurement units (PMUs) as the key devices to provide synchronized measurements on an electrical grid, enabling wide area monitoring and control. Due to the high cost of deploying and maintaining these devices, an efficient placement strategy is essential in enhancing the reliability of a power grid at a relatively low cost. In this paper, we propose a novel PMU deployment method based on the effectiveness of detecting line faults. We have carried out a sensitivity study of a PMU-based fault detection method using three different distance metrics and used the study as a guideline for efficient PMU deployment. To illustrate the effectiveness of this approach, we have derived a number of alternative PMU placement plans for a power grid from a protection perspective. Experimental results show that many of our PMU placement plans greatly reduce the required PMU deployment (up to 80 %) as compared to the original placement, yet still provides similar level of accuracy in fault detection.

Keywords: Smart grid · PMU deployment · Sensitivity · Fault detection · Accuracy

1 Introduction

Phasor measurement units (PMUs), or synchrophasors, are devices that are deployed in power systems to measure phase angles and magnitudes of the electrical waves in real time, for monitoring the health of the power grid. A significant amount of work has been done in analyzing real-time PMU data for detecting faults [15,16], oscillations [18], as well as tracking fault locations [7]. However, these approaches assume a comprehensive coverage of PMUs on the power grid. Due to the installation cost, instrumenting every bus with PMUs is not always practical. Therefore, it is critical to efficiently deploy a limited number of PMUs so that comprehensive coverage in terms of fault detection can be provided.

© Springer International Publishing Switzerland 2015
M. Helfert et al. (Eds.): Smartgreens 2015 and Vehits 2015, CCIS 579, pp. 199–215, 2016.
DOI: 10.1007/978-3-319-27753-0_11

Instead of developing fault detection methods based on a known topology of PMUs on a power grid, we take a different approach in which we use an existing fault detection algorithm as a guideline to derive more efficient PMU placement plans.

As the first step toward better deployment of PMUs, it is essential to quantitatively analyze how the distance between a fault and the PMU(s) used to detect that fault impact the detection process itself. To this end, we have carried out a sensitivity study of distances in PMU-based fault detection. Specifically, we use a PMU-based fault detection method that we previously developed as a baseline, and investigate the accuracy of this method with respect to the distance between the fault location and the PMUs being utilized. Here, three distance metrics are studied: topological distance, logical distance, and electrical distance. Topological distance is derived from the system schema of the grid, i.e., number of *hops* between two sites. Logical distance is the Pearson correlation coefficient which is derived from two PMU data streams. Electrical distance is derived from the Ybus of the power grid, representing another way to elucidate the electrical structure of a power grid [14].

The results of the sensitivity study indicate that there is a potential to accurately detect faults even when no PMU is placed on a bus immediately adjacent to the fault. Rather, fault detection remains accurate within a small neighborhood near the fault, and then accuracy falls off as distance from the fault increases. This relationship creates an opportunity for efficient PMU deployment. Specifically, we use the results of the sensitivity study as a guideline and develop a PMU placement algorithm which derives deployment solutions based on distance constraints. We verified our algorithm using PMU data collected from a power grid; experimental results show that our PMU placement plan uses 80 % fewer PMUs compared to the original placement; however, it provides similar level of accuracy in detecting faults.

The remainder of the paper is organized as follows. Section 2 reviews related work in both PMU-based fault detection and PMU placement in a smart grid. Section 3 introduces the background of this work, including the fault detection method we use in this study, as well as a description of the dataset we use. The experimental results from the sensitivity study we carried out on three different distances are presented in Sect. 4. In Sect. 5, we develop a new PMU deployment algorithm which derives possible PMU placement solutions based on the results from the sensitivity study. Section 6 concludes the paper and proposes future directions for this work.

2   Related Work

With the growing popularity of using phasor measurement units (PMUs) to monitor power systems and enhance their reliability, there is increasing interest in analyzing real-time PMU data to detect and locate faults in the power grid. A significant amount of work has been done to detect or monitor certain conditions of a power grid by leveraging information extracted from PMU data.

Jiang et al. propose an online approach for fault detection and localization using SDFT (smart DFT) [15]. Liu et al. use Frequency Domain Decomposition for detecting oscillations [18]. Kazemi et al. propose a multivariable regression model to track fault locations using PMU data [7]. A more comprehensive survey can be found in [11]. These approaches assume a comprehensive PMU deployment across the smart grid. Most recently, with the emergence of big data analytics, a variety of machine learning techniques have been applied to analyze PMU data in power grid systems, including classification [1], clustering [4], artificial neural networks [21], Support Vector Machines [12], and regression trees [23].

Along with the work of monitoring the power grid using PMUs, the challenge of optimizing PMU placement has also attracted much attention. This is because deploying PMUs is expensive and a per-bus coverage of PMU deployment is not always practical [20]. Traditional approaches formulate PMU deployment as an optimization problem, in which the power grid is modeled as a graph, and the objective is to deploy PMUs at a minimum number of nodes so that the state of the whole power grid is observable [2,3,5,13]. This problem has been proven to be NP-complete. It has also been proven that no more than 1/3 of the nodes in a connected graph of at least 3 nodes are requirement to be equipped with PMUs in order to provide coverage for the whole power grid [6].

Besides these graph-theoretic approaches, simulation based methods have also been used in developing optimal placement for PMUs. For instance, in [19], a generic algorithm is proposed to find optimal deployment for heterogeneous measurement devices, including both PMUs and smart metering systems. The results are tested using simulation. Similar simulation approaches are used in [24] to evaluate a PMU placement method which aims for improving the accuracy of state estimation of the grid. In [17], a concept of fault-location observability is proposed. PMUs are placed on buses based on the one-bus spaced deployment strategy, and then the results are tested using simulation. In [22], generation from renewable sources are considered in the deployment of PMU and smart metering.

In this paper we propose a novel approach to derive an anytime-optimal PMU placement plan guided by a sensitivity study of a PMU-based fault detection method. Our work differs from the previous work in the following aspects. First, instead of proposing a theoretical deployment algorithm, we take a practical approach by developing a fault detection algorithm first, and then carrying out a sensitivity study which serves as the guideline for PMU deployment. Second, instead of using simulation, we used real PMU data collected over one-year period on a smart grid in Pacific Northwest region of the United States of America.

3 Background

In order to derive efficient PMU deployment plans for a smart grid, we first develop a simple fault detection method, and verify this method using a year of real PMU data collected from a smart grid in the Pacific NorthWest of the United States of America. The dataset we used in this study, as well as the fault detection method are presented in the following sections.

3.1 Dataset

The dataset we use in this research is from Bonneville Power Administration, the first utility agency that implements a comprehensive adoption of synchrophasors in their wide-area monitoring system. The smart grid is located in pacific northwest area in the United States, and it contains both 500 KV and 230 KV buses. In this grid, there are 31 sites which are equipped with PMUs to measure voltage, current, and frequency data. The dataset we use in this paper is collected from October 17, 2012 to September 16, 2013. During this time period, there are 107 documented faults, including single-line-to-ground faults, line-to-line faults, and three-phase faults.

3.2 Fault Detection Method

The fault detection method used in this study was developed based on a theoretical analysis on the characteristics of faults, as well as the BPA datasets [16]. The algorithm is a threshold based decision tree, which classifies faults into the three fault types – single-line-to-ground, line-to-line, and three-phase – using the voltage sag values on all three phases. This fault detection method classifies faults based on a set of pre-defined threshold values on voltage sags, which are calculated by surveying the dataset for the voltage sag values during the same type of faults. The voltage sag values are in the *per-unit* system of measurement (p.u.), which is to say that voltages have been normalized with respect their steady state values. For the scenario presented here, we calculate the steady state voltages for each individual phase as follows: (1) use a sliding window to scan a period before the fault occurs; (2) move the window backward in time

---

Algorithm 1. SteadyVoltage(dataMinute, bus, phase, t).

$steadyData$ = grab a sufficient window of data prior to the fault at time t;
$end = t$
while *steadyData contains a one second window ending at end* **do**
    $window$ = a one second window ending at end
    m = average($window$)
    mn = min($window$)
    /* check the window minimum for smoothness */
    if $mn \leq 0.9m$ **then**
        move end one cycle earlier in time
        continue
    end
    /* check the window edges for smoothness */
    if $window\ edges < 0.99m$ **then**
        move end one cycle earlier in time
        continue
    end
    return m
end
return $error$ /* out of data */

(away from the fault), until the signal within the window satisfies a steadyness criteria; (3) return the average voltage over the window. Algorithms 1 and 2 show how the voltage steady state and voltage sag values are calculated, respectively.

Algorithm 2. VoltageSagCalculation (faultlist, steadyCheckingPeriod, fluctuation).

---

for *each fault i in the faultlist* **do**

    $data_i$ = the minute data in which the fault occurs;

    `/* grab the fault minute data where the fault occurs */`

    for *each bus j* **do**

        for *each phase k* **do**

            $V_{min} = \min(data_{i,j,k})$;

            `/* grab the minimum voltage value from the fault`
            `minute, use that as the voltage sag*/`

            $T_{min} = \mathrm{argmin}(data_{i,j,k})$;

            `/* grab the time (cycle), at which the minimum`
            `voltage above was found*/`

            $V_{ss} = \mathrm{SteadyVoltage}(data_i, j, k, T_{min})$;

            `/* calculate steady voltage prior to the fault`
            `shown in Algorithm 1*/`

            $Vsag_{i,j,k} = V_{min}/V_{ss}$;

            `/* ` V_{sag} ` (in p.u.) for the fault*/`

        end

    end

end

It has been shown that the accuracy of this method is more than 96 % [16]. Further, it is worth noting that we develop this simple fault detection technique to serve as a baseline for our sensitivity study, but the approach presented in this paper is not limited to this fault detection method. Any other approaches for fault detection could also be used for this purpose.

4 Sensitivity Study

When a fault occurs on a power grid, the signature is typically visible at nearby locations although the signature is typically reduced in magnitude. This fact makes it possible to optimize the PMU placement by removing PMUs which provide redundant coverage. To fully understand the impact of distances on smart grid fault detection, we have carried out a sensitivity study on the fault detection method described in Sect. 3. Specifically, we have investigated the accuracy of the method when fault signatures are observed by PMUs at different locations on the power grid.

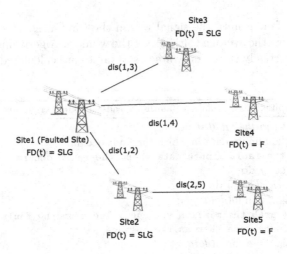

Fig. 1. Impact of a fault on smart grid.

4.1 Distance Metrics

A smart grid consists of a large number of interconnected sites. In order to efficiently deploy PMUs across the grid, we must first analyze the impact of various types of faults on the entire grid. Figure 1 shows an example grid which includes 5 sites. Suppose at certain point in time, a single-line-to-ground fault (SLG) occurs at Site 1, the impact of this fault is usually observable from other locations of the grid. As shown in Fig. 1, this impact can be captured by our fault detection method *FD* which is executed on various sites. Here in this example, the fault type (SLG) is successfully detected at sites 1, 2, and 3. However, as indicated in Fig. 1, Site 4 and 5 have failed to detect the fault, simply because they are further away. In this specific example, if a PMU is deployed on any of the sites 1, 2, or 3, this particular single-line-to-ground fault can be detected.

As the first step toward efficient deployment of PMUs across a power grid, we have carried out a sensitivity study of our fault detection method with respect to the distances to the faulted locations (sites) using real PMU data gathered from BPA's smart grid. Note that the *distance* between two sites can be represented in different ways. In our work, we have investigated three different distance metrics: topological distance, logical distance, and electrical distance.

Topological distance, or *hop distance*, is a distance metric for estimating geographical distances. To calculate the topological distance between two sites, we represent the grid as a graph with interconnected nodes. Each node is a site with a functioning PMU and edges between nodes are transmission lines that are also monitored by one or more PMUs[1]. We then use Dijkstra's algorithm [10] to derive the shortest path between any two sites, and construct a distance matrix

---

[1] Note that this method of deriving the connectivity graph ensures that our representation is a subset of the underlying power grid's full connectivity (other paths between sites may exist).

for the grid. Note that the topological distance matrix is static for a given smart grid, because it is derived from the topology of the grid.

Logical distance is a dynamic distance metric representing the linear correlation between two data streams. In this work, we use *Pearson correlation coefficient (PCC)* as the metric for logical distance. The PCC of two data streams $X(x_1, x_2, ..., x_n)$ and $Y(y_1, y_2, ..., y_n)$ can be calculated as follows:

$$PCC = \frac{\sum_{i=1}^{n} (x_i - \overline{X})(y_i - \overline{Y})}{\sqrt{\sum_{i=1}^{n} (x_i - \overline{X})^2}\sqrt{\sum_{i=1}^{n} (y_i - \overline{Y})^2}} \tag{1}$$

The value of PCC ranges from -1 to 1, representing the linear relationship between the two PMU data streams: 0 indicates no linear relationship, 1 and -1 indicate linear relationships, in positive or negative direction.

Electrical distance is an electrical cohesiveness metric, as proposed in [8]. The electrical distance between buses i and j is obtained from the quadrant of the ac power flow Jacobian that measures the incremental change in voltage phase angle difference between i and j for an incremental active power transaction between i and j. This power flow Jacobian is itself computed from a combination of the Y_{bus} (nodal admittance matrix), and generation and load information. In this particular set of experiments we build a 'nominal' power flow Jacobian by assuming that power injections are small increments, whereby the Jacobian is basically inherited from the Y_{bus} structure (this is analogous to a 'flat start' before solving the power flow problem).

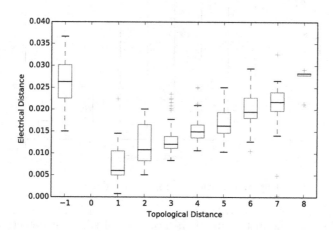

Fig. 2. Topological distance vs. electrical distance.

The above three metrics represent distances between sites in different ways. However, they are also related. For example, the topological distance, i.e., hop distance, has been shown to be a good indicator for electrical distance. Figure 2 shows a boxplot which depicts the relationship between these two types of distances derived from our dataset. As shown in Fig. 2, the electrical distance increases when the topological distance increases. Note that a topological distance of −1 indicates that the two sites are not connected by a path that is monitored by PMUs. Those sites generally have higher electrical distances too, as shown in the figure.

4.2   Fault Detection Sensitivity

With the three distance matrices being calculated, we can then analyze the accuracy of our fault detection algorithm presented in Sect. 3 across the whole smart grid, with respect to the distance to the faulted site.

Topological Distance. For each documented fault in our dataset, we first execute our fault detection algorithm on every PMU site, using the data being recorded during the time of the fault, then we compare the results with the ground truth (the recorded fault type), to determine whether the fault is correctly detected on each site. We then associate each result with the topological distance between the site where the data is collected and the faulted site. After all the faults have been analyzed, we calculate the accuracy of our fault detection method on a certain topological distance.

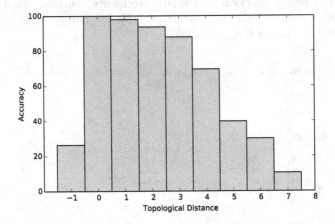

Fig. 3. Accuracy vs. topological distance.

Figure 3 shows the histogram of the accuracy of the fault detection method at various of distances away from the location of the fault. There is a clear correlation between the accuracy of the fault detection method and the topological distance from the fault location to the PMU where the data is collected. Specifically, if the PMU is located within 2 hops from the fault location, the accuracy of our fault detection method is above 80 % for all 107 recorded faults in the dataset. The accuracy decreases as topological distance increases.

Logical Distance. We represent logical distance between two sites using Pearson correlation coefficient (PCC) as shown in Eq. 1.

The logical distance metric models the similarity of two data streams within a certain period of time, therefore it is a dynamic metric which changes over time. In our study, we calculate logical distance using a 15-second time window preceding a fault, and analyze the accuracy of the fault detection method with respect to this distance metric. Specifically, for each fault, we first calculate the logical distance between the fault location and any other PMU site using the 15-second time window before the fault, then we execute the fault detection method using the data collected at each of the non-fault site, and associate the accuracy with the logical distance.

The results of the sensitivity analysis with respect to the logical distance are shown in Fig. 4. In general, the fault detection methods has higher accuracy when it is executed on a PMU site which has higher correlation with the fault location.

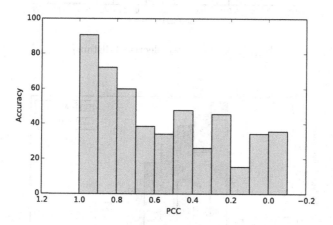

Fig. 4. Accuracy vs. logical distance

Electrical Distance. Similarly, we have carried out a sensitivity study on electrical distance, which is a static distance metric derived from the schema of the smart grid, as described in Sect. 4.1. The results are shown in Fig. 5. As expected, the accuracy of our fault detection method decreases when the electrical distance to the fault location increases. However, the accuracy is close to 100 % when the electrical distance is within 0.010.

To further investigate the electrical distance, we have calculated the number of added signals when we gradually increase the electrical distance boundary. Figure 6 shows the results. Light gray indicates the signals on which the fault detection method can accurately detect faults, while dark gray bars indicate the total set of signals for within a specific electrical distance from the fault's source. When the electrical distance is within 0.010, the fault detection method is accurate for the vast majority of signals. As the boundary's electrical distance increases from the fault's origin, however, the fraction of signals contributing to a correct classification tends to decrease. This loss of signal to noise follows intuition.

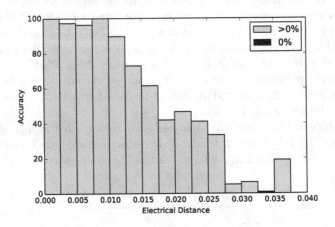

Fig. 5. Accuracy vs. electrical distance.

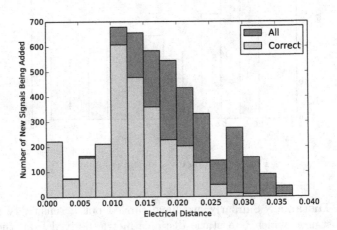

Fig. 6. Electrical distance vs. sites.

The sensitivity study presented in this section indicates that it is not necessary to deploy PMUs at every site in a smart grid. This is simply because most of the faults can be detected from a site which is within a certain distance from the fault location.

5 Sensitivity Based PMU Deployment

Based on the sensitivity study, we can derive an improved PMU deployment plan for the smart grid, so that fewer PMUs are required to provide similar level of accuracy in fault detection. Note that here we use the topological distance as an example to illustrate this approach, but the other two distance metrics can also be used in similar way.

5.1   PMU Placement Algorithm

The sensitivity study suggests that the accuracy of our fault detection method is reasonably good when the PMU is located within two hops from the fault. Based on this observation, we have developed a PMU placement algorithm which deploys PMUs in the way that each site in the smart grid is less than or equal to n hops away from a PMU. Algorithm 3 shows how a PMU placement plan is derived.

The algorithm randomly picks a starting site to place a PMU, then traverses the grid while iteratively placing PMUs on the sites as needed. Depending on the staring site, and choices made during the course of execution, the algorithm may return different solutions. Figure 7 shows an example placement solution which uses only 6 PMUs (highlighted in gray in the figure), as opposed to 31 in the original smart grid schema.[2] The placement is derived with a topological distance constraint of 3, which means that any site on the smart grid is less than or equal to 3 hops away from a site with a PMU.

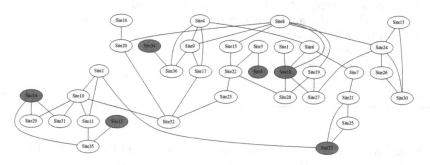

Fig. 7. An example PMU placement plan (PMU sites are highligthed in gray).

To evaluate the PMU placement plan shown in Fig. 7, we have simulated a smart grid with these 6 PMUs, and execute our fault detection method using data from these 6 PMUs. For the 107 recorded faults, the accuracy of the fault detection on the 6-PMU smart grid is 93.9 %, only 2.1 % less than the accuracy of the original smart grid with 31 PMU-equipped sites (96 %). These results illustrate that it is possible to accurately detect faults using significantly less PMUs, creating the opportunities of cost savings for PMU deployment.

---

[2] The actual site names are not displayed in Fig. 7 due to security reasons. Figure 7 shows 36 sites because we included 5 sites which do not have PMUs installed in the original grid, in order to maintain the original topology. Note that the new PMU deployment plan we generated only places PMUs on the sites that are PMU-equipped in the original power grid.

Algorithm 3. PMU Placement.

```
randomly pick a site S₀;
place PMU at S₀;
S₀.distance = 0;
Queue.push(S₀);
while Queue is not empty do
    nextSite = Queue.pop();
    currentDistance = nextSite.distance;
    if nextSite.distance ≤ 2 then
        Visited.append(nextSite);
        for neighbor in nextSite's neighborset do
            if neighbor is not visited then
                neighbor.distance = nextSite.distance+1;
                Queue.push(neighbor);
            end
        end
    end
    else
        place PMU at nextSite;
        nextSite.distance = 0;
        Queue.push(nextSite);
    end
    if Queue is empty && not all sites are visited then
        randomly pick an unvisited site;
        Place PMU at newSite;
        newSite.distance = 0;
        Queue.push(newSite);
    end
end
```

Similarly, we randomly picked some placement solutions generated by our PMU deployment algorithm using various of distance constraints, and calculated their accuracy. Figure 8 shows a comparison of the accuracy of these solutions with respect to their distance constraints. The number of PMUs of each solution is also noted in the figure. As shown in the figure, it is possible to achieve more than 90 % of accuracy in fault detection with only 6 PMUs. As expected, when the distance constraint increases, the accuracy decreases, so does the number of required PMUs.

Comparing to the original PMU deployment in the smart grid, where 31 PMUs are used, we have demonstrated alternative PMU placement plans that utilize many fewer PMUs while providing equivalent or similar quality of coverage in terms of detecting line faults. Based on a recent cost analysis report by Department of Energy [9], the average cost per PMU ranges from $40k to $180k, which includes cost for procurement, installation and commissioning. Therefore, our work can potentially result in significant cost savings for a smart grid.

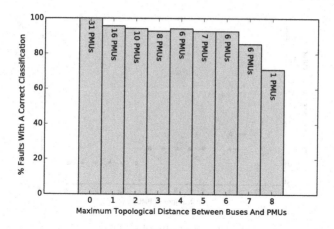

Fig. 8. Comparison of PMU placement plans.

5.2   Evaluation

Experiments have been carried out to evaluate the accuracy of potential PMU placement plans with various numbers of PMUs, and the effectiveness of our PMU placement algorithm.

Figure 9 shows the fault-detection accuracy of randomly generated PMU placement plans, with respect to number of PMUs placed. For each x-value, we generate approximately 1000 unique placement plans except for the 1-PMU and 2-PMU cases where we generated all possible unique placements. Recalling the plot in Fig. 8, note that a placement plan with 6 PMUs will include placements in which the maximum topological distance between two PMUs varies, perhaps widely. For 6 PMUs, the maximum topological distance ranges between 4–7 hops; perhaps more. The boxes in Fig. 9 show the 1st through 3rd quartile accuracy while the line within the box shows the median accuracy. As expected,

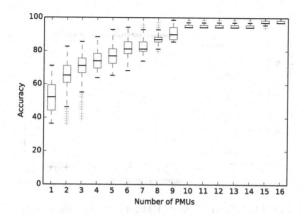

Fig. 9. Quality vs. number of PMUs.

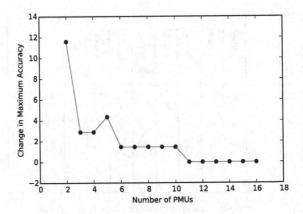

Fig. 10. Effect of adding PMUs.

increasing number of PMUs increases both average accuracy and maximum accuracy, although even solutions with few PMUs can achieve relatively high accuracy. Additionally, the distribution of placement accuracies dramatically narrows once 10 PMUs have been placed and median accuracy becomes much more stable.

Figure 10 shows the impact of adding each successive PMU after the first for the grid topology illustrated in Fig. 7. Impact, here, is the change in accuracy of the best observed placement for a given number of PMUs. A negative value would indicate that the best placement has become less accurate as a result of adding a PMU. Negative values are possible because the search space of possible PMU placements is extremely large and only partially explored by our experiment. However, the exploration presented here is sufficient to produce a monotonically improving accuracy as one would intuitively expect from an iterative placement scheme.

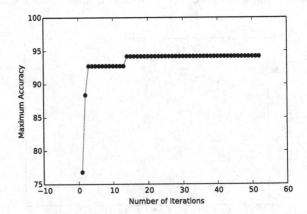

Fig. 11. Effectiveness of PMU placement algorithm.

We have also carried out a set of experiments to evaluate the effectiveness of our PMU placement approach (Algorithm 3) in generating high quality solutions. Specifically, we run the algorithm for multiple iterations, and in each iteration rotate across starting points. We then collect all the valid PMU placement plans generated by the algorithm, and calculate the maximum accuracy of all the placement plans. The results are shown in Fig. 11. Note that in these experiments we set the maximum distance allowed from a bus to its closest PMU is 2. As shown in Fig. 11, running the algorithm for more iterations increases the quality of the solution, and the best solution is identified relatively quickly—here, on the 14th iteration.

6   Conclusion

Synchrophasors are widely used in power grids to enhance situation awareness, and robustness of power delivery. A significant amount of work has been done in fault detection using PMU data. However, these approaches assume a predefined PMU deployment scheme across the smart grid. Since deploying PMUs is costly, it is not necessarily practical nor scalable to equip every bus with a PMU. A more cost-effective solution for PMU deployment is needed.

While traditional approaches usually simulate the power grid and derive efficient PMU deployment plans, in this paper, we take a novel approach to investigate ways to efficiently deploy PMUs across a power grid based on the accuracy of detecting faults. The goal of this work is to deploy the fewest PMUs while still providing comprehensive coverage in terms of fault detection. Specifically, we first developed a fault detection method based on voltage sags of three phases, and then carried out a sensitivity study on the accuracy of this method, with respect to the distance from the fault location. To this end, we have investigated three different types of distances, namely topological distance, logical distance, and electrical distance. The sensitivity study shows that our fault detection method can achieve high accuracy when it is executed using data collected within certain distance to the fault location. This creates opportunities to detect faults using less PMUs. We then developed a PMU deployment algorithm which derives valid solutions for PMU deployment based on a pre-defined distance constraint. The evaluation results show that our new PMU deployment plan can achieve high accuracy with less than one-fifth of PMUs originally deployed in the smart grid.

Our work is ongoing in several directions. First, we will develop new fault detection approaches using machine learning techniques, such as classification and clustering. Second, we will create visualization tools based on our study, for enhancing the real-time situation awareness of a smart grid. Third, we will investigate the possibilities to repurpose our fault detection techniques for solving other problems on a smart grid, such as data conditioning, and cyber-security challenges.

Acknowledgement. The generous support from Bonneville Power Administration and Oregon BEST through the NW Energy XP Award is gratefully acknowledged.

The authors also would like to thank Bonneville Power Administration for providing PMU data used in this research.

References

1. Alsafasfeh, Q.H.: Pattern recognition for fault detection, classification, and localization in electrical power systems. Ph.D. thesis, Kalamazoo, MI, USA (2010)
2. Anderson, J., Chakrabortty, A.: A minimum cover algorithm for PMU placement in power system networks under line observability constraints. In: IEEE Power and Energy Society General Meeting, pp. 1–7, July 2012
3. Anderson, J., Chakrabortty, A.: Graph-theoretic algorithms for PMU placement in power systems under measurement observability constraints. In: The 3rd IEEE International Conference on Smart Grid Communications (SmartGridComm), pp. 617–622, November 2012
4. Antoine, O., Maun, J.C.: Inter-area oscillations: identifying causes of poor damping using phasor measurement units. In: IEEE Power and Energy Society General Meeting, pp. 1–6, July 2012
5. Brueni, D.J.: Minimal PMU Placement for Graph Observability: A Decomposition Approach (1993)
6. Brueni, D.J., Heath, L.S.: The PMU placement problem. SIAM J. Discret. Math. **19**(3), 744–761 (2005)
7. Chang, G., Chao, J.P., Huang, H.M., Chen, C.I., Chu, S.Y.: On tracking the source location of voltage sags and utility shunt capacitor switching transients. IEEE Trans. Power Deliv. **23**(4), 2124–2131 (2008)
8. Cotilla-Sanchez, E., Hines, P., Barrows, C., Blumsack, S.: Comparing the topological and electrical structure of the north american electric power infrastructure. IEEE Syst. J. **6**(4), 616–626 (2012)
9. Department of Energy: Factors Affecting PMU Installation Costs (2014). https://www.smartgrid.gov/sites/default/files/doc/files/PMU-cost-study-final-10162014.pdf. Accessed 24 March 2015
10. Dijkstra, E.: A note on two problems in connexion with graphs. Numerische Mathematik **1**(1), 269–271 (1959)
11. Glavic, M., Van Cutsem, T.: A short survey of methods for voltage instability detection. In: IEEE Power and Energy Society General Meeting, pp. 1–8, July 2011
12. Gomez, F., Rajapakse, A., Annakkage, U., Fernando, I.: Support vector machine-based algorithm for post-fault transient stability status prediction using synchronized measurements. IEEE Trans. Power Syst. **26**(3), 1474–1483 (2011)
13. Haynes, T.W., Hedetniemi, S.M., Hedetniemi, S.T., Henning, M.A.: Domination in graphs applied to electric power networks. SIAM J. Discret. Math. **15**(4), 519–529 (2002)
14. Hines, P., Blumsack, S., Sanchez, E.C., Barrows, C.: The topological and electrical structure of power grids. In: Proceedings of the 43rd Hawaii International Conference on System Sciences (HICSS), pp. 1–10 (2010)
15. Jiang, J.A., Yang, J.Z., Lin, Y.H., Liu, C.W., Ma, J.C.: An adaptive pmu based fault detection/location technique for transmission lines. i. theory and algorithms. IEEE Trans. Power Deliv. **15**(2), 486–493 (2000)
16. Liang, X., Wallace, S., Zhao, X.: A technique for detecting wide-area single-line-to-ground faults. In: Proceedings of the 2nd IEEE Conference on Technologies for Sustainability (SusTech 2014), SusTech 2014, pp. 1–4. IEEE (2014)

17. Lien, K.P., Liu, C.W., Yu, C.S., Jiang, J.A.: Transmission network fault location observability with minimal PMU placement. IEEE Trans. Power Deliv. **21**(3), 1128–1136 (2006)
18. Liu, G., Venkatasubramanian, V.: Oscillation monitoring from ambient pmu measurements by frequency domain decomposition. In: IEEE International Symposium on Circuits and Systems (ISCAS 2008), pp. 2821–2824, May 2008
19. Liu, J., Tang, J., Ponci, F., Monti, A., Muscas, C., Pegoraro, P.: Trade-offs in PMU deployment for state estimation in active distribution grids. IEEE Trans. Smart Grid **3**(2), 915–924 (2012)
20. Mili, L., Baldwin, T., Adapa, R.: Phasor measurement placement for voltage stability analysis of power systems. In: Proceedings of the 29th IEEE Conference on Decision and Control, pp. 3033–3038, December 1990
21. Mishra, S., Bhende, C., Panigrahi, K.: Detection and classification of power quality disturbances using S-transform and probabilistic neural network. IEEE Trans. Power Deliv. **23**(1), 280–287 (2008)
22. Pegoraro, P., Tang, J., Liu, J., Ponci, F., Monti, A., Muscas, C.: Pmu and smart metering deployment for state estimation in active distribution grids. In: IEEE International on Energy Conference and Exhibition (ENERGYCON), pp. 873–878, September 2012
23. Zheng, C., Malbasa, V., Kezunovic, M.: Regression tree for stability margin prediction using synchrophasor measurements. IEEE Trans. Power Syst. **28**(2), 1978–1987 (2013)
24. Zhu, K., Nordstrom, L., Ekstam, L.: Application and analysis of optimum PMU placement methods with application to state estimation accuracy. In: IEEE Power Energy Society General Meeting, pp. 1–7, July 2009

Using Flexibility Information for Planning the Energy Demand of Households

Sandford Bessler[1]([⊠]), Domagoj Drenjanac[1], Eduard Hasenleithner[1], and Nuno Silva[2]

[1] FTW Telecommunications Research Center, Donau-City 1, 1220 Vienna, Austria
{bessler,drenjanac,hasenleithner}@ftw.at
[2] EFACEC Energia Máquinas e Equipamentos Eléctricos, S.A, PO Box 3078, 4471-907 Moreira Maia, Portugal

Abstract. Energy flexibility information describes the energy minimum and the maximum consumption profiles of a flexible load, and has been recently recognized as a significant enabler for smart energy management in the grid. In this paper we describe an energy management architecture in a residential grid that allows a flexibility operator to use the flexibility of household consumption. Among the benefits of this setting are, for instance, that the demand management can cope with higher household loads due to house heating, electric vehicle charging, and schedule the loads while respecting the total consumption limit. Another benefit of the architecture is the robustness of the system in case the communication between flexibility operator and households is disrupted. In addition to system architectural aspects, the paper describes the optimization problems in both controllers and presents numerical results from the use of a benchmark grid.

Keywords: Flexibility models · Load predictive models · Optimization models · Energy scheduling · EV charging · HVAC · PV generation · Demand response · OADR 2.0 · Day-ahead pricing · Setpoint following

1 Introduction

The intensive deployment of photovoltaic power generation modules in private homes has caused that most Distribution System Operators (DSO) come out with rules to limit further installations that would otherwise lead to over-voltages in the grid during the sunny hours. In the same time, a number of flexible loads such has HVAC for heating, air conditioning, combined heat pumps, and electric vehicles multiplicate the peak household consumption from 2 kW to more than 7 kW, a level which, if reached simultaneously by many consumers, would overload the grid. We mention these cases in order to underline the need for energy demand control for maintaining the power quality.

At the basis of this work we use the concept of power and energy flexibility, a time-varying information that is usually calculated by a distributed energy resource (DER) and reported to a DSO, a utility or a third party aggregator.

© Springer International Publishing Switzerland 2015
M. Helfert et al. (Eds.): Smartgreens 2015 and Vehits 2015, CCIS 579, pp. 216–233, 2016.
DOI: 10.1007/978-3-319-27753-0_12

The latter may use this information for various services, in particular for direct demand control. For alowing this kind of remote control, the DER owner might benefit monetarily, however contract and tariff aspects are beyond the scope of this paper.

The main objective of this work is to investigate the feasibility of a number of demand control schemes in a residential low voltage grid with both rigid and flexible intelligent loads, storage and generation [13]. The household controllers (CEMS) report periodically flexibility information to an aggregation controller, which uses it to optimally schedule the power level of those households. Flexibility information and actuation messages form a closed loop in which energy demand can be centrally shedded, shifted in time, balanced or scheduled among the CEMS. The information exchange between controllers is realized by means of a standardized web service interface for demand response applications, Open Automated Demand Response (OADR) verson 2.0, however the intended demand side mangement applications go beyond demand response, see [12] for a comparison of DR schemes.

The major contributions of this work are:

- to define flexibility models for EV charging, heating ventilation and air conditioning (HVAC) and aggregated CEM flexibility,
- to formulate a CEMS optimization model that uses the flexibility to control its flexible assets,
- to formulate the optimization model of an aggregation controller,
- to build and evaluate a system of communicating controllers for demand management.

1.1 Previous Work on Flexibility

With the emerging of Distributed Energy Resources (DER) in the last two decades, the decentralization of the energy network has started. Within their work to integrate the DER into the energy network, the M490 Working Group (SG-CG/RA and SG-CG/SP) introduced the concept of flexibility, which groups together consumption, production and storage in one entity [4]. In the project iPower [10] the flexibility interface is an information model designed for Direct Control of Distributed Energy Resources (DER), i.e. it conveys the characteristics that a DER exposes to an aggregator or virtual power plant. DERs are equipped with local controllers that follow also local goals, [1]. An aggregator manages multiple DERs.

Flexibility concepts have been used in the context of electric vehicle charging [3] and flexible home consumption. Sundstrom and Binding [2] use the energy stored in the EV fleet and the bounds of this energy to optimize the charging schedules at the fleet (aggregator) level. In [8] the authors present FlexLast, a solution for management the consumption of power for cooling in supermarkets, based on the flexibility reporting and control. Energy prices together with flexibility information have been used in a scheduling model in [11]. The Danish project iPower, see [5], goes a step further by defining flexibility services contracted between players in which the aggregator manages a portfolio with flexible consumers with low marginal flexibility costs.

The rest of the paper is organized as follows: in Sect. 2 we define the flexibility of a charging EV, an HVAC used for house heating and aggregate them to household flexibility. In Sect. 3 we describe the system architecture and introduce the optimization problem at the household level. In Sect. 4 we introduce the LV aggregation controller and formulate the scheduling problem at the LV grid level. In Sect. 5 we report on numeric experiments in the simulation environment and discuss the results. Finally we conclude and present directions for further research.

2   Flexible Asset Models

Flexibility information is usually a time series of predicted power and energy values over a forecast time horizon. Assume that time is discretized to N periods of duration T, where the set $N = 0, 1, \ldots N-1$ defines a forecast time horizon of duration NT. In order to calculate the asset flexibility, an energy consumption and storage model is used. It is important to mention that the considered processes are relatively slow, they do not "see" transients, abrupt voltage or power changes, therefore the mechanisms proposed are not suitable for voltage control. If the period T is set to 15 min, the values.

In the next subsection we present simple asset models: the electric vehicle and the HVAC used here for heating a house. In the rest of the paper we will use the following notation for the energy flexibility $\underline{E}_j^{asset}$ and $\overline{E}_j^{asset}$, and for the power flexibility $\underline{P}_j^{asset}$ and $\overline{P}_j^{asset}$, where j is the time period index, and the underline/overline notation means the minimum respectively maximum flexibility.

2.1   The Electric Vehicle (EV) Predictive Load Model

In a simplified world, charging an EV i is equivalent to a load which can be activated from the plug-in time until the leave-time. In a residential scenario the plug-in and plug-out/leave time at the charging point can be individually configured or obtained from history data. In this paper we will restrict to the residential case in which the EV is controlled by the Customer Energy Management System (CEMS).

The charging power varies from period to period, $p \in [0, P_{max}]$, but is constant during a period. At the end of the stay, the total charged energy should be between a minimum demand and a maximum demand value (full charged): $E^{EV} \in [D_{min}, D_{max}]$. This provides additional freedom in the charging process and expresses the fact that users do not have to fully charge the battery.

The energy flexibility is initially zero and represents the *cummulative* energy charged by the EV. The convention used is that the power consumed during period i corresponds to the cummulative energy at the end of this period. Figure 1 illustrates the flexibility of a charging load with $P_{max}^{EV} = 8\,kW$, $D_{min} = 4\,kWh$ and $D_{max} = 8\,kWh$. In Fig. 1 we depict the minimum and maximum energy for the next eight periods, calculated one period before EV arrival and 2 periods later, where 2.5 kWh have been actually charged.

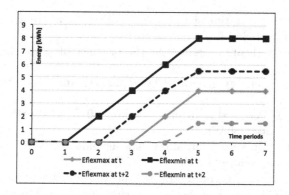

Fig. 1. EV energy flexibility at time t and t+2 (top) and power flexibility (bottom).

If we denote the already charged energy with D_c, the arrival period with a and the leave period with l, then the maximum power and energy flexibility are

$$\overline{P}_j^{EV} = \begin{cases} P_{max}, & \text{if } \overline{E}_{j-1}^{EV} + TP_{max} < D_{max} - D_c, j = a, \dots, l \\ 0, & \text{otherwise.} \end{cases} \tag{1}$$

$$\overline{E}_j^{EV} = \overline{E}_{j-1}^{EV} + T\overline{P}_j^{EV}, j = a, \dots, l \tag{2}$$

The minimum flexibility represents the latest time to start charging in order to satisfy the remaining demand $D_{min} - D_c$

$$\underline{P}_j^{EV} = \begin{cases} P_{max}, & \text{if } l - [(D_{min} - D_c)/T/P_{max}] \le j < l. \\ 0, & \text{otherwise.} \end{cases} \tag{3}$$

$$\underline{E}_j^{EV} = \underline{E}_{j-1}^{EV} + T\underline{P}_j^{EV}, j = a, \dots, l \tag{4}$$

2.2 The HVAC Predictive Load Model

Heating and air conditioning are good examples of thermal storage. Since a house is a complex thermal system, a complete model is impractical. We use however the first law of thermodynamics and describe as example the energy consumption and storage capacity of a simple house in Austria with two floors and a total size of $128\,m^2$. The house is well isolated and the majority of windows are facing south resulting in a total annual energy demand of around $60\,\text{kWh}/m^2$. The mathematical equation, based on the first law of thermodynamics, describing the major thermal effects in the house is:

$$E^p + E^a + E^s + E_i^h - E^v - E_i^{trans} = mc\Delta Temp_i \tag{5}$$

where

- the heating energy at time i is $E_i^h = z_i P^{HVAC} T$, where $z_i \in \{0,1\}$ is the control signal in period i,
- E^p is the energy (heat) generated by the presence of people in the house, in our case 256 Wh,
- E^a is the caloric energy generated by appliances and lights; for $3W/m^2$, we obtain $E^a = 384\,Wh$,
- E^s is the energy received from sun (assuming 40 % glass surface, south orientation), in our case 560 Wh.
- E^v is the energy lost via ventilation that depends on the temperature difference between inside and outside, $E^v = 45$ Wh,
- $E^{trans} = UP\Delta Temp_i$ is the energy lost due to window and wall conductivity at time i. $U[W/m^2/K]$ is a measure of the thermal resistance and $P[m^2]$ is the surface of the specific material, $\Delta Temp_i$ is the temperature difference to outside.

Using the Eq. (5), the model estimates the inside temperature for the planning horizon, based on a heating schedule. A temperature range of e.g. $18 - 22°C$ determines the point in which heating has to be switched on, respectively has to be switched off.

In order to calculate the flexibility, the HVAC uses the current state: to follow the maximum flexibility curve, it heats continuously up to the maximum temperature, then keeps the upper limit. For the minimum, the heating remains off until the low temperature limit is reached, then it must heat for a minimum time, see Fig. 2.

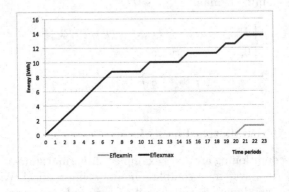

Fig. 2. 5 kW HVAC energy flexibility.

Given the ON-OFF operation of the HVAC heating in this example, the power flexibility is straightforward: $\underline{P}_j^{HVAC} = 0$ and $\overline{P}_j^{HVAC} = P^{HVAC}$, the heating power.

In the considered smart households, photovoltaic power generation is also available. Although this energy cannot be stored, the generated active power can be derated and/or curtailed. For a simple active power control, the ideal photovoltaic output p is first limited by the inverter maximum power, P_{rated}.

$P^{gen} = \min(P_{rated}, \eta A I_{solar})$, where η is the efficiency of the solar cells and A is their area in m^2. To control a certain range of this power output, we introduce the generation factor $gf \in [gf_{min}, 1]$ with $gf_{min} < 1$. For an available power P^{gen}, the PV generates therefore the power $p = gf P^{gen}$ with $gf_{min} P^{gen} \leq p \leq P^{gen} \leq P_{rated}$. This model can be easily mapped to the industrial modes of control using derated power and curtailing [6].

Finally, in the household there is also the non-flexible consumption, which is characterized by an individual profile P^{load}. To calculate the CEMS flexibility, we aggregate the asset flexibilities, the non-flexible consumption and the generated energy $P^{gen} > 0$ as follows:

$$\underline{E}_j^{CEMS} = \underline{E}_j^{EV} + \underline{E}_j^{HVAC} + 1/T \sum_{k=0}^{j} (P_k^{load} - P_k^{gen}), j \in N \qquad (6)$$

$$\overline{E}_j^{CEMS} = \overline{E}_j^{EV} + \overline{E}_j^{HVAC} + 1/T \sum_{k=0}^{j} (P_k^{load}), j \in N \qquad (7)$$

3   Energy Management Architecture

We consider a radial low voltage grid supplying a residential area, where each home is configured with the assets described in the previous sections: an HVAC used for heating, an EV charging point, PV generation and non-flexible loads. These assets are connected to a local controller, the CEMS, via a bidirectional data interface. The assets deliver the energy flexibility forecast to CEMS, which solves a planning problem resulting in a forecast of the house consumption and the charging and heating control profiles to be applied to the assets. The aggregated household flexibility and the consumption forecast are sent periodically to an Aggregation Controller as depicted in Fig. 3.

For the realisation of different demand control strategies such as direct load control, demand shifting, load scheduling, a bidirectional interface between the Aggregation controller and the CEMS controller is needed. We have chosen the Open Automated Demand Response (OADR) version 2.0, a standardized web service interface. In the demand response terminology the demand management control (DMC) represents to the aggregation controller and the virtual end node (VEN) represents the CEMS controller. OADR supports perfectly the main interactions: the Report message from VEN to DMC contains the flexibility and consumption active power forecast arrays, whereas the OADR Event message task is to distribute power setpoints to the VENs.

Additional input information needed by the CEMS optimization model is provided via the Head-end (Virtual Top Node VTN in the OADR architecture): solar irradiation forecasts, predicted household consumption and energy market clearing prices.

3.1   CEMS Energy Optimization

As mentioned at the beginning, the basic idea of reporting flexibility is to transfer the control of the house energy management, up to a certain extent, to an

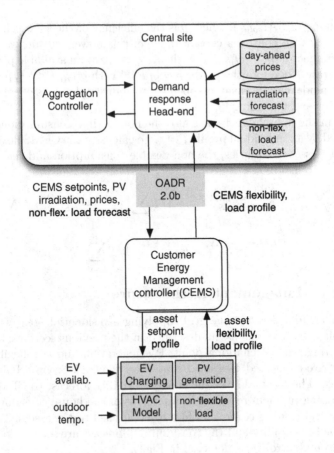

Fig. 3. Energy management architecture.

energy aggregator or utility. Nevertheless, the CEMS follows local management objectives as well.

In optimization terms this leads to a multi-objective function with three terms: the first term in (8) causes the CEMS consumption to follow the setpoints imposed at the LV grid level, and does so by minimizing the deviation between the CEMS net consumption (power from the grid) and the CEMS setpoint reference P^{ref}, similarly to the objective used in [2,9]. The second term maximizes the own generated power $gf\,P^{gen}$ over the prediction time horizon, so that more energy is locally stored. Finally, the third term uses energy prices to minimize the energy cost over the planning period. We use MCP (market clearing prices) c_j that are published and available the day before, for the whole grid. Besides the savings in buying more energy when prices are low, prices can be used to discourage usage during peak consumption periods.

If the original positive prices are used, the minimization goal in (8) will cause also the minimization of the consumed energy, an effect which is not always desired: for instance the EV will be always charged with the amount D_{min}, the house temperature will be kept at the minimum value. If we derive a relative price by substracting from the full price the daily average (base value), we obtain both positive and negative terms for the third term of the objective 8. Table 1 provides the used notation.

Table 1. Notation summary.

Notation	Description
y_j	charging power in kW during period j
z_j	HVAC heating binary control during period j
gf_j	generation factor during period j
gf_{min}	parameter defining the maximal curtailment of PV active power
E_j^{EV}	EV charged energy starting with j = 0
E_j^{HVAC}	electric energy consumed for heating, starting with j = 0
P^{HVAC}	heating power (in this example $-5\,$kW)
P_{max}^{EV}	maximum EV charging power, e.g. $6\,$kW
P_j^{in}	net power from or to the grid during period j
P^{in+}	$P^{in+} = P_j^{in}$ if $P_j^{in} > 0$ and zero else.
P_j^{load}	non-flexible average active power during period j
P_j^{gen}	uncurtailed PV generated power in period j
c_j	MCP energy price during period j
P_j^{ref}	reference power or setpoint imposed on the CEMS in period j
LV_{maxp}	limiting power constraint for the whole grid

The optimization program in Eqs. (8)–(16) is quadratic and has integer (binary) variables. The constraint (9) expresses the power flows balance at the house grid connecting point. The constraints (10) and (11) express the accumulation of energy in the battery, such that is has to be within the flexibility limits. Similarly, the HVAC in constraints (12) and (13).

minimize

$$K_1(\sum_{j \in N}(P_j^{in} - P_j^{ref})^2 - K_2 \sum_{j \in N} gf_j P_j^{gen} + K_3 \sum_{j \in N} c_j P_j^{in+} \qquad (8)$$

subject to:

$$P_j^{in} + gf_j P_j^{gen} - y_j - P_j^{load} - z_j P^{HVAC} = 0, j \in N \qquad (9)$$

$$E_j^{EV} = E_{j-1}^{EV} + y_{j-1}T, j \in N - \{0\}, E_0^{EV} = 0 \qquad (10)$$

$$E_j^{EV} \in [\underline{E}_j^{EV}, \overline{E}_j^{EV}], j \in N \qquad (11)$$

$$E_j^{HVAC} = E_{j-1}^{HVAC} + z_{j-1}P^{HVAC}T, j \in N - \{0\}, E_0^{HVAC} = 0 \qquad (12)$$

$$E_j^{HVAC} \in [\underline{E}_j^{HVAC}, \overline{E}_j^{HVAC}], j \in N \tag{13}$$

$$y_j \in [0, P_{max}^{EV}], j \in N \tag{14}$$

$$z_j \in \{0, 1\}, j \in N \tag{15}$$

$$gf_j \in [gf_{min}, 1], j \in N \tag{16}$$

The result of the CEMS optimization consists of:

- a plan of active power consumption $P_j^{in}, j \in N$ (respectively power injection into the grid if the values are negative).
- a plan of control actions: (a) $z_j, j \in N$ towards the HVAC, (b) $y_j, j \in N$ towards the EV charging point, (c) $gf_j, j \in N$ towards the PV inverter.

4   Aggregated Energy Management in the LV Grid

In this section we describe the optimization model of the aggregation controller, see Fig. 3. Its main role is to compute power reference values (setpoints) for each CEMS. In [16] we assumed that the grid topology is known, and we imposed voltage and current limits on each of the buses using power flows equations. In practice, the entity responsible for demand control, which is usually different from the DSO, has no access to grid topology information, except key parameters such as the nominal power at the secondary station, LV_{maxp}.

As long as the total requested load is below LV_{maxp}, we simply allocate it among the CEMS by calculating the setpoints, such that the error deviation from the planned demand P^{in} is minimized. The problem arises in an overload situation: the mean square error objective leads to a reduced setpoint value which is propotional to the severity of the overload. Such a solution is however not appropriate for high domestic on-off loads such as the 5 kW heating system. In this case we need a discrete model to determine which houses should be "on" and which ones should be "off". The algorithm sets the setpoint of an "on" house to the maximum required power defined in the reported flexibility, and the setpoint of an "off" house is the minimum required power, see Eqs. (19) and (20). For this purpose we define the binary variable $x_i \in 0, 1, i \in B$ and the maximum and minimum power p_i^{max} and p_i^{min} at period j as follows:

$$p_i^a = (\underline{E}_{ij}^{CEMS} - \underline{E}_{i(j-1)}^{CEMS})/T, i \in B, j \in N - 0$$

$$p_i^b = (\overline{E}_{ij}^{CEMS} - \overline{E}_{i(j-1)}^{CEMS})T, i \in B, j \in N - 0$$

$$p_i^{min} = min\{p^a, p^b\}$$

$$p_i^{max} = max\{p^a, p^b\}$$

The setpoint for household (and CEMS) i is defined as $P_i^{ref} = P_i^{in} + \beta_i$, where β_i has to be determined.

The objective (17) of the optimization problem has two terms: (a) to minimize the total squared error between requested loads and the estimated setpoint values, and (b) to minimize the setpoint fluctuation between subsequent time periods. For the latter goal, we store the setpoint calculated for $j - 1$, use it in period j and denote it P_i^{ref-}. α is a parameter to tune the relative importance of the goals. For each *period j* we solve the following problem:
minimize

$$\alpha \sum_{i \in B} \beta_i^2 + (1 - \alpha) \sum_{i \in B} (P_i^{in} + \beta_i - P_i^{ref-})^2; \tag{17}$$

subject to:
if $(\sum_{i \in B} P_i^{in} \le LV_{maxp})$:

$$\sum_{i \in B} (P_i^{in} + \beta_i) \le LV_{maxp} \tag{18}$$

else:{

$$\beta_i + P_i^{in} = p_i^{max}(1 - x_i) + p_i^{min} x_i), i \in B \tag{19}$$

$$\sum_{i \in B} (p_i^{max}(1 - x_i) + p_i^{min} x_i) \le LV_{maxp} \tag{20}$$

}

5   Simulation Experiments

5.1   Scenario

In the FP7 project SmartC2net [14] we used a scaled down version benchmark residential LV grid in a rural area in Denmark with 53 buses, to which a number of 38 households are connected, see Fig. 4. Smart meter measurements have been used to derive the non-flexible load for each household. The original grid was already quite loaded in the winter evening hours, as the voltages at some buses reached a low of 0.95 pu.

In the simulation, all the households have been enhanced with 5 kW HVACs for heating and PV panels with $P_{rated} = 4$ kW. Ten houses have been configured with EV charging points associated to various parking periods and $P_{max} = 6$ kW. The HVACs' initial indoor temperature was randomly distributed between 19.1 and 20.9 degrees, the outside temperature was 1°C(January). The simulation experiments have been performed for a duration of 96 periods (24 h) and a planning horizon of 6 h.

The test system in Fig. 3 has been distributed on two computers, one for the 38 CEMS controllers (VEN role in OADR) and house models, the other for the DMC controller and the VTN functionality. Between the VTN and VENs we deployed the OADR 2.0b web service. The controllers were implemented in java using for the optimization tasks the Gurobi MIP solver [15].

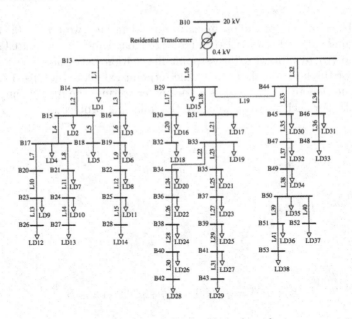

Fig. 4. Low voltage benchmark grid.

5.2 Simulation Results

Both the DMC and the CEMS controllers are event based and would interact every 15 min, in a real deployment. In a fast simulation mode we run the cycle every 100 s to eliminate any timing problems.

We performed a series of measurements to address the following questions:

1. What are the benefits of conveying flexibility information to the DMC?
2. How does the system cope with the obvious higher household power consumption (5 kW heating and eventually EV charging) and what is the impact on the power quality?
3. How robust is the CEMS against a failure of its connection to the DMC?
4. How do the energy prices affect the demand allocation and total costs?
5. How does the CEMS load follow the setpoints, in particular in presence of unexpected load fluctuations?
6. Which factors have an impact on the EV charging performance?

Benefits of Reporting Flexibility. We concentrate in this work on just two benefits from conveying flexibility information to the demand management operator: (a) by calculating p_i^{max} and p_i^{min} from the flexibility data, the aggregation controller knows exactly the range of the reference power signals it can send, and in addition it can satisfy the LV grid limit, and (b) robustness in case of communication failures. Both will be discussed in the following sections.

Coping with Higher Household Power Demand Levels. The simulation of the controller operation shows that we can schedule higher loads than those measured in the benchmark grid, without the need to enchance the grid. The simulation considers 38 households during one day in January. In order to show the effect of the toal consumption constraint in Eq. 20 we compare two runs with $LV_{maxp} = 110$ and 80 kW. Figures 5 and 6 show the total load and total reference power (setpoint) in each period.

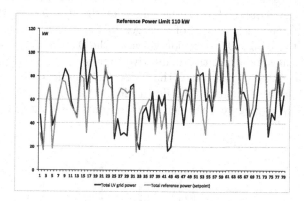

Fig. 5. Total LV grid power and reference, with $LV_{maxp} = 110$ kW.

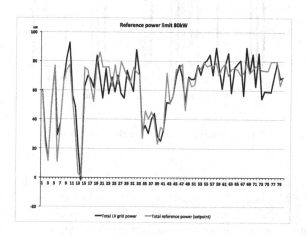

Fig. 6. Total LV grid power and reference, with $LV_{maxp} = 80$ kW.

It can be seen that the reference follows exactly the limit, however for the load there are a few outliers that exceed the limit. While the reference levels are adapted in case of an overload, the plan of the CEMS cannot always follow, leading to those outliers. Comparing the two figures, the limitation however is effective and the energy is shifted as much as possible to consumption valeys.

An overload period is illustrated in Fig. 7. In this period 17 houses request heating. Most of those households could consume even more power (e.g. for EV charging), maximum 7 kW, but they could also defer heating. The DMC algorithm selects 8 households to which it allocates the maximum power, so that the 80 kW limit is satisfied.

In order to derive the power quality from the power consumption, the simplest way is to calculate the power flows, given the grid topology in Fig. 4 and derive the bus voltages and angles. We compared two simulation runs, with different values of LV_{maxp}: 80 and 110 kW. Although for the transformer the toal load increase is 37 %, the distribution of voltages in Fig. 8 shows a decent shift to the left: from the 0.93–0.97 pu region towards the 0.89–0.92 pu under voltage region. Here we have to admit the qualitative superiority of the approach in [16] in which the aggregator that takes the individual bus loads in consideration, when calculating the setpoints. The downside of that is the required topology information at the aggregator, an operational requirement that is hard to satisfy.

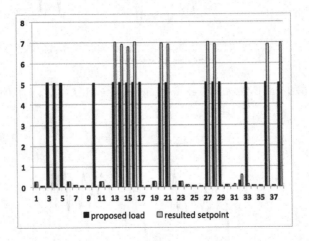

Fig. 7. Example of an overloaded period.

CEMS Planning Strategies in Case of Communication Failures. In this scenario all CEMS become suddenly disconnected from the DMC. Since the demand of each CEMS is remotely controlled, it is important to make sure that during the interruption the total consumption does not increase beyond limit and that power is not injected into the grid without control. This would lead to a CEMS "safe mode" with the following startegy: (a) switch off home heating (in order to allow cooling and still be feasible, we relax the low temperature limit from 19 to 16 degrees Celsius), (b) allow EV charging, but only as much as to compensate PV generation, (c) do not discontinue non-flexible loads.

The simulation of a three hour failure affecting 28 households is depicted in Fig. 9. A bouncing effect can be observed after the interruption, however the load converges quickly to the plan before the failure. We argue that the relative

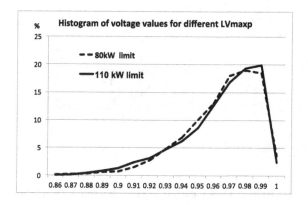

Fig. 8. Distribution of bus voltages for simulations with different LV_{maxp}.

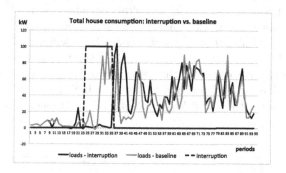

Fig. 9. Comparison of total loads if the CEMS-DMC communication is interrupted between 12:00-15:00.

robustness is due to the fact that the reference power values for the next six hours have been buffered at the CEMS before the failure and provide a certain planning guidance during the disconnection period.

The Impact of Day Ahead Prices. The tests have been done with quarterly hour market clearing prices (MCP). We used the relative prices (same effect is obtained with full prices, however they minimize also the consumed energy), see Fig. 10. At a total consumption in 24 h of 0.762 MWh, the energy cost at an average price of 44,23 Euro/MWh would be 33,71 Euro, whereas the cost after our optimized allocation is 30,86 Euro. This corresponds to a saving of roughly 10 %. the relative prices are shown.

Setpoint Following Objective and Disturbances. Setpoints are not hard constraints for the CEMS model. The design was carefully conducted in order to exclude non feasible solutions, even when the actually measured consumption values P^{load} are far from the predicted ones. This prediction error affects the

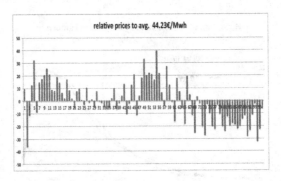

Fig. 10. 15 min market clearing prices relative to the day average.

PV generated power, the non-flexible loads, the EV charging when the vehicle is not available as planned, etc. Prediction errors have been simulated by adding to the non-flexible power value P_0^{load} a normal distributed "noise" with zero mean. We observe the setpoint following performance by calculating the mean square error $1/N \sum_j^N (P_j^{in} - P_j^{ref})^2, j = 0, N - 1$. In a simulation with two houses we inject the prediction error only in the period $j = 0$. For zero noise (perfect plan), see Fig. 11 we still obtain a MSE of 1.85, for $\sigma = 0.25$ kW, the MSE is 1.98, and by doubling the error to $\sigma = 0.5$ kW, we observe a stronger deterioration with MSE = 3.09.

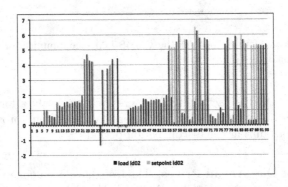

Fig. 11. Load and setpoint at LD2 during the simulation.

Impact on the EV Charging Performance. The CEMS local objectives are to maximize the use of PV generated energy, minimize energy costs, satisfy the EV minimum demand and maintain the indoor temperature range. As a result, the EV charging power in a certain period will depend on the several factors. Thus, if heating is switched on, if the setpoint value is low, and if energy price is high, then the charging power is reduced. If PV generation is high, then the charging power increases.

The ten houses with EV could all charge the minimum demand, see Fig. 12, but did not charge the maximum demand, mainly because of the relative short vehicle availability time at the charging point, in combination with the low maximum charging power of 6 kW, the low maximum household consumption of 6.9 kW, and the imposed total load limit $LV_{maxp} = 80$ kW.

House	period	Minimum demand kWh	Charged kWh
Id01	8-12	4.73	5.05
Id02	9-13	5.45	5.57
Id02	16-22	6.39	6.92
Id03	13:30-23:30	3.92	3.92
Id05	15-18	3.66	3.85
Id13	11-16	2.54	2.72
Id30	9:30-15:30	4.35	4.47
Id32	8-12	3.0	3.32
Id32	16-20	4.64	4.65
Id33	11-16	3.78	3.82

Fig. 12. Households with EV.

6   Concluding Remarks and Further Research

In this work we address the remote demand control of distributed energy resources using flexibility information. For the selected residential scenario, the demand management is realized by the interworking of CEMS controllers and the aggregated energy controller. The computation approach is based on forward planning and optimized scheduling.

Although additional, two-way communication is needed between the controller entities, the OADR protocol and demand response framework can be used as standardized technology to transport the flexibility information, which has currently a very simple structure.

During normal operation, the demand control scheme provides peak shaving, and in case on-off offered loads exceeds the capacity, it schedules the CEMS individually. The CEMS controls locally the flexible loads and the renewable generation.

The advantage of the planning approach becomes visible if the communication links fail: although the CEMS is remotely controlled, the "safe" operation of its assets would continue for a longer time in our proposed system than in a system without flexibility information exchange.

Future work is needed to build additional load predictive models for various flexible and intelligent loads, such as batteries, combined heat and electricity generators, pumps, etc. and study the deployment of the system for buildings, public charging stations, industrial environments.

Acknowledgements. The research leading to these results has received funding from the European Community Seventh Framework Programme (FP7/2007–2013) under grant agreement no. 318023 for the SmartC2Net project.

References

1. Biegel, B., Andersen, P., Stoustrup, J., Hansen, L.H., Tackie, D.V.: Information modeling for direct control of distributed energy resources. In: 2013 American Control Conference (ACC), pp. 3498–3504. IEEE, June 2013
2. Sundstrom, O., Binding, C.: Flexible charging optimization for electric vehicles considering distribution grid constraints. IEEE Trans. Smart Grid $3(1)$, 26–37 (2012)
3. Lopes, J.A.P., Soares, F.J., Almeida, P.M.R.: Integration of electric vehicles in the electric power system. Proc. IEEE $99(1)$, 168–183 (2011)
4. CEN-CENELEC-ETSI Smart Grid Coordination Group: Sustainable Processes (2012)
5. Harbo, S., Biegel, B.: Contracting flexibility services. In: 2013 4th IEEE/PES Innovative Smart Grid Technologies Europe (ISGT EUROPE), pp. 1–5. IEEE, October 2013
6. Pedersen, R., Sloth, C., Andresen, G.B., Wisniewski, R.: DiSC - a simulation framework for distribution system voltage control (2014)
7. Andersson, G.: Dynamics and control of electric power systems. Lecture notes, 227–0528 (2012)
8. Binding, C., Dykeman, D., Ender, N., Gantenbein, D., Mueller, F., Rumsch, W.C., Tschopp, H.: FlexLast: an IT-centric solution for balancing the electric power grid. In: IECON 2013–39th Annual Conference of the IEEE Industrial Electronics Society, pp. 4751–4755. IEEE, November 2013
9. Molderink, A., Bakker, V., Bosman, M.G., Hurink, J.L., Smit, G.J.: Management and control of domestic smart grid technology. IEEE Trans. Smart Grid $1(2)$, 109–119 (2010)
10. Orda, L.D., Bach, J., Pedersen, A.B., Poulsen, B., Hansen, L.H.: Utilizing a flexibility interface for distributed energy resources through a cloud-based service. In: 2013 IEEE International Conference on Smart Grid Communications (SmartGridComm), pp. 312–317. IEEE, October 2013
11. Tušar, T., Dovgan, E., Filipic, B.: Scheduling of flexible electricity production and consumption in a future energy data management system: problem formulation. In: Proceedings of the 14th International Multiconference Information Society IS 2011, pp. 96–99 (2011)
12. Palensky, P., Dietrich, D.: Demand side management: demand response, intelligent energy systems, and smart loads. IEEE Trans. Ind. Inf. $7(3)$, 381–388 (2011)
13. DeRidder, F., Hommelberg, M., Peeters, E.: Four potential business cases for demand side integration. In: Proceedings of the 6th European International Conference on Energy Market, EEM 2009, pp. 1–6, May 2009

14. SmartC2Net official webpage. http://www.SmartC2Net.eu
15. Gurobi Solver webpage. www.gurobi.com
16. Bessler, S., Drenjanac, D., Hasenleithner, E., Ahmed-Khan, S., Silva, N.: Using flexibility information for energy demand optimization in the low voltage grid. In: SmartGreens Conference, Lisbon, Portugal (2015)

Vehicle Technology and Intelligent Transport Systems

Laser Scanner and Camera Fusion
for Automatic Obstacle Classification
in ADAS Application

Aurelio Ponz[1(✉)], C.H. Rodríguez-Garavito[2], Fernando García[1],
Philip Lenz[3], Christoph Stiller[3], and J.M. Armingol[1]

[1] Intelligent Systems Lab, Universidad Carlos III de Madrid, Butarque 15,
Leganés, Madrid, Spain
{apv, fegarcia, armingol}@ing.uc3m.es
[2] Automation Engineering Department, Universidad de La Salle, Bogotá,
Colombia
cerodriguez@unisalle.edu.co
[3] Institut für Mess- Und Regelungstechnik, Karlsruher Institut für Technologie,
Karlsuhe, Germany
{lenz, stiller}@kit.edu

Abstract. Reliability and accuracy are key in state of the art Driving Assistance Systems and Autonomous Driving applications. These applications make use of sensor fusion for trustable obstacle detection and classification in any meteorological and illumination condition. Laser scanner and camera are widely used as sensors to fuse because of its complementary capabilities. This paper presents some novel techniques for automatic and unattended data alignment between sensors, and Artificial Intelligence techniques are used to use laser point clouds not only for obstacle detection but also for classification.. Information fusion with classification information from both laser scanner and camera improves overall system reliability.

Keywords: ADAS · Computer vision · Lidar · Advanced driving assistance system · Laser · Stereo camera · Sensor fusion

1 Introduction

Traffic accidents are among the most important avoidable risks for human life. About 1.2 million people die and 50 million people are disabled every year in the world as a consequence of traffic accidents [16]. Advanced Driving Assistance Systems (ADAS) can reduce the number and severity of traffic accidents by using Computer Vision (CV) technologies, Artificial Intelligence (AI) and Laser. ADAS use widely laser scanners and cameras to detect and classify obstacles on the road. These sensors are complementary, as the laser's ability to detect obstacles regardless of the light quality and to select Regions of Interest (ROI) for camera classification, improves remarkably the speed and accuracy of the Computer Vision classification in the images from the camera.

The present work has been developed using the Intelligent Vehicle based on Visual Information 2.0 (IVVI 2.0), as seen in Fig. 1, the Intelligent Systems Lab's research platform, designed to develop and test ADAS technologies [10].

© Springer International Publishing Switzerland 2015
M. Helfert et al. (Eds.): Smartgreens 2015 and Vehits 2015, CCIS 579, pp. 237–249, 2015.
DOI: 10.1007/978-3-319-27753-0_13

The article is divided in the following sections:

Section 2 provides scientific context of the state of the art in the related domain. Section 3 is a general description of the system. Section 4 describes the method for laser point cloud clustering, which is the initial part of obstacle detection. Section 5 outlines the data alignment process, essential for a correct data association between the camera and the laser system. Section 6 depicts the strategy for obstacle classification using laser point clouds and images, with a Support Vector Machine (SVM). Finally, Sect. 7 presents conclusions for the present work.

2 Related Work

The work described in the present paper covers several fields with interesting state of the art. Regarding the automatic and unattended data alignment phase in our system, [8] proposed a method for calibration using a chessboard pattern, [13] proposed a method for automatic camera and laser calibration, based on point cloud reconstruction of the road surface. Other approaches such as [7] and [6] projects the features into a 2D plane to minimize the distance among the features in the different sensors. [9] presents a CAD model based calibration system for inter-sensor matching. Similar approach based on triangular model is presented in [1] and based on circular models in [3].

Once the different systems are aligned, next step is obstacle detection and classification. Data fusion detection approaches can be divided in centralized and decentralized schemes. First perform a single detection based on the information provided by the different sensors. Some examples of decentralized schemes can be found in [11] and [12] with different algorithms to combine the features from computer vision and laser scanner, such as Naïve Bayes, GMMC, NN, FLDA. Decentralized schemes implements detection and classification on each sensor independently and a further fusion stage combines the detection according to the certainty provided by each sensor. [15] provides high level fusion based on multidimensional features for laser scanner and Histogram of Oriented Gradients (HOG) for computer vision. [4] provides pedestrian detection based on pedestrian's leg model for laser scanner and HOG features for computer vision for distributed pedestrian detection and danger evaluation. [5] takes advantage of advance fusion techniques (i.e. Joint Probabilistic Data Association Filter) to enhance decentralised laser and computer vision pedestrian detection.

3 General Description

The presented work uses sensor fusion between laser scanner and computer vision for obstacle detection and classification in automotive applications.

This work is included in the IVVI 2.0 project (Fig. 1). IVVI 2.0 is the second platform for development and research of ADAS technologies of the Intelligent Systems Lab, at Universidad Carlos III de Madrid.

In the presented application, a Sick LDMRS 4-layer Laser Scanner and a trinocular camera are used. Laser scanner for primary obstacle detection and later for classification, and stereo capability from the trinocular camera is used for point cloud ground

Fig. 1. IVVI 2.0 research platform.

representation and data alignment parameters estimation; later one of the cameras from the trinocular camera is used as a monocular camera for image capturing.

The laser scanner generates a point cloud in which the system extracts the obstacles as clusters of points. These clusters are used both for ROI generation in the images and as information for obstacle classification (Fig. 6). The extracted ROIs in the image are processed for obstacle classification using AI methods applied to Computer Vision. The last step in the process performs further information fusion between laser and camera for a final obstacle classification based on machine learning.

A database with manually labeled images and point clouds is used for SVM training and testing in the classification process.

4 Point Cloud Clustering for Laser Detection

The first step in our system is the obstacle detection using laser generated point clouds. This is the most reliable sensor in our system, as it is not affected by illumination conditions but only by some meteorological conditions.

The four layer laser sensor obtains a point cloud representing some of the reality in front of the vehicle. Obstacles are part of this reality and can be located as local concentrations of points in the point cloud that can be mathematically categorized as clusters.

Several clustering techniques have been studied in order to obtain the highest and most reliable amount of information from the point cloud. It is important to note that obstacles to be detected will be represented by very few points in the point cloud, typically from four points to not much more than fifty depending on the distance to the vehicle, due to laser limitations. Most of the clustering strategies already available are designed for highly populated point clouds, obtained from high resolution multilayer laser scanners or stereo cameras, and do not adapt well to our outdoor, sparse point clouds offering limited information.

Our SICK LD-MRS laser scanner offers some scanning frequencies with different angular resolution. The smallest frequency, 12.5 Hz, with variable angular resolution between 0.125° in front of the vehicle, 0.25° between the 10° and the 30° and 0.5° between 30° and 50° (60° in the right side of the scene) as seen in Fig. 2. This configuration increases the ability for long range detection in front of the vehicle, where obstacles tend to be further. For automotive applications, lower resolutions in the sides are acceptable, as the obstacles of our concern are closer than in the front and will be represented by many points even at lower resolutions.

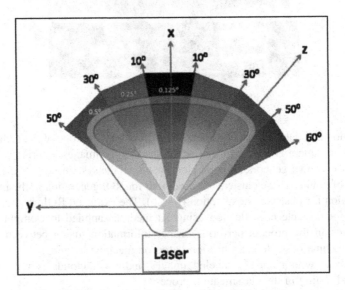

Fig. 2. Angular resolutions by sector in the laser scanner.

Distances between measured points in Y explain the need for adaptation of cluster threshold according to the distance from the obstacle to the laser, in order to obtain the most populated possible clusters.

The meaning of the values in Table 1 are:

Table 1. Distances between measured points at angular resolutions of 0.125°.

Dist (m)	Y_S	Y_G1	Y_G2	X_Layer
10	0.014	0.029	0.007	0.139
25	0.035	0.074	0.019	0.349
50	0.069	0.148	0.039	0.698
100	0.139	0.296	0.078	1.396

Y_S is the width of the measured point, Y_G1 is the distance between measured points in one measurement plane, Y_G2 is the distance between measured points between two laser pulses, and X_Layer is the height of the measured point [14].

Further sections deploy the different techniques developed for advanced automatic cluster detection.

4.1   Adapted Euclidean Distance and Geometrically Constrained Clusters

In this approach, a classical Euclidean distance clustering strategy has been adopted, modulated by several parameters in order to modify the clustering behavior, such as distance from the sensor to the obstacle, geometrical constraints, allowed number of points in every cluster, etc.

Additionally, some parameters used in the clustering process such as maximum distance between candidate points, are modified according to the shapes detected in the point cloud near to the cluster, to improve oblique obstacle detections.

An alternative strategy has been tested, using Mahalanobis distance, as the normalized Euclidean distance from the cluster's centroid to candidate points. This method tends to obtain compact clusters and ignores increasingly further points belonging to oblique obstacles. Taking into account that our scenario will produce small clusters, that is the reason why it has been discarded.

In this approach, clusters are defined as the set of points separated a certain distance, which varies as a function of several parameters, plus some points that does not meet the distance requirements, but some geometric constraints, such as belonging to the same line in the space than some of the points in the cluster.

The strategy is defined as an iterative addition of points to the cluster with the following steps:

First point in the point cloud is taken as the first point in the cluster.

All the other points in the point cloud are checked to have a distance smaller than the cluster threshold *ClusterTh*

$$ClusterTh = BaseTh + DistCorr(x)$$

$$DistCorr(x) = \sqrt{(x\,tan(\alpha_y))^2 + (x\,tan(\alpha_z))^2}$$

$$\text{if } \left|arctan\left(\frac{y}{x}\right)\right| < 2\pi \frac{10}{360} \text{ then } \alpha_y = 2\pi \frac{0.125}{360}$$

$$\text{if } 2\pi \frac{10}{360} \leq \left|arctan\left(\frac{y}{x}\right)\right| < 2\pi \frac{30}{360} \text{ then } \alpha_y = 2\pi \frac{0.25}{360} \tag{1}$$

$$\text{if } 2\pi \frac{30}{360} \leq \left|arctan\left(\frac{y}{x}\right)\right| < 2\pi \frac{60}{360} \text{ then } \alpha_y = 2\pi \frac{0.5}{360}$$

x,y,z are point's coordinates.
Due to laser scanner restrictions, α_z is always 0.8°

where *BaseTh* is a parameter experimentally determined as the base threshold. *DistCorr (x)* is a function of the x coordinate which ensures that no distance smaller than the minimum physically possible distance will be required, as seen in Eq. 1, and depending on the different angular resolutions seen in Fig. 2. *DistCorr(x)* is computed as the minimum distance possible between two consecutive points in z and y coordinates. α_y Represents the angle between two consecutive laser reads in horizontal (y axis) and α_z is the angle between two consecutive laser reads in vertical (z axis) (Fig. 3).

Fig. 3. IVVI 2.0 research platform with axis represented in the image: X = laser-obstacle distance, Z = detection height, Y = horizontal deviation from the laser.

All the points in the point cloud are checked for cluster inclusion. The same iteration is performed for every point added to the cluster until all cross checks are performed. Then, points close to the obstacle but not belonging to the cluster are included into a temporary new point cloud together with the obtained cluster, and then lines are searched in the new cluster using RANSAC. If lines are found containing a determined minimum of points belonging to the original cluster and points not belonging to it, then these points are added to the cluster. This strategy has proven to be effective for oblique obstacles.

Figure 4 shows the result of the algorithm. Red dots are the cluster created by Euclidean Adapted distance. Blue dots are the points close to the cluster but not belonging to it. Yellow lines are 3D lines found by RANSAC, including points from the original cluster and points from the extended cluster.

Upon completion of cluster extraction, it is checked against the parameters *ClusterTolerance* for maximum width of cluster in meters, and *minClusterSize* and *maxClusterSize* for minimum and maximum number of points, respectively. These parameters are also a function of the distance to the obstacle.

The strategy is addressed to obtain the most populated clusters possible, taking into account that we are using a low resolution multilayer laser. The threshold distance must be adapted to the distance x from the laser sensor to the obstacle, as the distance between consecutive laser points grows with x. Due to laser construction limitations,

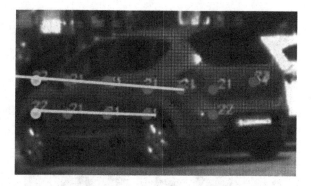

Fig. 4. Extended cluster using geometrical constraints.

the minimum distance detected in y and z in consecutive points will be greater than the initial threshold if not adapted following Eq. (1).

4.2 Ground Detection and Removal from Point Cloud

As outlined in Sect. 5, our system can compute the plane corresponding to the road surface, so it is possible to remove ground plane points from the list of detected clusters. Figure 5 shows the result of the algorithm, ignoring as cluster candidates all the points located in the ground plane obtained with RANSAC.

Fig. 5. Cluster removal in ground plane.

Fig. 6. Obstacle detection based on cluster computation.

5 Data Alignment

Our system is based in data fusion between several sensors, based on different physical phenomena. Thus each of these sensors has its own system of reference, and extrinsic parameters between sensors system of reference must be estimated in order to perform the data alignment.

To achieve the necessary alignment, rotation and translation between sensors must be estimated. Some methods have already been proposed by other authors, involving chessboards or specific patterns [8] detectable by all of the sensors involved in the fusion [6]. This is cumbersome and requires driver implication or some help from others, needs specific and stationary environment and to be performed manually again in case of change of orientation or translation between sensors.

Our approach estimates the extrinsic parameters of all the sensors involved, and calibration between them, assuming flat surface in front of the vehicle, thus sensor's height and two rotation angles can already be determined. For the third angle computation, any identifiable obstacle located in the road surface can be used.

Applying the M-estimator-Sample-Consensus (MSAC) algorithm for plane detection in the point clouds obtained from the stereo camera and from the laser scanner, the most populated planes are found from the clouds in the form

$$\pi_{(X)} : ax_c + by_c + cz_c + d = 0 \tag{2}$$

which can be written in the Hessian form

$$\pi_{(X)} : \vec{n}.\vec{p} = h \tag{3}$$

where $\vec{n}$ is the vector normal to the road plane, and the relation between this vector and the camera and laser rotation angles can be computed as in [13].

Once all the calibration parameters, i.e. roll, pitch, yaw and x,y,z translations between sensors have been computed, the system is able to translate from laser coordinates into camera coordinates in the image for obstacle classification using Computer Vision.

The conversion between laser and image coordinate systems can be performed as in Eq. (4)

$$\begin{bmatrix} x \\ y \\ z \end{bmatrix} = R(\begin{bmatrix} x_0 \\ y_0 \\ z_0 \end{bmatrix} + T)$$

$$R = \begin{bmatrix} \cos(\delta) & 0 & \sin(\delta) \\ 0 & 1 & 0 \\ -\sin(\delta) & 0 & \cos(\delta) \end{bmatrix} \cdot \begin{bmatrix} 1 & 0 & 1 \\ 0 & \cos(\varphi) & -\sin(\varphi) \\ 0 & \sin(\varphi) & \cos(\varphi) \end{bmatrix} \cdot \begin{bmatrix} \cos(\theta) & -\sin(\theta) & 0 \\ \sin(\theta) & \cos(\theta) & 0 \\ 0 & 0 & 1 \end{bmatrix},$$

(4)

$$T = \begin{bmatrix} x_t \\ y_t \\ z_t \end{bmatrix},$$

where T represents the translation vector and R the rotation matrix between sensors.

6 Obstacle Classification Using Laser and Image Information Fusion

Obstacle classification in this work can be performed with single sensor information or using sensor fusion information. The automated environment developed will allow direct comparison of results and fast training improvements.

6.1 SVM Classification

Classification is performed using the SVM implementation from the Computer Vision OpenCV library. SVM algorithm was developed by Vapnik & Cortes [2] and is widely used in machine learning as a classification method. In the present work, a database of manually labelled images and clusters obtained from a capture with the IVVI platform is used to execute a supervised learning process. Image database also includes images from sources other than the IVVI. After the training process, the SVM structures are stored and used for classification of images and clusters as seen in Figs. 8 and 9.

6.2   Laser Scanner Feature Vector

Clusters detected in laser scanner generated point clouds are used to determine a Region of Interest in the image where we can perform obstacle classification applying Computer Vision and Artificial Intelligence techniques, but can also be used for obstacle classification without image support [11].

Clusters are converted into a mesh structure by Delaunay triangulation in order to reconstruct the shape of the obstacle and to extract relevant features according to the 3d shape of the cluster, as seen in Fig. 7. These obstacles are detected by the system as clusters, which have some characteristics suitable for further SVM training following the process outlined in Fig. 8. Clusters obtained from the test sequences are stored and manually labeled using the corresponding images for training. These clusters are manually labeled as frontal view, back view, side view, frontal oblique view and back oblique view.

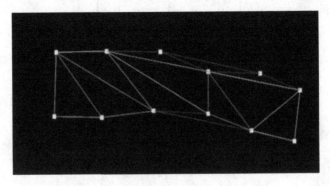

Fig. 7. Mesh representation of a cluster.

Training Process for clusters

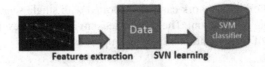

Classification process for clusters

Fig. 8. SVM learning process for clusters: training and classification.

Previous works [11] have considered 2D point clouds for classification, but the present work is intended to extract features from a 3D point cloud, in an effort to maximize the use of the available information. The features considered are described in Table 2.

Table 2. Features considered for cluster classification.

Concentration: Normalized mean distance to the centroid 3D
Y-Z concentration: normalized mean distance to the centroid excluding x
X-Z concentration: normalized mean distance to the centroid excluding y
X-Y concentration: normalized mean distance to the centroid excluding z
Planicity: normalized mean distance to the most populated plane found in the cluster
Sphericity: normalized mean distance to the most populated sphere
Cubicity: measures how far are the planes containing the mesh triangles from being the same plane or from being perpendicular
Triangularity: measures the uniformity of the triangles composing the mesh bye the relation between sides' lengths
Average deviation from the median in x, y, z

Training Process for images

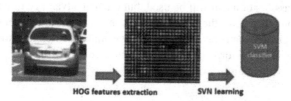

HOG features extraction   SVN learning

Classification process for images

Classification depending on the training process.
Car/No Car
Pedestrian/Other
Front view/Side view/Oblique

Fig. 9. SVM learning process for images: Training and classification.

6.3 Computer Vision Feature Vector

As pointed before, obstacles found in the Laser Scanner Point Cloud as clusters are used to determine a ROI in the image suitable for applying SVM for obstacle classification in images.

An image database has been created using both the ROIs obtained from obstacles detected by laser and images from public databases, from any point of view.

These images have been manually labeled as frontal view, back view, side view, frontal oblique view and back oblique view. Later, Histogram of Oriented Gradients (HOG) features are extracted from every image (Fig. 10), and SVM training is performed following the process outlined in Fig. 9, in order to obtain the SVM classifier [17].

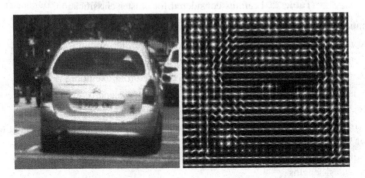

Fig. 10. Original image and representation of HOG features.

6.4 Information Fusion

In poor illumination conditions, when the camera offers no help, laser scanner obstacle detection and classification can still be used, but the real advantage of the sensor fusion resides in the combination of the information obtained from several sensors to obtain a result which is greater than the mere sum of the individual contributions. [5]. Information fusion will be performed with SVM and results will be compared with individual sensor classifications.

7 Preliminary Results and Discussion

The presented work is currently under development but its results have been preliminarily tested, showing better figures using sensor fusion for classification than single sensor classification, as presumed, and very promising expectations. Future tests will present complete quantitative results and comparisons.

Acknowledgements. This Work Was Supported by the Spanish Government through the CICYT Project (TRA2013-48314-C3-1-R).

References

1. Debattisti, S., Mazzei, L., Panciroli, M.: Automated extrinsic laser and camera inter-calibration using triangular targets. In: 2013 Intelligent Vehicles Symposium (IV), pp. 696–701. IEEE (2013)
2. Cortes, C., Vapnik, V.: Support vector network. Mach. Learn. **20**, 1–25 (1995)

3. Fremont, V., Bonnifait, P.: Extrinsic calibration between a multi-layer lidar and a camera. In: 2008 IEEE International Conference on Multisensor Fusion and Integration for Intelligent Systems (2008)

4. García, F., Jiménez, F., Naranjo, J.E., Zato, J.G., Aparicio, F., Armingol, J.M., de la Escalera, A.: Environment perception based on LIDAR sensors for real road applications. Robotica 30, 185–193 (2012)

5. García, F., García, J., Ponz, A., de la Escalera, A., Armingol, J.M.: Context aided pedestrian detection for danger estimation based on laser scanner and computer vision. Expert Syst. Appl. 41(15), 6646–6661 (2014)

6. Kwak, K., Huber, D.F., Badino, H., Kanade, T.: Extrinsic calibration of a single line scanning lidar and a camera. In: IEEE/RSJ International Conference on Intelligent Robots and Systems, pp. 3283–3289 (2011)

7. Li, Y., Ruichek, Y., Cappelle, D.: 3D triangulation based extrinsic calibration between a stereo vision system and a LIDAR. In: 14th International IEEE Conference on Intelligent Transpprtation Systems, pp. 797–802 (2011)

8. Li, Y., Liu, Y., Dong, L., Cai, X.: An algorithm for extrinsic parameters calibration of a camera and a laser range finder using line features. In: IEEE/RSJ International Conference on Intelligent Robots and Systems (2007)

9. Lisca, G., Jeong, P.J.P., Nedevschi, S.: Automatic one step extrinsic calibration of a multi layer laser scanner relative to a stereo camera. In: 2010 IEEE International Conference on Intelligent Computer Communication and Processing (ICCP) (2010)

10. Martín, D., García, F., Musleh, B., Olmeda, D., Marín, P., Ponz, A., Rodríguez, C.H., Al-Kaff, A., de la Escalera, A., Armingol, J.M.: IVVI 2.0: an intelligent vehicle based on computational perception. Expert Syst. Appl. 41, 7927–7944 (2014)

11. Premebida, C., Ludwig, O., Nunes, U.: LIDAR and vision-based pedestrian detection system. J. Field Robot. 26, 696–711 (2009)

12. Premebida, C., Ludwig, O., Silva, M., Nunes, U.: A cascade classifier applied in pedestrian detection using laser and image-based features. In: Transportation, pp. 1153–1159 (2010)

13. Rodríguez-Garavito, C.H., Ponz, A., García, F., Martín, D., de la Escalera, A., Armingol, J. M.: Automatic laser and camera extrinsic calibration for data fusion using road plane (2014)

14. Sick, LD-MRS Manual. SICK AG Waldkirch, Reute, Germany (2009)

15. Spinello, L., Siegwart, R.: Human detection using multimodal and multidimensional features. In: IEEE International Conference on Robotics and Automation, pp. 3264–3269 (2008). doi:10.1109/ROBOT.2009.4543708

16. WHO, Global status report on road safety. Time for action. WHO library cataloguing-in-publication data, World Health Organization, Geneva, Switzerland (2009). ISBN 978-9-241563-84-0

17. Zezhi, C., Pears, N., Freeman, M., Austin, J.: Road vehicle classification using support vector machines. 2009 IEEE Int. Conf. Intell. Comput. Intell. Syst. ICIS 2009 4, 214–218 (2009). doi:10.1109/ICICISYS.2009.5357707

Vehicle Routing to Minimizing Hybrid Fleet Fuel Consumption

Fei Peng[1]([✉]), Amy M. Cohn[2], Oleg Gusikhin[3], and David Perner[4]

[1] Computer Science Department, Carnegie Mellon University,
Pittsburgh, PA, USA
fpeng@cs.cmu.edu
[2] Department of Industrial and Operations Engineering,
University of Michigan, Ann Arbor, MI, USA
[3] Research and Advanced Engineering, Ford Motor Company,
Dearborn, MI, USA
[4] Ford Motor Company, Dearborn, MI, USA

Abstract. In this paper, we address a variant of the Vehicle Routing Problem (VRP) where the fleet contains vehicles that not only vary in performance, but this variation is a function of the arc type, such that a given vehicle might have costs lower on some arcs but higher on others. We refer to this as the Hybrid Fleet Vehicle Routing Problem. This is more realistic than the common assumption that all vehicles are identical. In many cases, fleets are made up of different vehicle types, varying in size, engine/fuel type, and other performance-impacting factors. Even in a homogeneous fleet, vehicles often differ by age and condition, which can greatly impact performance. We propose two heuristic methods that take into account the vehicle-specific cost structures. We provide computational results to demonstrate the quality of our solutions, and a comparison with a Genetic Algorithm based method.

Keywords: Vehicle routing problem · Heterogeneous feet · Heuristics

1 Introduction

In this paper, we present models and algorithms for solving the Hybrid Fleet Vehicle Routing Problem (HFVRP). In the traditional VRP, a collection of identical vehicles must be routed so as to visit every customer in a given set while minimizing transportation cost; it is assumed that the cost to traverse an arc between any pair of customers is the same for all vehicles in the fleet. The HFVRP is a variation of VRP in which vehicles in the fleet may differ, and we allow the arc cost to vary by vehicle type.

HFVRP has applicability in many real-world contexts. It is quite common, for example, that vehicles within a given fleet will vary in age and thus in fuel efficiency (and associated cost). Moreover, fleet managers in many industries are gradually moving towards more fuel-efficient, environmentally-friendly vehicle types within their fleet. As older vehicles with traditional combustion-based

© Springer International Publishing Switzerland 2015
M. Helfert et al. (Eds.): Smartgreens 2015 and Vehits 2015, CCIS 579, pp. 250–266, 2016.
DOI: 10.1007/978-3-319-27753-0_14

engines are retired, they are being replaced with hybrid or electric vehicles. Not only do these vehicle types vary in efficiency, but this variation may depend on driving conditions – one vehicle may be more efficient in city driving, for example, while another is more efficient in highway driving. Furthermore, in some countries, electric vehicles are given privileges such as being allowed to pay less toll. In such cases, no one vehicle type will be Pareto-dominant over the others. Thus, the extension from VRP to HFVRP is not only in determining which vehicle type to place on which routes but also in actually designing the routes to leverage the strengths of the different vehicle types [1]. Finally, recent interests in system-wide costs, including environmental as well as economic, has emerged in a variety of problems concerning Green Transportation, such as topics related to electric vehicles, alternative fuels, and intelligent transportation systems and infrastructure [2,3]. Tying directly to these issues is the better utilization of vehicles and better routing solutions.

VRP is known not only to be NP-hard in theory (the Traveling Salesman Problem is a special case of VRP, in which there is only one vehicle to be scheduled), but also to often be computationally challenging in practice as well. It is therefore frequently solved with heuristics, as we discuss in Sect. 2. However, these heuristics often rely on approaches that target the minimization of total mileage traveled in the system. In HFVRP, circuitous mileage may lead to better matching of vehicle types to driving conditions, and thus the solution with minimum total distance traveled may not be the minimum-cost solution.

In this research, we begin by posing an explicit mathematical programming approach to solving HFVRP, and demonstrate the computational challenges of this approach. We then introduce two heuristics for solving this problem, one which can be solved very quickly and without the use of any commercial solvers, and the other which can be used in contexts where there is more run time – and access to a commercial mixed integer programming solver – available. We then provide comparison with a GA based algorithm, and experiments to gain insights into both the computational performance and the solution quality.

The contribution of this research is in: investigating an important variation of the classical VRP with real-world relevance; identifying structural challenges that impact the tractability of this problem; presenting heuristic approaches to find quality solutions in tolerable run times; and conducting computational experiments to assess performance and solution characteristics.

2   Motivation and Literature Review

The VRP is a classical problem that has been studied extensively in the literature. Given a fleet of identical vehicles and a group of customers that need to be served, VRP seeks the best assignment of routes to vehicles such that all customers are covered while the overall cost (usually measured in distance traveled) is minimized. This problem was first introduced some fifty years ago [4]. Since then, many aspects of the problem have been studied [5–7]. VRP is not only theoretically interesting but also has broad applicability in real-world practices, from transportation, distribution and logistics to scheduling [8,9].

In practice, exact solutions to VRP can typically only be obtained for relatively small sized problems [10], with problems having even as few as a hundred customers often not guaranteed to be solvable. Therefore a myriad of heuristics have been developed to tackle this problem, including the savings heuristic [11,12], giant-tour based heuristic [13], and many augmented methods [14,15].

Many variants of the classical VRP have been investigated as well. For example, in the capacitated version of VRP, each vehicle can only carry a limited amount of goods [16–18]. In the VRP with time windows, some or all of the customers/depot can accept delivery only during a specified time period [19–22]. In VRP with stochastic supply/demand, supply/demand are not deterministic but have some variability [23].

We are interested in a variation of VRP that we call the Hybrid Fleet Vehicle Routing Problem (HFVRP). Unlike VRP, HFVRP does not assume that all vehicles have identical characteristics. Variants of HFVRP have appeared in the literature in various forms and under other names, such as the heterogeneous vehicle routing problem [24], the fleet size and mix vehicle routing problem [13], mix fleet vehicle routing problem [25], etc. These usually differ in whether fixed cost is considered, and whether the fleet size is limited. Various algorithms have been proposed for this family of problems. [16] worked with a route based formulation (similar to the one we describe in Sect. 3.3) and proposed several lower bounding techniques that effectively eliminated many candidate routes while still maintaining optimality. The authors were able to solve optimality several problems of size up to 75 customers. In terms of heuristic methods, Taillard [26] first solved the VRP problem for each vehicle type, then use a column generation-based approach to generate and store an augmented set of routes, then within this set of routes solve a set partitioning problem to obtain the final solution. Choi and Tcha [24] performed column generation on the case where a customer can be visited more than once, where a dynamic programming approach was used to solve the sub-problems and find new columns. Meta-heuristics have also been explored: Ochi et al. [27] used the petal genetic algorithm; Wassan and Osman [25] and Tarantilis et al. [28] applied tabu search method to this problem.

Our interest is in the specific version where the cost of traversing an arc varies by vehicle, and the time/length of the route is limited (this problem is sometimes referred to as the Heterogeneous VRP with Vehicle Dependent Routing Costs [5]. These conditions are almost always the situation in practice – different vehicles have different engines and thus different fuel efficiency; even within a fleet of the same vehicles, age can sometimes cause fuel efficiency to vary substantially. Such problems are particularly challenging because cost is no longer so directly tied to distance. Instead, we might be willing to travel circuitous mileage if that excess mileage led to the use of lower-cost arcs.

Being a generalization of VRP, HFVRP is an NP-hard problem, and in industrial applications it is in general solved heuristically. One approach would be to start by assuming a common cost, across all vehicles, for each given arc, and solve the traditional VRP using known heuristics. Then, in a second phase, the true cost of assigning each vehicle to each of the chosen routes could be calculated and the actual matching of vehicles to routes could be done optimally. However, this can lead to sub optimal solutions, because of the fact that the shortest distance routes are no longer necessarily the cheapest, and that the routes good for one vehicle may be bad for another.

Therefore we need to develop new heuristics that specifically address the challenges of HFVRP. In the remainder of the paper we present first an exact formulation, then two heuristics: a randomized greedy heuristics and a set-partitioning based approach. Finally we present computational results to compare the heuristics and identify appropriate contexts for the use of each.

3 Formulations and Heuristic Methods

3.1 Connection Based Formulation

We begin by presenting a connection based approach to solving HFVRP. Note that the same technique can also be used in formulating problems such as capacitated vehicle routing [13]. Let T be the set of vehicle type indices, N be set of nodes, where node 0 is the depot, and let $N_0 = N \backslash \{0\}$ be the set of all customer nodes. We use variables x_{ij}^t to denote whether a vehicle of type t travels directly from node i to j, $i, j \in N, t \in T$. Moreover, let M_t be the number of routes vehicles of type $t \in T$ can serve. This restriction stems from the fact that drivers have only limited work time available in a given period. M_t is simply the number of vehicles of type t if each driver can drive only one trip over the time horizon under consideration. We use Q_t to represent the length of time a driver can spend working for vehicle $t \in T$, and use d_{ij}^t to denote the time it takes for vehicle of type t to travel from node i to j. Finally, let c_{ij}^t be the cost of traveling from customer i to j, $i, j \in N$. $c_{ii}^t = 0 \ \forall i \in N$. HFVRP can be formulated as:

$$(C) \quad \text{minimize} \sum_{t \in T} \sum_{i \in N} \sum_{j \in N} c_{ij}^t x_{ij}^t \tag{1}$$

subject to:

$$\sum_{t \in T} \sum_{i \in N} x_{ij}^t = 1 \qquad\qquad j \in N_0 \tag{2}$$

$$\sum_{j \in N_0} x_{0j}^t \leq M_t \qquad\qquad t \in T \tag{3}$$

$$\sum_{i \in N} x_{ij}^t = \sum_{i \in N} x_{ji}^t \qquad\qquad t \in T, j \in N \tag{4}$$

$$\sum_{i \in S} \sum_{j \in S} x_{ij}^t \leq |S| - 1 \qquad\qquad \forall S \subset N_0, |S| \geq 2 \tag{5}$$

$$x_{ij}^t \in \{0, 1\} \qquad\qquad i, j \in N, t \in T. \tag{6}$$

Here Constraints (2) ensures that each customer is covered. Constraints (3) specify that no more than the maximum number of each vehicle type can be used. Flow conservation constraints (4) specify that for each node, any vehicle entering this node must also leave. Here (5) helps eliminate subtours in the solution. In addition, to impose the route length restriction, consider a *path p* of k^p nodes:

$$n_1^p \rightarrow n_2^p \rightarrow \ldots, \rightarrow n_{k^p}^p, \tag{7}$$

if for vehicle $t \in T$, a route starting from the depot that traverses the path and returns to the depot violates the route length restriction, in other words:

$$\sum_{j=1}^{k^p-1} d_{n_j^p, n_{j+1}^p}^t > Q_t, \tag{8}$$

but removing either end points does not, we call such path a *minimal violating path* (MVP). We include one constraint:

$$\sum_{j=1}^{k^p-1} x_{n_j^p, n_{j+1}^p}^t \leq k^p - 1 \tag{9}$$

for each MVP to ensure no route takes longer than Q_t. Note that here we implicitly assume it is always faster to go directly between two nodes than through a third node).

This formulation can also be applied to HFVRP with vehicle-dependent capacities, in which case we can use Q_t to represent the capacity of vehicle $t \in T$, and d_{ij} to represent the load at node j for all i. As is often the case with VRP, we have observed significant fractionality in our computational experiments, leading to very slow convergence of the branch-and-bound tree and/or incompletion due to running out of memory. For example, we tested an instance with 58 customers and 4 vehicle types. We pre-processed out routes that exceed the time limit before formulating this problem in Cplex. After solving for more than 15 h with Cplex version 12.1 on a Mac Pro with two 2.8 GHz Intel Xeon CPUs and 10 GB of RAM, 161,400 nodes of the branch-and-bound tree had been explored with 160,031 nodes still pending, and no integer-feasible solutions had yet been found.

3.2 Greedy Heuristic

The lack of efficient methods to solve the mixed integer programming (MIP) formulation for all but fairly small problem instances forces us to investigate in heuristic approaches. We next present a method that can find high quality solutions quickly for many problem instances. As illustrated in Fig. 1, this heuristic (Heuristic 1) can be summarized as a randomized greedy algorithm. The algorithm works as follows:

1. if no customer is outstanding, stop; otherwise identify the smallest cost from all vehicles to all outstanding customers, without loss of generality, say customer i, vehicle number j with cost c
2. find the second smallest cost from i to all vehicles, record vehicle number j', and cost c'

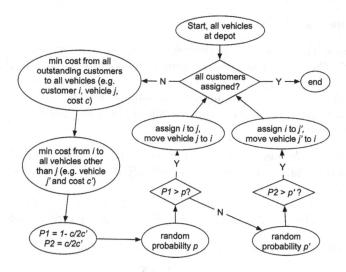

Fig. 1. Flow chart for the greedy heuristic.

3. for j, accept customer i with probability $P_1 = 1 - c/2c'$ and reject i with probability $1 - P_1$, so that the smaller c is compared to c', the bigger chance j will be selected to serve i. On the other hand if $c = c'$, or the costs of using j and j' are equivalent, the probability becomes $1/2$;
4. if customer rejected in (3), it is then assigned to vehicle j' with probability $P_2 = c/2d$
5. if the customer is assigned to neither vehicles, the process restarts, and in the immediate next iteration, i will not be considered for selection to avoid repeating the same situation; otherwise, move the chosen vehicle to i and go to (1).

This approach has certain resemblance to the greedy heuristic, because priority is always given to the assignment with the smallest arc cost. In every stage of the algorithm, we keep track of the cumulative service time of each vehicle, and returns a vehicle to the depot if no more assignment is possible.

Each iteration of the algorithm takes very little time, so we can run it many times and keep the best solution. We will provide empirical studies in Sect. 4. We also emphasize that this is an approach that can be implemented fairly easily, and does not require the use of an underlying MIP solver, thus has great value for many small fleet managers with limited resources for sophisticated implementations.

Nonetheless, the randomized approach clearly runs the risk of sub-optimal solutions. In particular, the number of feasible routes is exponentially large, with only a small fraction of these being generated in the randomized runs. This therefore motivates us to consider a hybrid approach, blending the route-based approach with an underlying MIP structure for combining routes effectively, with the aim of being able to find higher-quality solutions when more sophisticated implementations are viable.

3.3   Route Based Formulation

In some cases, when more time is allowed to find good solutions and more sophisticated technology is available, we can expand our idea to leverage the strength of
an optimization-based approach, and take advantage of the randomized approach
to reduce the problem size and improve tractability. We present the route-based
model (also referred to as the composite variable model [29,30]). We need the
following additional notations:

- R_t: set of possible routes of customers that can be served by a vehicle of type t;
- w_{rt}: binary variable that equals 1 if and only if route $r \in R_t$ is served by a
  vehicle of type $t \in T$; 0 otherwise
- C_{rt}: cost associated with assigning route $r \in R_t$ to a vehicle of type $t \in T$
- δ_{ri}: binary indicator of whether a node $i \in N_0$ is covered by a route $r \in R_t$;

The route-based model can then be formulated as follows:

$$(S) \quad \text{minimize} \sum_{t \in T} \sum_{r \in R_t} C_{rt} w_{rt} \tag{10}$$

subject to:

$$\sum_{t \in T} \sum_{r \in R_t} \delta_{ri} \cdot w_{rt} = 1 \qquad\qquad i \in N_0 \tag{11}$$

$$\sum_{r \in R_t} w_{rt} \leq M_t \qquad\qquad t \in T \tag{12}$$

$$w_{rt} \in \{0, 1\} \qquad\qquad r \in R_t, t \in T. \tag{13}$$

Here constraint (11) ensures that each customer is covered by one and only one
route. Constraint (12) forces the number of vehicles of each type used to be no
more than the total number of that type.

  Observe that if we were to enumerate all routes, solving this problem would
lead to an optimal solution. In reality, this is impractical for all but very small
instances. Techniques such as column generation and branch-and-price [31] may
be applied to problems like this, and iteratively generate only routes that appear
promising. However, the problems for finding such routes are essentially VRP
type and NP-hard. In the Appendix, we show that formulation (S) is stronger
than (C) and another explicit, connection based formulation, and it is therefore
advantageous to work with (S).

  We leverage the speed of the randomized approach from Sect. 3.2 with the
power of the route-based formulation above to improve the solution quality.
First we run the randomized heuristic for a large number of iterations. Instead
of keeping only the set of routes with the smallest cost, all routes generated in
each iteration are put into a pool of routes. Once the route generation is finished,
we will have many candidate routes that are cost efficient. Then we formulate
problem (S) with the poll of candidate routes, and solve it to find the best route
combination.

4 Results and Discussion

4.1 Baseline — Genetic Algorithm

In order to provide a comparison for the proposed algorithm against an existing class of algorithms, a genetic algorithm (GA) [32] was developed. GA is suitable for a wide range of combinatorial problems, including VRP. Recent applications of the GA to various VRP problems have shown its competitiveness with other heuristic techniques in both computation time and quality [33]. Our implementation of the GA is based on the "pure GA" described in Baker and Ayechew [33]. In this approach, the problem is decomposed into two steps. The first, controlled by the GA, assigns customers to individual vehicles and over time moves the solution space to be less infeasible and lower in cost. Since this does not establish the order in which customers assigned to a vehicle are to be visited, a 2-opt algorithm [34] is employed to solve the corresponding TSP for each individual vehicle.

Our GA implementation is performed in Matlab on a Windows machine with an Intel Core i5-2520M processor at 2.5 GHz and 8 GB RAM. In order to test the quality of the developed algorithm, several test datasets were chosen from *branchandcut.org*, themselves cases from published articles. The results for these experiments, with the alphanumeric naming convention given, are shown in Table 1. Moreover, we considered one more dataset that was extracted from the actual daily service routes of a food-gathering company. We randomly selected five of their existing routes (spanning 58 customers) as well as the vehicles serving these routes, calculated the travel time between each pair of locations and compiled this into a travel-time matrix. To obtain cost information, we used average costs per mile for each individual vehicle (this information can be obtained by multiplying the fuel consumption per mile and corresponding fuel price. One of the methods for accurate fuel consumption estimation is presented in Kolmanovsky et al. [35]. We assume the maximum work time for a vehicle/driver is eight hours.

Table 1. Performance of GA solution vs. the best known solution on test cases.

Case	Best solution	GA solution	Difference
A-n37-k5	669	731.9	9.41 %
E-n23-k3	569	569.7	0.13 %
E-n30-k3	534	557.8	4.47 %
P-n16-k8	450	451.9	0.43 %
P-n55-k8	588	677.8	15.27 %
58-Node	N/A	187.1	N/A

4.2 The Value of Explicitly Considering Heterogeneous Arc Costs, and Our Heuristics Compared with the GA

In current practices, HFVRP is often solved using a single cost across all vehicles for each arc, for example, the minimum cost, maximum cost, or average cost. Once the routes have been constructed, they are then assigned to individual vehicles and the true costs of assigning vehicles to routes can be accurately calculated. In this experiment, we consider the value of considering the true (vehicle-specific) costs explicitly when designing the vehicle routes. The following experiments were performed with c++ on a Mac Pro with two 2.8 GHz Intel Xeon CPU and 10 GB of RAM.

The food-gathering company data is a simplification that assumes Pareto dominance across vehicles — that is, if Vehicle A is more cost-effective on one arc than Vehicle B, then it will be more cost-effective on all arcs. This is often not the case and, in fact, the motivation for our research comes from cases where this is not true. Thus, we generated three additional instances that are not Pareto-dominant. Cost perturbation was done by multiplying each entry in the cost matrix by a random number. For slight cost perturbation, the random number was uniformly taken between 0.8 and 1.2; for medium cost perturbation, the random number was uniformly taken between 0.5 and 1.5; and for large perturbation, the random number was uniformly taken between 0.3 and 1.7.

For each of these four instances, we solve the HFVRP four times. In the first, we apply the solver-free heuristic from Sect. 3.2 (H1), using the average cost data (i.e., for each arc, we take the average across all vehicle types for that arc). After constructing the routes, we then assign them to specific vehicles: the most fuel-efficient vehicle gets the longest route, the second most fuel-efficient vehicle gets the second longest route, etc. Fuel efficiency is measured by average fuel cost across all arcs. Finally, we compute the final cost using each vehicles specific arc costs. In the second approach, we apply Heuristic 1 using the true arc costs within the heuristic. In both of these two approaches, we set a one-hour time limit on run time. In the third approach, we use the solver-based heuristic from Sect. 3.3 (H2) with the average cost data. In the fourth, we use the true cost data. For both solver-based heuristic runs, we use 100,000 randomly generated columns.

Results appear in Table 2. Observe that in all four instances, for either heuristic, incorporating true costs in the initial route construction reduces cost (by as much as 33 % in one instance). This shows that, with the same algorithm, explicitly considering the cost of individual vehicles provides an advantage over using an uniform cost for all vehicles in the route generation process. Moreover, Heuristic 2 always achieves better solutions compared with Heuristic 1 on the same datasets, which is no surprise given the much larger set of routes available for selection in the set partitioning model. Furthermore, compared to results in Table 1, all four implementations of our heuristics outperformed the GA, sometimes by as much as 22 %.

It is not surprising that the additional value of applying our approaches improves as the data becomes less Pareto-dominant. We therefore focus on the most highly non-Pareto instance for the remainder of our computational experiments.

Table 2. Absolute and relative costs of solutions from different cost structure between VRP and HFVRP.

	Pareto	Low None-Pareto	Medium	High
H1 with avg. cost	150	152	153	122
	104 %	107 %	124 %	132 %
H1 with true cost	149	145	126	95
	103 %	102 %	103 %	103 %
H2 with avg. cost	146	145	142	123
	101 %	102 %	116 %	133 %
H2 with true cost	145	142	123	93
	100 %	100 %	100 %	100 %

4.3 The Effect of Randomness/Heuristic Parameters on Performance

Because our two heuristics both have significant random components, we next test to see the variation in outcomes.

Returning to the complete data set (again with the least-Pareto dominant arc costs), we apply solver-free Heuristic 1 fifty times using a run time limit of one hour for each run. Figure 2 shows the variation in objective value. Note the limited range in solution values. We repeat the previous experiment using solver-based Heuristic 2 with a limit of 100,000 columns. Results appear in the Fig. 3.

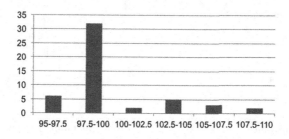

Fig. 2. Histogram of objective values from 50 runs of heuristic 1 using true cost.

Recognizing that the solution quality of the heuristics depends in part on the algorithmic parameters, we conduct the following experiments: we run the solver-free heuristic with five different time limits: 1 min, 15 min, 30 min, 45 min, and 60 min. For each time limit, we run ten random instances of the heuristic. Results are displayed in Fig. 4. Observe that increased runtime improves performance both in reducing objective value and variation between individual tests.

Finally, we run the solver-based heuristic with 100, 1,000, 10,000, 50,000, and 100,000 columns. For each column limit, we run ten random instances of

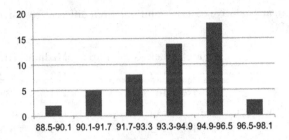

Fig. 3. Histogram of objective values from 50 runs of heuristic 2 using true cost.

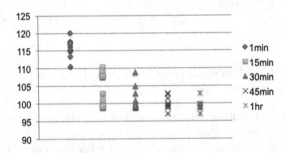

Fig. 4. Objective values from heuristic 1 under different time limits, 10 runs for each instance.

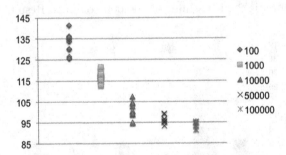

Fig. 5. Objective values from Heuristic 2, with different number of starting routes, 10 runs for each instance.

the heuristic. Results are displayed in Fig. 5. Clearly, there is benefit in increasing the number of columns, with both minimum value, the average value, and the variance all decreasing as the number of columns increases.

5   Conclusions and Future Research

In virtually every realistic context, vehicles within a fleet can have some variation in efficiency as a function of e.g. vehicle age and drivetrain types. With the current push towards more fuel-efficient and environmentally-friendly vehicles, even greater variations are being observed, as fleet operators are gradually replacing older vehicles with new vehicles that vary substantially from the original fleet composition. Many traditional VRP algorithms are no longer suited for HFVRP, where matching vehicle types to driving conditions is critical (especially when no one vehicle type demonstrates Pareto dominance over all the others). We have thus proposed three approaches that explicitly consider the difference in the cost structure. We start with an exact approach and showed empirically that it is intractable in realistic settings. We also proved that this exact formulation is not as tight as a route based, abstract formulation. Next we consider a greedy approach that can quickly and easily be implemented, as well as having very fast run times. This approach shows great promise for those environments in which the planning time and the optimization capabilities of the fleet operator are limited. Finally, we extend this randomized approach into a hybrid heuristic that incorporates the randomization within an optimization-based framework, typically leading to higher-quality solutions without a significant increase in run-time. In our experiments both of our heuristic approaches outperformed the genetic algorithm in solving a real-world HFVRP problem. Moreover, our experiments showed that the more non-Pareto the cost structure becomes, the more benefit HFVRP algorithms can bring compared to considering all vehicles as identical.

A number of promising investigations into the study of HFVRP remain. The first is to expand our experiments to include comparison with algorithms other than the GA, and to include larger test instances. The second is to replace the randomization component of the route-based problem with an optimization-based column generation routine, where the subproblems are solved with specialized VRP algorithms (this is also referred to as price-and-branch). The third, building on the proposed technique for column generation, is to develop a branch-and-price framework for doing an optimal tree search, and with that primal heuristics and upper bounding techniques. Finally, we observe that VRPs are typically assumed to be additive – i.e. the cost of a route is simply the sum of the individual costs of the arcs comprising that route. This assumption is not realistic in some cases. For example, a vehicle picking up different loads at different locations will have changing weight and correspondingly fuel consumption as loads accumulate, which depends on the arcs traversed thus far. We thus propose to investigate a variation of HFVRP in which the cost of traversing a route may be non-additive relative to the individual arc costs.

Appendix

We denote the LP relaxation to problem (S) as (SL), and the LP relaxation to problem (C) as (CL).

Theorem 1. *The lower bound generated by problem (SL) is at least as tight as the lower bound generated by problem (CL).*

Proof. We first show that, for any feasible solution to (SL), there is a corresponding feasible solution to (CL) with the same objective function value. For any feasible solution, say $\hat{w}$, to problem (SL), let $\hat{x}_{ij}^t = \sum_{r \in R_t} \delta_{ri} \hat{w}_{rt}$. It is easy to see that (2) and (3) are satisfied since (11) and (12) are. Moreover, this solution also satisfies (4), since each route $r \in R_t$ already guarantees the flow conservation constraint (4) for all its nodes. Assuming the connection costs are additive, the objective function value corresponding to $\hat{x}$ will equal the objective value for $\hat{w}$. To see that this solution also satisfies (9), first note that since any route in (SL) satisfies this constraint, the maximum number of legs a route r can overlap with a MVP p is $k^p - 1$. Therefore along the direction of r, there will be at least one leg on p, either right before the start or after the end point of the overlapping section or both, that is exposed (i.e., not covered by r). Because of (11), the sum of the flow on the exposed leg is at most $1 - \hat{w}_{rt}$. The sum of all "lost" flows on all exposed legs along p is therefore $\geq \sum_{r \in R_t} \hat{w}_{rt} \geq 1$. The right inequality holds whenever at least one vehicle of type t is used. We can show that (5) is satisfied by $\hat{x}$ in a similar way.

To complete the second half of this proof, we show that not all solutions to (SL) are feasible to (CL). Consider a simple problem with 3 customers besides the depot and 3 vehicles of the same type. Assuming that the trip length limit is large enough, a solution to (CL) can make a round-trip between each pair of customers with "half" a vehicle (i.e., the weight of the connection is 0.5 for both legs of the trip). This solution will satisfy all the constraints in (CL), but will not have a corresponding solution in (SL) since it skips the depot altogether. □

Theorem 2. *The lower bound generated by problem (SL) is at least as tight as the lower bound generated by the relaxation of problem (C1) below.*

$$(C1) \quad \text{minimize} \sum_{t \in T} \sum_{i \in N} \sum_{j \in N} c_{ij}^t x_{ij}^t \tag{14}$$

subject to:

$$\sum_{t \in T} \sum_{j \in N} x_{ji}^t = 1 \qquad\qquad i \in N_0 \tag{15}$$

$$\sum_{j \in N_0} x_{0j}^t \leq M_t \qquad\qquad t \in T \tag{16}$$

$$\sum_{i \in N} x_{ip}^t - \sum_{j \in N} x_{pj}^t = 0 \qquad\qquad t \in T, p \in N \tag{17}$$

$$x_{ij}^t \in \{0,1\} \qquad\qquad i,j \in N, t \in T \tag{18}$$

$$y_0^t = 0 \qquad\qquad t \in T \tag{19}$$

$$y_j^t \leq Q_t - d_{j0}x_{j0}^t \qquad\qquad j \in N_0, t \in T \tag{20}$$

$$y_j^t - y_i^t \geq d_{ij}x_{ij}^t - (1 - x_{ij}^t)Q_t \qquad i \in N, j \in N_0, t \in T \tag{21}$$

$$y_i^t \geq 0 \qquad\qquad i \in N, t \in T. \tag{22}$$

Here variable y_i^t represents the time a vehicle of type t has spent on the road right after serving customer $i \in N$. For constraints (21), if x_{ij}^t is equal to 0, or no vehicle of type t serves a route that goes from i to j, then $y_j^t - y_i^t$ can take any value $\geq -Q_t$, i.e. their relative significance is not constrained; on the other hand, if $x_{ij}^t = 1$, or there is some vehicle that serves this route, then the constraint becomes $y_j^t - y_i^t \geq d_{ij}$, which specifies that y_j^t is larger than y_i^t by d_{ij}. Constraints (21) also eliminate subtours from the solution. Constraints (20) help ensure that the overall travel time for any route is no more than Q_t.

By employing the y variables, formulation (C1) avoids having to write constraints (5) that have number exponential in the number of nodes. A similar formulation has been used in modeling the capacitated VRP [13]. However, as with formulation (C), severe fractionality in the solution to the LP relaxation usually causes convergence issues for this problem for reasonably sized problems in our tests. Here we provide a proof for the relative strength of formulations (S) vs. (C1).

Proof. The proof is based on a Dantzig-Wolf reformulation of (C1). Consider a decomposition of (C1) where constraints (15) and (16) are part of the master problem, and constraints (17)–(22) are included in $|T|$ subproblems, each for a different vehicle type $t \in T$. The master problem then reads:

$$(M) \quad \text{minimize} \sum_{t \in T} \sum_{r \in R_t} \left(\sum_{i \in N} \sum_{j \in N} c_{ij}^t z_{ij}^{rt} \right) \omega_{rt}$$

subject to:

$$\sum_{t \in T} \sum_{r \in R_t} \left(\sum_{j \in N} z_{ji}^{rt} \right) \cdot \omega_{rt} = 1 \qquad i \in N_0$$

$$\sum_{r \in R_t} \left(\sum_{j \in N_0} z_{0j}^{rt} \right) \omega_{rt} \leq M_t \qquad t \in T$$

$$\omega_{rt} \in \{0,1\} \qquad t \in T, r \in R_t,$$

where the entries of a column, $(z_{ij}^{rt})_{i \in N, j \in N}$, form a feasible solutions to the single vehicle routing constraints:

$$\sum_{i \in N} z_{ip}^t - \sum_{j \in N} z_{pj}^t = 0 \qquad p \in N$$

$$z_{ij}^t \in \{0,1\} \qquad i,j \in N$$

$$\zeta_0^t = 0$$

$$\zeta_j^t \leq Q_t - d_{j0} z_{j0}^t \qquad j \in N_0$$

$$\zeta_j^t - \zeta_i^t \geq d_{ij} z_{ij}^t - (1 - z_{ij}^t) Q_t \qquad i \in N, j \in N_0, i \neq j$$

$$\zeta_i^t \geq 0 \qquad i \in N,$$

and R_t is the set of feasible solutions to the constraints above for each $t \in T$. By noting that

$$\sum_{i \in N} \sum_{j \in N} c_{ij}^t z_{ij}^{rt} = C_{rt} \qquad\qquad r \in R_t, t \in T$$

$$\sum_{j \in N} z_{ji}^{rt} = \delta_{ri} \qquad\qquad i \in N_0, r \in R_t, t \in T$$

$$\sum_{j \in N_0} z_{0j}^{rt} = 1 \qquad\qquad r \in R_t, t \in T,$$

we see that (M) is equivalent to the route based formulation (S). Since fractional solutions to the single vehicle routing constraints are not part of R_t, and thus any solution that is not convex combinations of routes in R_t will not be feasible to (S), the LP relaxation to (S) is at least as strong as that to (C1).   □

References

1. Gusikhin, O., MacNeille, P., Cohn, A.: Vehicle routing to minimize mixed-fleet fuel consumption and environmental impact. In: Proceedings of 7th International Conference on Informatics in Control, Automation and Robotics, vol. 1, pp. 285–291, Funchal, Madeira, Portugal (2010)
2. Lin, C., Choy, K.L., Ho, G.T., Chung, S., Lam, H.: Survey of green vehicle routing problem: past and future trends. Expert Syst. Appl. **41**, 1118–1138 (2014)
3. Minett, C.F., Daamen, W., Van Arem, B., Kuijpers, S., et al.: Eco-routing: comparing the fuel consumption of different routes between an origin and destination using field test speed profiles and synthetic speed profiles. In: 2011 IEEE Forum on Integrated and Sustainable Transportation System (FISTS), pp. 32–39. IEEE (2011)
4. Dantzig, G.B., Ramser, J.H.: The truck dispatching problem. Manage. Sci. **6**, 80–91 (1959)
5. Baldacci, R., Battarra, M., Vigo, D.: Routing a heterogeneous fleet of vehicles. In: Golden, B., Raghavan, S., Wasil, E. (eds.) The Vehicle Routing Problem: Latest Advances and New Challenges, vol. 43, pp. 3–27. Springer US, New York (2008)
6. Laporte, G.: Fifty years of vehicle routing. Transp. Sci. **43**, 408–416 (2009)
7. Toth, P., Vigo, D. (eds.): The Vehicle Routing Problem. Society for Industrial and Applied Mathematics (SIAM), Philadelphia (2001)
8. Baldacci, R., Bartolini, E., Laporte, G.: Some applications of the generalized vehicle routing problem. J. Oper. Res. Soc. **61**, 1072–1077 (2010)
9. Tahmassebi, T.: Vehicle routing problem (VRP) formulation for continuous-time packing hall design/operations. Comput. Chem. Eng. **23**(suppl S), 1011–1014 (1999)
10. Hasle, G., Kloster, O.: Industrial vehicle routing. In: Hasle, G., Lie, K.-A., Quak, E. (eds.) Geometric Modelling, Numerical Simulation, and Optimization, pp. 397–435. Springer, Berlin (2007)
11. Clark, G., Wright, J.W.: Scheduling of vehicles from a central depot to a number of delivery points. Oper. Res. **12**, 568–581 (1964)
12. Desrochers, M., Verhoog, T.W.: A new heuristic for the fleet size and mix vehicle routing problem. Comput. Oper. Res. **18**, 263–274 (1991)

13. Golden, B., Addad, A., Levy, L., Gheysens, F.: The fleet size and mix vehicle routing problem. Comput. Oper. Res. **11**, 49–66 (1984)
14. Li, F., Golden, B., Wasil, E.: A record-to-record travel algorithm for solving the heterogeneous fleet vehicle routing problem. Comput. Oper. Res. **34**, 2734–2742 (2007)
15. Salhi, S., Rand, G.K.: Incorporating vehicle routing into the vehicle fleet composition problem. Eur. J. Oper. Res. **66**, 313–330 (1993)
16. Baldacci, R., Mingozzi, A.: A unified exact method for solving different classes of vehicle routing problems. Math. Program. Ser. A **120**, 347–380 (2009)
17. Campos, V., Mota, E.: Heuristic procedures for the capacitated vehicle routing problem. Comput. Optim. Appl. **16**, 265–277 (2000)
18. Ralphs, T.K., Kopman, L., Pulleyblank, W.R., Trotter, L.E.: On the capacitated vehicle routing problem. Math. Program. **94**, 343–359 (2003)
19. de Oliveira, H.C.B., Vasconcelos, G.C.: A hybrid search method for the vehicle routing problem with time windows. Ann. Oper. Res. **180**, 125–144 (2010)
20. Kim, B.I., Kim, S., Sahoo, S.: Waste collection vehicle routing problem with time windows. Comput. Oper. Res. **33**, 3624–3642 (2006)
21. Kritikos, M.N., Ioannou, G.: The balanced cargo vehicle routing problem with time windows. Int. J. Prod. Econ. **123**, 42–51 (2010)
22. Li, X., Tian, P., Leung, S.C.: Vehicle routing problems with time windows and stochastic travel and service times: models and algorithm. Int. J. Prod. Econ. **125**, 137–145 (2010)
23. Novoa, C., Storer, R.: An approximate dynamic programming approach for the vehicle routing problem with stochastic demands. Eur. J. Oper. Res. **196**, 509–515 (2009)
24. Choi, E., Tcha, D.W.: A column generation approach to the heterogeneous fleet vehicle routing problem. Comput. Oper. Res. **34**, 2080–2095 (2007)
25. Wassan, N., Osman, I.: Tabu serach variants for the mix fleet vehicle routing problem. J. Oper. Res. Soc. **53**, 768–782 (2002)
26. Taillard, É.D.: A heuristic column generation method for the heterogeneous fleet VRP. Oper. Res. - Recherche Opérationnelle **33**, 1–14 (1999)
27. Ochi, L.S., Vianna, D.S., Drummond, L.M.A., Victor, A.O.: An evolutionary hybrid metaheuristic for solving the vehicle routing problem with heterogeneous fleet. In: Poli, R., Schoenauer, M., Fogarty, T.C., Banzhaf, W. (eds.) EuroGP 1998. LNCS, vol. 1391, pp. 187–195. Springer, Heidelberg (1998)
28. Tarantilis, C., Zachariadis, E., Kiranoudis, C.: A guided tabu search for the heterogeneous vehicle routing problem. J. Oper. Res. Soc. **59**, 1659–1673 (2008)
29. Armacost, A., Barnhart, C., Ware, K.: Composite variable formulations for express shipment service network design. Transp. Sci. **35**, 1–20 (2002)
30. Barlatt, A., Cohn, A., Fradkin, Y., Gusikhin, O., Morford, C.: Using composite variable modeling to achieve realism and tractability in production planning: an example from automotive stamping. IIE Trans. **41**, 421–436 (2009)
31. Barnhart, C., Johnson, E.L., Nemhauser, G.L., Savelsbergh, M.W., Vance, P.H.: Branch-and-price: column generation for solving huge integer programs. Oper. Res. **46**, 316–329 (1998)
32. Holland, J.: Adaptation in Natural and Artificial Systems, p. 5. University of Michigan Press, Ann Arbor (1975)
33. Baker, B., Ayechew, M.: A genetic algorithm for the vehicle routing problem. Comput. Oper. Res. **30**, 787–800 (2003)

34. Lin, S., et al.: Computer solutions of the traveling salesman problem. Bell Syst. Tech. J. **44**, 2245–2269 (1965)
35. Kolmanovsky, I., McDonough, K., Gusikhin, O.: Estimation of fuel flow for telematics-enabled adaptive fuel and time efficient vehicle routing. In: Proceeding of 11th IEEE International Conference on Intelligent Transportation Systems Telecommunications, pp. 139–144, St. Petersburg, Russia (2011)

Service Oriented Big Data Management for Transport

Gavin Kemp[1(✉)], Genoveva Vargas-Solar[2,3], Catarina Ferreira Da Silva[1],
Parisa Ghodous[1], and Christine Collet[2]

[1] Université Lyon 1, LIRIS, CNRS, UMR5202, bd du 11 novembre 1918, 69621 Lyon,
Villeurbanne, France
gavin.kemp@univ-lyon1.fr
[2] Grenoble Institute of Technology, LIG, 681 rue de la Passerelle, Grenoble,
Saint Martin d'Hères, France
[3] LIG-LAFMIA, CNRS, 681 rue de la Passerelle, Grenoble, Saint Martin d'Hères, France

Abstract. The increasing power of computer hardware and the sophistication of computer software have brought many new possibilities to information world. On one side the possibility to analyze massive data sets has brought new insight, knowledge and information. On the other, it has enabled to massively distribute computing and has opened to a new programming paradigm called Service Oriented Computing particularly well adapted to cloud computing. Applying these new technologies to the transport industry can bring new understanding to town transport infrastructures. The objective of our work is to manage and aggregate cloud services for managing big data and assist decision making for transport systems. Thus this paper presents our approach to propose a service oriented architecture for big data analytics for transport systems based on the cloud. Proposing big data management strategies for data produced by transport infrastructures, whilst maintaining cost effective systems deployed on the cloud, is a promising approach. We present the advancement for developing the Data acquisition service and Information extraction and cleaning service as well as the analysis for choosing a sharding strategy.

Keywords: ITS · Big data · Cloud services · NoSQL · Service oriented architecture

1 Introduction

During the last five years, the problem of providing intelligent real time data management using cloud computing technologies has attracted more and more attention from both academic researchers, e.g. P. Valduriez team in France [1], Freddy Lecue's work at Ireland IBM Research Lab [2], Big Data Initiative CSAIL Laboratory in MIT, USA, Cyrus Shahabi's team University of Southern California in USA [3] and industrial practitioners like Google Big Query, IBM, Thales. They mostly concentrate on modelling stream traffic flow, yet they barely combine different data flows with other big data to provide new intelligent transport services (ITS). ITS apply technology for integrating computers, electronics, satellites and sensors for making every transport mode (road, rail, air, water) more efficient, safe, and energy saving. ITS effectiveness relies on the

© Springer International Publishing Switzerland 2015
M. Helfert et al. (Eds.): Smartgreens 2015 and Vehits 2015, CCIS 579, pp. 267–281, 2015.
DOI: 10.1007/978-3-319-27753-0_15

prompt processing of the acquired transport-related information for reacting to congestion, dangerous situations, and, in general, optimizing the circulation of people and goods. Integration, storage and analysis of huge data collections must be adapted to support ITS for providing solutions that can improve citizens' lifestyle and safety.

In order to address these challenges it is important to consider that big data introduce aspects to consider according to its properties described by the 5V's model [4]: Volume, Velocity, Variety, Veracity, Value.

Volume and velocity (i.e., continuous production of new data) have an important impact in the way data is collected, archived and continuously processed. Transport data are generated at high speed by arrays of sensors or multiple events produced by devices and transport media (buses, cars, bikes, trains, etc.). This data need to be processed in real-time, near real-time or in batch, or as streams. Important decisions must be made in order to use distributed storage support that can maintain these data collections and apply on them analysis cycles. Collected data, involved in transport scenarios, can be very heterogeneous in terms of formats and models (unstructured, semi-structured and structured) and content. Data variety imposes new requirements to data storage and database design that should dynamically adapt to the data format, in particular scaling up and down. ITS and associated applications aim at adding value to collected data. Adding value to big data depends on the events they represent and the type of processing operations applied for extracting such value (i.e., stochastic, probabilistic, regular or random). Adding value to data, given the degree of volume and variety, can require important computing, storage and memory resources. Value can be related to quality of big data (veracity) concerning (1) data consistency related to its associated statistical reliability; (2) data provenance and trust defined by data origin, collection and processing methods, including trusted infrastructure and facility.

Processing and managing big data, given the volume and veracity and given the greedy algorithms that are sometimes applied to it, for example, giving value and making it useful for applications, requires enabling infrastructures. Cloud architectures provide unlimited resources that can support big data management and exploitation. The essential characteristics of the cloud lie in on-demand self-service, broad network access, resource pooling, rapid elasticity and measured services [5]. These characteristics make it possible to design and implement services to deal with big data management and exploitation using cloud resources to support applications such as ITS.

The objective of our work is to manage and aggregate cloud services for managing big data and assist decision making for transport systems. Thus this paper presents our approach for developing data storage, data cleaning and data integration services to make an efficient decision support system. Our services will implement algorithms and strategies that consume storage and computing resources of the cloud. For this reason, appropriate consumption models will guide their use.

The remainder of the paper is organized as follows. Section 2 describes work related to ours. Section 3 introduces our approach for managing transport big data on the cloud for supporting intelligent transport systems applications. Section 4 presents a case study of the application that validates our approach. Finally, Sect. 5 concludes the paper and discusses future work.

2   Related Work

2.1   Big Data Transport Systems

This section focuses on big data transport projects, namely to optimize taxi usage, and on big data infrastructures and applications for transport data events.

Transdec [3] is a project to create a big data infrastructure adapted to transport. It is built on three tiers comparable to the MVC (Model, View, Controller) model for transport data. The presentation tier, based on GoogleTM Map, provides an interface to express queries and expose the result, the query interface provides standard queries for the presentation tier and a data tier is spatiotemporal database built with sensor data and traffic data. This work provides an interesting query system taking into account the dynamic nature of town data and providing time relevant results in real-time.

Urban insight [6] is a project studying European town planning. In Dublin they are working event detection through big data, in particular on an accident detection system using video stream for CCTV (Closed Circuit Television) and crowdsourcing. Using data analysis they detect anomalies in the traffic and identify if it is an accident or not. When there is an ambiguity they rely on crowdsourcing to get further information. The project RITA [7] in the United States is trying to identify new sources of data provided by connected infrastructure and connected vehicles. They work to propose more data sources usable for transport analysis. L. Jian and co [8] propose a service-oriented model to encompass the data heterogeneity of several Chinese towns. Each town maintains its data and a service that allows other towns to understand their data. These services are aggregated to provide a global data sharing service. These papers propose methodologies to acknowledge data veracity and integrate heterogeneous data into one query system. An interesting line to work on would be to produce predictions based on this data to build decision support systems.

N.J. Yuan and co [9], Y. Ge and co [10] and D.H. Lee and co [11] worked a transport project to help taxi companies optimize their taxi usage. They work on optimizing the odds of a client needing a taxi to meet an empty taxi, optimizing travel time from taxi to clients, based on historical data collected from running taxis. Using knowledge from experienced taxi drivers, they built a mapping of the odds of passenger presence at collection points and direct the taxis based on that map. These research works do not use real-time data thus making it complicated to make accurate predictions and react to unexpected events. They also use data limited to GPS and taxi usage, whereas other data sources could be accessed and used.

D. Talia [12] presents the strengths of using the cloud for big data analytics in particular from a scalability stand point. They propose the development of infrastructures, platforms and service dedicated to data analytics. J. Yu and co [13] propose a service oriented data mining infrastructure for big traffic data. They propose a full infrastructure with services such accident detection. For this purpose they produce a large database with the collected data by individual companies. Individual services would have to duplicate the data to be able to use it. This makes for highly redundant data as the same data is stored by the centralized database, the application and probably the data producers. What is more, companies could be reluctant to giving away their data with no control for its use.

The state of the art reveals a limited use of predictions from big data analytics for transport-oriented systems. The heavy storage and processing infrastructures needed for big data and the current available data-oriented cloud services make possible the continuous access and processing of real time events to gain constant awareness, produce big data-based decision support systems, which can help take immediate informed actions. Cloud based big data infrastructure often concentrate around the massive scalability but don't propose a cheap method to simply aggregate big data services.

2.2 Big Data Analysis

H.V. Jagadish and co [4] propose a big data infrastructure based on five steps: data acquisition, data cleaning and information extraction, data integration and aggregation, big data analysis and data interpretation. X. Chen and co [14] use Hadoop-gis to get information on demographic composition and health from spatial data. J. lin and D. Ryaboy [15] present their experience on twitter to extract information from log information. They concluded that an efficient big data infrastructure is a balancing speed of development, ease of analysis, flexibility and scalability. Proposing a big data infrastructure on the cloud will make developing big data infrastructures more accessible to small businesses for several reasons: little initial investment, ease of development through Service-Oriented Architecture (SOA) and using services developed by specialist of each service.

Satish Narayana Srirama and co [16] demonstrated their cloud infrastructure for scientific analysis. Using Hadoop mapreduce, they classified the scientific algorithms according to how easy they could be adapted to mapreduce. Thus class 1 is when an algorithm can be executed with one mapreduce, class 2 is when the algorithm needs sequential mapreduce, class 3 is when each iteration of an algorithm executes one map reduce and class 4 is when each iteration needs multiple mapreduce.

Kurt Thearling [17] has put online a document introducing to the main families and technics for data mining. Whilst he claims the statistical technics are not data mining under the strictest of definitions, he included them since they are very used. He classified into two main families. The classical technics include statistical models very good for making predictions, nearest neighbour, clustering and generally technics visualizing data as space with as many dimensions as variable. The second is the Next Generation Techniques that include decision trees, neural networks and rules induction, they view data analysis as a series of tests. There are also more advanced methods [18].

And finally, Ricardo [19] is a tool which proposes to integrate the R scripting language and Hadoop. The objective of this tool is to provide data analyst easy tools to use mapreduce. Ricardo provides an Application Programing Interface to R that connects to a Hadoop cluster. It can convert R object into JaQL [20] queries to analyse the data. Whilst this technique has been proven successful with analytical technics like Latent-Factor Model or principal component analysis it showed less efficient than a straightforward mapreduce, on the other hand this tools greatly reduce the time of development.

2.3 Service Oriented Big Data

Domenico Talia [12] proposes three levels of bIg data analytical service to the image of the three levels of services in cloud. The SaaS provides data mining algorithms and knowledge discovery tools. The PaaS provides a platform for the development of new data analytical services. The IaaS provides the low level tools to data mining. In the same way Zibin Zheng and co [21] have proposed a similar vision applied to analyzing logs.

H. Demirkan and D. Delen [22] proposes a service oriented decision support system using big data and the cloud. They do this by combining data from multiple databases into a single database then duplicate it to services.

Eric E. Schadt and co [23] demonstrate the efficiency that cloud computing could have for big data analytics, showing that analysis of 1 peta Byte of data in 350 minutes for 2040 dollars.

Zhenlong Li and co [24] proposed a service oriented architecture for geoscience data were they separate the modelling service for geoscience, the data services, processing service and the cloud infrastructure.

Several articles have demonstrated the strength of cloud and big data in particular for instancing large quantities of computing power [25, 26, 27].

2.4 Conclusion of the State of the Art

These papers have shown that using big data for transport can provide very interesting applications. Big data analytics is a domain combining both old methods and new technology, that the data expert hasn't necessarily mastered. The use of the cloud for big data analytics has shown great results in both analytical speed but also cost and more importantly provides great elasticity.

On the other hand these papers have shown that big data analytics is viewed as a single service and not as a family of services responsible for the individual steps in the data management and analysis. Also data experts being general expert in their area, providing tools to ease the use of the new technology is important. By proposing a service oriented architecture for big data analysis, we hope to propose easy to develops tools for transport.

3 Big Data on the Cloud

In cloud computing everything is viewed as a service (XaaS). As a consequence cloud software (SaaS) is built as an aggregate of services exploiting services available on the cloud infrastructure (IaaS). In this spirit, we build a big data architecture where individual services manage the treatment level of big data. This also means that the companies wanting a big data infrastructure will be able to simply build it from an aggregation of services proposed by specialized companies.

Following the 5 step in big data proposed by H.V. Jagadish and co [4], we will design 5 types services (Fig. 1) for both historical data and real time data. These data services are: data acquisition services, data cleaning and extraction service, data integration and

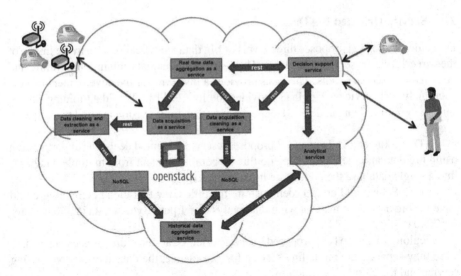

Fig. 1. Big data architecture

aggregation, data analytical services, and decision support services. The next paragraph will go into more detail for each service.

3.1   Data Acquisition Service

The first step of a big data infrastructure is well collecting the big data. This is basically hardware and infrastructure services that transfer, to NoSQL data stores adapted to the format of the data, the data acquired by the vehicles, users, and sensors deployed in cities (e.g. roads, streets, public spaces). This is done by companies and entities such as town or companies managing certain public spaces, who have data collecting facilities. These companies propose and sell their data on the cloud in our case the university Openstack infrastructure [28]. Using NOSQL storage like MongoDB [29], these companies will have a highly scalable and sharable data store. Also the sharding capability of these data stores offers high horizontal scalability but also faster analysis through MapReduce and data availability.

3.2   Information Extraction and Cleaning Service

The next step is cleaning and data extraction. This consists of both extracting the information from unstructured data and cleaning the data. This could be done by the company producing the data or an independent company depending on the level of structuration of the data. Highly structured data would likely be cleaned by the company producing the data as they understand best its production and thus know how best to clean it up. For highly unstructured data like sound or video data, highly specialized expert would be needed to extract the information.

This would be used to pot outliers in the data. Using MapReduce, the company acquiring the data or the company contracted to do it would perform statistical analysis to identify for example outliers in the data. This is important as, for example, a malfunction in a sensor loop could either ignore passing traffic or register non-existing traffic. Cleaning these events is important since inaccurate data produced by a dodgy sensor can break a model.

3.3   Integration and Aggregation Services

The objective of big data analytics is to use the large volume of data to extract new knowledge by searching, for example, for patterns in the data. This often has a consequence of data coming from a wide variety of sources. This means the data has to be aggregated into a usable format for the analytics tools to use. This service proposes services for real-time data aggregation and historical data aggregation.

The real-time data aggregation service gets the data from the individual data stores real-time data services and proposes a formatted file with the data from all the data acquiring service simply by fusing together the data provided by the real-time data acquisition services. Thus we aggregate data from the city, state of recharging stations, having location of people based on the time stamp or the GPS location.

The historical data aggregation will have to find a way to do similar action but with the data stores. The problem is that having data on several separate data stores is not a usable format. Importing all the data into a new huge data store would be redundant on already existing resources making this service potentially excessively expensive and as for temporary stores would be long to build when having to import terabytes of data as well as being expensive on network cost as well as time consuming. To solve this problem, this service will propose a query interface for simple querying and processing service to process the data mass by converting a form simple programing language into UNQL queries [30] to collect and pre-process the data before being integrated into a model.

3.4   Big Data Analytical and Decision Support Services

The whole point of big data is to identify and extract information from the mass of data. Predictive tools can be developed to anticipate the future. The role of this service is to provide a computer model of the historical data. It also provides the algorithm applied to the individual pieces of data. Thus using the model provided by the analytical service and the algorithm applied to the real-time data we can approach similar situations and act accordingly.

The decision support service composes several services. On the strategic level and using the model and the algorithm proposed by the big data analytical services, the decision support service provides an interface exposing the data situation in real-time but also predictions on events. For example, regularly observing an increase in the population in one place and traffic jams 30 minutes later we can deduct cause and effect and intervene in future situations so the taxis avoid and evacuate that area.

This service also generates data on the decision taken by the strategists to build more elaborate model including the consequence of this decision to then provide better decision support. On the vehicle level, services will provide advice to the vehicle for optimal economic driving based on the driving conditions. It also provides a database were the information on the dangers of the road is stored.

4 Managing Transport Big Data in Smart Cities

Consider the scenario where a taxi company needs to embed decision support in electric vehicles, to help their global optimal management. The company uses electric vehicles that implement a decision cycle to reach their destination while ensuring optimal recharging, through mobile recharging units. The decision making cycle aims at ensuring vehicles availability both temporally and spatially; and service continuity by avoiding congestion areas, accidents and other exceptional events. The taxis and mobile devices of users are equipped with video camera and location trackers that can emit the location of the taxis and people. For this purpose, we need data on the position of the vehicles and their energies levels, have a mechanism to communicate unexpected events and have usage and location of the mobile recharging station.

Figure 2 presents the general architecture of the transport data store as a service that we propose. It adopts a polyglot persistence [31] approach that combines several NoSQL systems for providing a storage support. Profiting from the cluster-oriented architecture of these systems our store uses a multi-cloud cluster based storage layer.

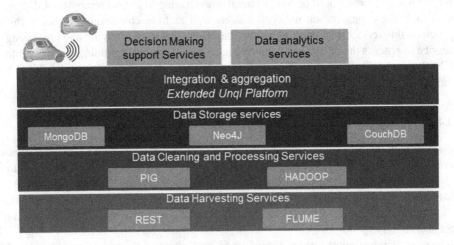

Fig. 2. Big data services

Our service extends an UnQL [30] layer with data processing operators including joins and filters for storing and retrieving data in an homogeneous way.

Furthermore, it exploits the sharding strategies of the NoSQL [29] systems for distributing and duplicating data, and ensuring availability. Shards are organized according to ranges of values of given attributes, or to hash functions and tags related to geographic zones. This induces request balancing and ensures better performance when data must be inserted and retrieved.

The service exploits also the persistence supports of clients (disk and cache) installed in mobile devices in order to distribute data processing and ensure data availability. For example, in our transport scenario, the service uses storage provided by devices used by taxis and users to process and manage data necessary for ITS services described in the previous section. In this way it avoids data transfer that can be penalizing in terms of response time and economic cost for accessing 3G or 4G networks.

Our data store service provides a global access to clusters providing NoSQL and relational support, and enables applications designers to configure their resources provision and non-functional properties according to given requirements and cloud subscriptions. An application defines the data structures that must persist in the UML eclipse plugin and then the tool Model2Roo (https://code.google.com/p/model2roo/) generates the necessary bindings to interact with different NoSQL stores. The application designer according to a profiling phase executed using the QDB benchmark (https://github.com/qdb-io) chooses the NoSQL stores.

4.1 Designing Transport Data Collections

The data collections "Evènement routier temps reel", "Etat du trafic temps reel", "Borne Criter", "Tronçon Web Criter", "Trafic historique", "plan Lyon", "Aménagement cyclable", "Caméra Web Criter" and "Station Velo'v", provided by the project Grand Lyon [33], are sought and stored by our service in order to be able to correlate collected data with data describing the city and its infrastructures (parks, roads, commercial zones, river). This data is highly heterogeneous in format, information and update rates. There are images in JPG, JSON, XML, and PDF formats. The data is also updated at varying rates going from yearly updates to real-time data passing by daily and minutely updates. GPS and location data in devices and vehicles are seen by our service as continuous data that can be correlated to other collected data useful for performing some decision making requests, such as which is the closest taxi (considering distance and time) to a client?, according to traffic and taxi-energy level, which are the possible destinations it can accept? Data are sharded by our service to perform this type of requests that require computing resources. Our service uses a MongoDB cluster to store these data.

Data stemming from social networks particularly Twitter and Waze of taxi users are collected and stored in NeO4J. This collection provides a real-time view of the traffic, road and zones status and events. Data are sharded thanks to our storage service locally on mobile devices and on NeO4J instances deployed in the cloud.

4.2 Making Global Transport Decisions

We conducted an experimental validation of our transport data store as a service for the scenario we described in Sect. 3. The experiment implements a polyglot multi-database that contains data collected from the French city Lyon. These data are retrieved by applications and infrastructure integrated by the project Grand Lyon. We then implement some important operations of the decision making cycle of the scenario (Fig. 3). The decision making cycle consists in:

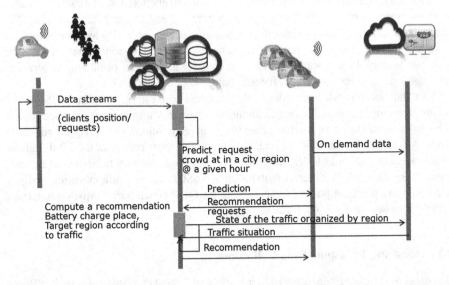

Fig. 3. UML sequence diagram of the decision making process.

Collecting data streams from taxis and users that are mobile data providers evolving in Lyon and feeding the data store service.

We focus particularly in three operations that use the transport data storage as a service approach, which are dissemination of events, optimization of energy recharging and scaling taxi provision of exceptional situations. We describe this use cases hereafter.

Disseminating Events. The applications deployed in taxis and users can be used for disseminating exceptional situation events, for example, unexpected dangers (Fig. 4). In our scenario a pedestrian is about to cross the road. "Vehicle A" is arriving in the same place but has no line of sight. "Vehicle B" in the area "sees" the pedestrian. The data sent from "Vehicle B" is then sent to data collection services and stored a NoSQL database. As the vehicle comes in the area, the vehicle computer will make HTTP query to a cloud which will access the data in the NoSQL database.

Depending on the nature of the danger the data store will make decisions on how long to keep that information and during which period it will re-execute the dissemination to taxis getting close to the zone.

Optimizing Battery Recharging. Part of the objective of taxi companies is use only electric vehicles. Unfortunately the lack of data makes it complicated to make good strategic solutions on the locations of the recharging stations that are also mobile (Fig. 5).

Fig. 4. Disseminating exceptional events

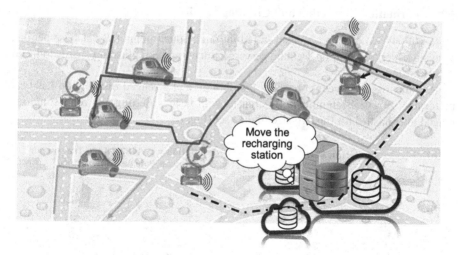

Fig. 5. Optimizing battery recharging

Using UnQL queries from the data integration service, the historical data stored in the NoSQL databases is periodically analyzed to extract information to build classification models or regression models for the real time data. Using this model and real-time data the system will make predictions on the location of taxi users and the traffic. As decision makers take decisions, this information is feed into the model to help the decision maker optimize the number of operational taxi, the location of these taxis and the location of the recharging stations by exposing the consequence previous similar decisions had.

The next section will present the state of development of the data collection service and the data storage services.

5   Implementation and Testing

In this section we present the data acquisition service and the information extraction and cleaning service. We also looked for the ideal sharding strategy for the MongoDB.

5.1   Data Acquisition Service

We have implemented and tested the data acquisition service. This services uses NodeJS module to acquire the city data from the Grand Lyon [33] but also from Twitter and from Bing search engine using REST requests. Still using REST requests these services will post the data onto a Mongodb database container to store as historical data. The service provides functions to access data via REST either with the key to the data store when wanting to query or analyses the historical data or the latest file acquired when using the real-time data service. The data is stored under XML, JSON or the original image file.

5.2   Information Extraction and Cleaning Service

So far 43 649 Kb of data has been stored into individual mongoDB database per data acquisition service built on 1 config server, 1 router, and 3 replicating shards to insure data persistence.

A comparison between a hashing distribution and a ranged distribution has been performed. It reveals significant differences with faster inserting and requesting data ranged over hashed for the two size of data set (Fig. 6).

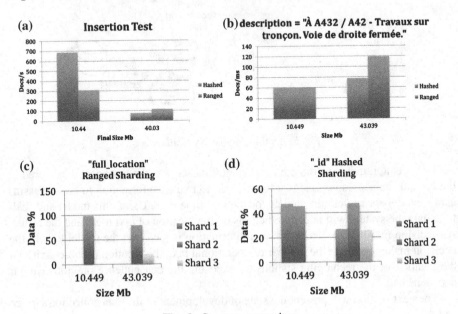

Fig. 6. Strategy comparison

We observer generally the data distribution between the shards is better for hashed IDs over ranged IDs (Fig. 6 C and D). This induces better performances (Fig. 6 A and B) for the hashed data since it allows a better distributed computing, where each individual shard has less data to analyses. The ranged show improved results when the data set becomes large, largely because, provided the query is related to the ordered variable, one does not have to analyses all the data longer.

Thus using ranged ids based on the coordinates of the data will be at least able to optimize location based queries.

6   Conclusion and Future Work

This paper proposes a transport data store as a service that implements a distributed storage approach. Our approach uses NoSQL systems deployed in a multi-cloud setting and makes sharding decisions for ensuring data availability.

The transport data store service is validated in a scalable and adaptable ITS for electric vehicles using big data analytics on the cloud. This provides a global view of current status of town transport, helps making accurate strategic decisions, and insures maximum security to the vehicles and their occupants.

For the time being our storage service concentrates in improving design issues with respect to NoSQL support. We are currently measuring performance with respect to different sizes of data collections. We have noticed that NoSQL provides reasonable response times once an indexing phase has been completed. We are willing to study the use of indexing criteria and provide strategies for dealing with continuous data. We will also be developing the other services for our big data architecture. These issues concern our future work.

Acknowledgement. We thank the Région Rhône-Alpes who finances the thesis work of Gavin Kemp by means of the ARC 7 programme (http://www.arc7-territoires-mobilites.rhonealpes.fr/), as well as the competitiveness cluster LUTB Transport & Mobility Systems, in particularly Mr. Pascal Nief, Mr. Timothée David and Mr. Philippe Gache for putting us in contact with local companies and projects to gather use case scenarios for our work.

References

1. Gulisano, V., Jiménez-Peris, R., Patiño-Martnez, M., Soriente, C., Valduriez, P.: StreamCloud: an elastic and scalable data streaming system. IEEE Trans. Parallel Distrib. Syst. **23**, 2351–2365 (2012)
2. Lecue, F., Tallevi-Diotallevi, S., Hayes, J., Tucker, R., Bicer, V., Sbodio, M.L., Tommasi, P.: STAR-CITY. In: Proceedings of the 19th international conference on Intelligent User Interfaces - IUI 2014, pp. 179–188 (2014)
3. Demiryurek, U., Banaei-Kashani, F., Shahabi, C.: TransDec: a spatiotemporal query processing framework for transportation systems. In: Proceedings of 26th IEEE International Conference on Data Engineering, pp. 1197–1200 (2010)
4. Jagadish, H.V., Gehrke, J., Labrinidis, A., Papakonstantinou, Y., Patel, J.M., Ramakrishnan, R., Shahabi, C.: Big Data and Its Technical Challenges, vol. 57, no. 7 (2014)

5. Mell, P., Grance, T.: The NIST definition of cloud computing recommendations of the national institute of standards and technology (2008)
6. Artikis, A., Weidlich, M., Gal, A., Kalogeraki, V., Gunopulos, D.: Self-Adaptive Event Recognition for Intelligent Transport Management, pp. 319–325 (2013)
7. Thompson, D., McHale, G., Butler, R.: RITA (2014). http://www.its.dot.gov/data_capture/data_capture.htm
8. Jian, L., Yuanhua, J., Zhiqiang, S., Xiaodong, Z.: Improved design of communication platform of distributed traffic information systems based on SOA. In: 2008 International Symposium on Information Science and Engineering, vol. 2, pp. 124–128 (2008)
9. Yuan, N.J., Zheng, Y., Zhang, L., Xie, X.: T-finder: a recommender system for finding passengers and vacant taxis. IEEE Trans. Knowl. Data Eng. **25**, 2390–2403 (2013)
10. Ge, Y., Xiong, H., Tuzhilin, A., Xiao, K., Gruteser, M., Pazzani, M.: An energy-efficient mobile recommender system. In: Proceedings of the 16th ACM SIGKDD international conference on Knowledge discovery and data mining - KDD 2010, p. 899 (2010)
11. Lee, D.-H., Wang, H., Cheu, R., Teo, S.: Taxi dispatch system based on current demands and real-time traffic conditions. Trans. Res. Rec. **1882**, 193–200 (2004)
12. Talia, D.: Clouds for scalable big data analytics. Computer (Long. Beach. California), vol. 46, no. 5, pp. 98–101 (2013)
13. Yu, J., Jiang, F., Zhu, T.: RTIC-C: a big data system for massive traffic information mining. In: 2013 International Conference on Cloud Computing and Big Data, pp. 395–402 (2013)
14. Chen, X., Vo, H., Aji, A., Wang, F.: High performance integrated spatial big data analytics. In: Proceedings of the 3rd ACM SIGSPATIAL International Workshop on Analytics for Big Geospatial Data - BigSpatial 2014, pp. 11–14 (2014)
15. Lin, J., Ryaboy, D.: Scaling big data mining infrastructure : the twitter experience. ACM SIGKDD Explor. Newsl. **14**(2), 6 (2013)
16. Tavakoli, S., Mousavi, A.: Adopting user interacted mobile node data to the flexible data input layer architecture. In: 2008 International Conference on Intelligent Sensors, Sensor Networks and Information Processing, pp. 533–538 (2008)
17. Berson, A., Smith, S., Thearling, K.: An overview of data mining techniques. Data Min. Appl. CRM, pp. 1–49 (2004)
18. Yan, W., Brahmakshatriya, U., Xue, Y., Gilder, M., Wise, B.: p-PIC: parallel power iteration clustering for big data. J. Parallel Distrib. Comput. **73**(3), 352–359 (2013)
19. Das, S., Haas, P.J., Beyer, K.S.: Ricardo: integrating R and hadoop categories and subject descriptors, pp. 987–998 (2000)
20. Lim, S.: Scalable SQL and NoSQL data stores, Statistics (Ber) (2008)
21. Zheng, Z., Zhu, J., Lyu, M.R.: Service-generated big data and big data-as-a-service: an overview. In: 2013 IEEE Proceedings of the International Congress on Big Data, pp. 403–410 (2013)
22. Demirkan, H., Delen, D.: Leveraging the capabilities of service-oriented decision support systems: Putting analytics and big data in cloud. Decis. Support Syst. **55**(1), 412–421 (2013)
23. Schadt, E.E., Linderman, M.D., Sorenson, J., Lee, L., Nolan, G.P.: Cloud and heterogeneous computing solutions exist today for the emerging big data problems in biology. Nat. Rev. Genet. **12**(3), 224 (2011)
24. Li, Z., Yang, C., Jin, B., Yu, M., Liu, K., Sun, M., Zhan, M.: Enabling big geoscience data analytics with a cloud-based, MapReduce-enabled and service-oriented workflow framework. PLoS One **10**(3), e0116781 (2015)
25. Abramova, V., Bernardino, J.: NoSQL databases: a step to database scalability in web environment. In: Proceedings of the International C* Conference on Computer Science Software Engineering - C3S2E 2013, pp. 14–22 (2013)

26. Hipgrave, S.: Smarter fraud investigations with big data analytics. Netw. Secur. **2013**(12), 7–9 (2013)
27. Tannahill, B.K., Jamshidi, M.: System of Systems and Big Data analytics – Bridging the gap. Comput. Electr. Eng. **40**(1), 2–15 (2014)
28. Sadalage, P.J., Fowler, M.: NoSQL Distilled (2012)
29. Open, "Openstack," (2015). http://www.openstack.org/
30. Buneman, P., Fernandez, M., Suciu, D.: UnQL: a query language and algebra for semistructured data based on structural recursion. VLDB J. **9**(1), 76 (2000)
31. Nance, C., Losser, T., Iype, R., Harmon, G.: NoSQL vs RDBMS - why there is room for both. In: Proceedings Southern Association Information System Conference, pp. 111–116 (2013)
32. Cattell, R.: Scalable SQL and NoSQL data stores. ACM SIGMOD Rec. **39**(4), 12 (2011)
33. GrandLyon: Smart Data (2015). http://data.grandlyon.com/

An Integrated Architecture for Simulation and Modeling of Small- and Medium-Sized Transportation and Communication Networks

Ahmed Elbery[1], Hesham Rakha[2(✉)], Mustafa Y. ElNainay[3], and Mohammad A. Hoque[4]

[1] Department of Computer Science, Virginia Tech,
Blacksburg, VA, USA
aelbery@vt.edu
[2] Department of Civil Engineering, Virginia Tech, Blacksburg, VA, USA
hrakha@vtti.vt.edu
[3] Department of Computer and Systems Engineering, Alexandria University, Alexandria, Egypt
ymustafa@alexu.edu.eg
[4] Department of Computing, East Tennessee State University, Johnson City, USA
hoquem@etsu.edu

Abstract. The emergence of Vehicular Ad-hoc Networks (VANETs) in the past decade has added a level of complexity to the modelling of Intelligent Transportation System (ITS) applications. In this paper, the Vehicular Network Integrated Simulator (VNetIntSim) is introduced as a new transportation network and VANET simulation tool by integrating transportation and VANET modelling. Specifically, it integrates the OPNET software, a communication network simulator, and the INTEGRATION software, a microscopic traffic simulation software. The INTEGRATION software simulates the movement of travellers and vehicles, while the OPNET software models the data exchange through the communication system. Information is exchanged between the two simulators as needed. The paper describes the implementation and the operation details of the VNetIntSim as well as the features it supports such as multiclass support and vehicle reuse. Subsequently, VNetIntSim is used to quantify the impact of mobility parameters (vehicular traffic stream speed and density) on the communication system performance considering Transmission Control Protocol (TCP) and User Datagram Protocol (UDP) applications. Specifically, the routing performance (packet drops and route discovery time), IP processing delay in case of a file transfer protocol (FTP) application, and jitter in case of a Voice over Internet Protocol (VoIP) application and evaluated.

Keywords: Vanet · Intelligent Transportation Systems · Transportation System Modelling · Simulation

1 Introduction

Vehicular Ad Hoc Networks (VANETs) and Intelligent Transportation Systems (ITSs) have a wide spectrum of applications, algorithms and protocols that are important for the public, commercial, environmental and scientific communities. From the communication

© Springer International Publishing Switzerland 2015
M. Helfert et al. (Eds.): Smartgreens 2015 and Vehits 2015, CCIS 579, pp. 282–303, 2015.
DOI: 10.1007/978-3-319-27753-0_16

perspective, these applications range from on-road-content-sharing Li, et al. [1], entertainment-based and location-based services [2]. From the transportation perspective, these applications include safety applications [3], cooperative driving and warning applications [4], traffic control and management [5], fuel consumption and carbon emission minimization applications [6], speed harmonization [7], road traffic congestion detection and management [8], and taxi/transit services [9]. This wide application spectrum demonstrates the importance of these systems.

On the other hand, evaluating these systems is challenging, not only because of the cost needed to implement these systems because of the need for a large number of vehicles equipped with communication devices, the required communication infrastructure and signal controllers, but also for the need for roads to run the required experiments. A third reason is that some applications/algorithms work in special conditions of either weather and/or traffic congestion, which are not easily provided. Fourthly, and most importantly, the failures in some of these applications may result in loss of lives of the participants.

Thus, currently, the best approach to study these systems is to use simulation tools. However, simulating ITS and VANET systems is challenging. The reason is that these systems cover two fields, namely the transportation field and the communication field. The transportation field includes the modeling of vehicle mobility applications including traffic routing, car-following, lane-changing, vehicle dynamics, driver behavior modeling, and traffic signal control modeling, in both macroscopic and microscopic modeling scales. The other main field is the data and communication network modeling that includes data packet flow, vehicle-to-vehicle (V2 V) communication as well as vehicle-to-infrastructure (V2I) communication, wireless media access, data transportation, data security and other components. These two fields are not distinct or isolated, but instead are interdependent and influence one another. For example vehicle mobility, speeds and density affect the communication links between vehicles [3] as well as the data routes, and hence the communication quality (i.e. reliability, throughput and delay) [10]. Another example is the attempt in [11] to model the multi-hop V2 V connectivity in urban vehicular networks using archived Global Positioning System (GPS) traces that revealed many interesting characteristics of network partitioning, end-to-end delay and reachability of time-critical V2 V messages. In the opposite direction, the number of packet losses between vehicles and the delivery delay will affect the accuracy of the data collected, and hence the correctness of the decisions made by the ITS's systems. Taking in consideration the complexity of each system (transportation and communication) in addition to the high and complex interdependency level between them, we can see how challenging the modeling and simulation of VANET and ITS.

Most of the previous efforts in simulating VANET and ITS platform are based on using fixed mobility trajectories that are fed to the communication network simulator. These trajectories may be generated off-line using a traffic simulator platform or extracted from empirical data sets. This simulation paradigm is useful for single directional influence (i.e. studying the effect of mobility on the network and data communication) such as data dissemination in a VANET. However, this approach cannot be used in case the opposite direction of interdependence is important (i.e. the effect of the communication system on the transportation system). Such as vehicle speed control in the vicinity of traffic signals, where vehicles and the signal controllers exchange information to compute and optimal vehicle trajectory. These interactions have to be run in real-time to accurately model the various component interactions.

In this paper, we introduce a new framework for modeling and simulating an integrated VANET and ITS platform. This new framework has the capability of simulating the full VANET/ITS system with full interdependence between the communication and transportation systems, and hence allows for the analysis of VANET and/or ITS applications and algorithms with any level of interaction or interdependence between them. This framework integrates two simulators, namely; the INTEGRATION [12] as microscopic traffic simulator and the OPNET modeler [13] as the data and communication simulator by establishing a two-way communication channel between the models. Through this communication channel, the two simulators can interact to fully model any VANET/ITS application. Subsequently, the developed framework is used to study the effect of different traffic characteristics (traffic stream speed and density) on V2 V and V2I communication performance.

The paper is organized as follows. Section 2 provides a brief description of related work. Subsequently, the VNetIntSim operation and how the two simulators interact is described in Sect. 3. The architecture of the VNetIntSim and the implementation of the proposed framework is presented in Sect. 4. A simulation case study is presented and discussed in Sect. 5, in which the VNetIntSim is used to study the effect of various traffic mobility measures on the communication performance. Finally, conclusions of the study and future research directions are presented in Sect. 6.

2   Literature Review

The necessity of integrating a full-fledged traffic simulator with a wireless network simulator to model the cooperative ITS systems built on V2X communication platform has been perceived since the past decade. A number of attempts have been made within recent years to develop an integrated traffic simulation platform that allows the vehicles' mobility conditions dynamically adapt to the wirelessly received messages. Two different approaches have been considered by the researchers to facilitate this interoperability.

One common approach was to embed the well-known vehicular mobility models into the established network simulators. These features are sometimes combined with the original simulator as separate functional modules or APIs. For example, Choffnes et al. [14] integrated the Street Random Waypoint (STRAW) model into the Java-built scalable communication network simulator SWANS, which allowed parsing of real street map data and modeling of complex intersection management strategies. A collection of application-aware SWANS modules, named as ASH, were developed to incorporate the car-following and lane-changing models providing a platform for evaluating inter-vehicle Geo-cast protocols for ITS applications [14, 15]. Following a similar approach, the communication network simulator NCTUns extended its features to include road network construction and microscopic mobility models [16]. More recently, NS-3 has been engineered to incorporate real-time interaction between a wireless communications module and vehicular mobility models using a fast feedback loop.

Another different approach is to integrate two standalone simulators - a traffic simulator coupled with a wireless network simulator. The choice of traffic simulators considered by the community for coupling in this manner included CORSIM, VISSIM, SUMO whereas network simulators ranged from NS-2, NS-3, QUALNET, and OMNET ++. Table 1 summarizes some of these integration attempts:

Table 1. Integrated simulators summary.

Traffic sim.	Network sim.	Integrated simulator
VISSIM	NS-2	MSIE [17]
SUMO	NS-2	TraNS [18]
SUMO	OMNET ++	VEINS [19]
SUMO	NS-3	OVNIS [20]
SUMO	NS-3	iTETRIS [21]

CORSIM is a commercial traffic simulator that does not provide dynamic routing capabilities, while VISSIM does provide some dynamic routing capabilities these are limited compared to the INTEGRATION software, which provides a total of ten different routing strategies ranging from feedback to predictive dynamic routing. Consequently, both CORSIM and VISSIM do not provide sufficient routing algorithms for testing in a connected vehicle environment. The first attempt of integrating two independent open source traffic and wireless simulators was TraNS (Traffic and Network Simulation Environment) [18], which combined SUMO and NS-2. Later, VEINS [19] also adopted the open source approach of TraNS by combining the network simulator OMNET ++ with SUMO. VEINS allowed for the interaction between the two simulators by implementing an interface module inside OMNET ++ that sends traffic mobility updating commands to SUMO. For example, VEINS could impose a given driving behavior to a particular vehicle upon receiving wireless messages from another vehicle. Most recently, the Online Vehicular Network Integrated Simulation (OVNIS) [20] platform was developed, that coupled SUMO and NS-3 together and included an NS-3 module for incorporating user-defined cooperative ITS applications. OVNIS extends NS-3 as a "traffic aware network manager" to control the relative interactions between the connected blocks during the simulation process. Last but not the least, iTETRIS [21] moves one step beyond the state-of-the-art solutions and overcomes one limitation that is present in Trans, VEINS and OVNIS by providing a generic central control system named iCS to connect an open-source traffic simulator with a network simulator, without having to modify the internal modules of the interconnected simulation platforms.

VNetIntSim uses the concept of separation between the internal simulators modules and the new modules that were added to support the model integration. This feature is actually inherited from the two simulators we selected for the VNetIntSim. INTEGRATION is fully built in modular fashion with a master module that manages and controls of all the modules. The interaction between the modules is modeled using interfaces between the modules. Consequently, updating any modules will not affect the others as long as this interface does not change. OPNET is built in a hierarchical modular fashion at all its levels (network, nodes, links and processes). The network consists of a set of nodes and links. Each node consists of a set of process modules. The process modules interact through interrupts and the associated Interface Control Information (ICI). The modules added to the simulators in this research effort maintain the same concept, so that updating the simulators does not affect the integration between them.

OPNET and INTEGRATION have their unique features compared to the other simulators. Compared to NS-2 and NS-3, OPNET has these features; (1) a well-engineered user interface that allows for easy building and managing of different simulation scenarios. (2) the OPNET modeler provides its powerful debugging capabilities. (3) OPNET supports a visualization tool that allows for tracking data packets within the nodes. OMNET ++ is a simulation framework that does not have modules. However, there are many open source frameworks based on OMNET ++ that implement different modules such as VEINS. In VEINS, the update interval is 1 s which is a long interval from the communication perspective. For example if the speed is the vehicle is 60 km/h (37.28 miles/h) which is a common speed in cities, this update interval corresponds to 16.6 m which is a long step that can affect the communication between vehicles.

From the traffic perspective, INTGRATION supports many features, such as dynamic vehicle routing and dynamic eco-routing [22], eco-drive systems, eco-cruise control systems, vehicle dynamics and other features that are not supported in other traffic simulation software, including SUMO. The INTEGRATION model has been developed over three decades and has been extensively tested and validated against empirical data and traffic flow theory. Furthermore, the INTEGRATION software is the only software that models vehicle dynamics, estimates mobility, energy, environmental and safety measures of effectiveness. The model also includes various connected vehicle applications including cooperative adaptive cruise control systems, dynamic vehicle routing, speed harmonization, and eco-cooperative cruise control systems.

3   VNetIntSim Operation

This section introduces the operation of the VNetIntSim platform which integrates two simulators; namely OPNET and INTEGRATION. First, a brief introduction about INTE-GRATION and OPNET is presented. Then, the VNetIntSim operation is described.

3.1   Integration Software

The INTEGRATION software is agent-based microscopic traffic assignment and simulation software [12]. INTEGRATION is capable of simulating large scale networks up to 10000 road links and 500,000 vehicle departures with time granularity of 0.1 s. This granularity allows detailed analyses of acceleration, deceleration, lane-changing movements, car following behavior, and shock wave propagations. It also permits considerable flexibility in representing spatial and temporal variations in traffic conditions. These are very important characteristics needed when studying the communication between these vehicles.

The model computes a number of measures of performance including vehicle delay, stops, fuel consumption, hydrocarbon, carbon monoxide, carbon dioxide, and nitrous oxides emissions, and the crash risk for 14 crash types [12].

3.2 OPNET Modeler

The OPNET modeler is a powerful simulation tool for specification, simulation and analysis of data and communication networks [13]. OPNET combines the finite state machines and analytical model. The modeling in OPNET uses Hierarchical Modeling, which has a set of editors (Network, Node and Process editors), all of which support model level reuse. The most important OPNET characteristic is that has been tested using implementations for many standard protocols. However, it does not yet support any VANET technology protocols (i.e. IEEE 802.11p DSRC [23], nor Vehicular Routing Protocols). Consequently, for now, the IEEE 802.11 g for wireless LAN simulation is used in the scenarios and AODV [24] for routing purposes.

3.3 Integrating OPNET and INTEGRATION

The main idea behind VNetIntSim is to use the advantages of both the INTEGRATION and OPNET platforms by establishing a two-way communication channel between them. Through this channel the required information is exchanged between the two simulators. The basic and necessary information that should be exchanged periodically is the vehicle locations. The locations of vehicles are calculated in INTEGRATION every deci-second and transmitted to the OPNET modeler, which updates the vehicle locations while they are communicating.

For this version of VNetIntSim, the communication channel between OPNET and INTEGRATION is established by using shared memory as we will explain in the next section. The shared memory supports the required speed and communication reliability between the two simulators.

Initialization and Synchronization. When starting the simulators, and before starting the simulation process, the two simulators should initialize the communication channel using two-way Hello Messages. After establishing the connection, the two simulators synchronize the simulation parameters; simulation duration, network map size, location update interval, maximum number of concurrent running vehicles and number of signals. In this synchronization phase the INTEGRATION serves as a master and OPNET serves as a slave, i.e. values of these parameters in OPNET should match those calculated in INTEGRATION. Mismatching in some of these parameters (such as simulation duration, number of fixed signal controllers and the maximum number of concurrent running vehicles) will result in stopping the simulators. In this case the OPNET software sends a Synchronization Error message to the INTEGRATION software. This behavior guarantees the consistency of the operation and the results collected in both system. Additional parameters allow some tolerances. For example, the map size in OPNET should be greater than or equal to that in INTEGRATION.

After successful synchronization, the simulation process should start by exchanging the simulation start message sent from OPNET. OPNET starts the simulation by initializing its scenario components and initializing the vehicles locations and status. The component initialization take place by sending start simulation interrupt to each module in each component in the scenario (i.e. routers, hosts, vehicles...etc.). The purpose of this interrupt is to read the configuration parameters, initialize the modules state variable and invoke the appropriate processes based on the configuration. After this initialization, OPNET finds all the vehicles nodes in the scenario and map each one to a vehicle ID in the INTEGRATION software. Using this mapping, each vehicle in OPNET corresponds to only one vehicle in the INTEGRATION. However, this behavior can be overridden as described in the next section. Then, OPNET disable all the vehicles, which means that all the vehicles will be inactive. After that, OPNET enables vehicles based on the information it receives from INTEGRATION. The vehicle in OPNET is a mobile node that we customized by adding new attributes such as speed, acceleration and movement direction. Also we added some modules to this this vehicle node to represent some vehicular applications such as eco-routing module that implement the eco-routing [22] algorithm for minimizing fuel consumption. However this is out of the scope of this article.

During the simulation phases, there are many types of messages that can be exchanged between the two simulators. Each message type has its unique Code. Based on the code, the message fields are determined. Table 2 shows the different message codes. The gaps between the code values allow for the addition of new functionalities in the future.

Table 2. Message codes.

Code	Function
01	Initialization; Hello Message
02	Initialization: Connection Refused
10	Parameter Synchronization
11	Synchronization Error
30	Signal Locations Request
31	Signal Locations Updates
40	Start Simulation
50	Locations Information Request
51	Locations Information Updates
60	Speed Information Request
61	Speed Information Updates
99	Termination Notification

Location Updating. During the simulation, the INTEGRATION software computes the new vehicle coordinates and sends them to the OPNET software, which in turn updates the location of each vehicle, as shown in Fig. 1. This cycle is repeated each update_interval, which is typically 0.1 s in duration. The time synchronization during the location updating is achieved in two ways, (1) using two semaphores (intgrat_made_update and opnet_made_update) one for each simulator, (2) at each update time step the INTEGRA-TION software sends the current simulation time to OPNET. If it does not match the OPNET time, OPNET will take the proper action to resolve this inconsistency. Figure 2 shows the flow chart for the basic location update process. In each location update cycle, the INTEGRATION software computes the updated vehicle locations. Subsequently, it checks whether the last update has been copied (intgrat_made_update = 0). If so, it writes the new update to the shared memory and sets the intgrat_made_update flag to 1.

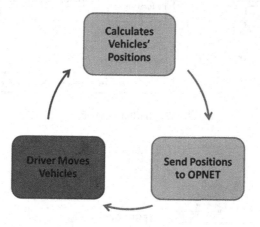

Fig. 1. Location update cycle.

OPNET waits for new updates. When it receives a new update, if the received time equals its current time, the driver process in OPNET will copy the locations, set the intgrat_made_update flag to 0, and then moves the vehicles to the new locations. If the received time is greater than the OPNET current time, it schedules the process to be executed again in the received time. If the received time is less than the current time, OPNET discards this update.

Application Communication. The basic operation described above is only for updating locations, which is the core of the VNetIntSim platform. However, ITS applications need the exchange of other types of information that reflect the communication results to INTEGRATION. This information and how/when it should be exchanged depend mainly on the application itself. Thus, the application specifications should define what other information as well as how and when it should be exchanged.

The applications will use the established communication channel to exchange the required information. VNetIntSim supports simultaneous multi-applications, where each application can use one or more codes to support its functionalities. Figure 3 shows the complete communication cycle when running an application.

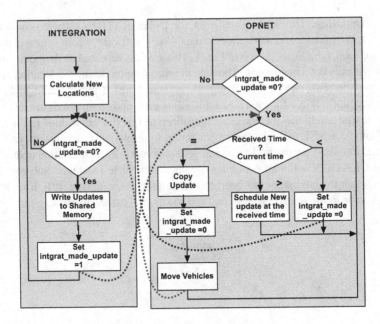

Fig. 2. VNetIntSim basic operation.

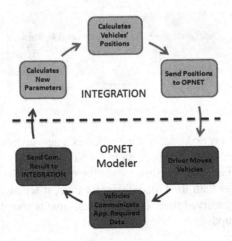

Fig. 3. Complete communication cycle.

For example, in variable speed control systems, INTEGRATION will move the vehicles. Then, in OPNET, the vehicles and signals communicate the speed information. Based on the exchanged information, each vehicle finds its new speed. These new speeds should be sent to the INTEGRATION software, which computes the updated parameters (i.e. acceleration or deceleration) and then computes the updated vehicle locations.

4   Architecture, Implementation and Features of VNetIntSim

This section describes the architecture and the detailed implementation of the modeler and then the supported features in the current version.

4.1   Architecture and Implementation

Figure 4 shows the VNetIntSim architecture and the modules that were added to each simulator (dashed boxes). Within INTEGRATION, the Configuration Reader Module reads the input files and based on the configuration generates an XML topology file for OPNET. This topology file contains the vehicle specifications, signal controller locations as well as the application and profile specifications. This file is used by OPNET to generate its scenarios.

The first issue that arises during implementation entails identifying the inter-process communication mechanism that should be used to connect the simulators. In VNetIntSim two methods were selected, namely; TCP sockets and shared memory. Each of these methods has its advantages over all the other methods. The shared memory approach supports very high speed communication, which is needed when modeling large simulation networks. In addition, the operating system manages the mutual execution of this shared memory so this does not need to be considered.

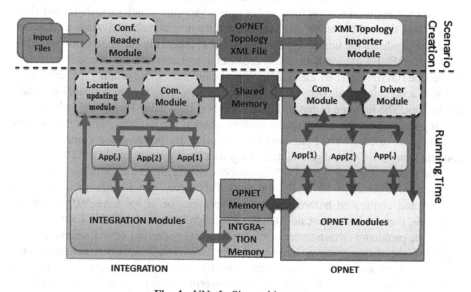

Fig. 4. VNetIntSim architecture.

However, it is limited by the machine capabilities in terms of processing speed and memory size. On the other hand, TCP sockets provide more flexibility so that the INTE-GRATION software can be connected to any other simulator on a different OS/machine, in addition to the processing capabilities that will be gained from the other machine. However, TCP sockets introduce the network dynamics, reliability and delay problems to the simulation process which may result in some communication delay. Consequently, the approach used in this paper is the shared memory approach. In future we plan to implement the TCP socket communication.

In each of the two simulators, a communication module was created. These two modules are responsible for (1) establishing the communication channel by creating a shared memory, (2) exchanging the information between the two simulators through the shared memory, (3) addressing the applications using the message codes shown in Table 2, based on the received code the communication module forwards the data to the appropriate application, and (4) synchronizing the communication against the data damages or losses by using intgrat_made_update and opnet_made_update semaphores, one for each direction.

The location updating module in INTEGRATION is responsible for calculating the location of each vehicle (because INTEGRATION works based on the distance on the link) and sending them along with the other parameters to the driver module in OPNET. The other parameters basically include the number of moving vehicles, the vehicle IDs, and the current time. Moreover, in the location updating message, the location updating module notifies OPNET about the vehicles that completed their trips.

The driver module in OPNET receives the location updating messages (code 51) from the communication module and then (1) checks the received simulation time from the other side, and in case of time mismatch it takes the appropriate decision to overcome this mismatch as shown in Fig. 2, (2) updates the location for the moving vehicles, (3) activates any required new vehicles, and (4) deactivates the vehicles which finished their trips. Using the number of moving vehicles and the activation/deactivation mechanism drastically reduces the processing time in OPNET, especially for large scenarios. That is because OPNET cannot dynamically create or delete communication nodes (vehicles) during the run time, and all the vehicles must be created before running the scenario.

We faced many challenges in the implementation. This section describes the main challenges. The first one is that INTEGRATION is built using FORTRAN which does not support any of the inter-process communication mechanisms. To overcome this problem, we used Mixed-Language Programming by building the communication module using the C language and then compiling its object file into FORTRAN.

The second problem is that OPNET cannot dynamically create or delete communication nodes (vehicles) during the run time. This means that all the vehicles must be created and configured before running the scenario i.e. if we have 50,000 vehicle scenarios, then we have to create 50,000 communication nodes in OPNET at the design time. The problem is this number of communication nodes in OPNET will result in a very slow simulation process. Here we used the Activation/Deactivation mechanism for communication nodes. This mechanism starts by deactivating all the communication nodes and when receiving location updates activating the required nodes. When INTE-GRATION sends a notification about a vehicle that completes its trip, the mechanism deactivates that vehicle. This mechanism drastically reduces the number of active vehicles in OPNET and thus enhances the simulation speed.

Moreover, most of the computations are made in the INTEGRATION software to take the advantage of the FORTRAN high computing speed. For example, one option was to send the vehicle speeds and directions and have OPNET compute the vehicle updated locations, however because FORTRAN is faster than C, all computations were made in the FORTRAN environment.

4.2 Modeler Features

VNetIntSim has some features that were added to achieve different objectives, as described in this section.

Vehicle Reuse. One of the main issues when simulating the vehicular network is scalability, which is mainly affected by the number of vehicles traveling along the network. As mentioned in the previous subsection, OPNET cannot create vehicles in run time. Consequently we have to create all the required vehicles in the design phase. In case of large network scenarios, the large number of vehicles will result in a very long initialization time when starting the simulation and also results in large memory usage. Subsequently, this limits the model scalability. To overcome this limitation VNetIntSim can make reuse of the same vehicle as a communication node to represent multiple moving vehicles, obviously in different time slots. In this way, the required number of vehicles in OPNET can be reduced from the total number of vehicles or trips (which may be thousands of vehicles) to the maximum number of concurrent vehicles which is much smaller than the total number of vehicles or trips. The vehicle reuse feature can significantly increase the scalability by reducing the number of vehicles simulated in OPNET, consequently, decreases the memory requirements and the execution time. This feature can be safely used when we are interested in studying the global system behavior. However, it is not suitable when studying the individual communication behavior of a vehicle or a connection.

Vehicles Multi-class Support. This capability is inherited from INTEGRATION which supports up to five classes of vehicles. Each class can be configured to run in different way and use different algorithms. We extend this feature to OPNET, where the class information is associated with the vehicle and transferred from INTEGRATION to OPNET. So, the user can implement communication protocols or configure them to work differently for different classes of vehicles. For example, in data dissemination in VANET, the user can chose to send the data only to specific vehicle class (i.e. Trucks). Using this feature also, routing protocol can prioritize next hop based on its class (i.e. vehicles of the same class move in similar speeds, thus their relative speeds are very low). Another application of this feature is the penetration ratio of a specified technology where we want to check the effect of the penetration ratio of some new technologies (i.e. cooperative driving).

Customizable Updating Interval. The location updating interval determines how frequently the location information are sent from INTEGRATION to OPNET. The shorter the updating interval, the higher the accuracy of the mobility. However, the shorter the updating interval the more the processing, and thus, the longer the execution time. VNetIntSim, enable the user to change this interval based on the network requirements. Its default is 0.1 s which is also the minimum updating interval. It can be changed to any value that is multiple of 0.1 s. Also, it is not necessary to be matched in the two sides of the VNetIntSim because the INTEGRATION can overwrite the updating interval setting n OPNET.

5 Case Study

Routing is one of the important protocols that are sensitive to vehicle mobility and density parameters. In this section, the VNetIntSim is used to study the effect of mobility measures on the AODV [24] routing, in case of FTP traffic. In addition, the effect of vehicle density on VIOP jitter is studied. Subsequently the scalability of the VNetIntSim modeling tool is tested because scalability is a critical drawback in existing simulators, including: VEINS and iTETRIS.

5.1 Simulation Setup

In this case study, the road network shown in Fig. 5 is used.

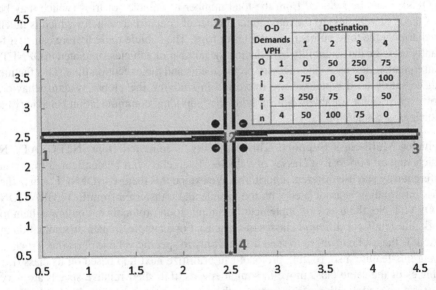

Fig. 5. Road network and O-D demands.

The road network consists of an intersection numbered 12, and four zones numbered 1, 2, 3 and 4. Each zone serves as a vehicle origin and destination. Each road link is 2 km in length. The vehicular traffic demand that was considered in the study is presented in Fig. 5. For example, the traffic rate from zone 2 to 1 is 75 Veh/h. The vehicles speeds are determined using two speed parameters, namely; the free-flow speed and the speed-at-capacity [25]. Throughout the paper, the notation Free/Capacity will be used to represent the ratio of free-flow speed to the speed-at-capacity. Two speed scenarios are considered, namely: 40/30 km/h and 80/50 km/h.

For the application we used File Transfer Protocol (FTP), in which we can control the connection time by deciding the file size. Also, in OPNET we can control the traffic rate of the FTP connections. The FTP server is located at the intersection. Starting from 250 s, the moving vehicles attempted to download a 100 Kbyte file from this server. The FTP clients re-established a new connection every 20 s. The FTP server is spatially fixed and modeled as a road side unit (RSU). The IEEE82.11 g was employed at the wireless communication medium with a data rate of 24 Mbps. For routing the AODV was used as the routing protocol for both scenarios.

5.2 Number of Moving Vehicles in the Network

The traffic simulation included three phases; two transient and one steady-state phase. The loading and unloading phases are transient phases, which represent the two shoulders of the peak period, as illustrated in the graphs in Fig. 6. In the loading phase, vehicles enter the road network, while in the unloading phase vehicles exit. Between them there is a steady-state phase in which some vehicles are entering the network, while others are exiting. In the steady-state phase, the change in the number of the vehicles in the network is not significant. While in the loading phase the network loading changes significantly. The length of these phases depends mainly on the speed distribution, vehicle departure rates, and the road map.

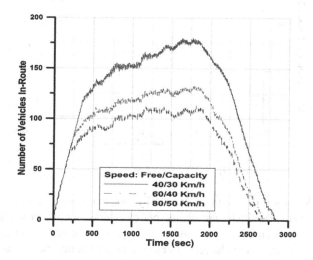

Fig. 6. Number of vehicles in the network.

Figure 6 shows the number of vehicles in the network for different speed parameters (Free/Capacity). The importance of determining these phases is that during the transient phases the communication network may be spatially partitioned without data routes that link these partitions together. While in the steady-state phase vehicles almost cover the entire road network, and most probably there is full connectivity between vehicles. Consequently, the network communication behavior during the transient phases is different from that during the steady-state phase.

By controlling the speed parameters and the departure rate distribution, we can control the network partitions during the simulation time. Using this methodology, we can model the delay tolerant communication networks (DTN) [26] and intermittently connected mobile networks [27].

Thirdly defining these phases gives us estimation for the vehicle density in the network at any instant in time. This density significantly influences the communication performance as will be shown later.

5.3 FTP Connections and AODV

In this section some results obtained from the FTP communication will be presented. As we described in the previous subsection the vehicle density significantly affects the communication performance. Figure 7 shows the cumulative number of packets dropped by AODV across the entire network due to the loss of a route to the destination.

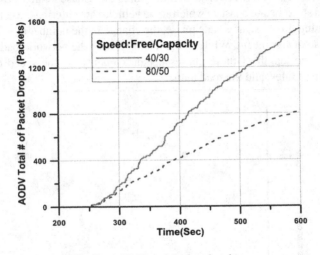

Fig. 7. AODV total # of packet drops.

The AODV packet drop can be caused by two main reasons: (1) the number of vehicles in the network; the larger the number of vehicles the larger the traffic. So any route missing will result in a larger number of drops. (2) The vehicle speeds; the higher the speed the faster the route changes, and so the larger the number of packet drops.

In an attempt to identify which of the two factors is more influential on the routing, Fig. 8 illustrates how the average number of drops vary across the network. It shows that around 300 s, both speeds have a similar average packet drop rate. During this interval the number of vehicles for both scenarios is very similar. While as the difference in vehicle density increases with time, the average number of drops also reflects the changes in traffic density.

The two figures demonstrate that for the two scenarios, despite the fact that the vehicle density is related to the traffic stream speed, the vehicle density has a more significant impact on the performance of the communication system. Consequently,

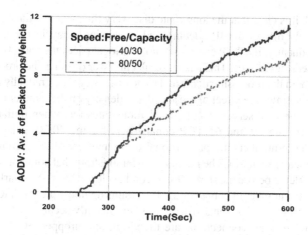

Fig. 8. AODV Av. # of Packet Drops per vehicles.

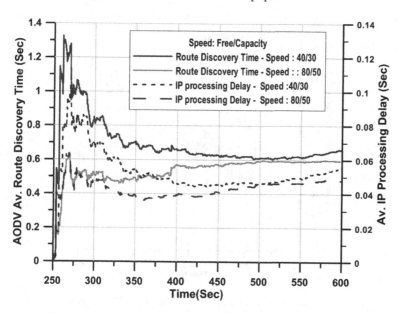

Fig. 9. AODV Av. route discovery time and Av. IP processing delay.

a change in the traffic stream density caused by other factors, such as traffic demand has a more significant impact on the routing than does changes in the traffic stream speed. Another important parameter in routing efficiency is the route discovery time which is shown in Fig. 9. It shows the correlation between the route discovery time and the IP processing and queuing delay on the vehicles. After 250 s each vehicle attempts to establish an FTP session with the server resulting in a flood of AODV route request packets. This flood increases the amount of IP packets being sent and processed at the IP layer in each vehicle, and thus increases the IP processing (queuing + processing) delay, which is reflected on the route discovery time.

From Fig. 9, it is clear that the long route discovery time when initiating the communication is mainly due to the IP queuing and processing delay in the higher density scenario. Subsequently, the TCP congestion control logic paces the packets based on the acknowledgements it receives. This pacing results in lower queuing and processing delay. Consequently, both the processing delay and route discovery time gradually decrease.

Figure 10 illustrates the effect of the speed and density on the number of active TCP connections on the FTP server. The figure demonstrates that when initiating the FTP connections there are 69 and 61 TCP connections for the 40/30 and 80/50 speeds, respectively. These numbers are proportional to the number of concurrent vehicles in the network for each scenario. The results also demonstrate that some of these connections were completed before the start of the second cycle (at 270 s). Similarly, the second cycle increases the number of connections. The results demonstrate that later the number of connections for the 80/50 scenario decreases significantly because some vehicles exit the network and so their connections are timed-out and dropped, while in the 40/30 scenario vehicles are still traveling on the network.

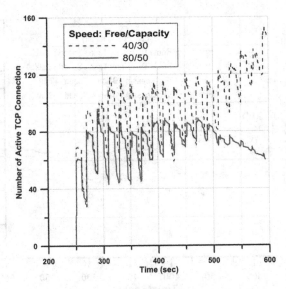

Fig. 10. Number of TCP connections of the FTP server.

The above results and analysis for the simple scenarios we used are realistic and consistent with the protocol behavior.

5.4 VOIP Jitter

This subsection focuses on the VOIP traffic and how the mobility parameters affect the performance of the voice application. The start time of the voice sessions is normally distributed with a mean and variance of 350 and 50 s, respectively. The session duration is 250 s. Figure 11 shows the average jitter across the entire network. Figure 11 shows that the jitter for the low speed is very high compared to the high speed.

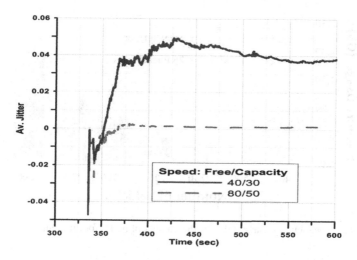

Fig. 11. Average VOIP jitter.

The results show that when the voice session starts around 350 s, the jitter in both scenarios is similar. Furthermore, as the number of sessions increases, the jitter increases gradually. For the 80/50 speeds the jitter increase seizes because the network enters a steady-state (the change in number of vehicles is not significant). While for the 40/30 scenario, the jitter continues to increase to unacceptable values because of the increase in the number of vehicles.

Figure 11 shows the importance of the vehicle density in the network and how influential it is on the VOIP connections. It shows that as the number of vehicles in the network reaches a specific value, the overall jitter across the network becomes unacceptable. Although the routes in lower speed are relatively more stable, the jitter is higher due to the vehicle density.

5.5   System Scalability

The scalability is the most critical drawback of existing platforms including the proposed platform. The two main scalability parameters are the memory usage and the execution time. The results show that the number of nodes and the data traffic rate per vehicle are key factors behind the scalability issue. Specifically, results show that, the memory usage grows exponentially with the number of vehicles in the network, as shown in Fig. 12. The result shows also that the execution time is mainly dependent on the average traffic rate per vehicle. As shown in Fig. 13.

Figure 12, shows that the memory utilization increases exponentially with the number of vehicles in the network. This possesses a scalability limitation to the modeler. This scalability problem is reasoned to the detailed implementation of the network simulation models. However, this detailed implementation is necessary when studying the behavior of individual vehicle, individual connection between two vehicles or the detailed behavior of a specific protocol.

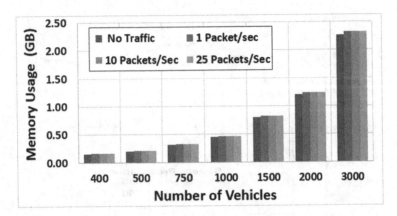

Fig. 12. The memory usage (GB) vs. the number of nodes for different traffic rates.

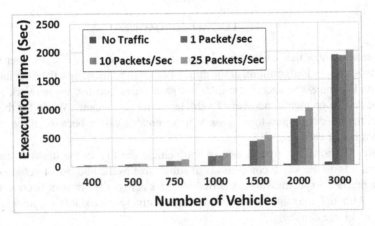

Fig. 13. The execution time (Sec) vs. the number of nodes and the traffic rate per vehicle.

On the other hand, in case of focusing on global analysis, where the individual detailed behavior is not important, we can reduce the number of vehicles in the network by reuse the vehicles as described earlier. In this case, the total number of vehicles we need in the simulation network become the maximum concurrent number of vehicles.

Figure 12 also shows that for a specific number of nodes, increasing the traffic rate has no significant effects on the memory usage. We argue that behavior to the ability of OPNET to destroy the packets after they arrived it destination application and so free its memory.

Figure 13 shows that the execution time is exponentially increasing with number of vehicles, and increases also with the average traffic rate per vehicle. We can notice the abrupt increase in the execution time when increasing the traffic rate to only one packet. This large increment is reasoned to the broadcast nature of the AODV protocol that used in this scenario. Where any application packet to a new source triggers the AODV to broadcast a route request message to all its neighbors. Each of these neighbors receives and processes this message and might rebroadcast it. Which results in a wave of broadcast that spans overall the network. Consequently, increasing the execution time.

We also notice that increasing the traffic rate per vehicle from 1 packet to 10 packets per vehicle does not result in such increase in the execution time. That is because the first packet only initiates the broadcast waves in the network. And any other packets to the same destination needs only the route maintenance.

These results are obtained on a machine of Intel Core-i7 Quad-core processor, 4 GB of memory, and running windows 7 Ultimate.

6 Conclusions and Future Work

VNetIntSim, is presented as an integrated platform for simulating and modeling vehicular networks. VNetIntSim integrates a transportation simulator (INTEGRATION) with a data communication network simulator (OPNET modeler). Results obtained from the simulation scenarios are realistic and consistent with protocol behavior. VNetIntSim has the capability to fully simulate the two-way interdependency between the transportation and communication systems, which is necessary for many applications. In addition it provides the power of both simulators to study global network parameters as well as very detailed parameters for each system at a microscopic level considering a 0.1 s granularity.

Subsequently, the VNetIntSim modeler is used to quantify the effect of mobility parameters on the communication performance. The results show that the effect of vehicle density is of higher significance than that of the speed. More specifically, the higher speed results in a lower drop ratio and lower jitter due to the lower traffic stream density.

Proposed future work entails enhancing the model scalability by creating a vehicle module with the necessary sub-modules. Further work entails implementing the DSRC module in the OPNET modeler. The most important future work is to implement some ITS applications such as speed harmonization, eco-driving, congestion avoidance and vehicle routing. A study of the effect of quality of services and different routing mechanisms on the performance of the transportation system and services offered for both users and vehicles is also warranted.

Acknowledgements. This effort was funded partially by the Tran*LIVE* and MATS University Transportation Centers and NPRP Grant # 5-1272-1-214 from the Qatar National Research Fund (a member of The Qatar Foundation). The statements made herein are solely the responsibility of the authors.

References

1. Li, M., Yang, Z., Lou, W.: CodeOn: cooperative popular content distribution for vehicular networks using symbol level network coding. IEEE J. Sel. A. Commun. **29**, 223–235 (2011)
2. Bruner, G.C., Kumark, A.: Attitude toward location-based advertising. J. Interact. Advertising **7**, 3–15 (2007)

3. Hafeez, K.A., Lian, Z., Zaiyi, L., Ma, B.N.: Impact of mobility on VANETs' safety applications. In: Global Telecommunications Conference (GLOBECOM 2010), pp. 1–5 (2010)
4. Van den Broek, T.H.A., Ploeg, J., Netten, B.D.: Advisory and autonomous cooperative driving systems. In: 2011 IEEE International Conference on Consumer Electronics (ICCE), pp. 279–280 (2011)
5. Baskar, L.D., De Schutter, B., Hellendoorn, H.: Hierarchical traffic control and management with intelligent vehicles. In: Intelligent Vehicles Symposium, pp. 834–839 (2007)
6. Xiao, Y., Zhao, Q., Kaku, I., Xu, Y.: Development of a fuel consumption optimization model for the capacitated vehicle routing problem. Comput. Oper. Res. **39**, 1419–1431 (2012)
7. Talebpour, A., Mahmassani, H., Hamdar, S.: Speed Harmonization. Transp. Res. Rec. J. Transp. Res. Board **2391**, 69–79 (2013)
8. Roy, S., Sen, R., Kulkarni, S., Kulkarni, P., Raman, B., Singh, L.K.: Wireless across road: RF based road traffic congestion detection. In: Third International Conference on Communication Systems and Networks (COMSNETS), pp. 1–6 (2011)
9. Hoque, X.H.M.A., Dixon, B.: Innovative taxi hailing system using DSRC infrastructure. In: ITS World Congress, Detroit (2014)
10. Alam, M., Sher, M., Husain, S.A.: VANETs mobility model entities and its impact. In: 4th International Conference on Emerging Technologies, ICET, pp. 132–137 (2008)
11. Hoque, M.A., Hong, X., Dixon, B.: Efficient multi-hop connectivity analysis in urban vehicular networks. Veh. Commun. **1**, 78–90 (2014)
12. Rakha, H.: INTEGRATION Rel. 2.40 for Windows - User's Guide, Volume I: Fundamental Model Features. https://sites.google.com/a/vt.edu/hrakha/software. Accessed August 2014
13. R. Technology: http://www.riverbed.com/products/performance-management-control/opnet.html. Accessed August 2014
14. Choffnes, D.R., Bustamante, F.E.: An integrated mobility and traffic model for vehicular wireless networks. In: Proceedings of the 2nd ACM International Workshop on Vehicular Ad Hoc Networks, pp. 69–78 (2005)
15. Ibrahim, K., Weigle, M.C.: ASH: application-aware SWANS with highway mobility. In: INFOCOM Workshops, pp. 1–6 (2008)
16. Wang, S.Y., Chou, C.L.: NCTUns tool for wireless vehicular communication network researches. Simul. Model. Pract. Theory **17**, 1211–1226 (2009)
17. Caliskan, C.L.M., Scheuermann, B., Singhof, M.: Multiple simulator interlinking environment for C2CC in VANETs. http://www.cn.hhu.de/en/our-research/msiecv.html. Accessed August 2014
18. Piorkowski, M., Raya, M., Lugo, A.L., Papadimitratos, P., Grossglauser, M., Hubaux, J.-P.: TraNS: realistic joint traffic and network simulator for VANETs. ACM SIGMOBILE Mob. Comput. Commun. Rev. **12**, 31–33 (2008)
19. Sommer, C., German, R., Dressler, F.: Bidirectionally coupled network and road traffic simulation for improved IVC analysis. IEEE Trans. Mob. Comput. **10**, 3–15 (2011)
20. Pigne, Y., Danoy, G., Bouvry, P.: A platform for realistic online vehicular network management. In: IEEE GLOBECOM Workshops (GC Wkshps), pp. 595–599 (2010)
21. Rondinone, M., Maneros, J., Krajzewicz, D., Bauza, R., Cataldi, P., Hrizi, F., et al.: iTETRIS: a modular simulation platform for the large scale evaluation of cooperative ITS applications. Simul. Model. Pract. Theory **34**, 99–125 (2013)
22. Ericsson, E., Larsson, H., Brundell-Freij, K.: Optimizing route choice for lowest fuel consumption – potential effects of a new driver support tool. Transp. Res. Part C Emerg. Technol. **14**, 369–383 (2006)

23. Jiang, D., Taliwal, V., Meier, A., Holfelder, W., Herrtwich, R.: Design of 5.9 GHz DSRC-based vehicular safety communication. IEEE Wirel. Commun. **13**, 36–43 (2006)
24. Perkins, C., Belding-Royer, E., Das, S.: RFC 3561-ad hoc on-demand distance vector (AODV) routing. Internet RFCs, pp. 1–38 (2003)
25. Van Aerde, M., Rakha, H.: Multivariate calibration of single regime speed-flow-density relationships. In: Proceedings of the 6th Vehicle Navigation and Information Systems Conference, pp. 334–341 (1995)
26. Fall, K.: A delay-tolerant network architecture for challenged internets. In: Proceedings of the Conference on Applications, Technologies, Architectures, and Protocols for Computer Communications, Karlsruhe, Germany, pp. 27–34 (2003)
27. Lindgren, A., Doria, A., Schel, O.: Probabilistic routing in intermittently connected networks. SIGMOBILE Mob. Comput. Commun. Rev. **7**, 19–20 (2003)

Privacy Endangerment from Protocol Data Sets in VANETs and Countermeasures

Sebastian Bittl[(⊠)] and Arturo A. Gonzalez

Fraunhofer ESK, 80686 Munich, Germany
{sebastian.bittl,arturo.gonzalez}@esk.fraunhofer.de

Abstract. Wireless vehicular networks are about to be deployed within the next years. Important progress towards practical usage of such networks is being made by standardization in Europe and the USA. Thereby, one of the core concerns is privacy of vehicles and their drivers, especially in Europe. Prior work has regarded only a small sub-set of the information exposed by current standards to an attacker for vehicle tracking. Thus, we take a close look on the data contained on different protocol layers of an ETSI ITS system. We find that much data is very distinctive and can be used to identify static vehicle properties such as manufacturer or even model. We call these data sets volatile constant data. Its presence is shown to greatly reduce usability of formerly proposed cooperative pseudonym switching strategies. Thereby, a privacy metric called vehicular uniqueness is introduced. The provided analysis shows that more constraints have to be applied for selecting appropriate cooperation partners for pseudonym switching, which significantly reduces their availability. Therefore, current techniques cannot provide the level of privacy defined in VANET standards. Suggestions for improving the data sets used by security entity and facility layer of ETSI ITS are given to limit the impact of the found issues. Effectiveness of the proposed mechanisms is shown in the provided evaluation.

Keywords: VANET · ETSI ITS · Privacy · Security

1 Introduction

Wireless intelligent transport systems (ITS) are about to enter the mass market in upcoming years. Important examples are ETSI ITS in Europe [2] and WAVE in the USA [20]. Thus, these systems' security and privacy aspects are gaining increased attention. Thereby, the possibility to track vehicles is a core point of concern, especially in Europe [26]. Many approaches for realizing such tracking exist. Typically, such attacks use the temporarily fixed pseudonym certificate, used by vehicles to authenticate their broadcast messages. However, higher level protocol information, e.g., identifiers or current position and velocity of a vehicle, is regarded for this purpose as well [17].

Many studies have shown the possibility to track vehicles in ITS systems based on the mentioned data sets, e.g. [28]. Tracked vehicle movement paths

© Springer International Publishing Switzerland 2015
M. Helfert et al. (Eds.): Smartgreens 2015 and Vehits 2015, CCIS 579, pp. 304–321, 2016.
DOI: 10.1007/978-3-319-27753-0_17

can be well correlated to homes of their drivers [18]. Thus, tracking of vehicles limits privacy of drivers. Therefore, a number of countermeasures has been published. These include context aware pseudonym changes [17] and time synchronized pseudonym switching [29]. Unfortunately, these mechanisms require the exchange of further messages between vehicles cooperating during the pseudonym change. This clearly increases the already significant overhead introduced by security mechanisms (see e.g., [13]). Moreover, none of these works studies the influence of metadata contained in the security envelope of current ETSI ITS and WAVE systems on the privacy of vehicles. Additionally, only a fraction of the vast number of data fields from higher level applications is taken into consideration in this prior work.

Thus, a first look on the privacy impact of such additional data fields has been provided in [12]. This work extends the one given in [12], especially regarding recently updated ETSI ITS standards and a significantly increased evaluation of suggested privacy improvement mechanisms.

Our contribution focuses on the influence on the privacy of information broadcast by vehicles in ETSI ITS conforming VANETs. Thereby, we especially study the metadata contained in the security envelope of broadcast messages apart from the used pseudonym. Furthermore, we take a close look on the high number of data sets used by higher level protocols regarding their possibility to ruin the privacy efforts taken elsewhere. For the sake of compactness we focus the study of the ETSI ITS facility layer on Cooperative Awareness Messages (CAMs). However, much similarity between ETSI ITS and WAVE exists on the different protocol layers. Thus, we especially point out the cases which also apply for WAVE based systems.

The further outline is as follows. Section 2 reviews related work. Afterwards, Sect. 3 provides the in detail study of the impact of individual data fields on privacy of broadcasting vehicles. In Sect. 4, the achieved results are used to determine a metric for vehicle uniqueness within its vehicular environment. Finally, a conclusion is provided in Sect. 6 alongside with possible topics of future work.

2   Related Work and Attacker Model

Recent work on privacy in vehicular area networks (VANETs) or intelligent transport systems (ITSs) includes [11,15–17,25,28,29]. Basically, privacy in such networks relies on a pseudonym scheme which changes the identifiers (IDs) of a vehicle (or ITS-station (ITS-S)) on all protocol layers on a regular basis to avoid tracking [26]. A general overview of security and privacy mechanisms in VANETs is given in [24,26,27].

Both ETSI ITS and WAVE do not use dedicated messages to distribute security related data sets like pseudonym certificates. Instead piggybacking of such information on cyclically (CAM, BSM) or on demand distributed (DENM) messages is used [3,9].

There are mainly two kinds of attacks on privacy in VANETs. Simple attacks just use identifiers like the station ID and a very limited set of additional information about the ITS-S, typically only the vehicle position. Advanced attacks include more context information for tracking, e.g., behavior of other vehicles [17,28]. Bayesian traffic analysis to re-identify vehicles after cooperative pseudonym changes is proposed in [14]. Thereby, it has been shown that simple pseudonym change, like in ETSI ITS and WAVE, cannot avoid tracking. The probability of two (or even more) vehicles changing their pseudonym in close vicinity just by chance, confusing an attacker, is just to small.

Many approaches to confuse an attacker trying to track vehicles have been proposed. A simple pseudonym scheme based on per-trip certificate usage is given in [11]. Advanced pseudonym switching schemes apply concepts like *Mix-Zones* [25], silent periods, *SLOW* [15], context aware pseudonym changes [17] and time synchronized pseudonym switching [29] (see also [28] and references within). A common requirement of all these concepts is that vehicles must find indistinguishable partners in their vicinity with whom they cooperate to perform a secure pseudonym change. All vehicles should change all of their identification parameters together to confuse the attacker [26]. However, we show that finding such partners is quite unlikely to happen in VANETs using current ETSI ITS and WAVE standards.

A commonly assumed attacker model is the global passive adversary [28]. This passive attacker can monitor all messages in the whole ITS system. This model is also assumed in the following.

Even advanced attacks from prior work (e.g., [28,29]) have so far not included usage of the biggest share of metadata from the security envelope and higher protocol level data from cyclic messages in VANETs following current standards. Thus, we study the usability of these data for more advanced attacks.

Properties of the studied standards from the ETSI ITS and WAVE frameworks are explained in the next Sect. 3, alongside with their impact on privacy aspects.

3   Data for Vehicle Identification

ETSI ITS and WAVE use Cooperative Awareness Messages (CAMs) and Basic Safety Messages (BSMs) for the main data exchange in their VANET systems, respectively. Therefore, our focus is on the contents of theses messages on the different protocol layers.

When looking for possible privacy issues regarding vehicle tracking, the core focus is on data within messages which differs for different groups of vehicles, but is also constant for the individual vehicle for a long time. One example is vehicle dimensions which are identical for all vehicles of the same model but different for other models with high probability. We call that kind of data *volatile constant data*. Thereby, volatile is meant in the sense of the data being accessible by all receivers and constant with respect to a long time period.

Within typical traffic scenarios many different vehicle types and models are present in the vicinity of a vehicle intending to perform a secure pseudonym change. To do so, the above described cooperative pseudonym strategies select partners whose broadcast information is as similar as possible to confuse the attacker. The presence of volatile constant data clearly makes it less probable to find such proper partners leading to possibly insecure pseudonym changes. Thus, the presence of such data should be avoided as far as possible.

Current standards bind the lifetime of MAC address, network layer address and station ID of the facility layer to the one of the pseudonym. This means, once the pseudonym gets changed the other identifiers get changed, too. Therefore, an attacker cannot profit from looking on more than one of these identifiers at once as they all provide the same temporarily valid information. Moreover, for the simple case of single hop broadcast, like it is used for CAMs and BSMs, the network and access layer only add information to the transmitted messages which cannot be used to track their senders.

In the next section metadata from the security envelope will be studied. The impact of data from access and network layer is looked at in Sect. 3.2. Afterwards, the content of CAMs at the facility layer will be discussed.

3.1   Metadata in Security Envelope

The security envelope is used to secure content from the facility and network layer protocols by embedding them into a dedicated header and trailer, each consisting of different sub-parts. Thereby, content handed over to the security entity is treated in accordance to a so called security profile. These profiles determine the required header fields as well as the used cryptographic techniques, which can be digitally signing and/or encryption. The definition of the security envelope is quite similar in ETSI ITS [9] and WAVE [3].

In ETSI ITS the sets of mandatory header fields for security profiles *CAM* and *Generic* are subsets of the one for *DENM* (used for Decentralized Environment Notification Messages (DENMs)). Thereby, the location stamp in profiles *DENM* and *Generic* carries the same information as the vehicle position inside a CAM [5,7]. Thus, this field is not discussed separately and the reader is referred to Sect. 3.3 for details.

We focus the further discussion on mandatory header fields from the CAM security profile. Privacy issues resulting from such fields are more severe than those from optional ones, as these can be simply skipped in practical implementations. In contrast, to fix issues regarding mandatory fields the standard has to be changed. Furthermore, [23] suggests to remove the possible inclusion of optional fields. We support this proposal, as differing combinations of data sets in the envelope by different implementations clearly give an attacker a possibility to easily distinguish vehicles independently from their pseudonyms.

The following sections discuss the different header fields' privacy implications in detail.

Protocol Version. The used protocol version will be constant for all vehicles at the beginning of the deployment phase. However, over time it is very likely that multiple versions will be present in VANETs. As this value is constant for an individual vehicle over a long time, it is clearly volatile constant data. Thus, the presence of many different versions should be avoided even if they are otherwise compatible.

Signer Info. The signer information of a message may hold different contents. Thus the available information for the attacker differs. However, one can always uniquely determine the signer (and sender) of the message. Therefore, this is often called the pseudonym ID of the sender. In both CAMs and BSMs the field's content can either be the hash of the used pseudonym certificate (PSC) or the full certificate [3,9]. Both systems use cyclic inclusion of the full certificate every 0.5 or 1 second, respectively. In case of security profiles *DENM* and *Generic* the full certificate is always present [9].

In case of an included PSC within the security envelope the following data is available to the receiver [3,9].

Signer Info of Pseudonym Certificates. A signer info field in a PSC identifies its signer, which is an authorization authority (AA). This can be done either by a hash digest or by the full AA certificate (AAC). Both uniquely identify the AA. Current standards allow for a possible multitude of such entities to exist. In practice this will be probably done by the car manufacturers (OEMs). However, this leads to a privacy issue as the signer information is volatile constant data. An attacker can directly determine the OEM and use this to distinguish PSCs and thereby vehicles. PSCs signed by different AAs are very unlikely to be used by the same vehicle and a vehicle will very likely use only PSCs issued by the same AA. Clearly, vehicles of low volume OEMs will be particularly vulnerable.

To limit the usability of the AA's identity for an attacker one can think of mainly two countermeasures. Firstly, one could increase the number of AA certificates and make a single AA use a multitude of them. Thereby, the effort for an attacker to keep track of all certificates would increase. However, this would significantly increase the effort for AA certificate distribution to all ITS-S for a small security gain.

Secondly, one could limit the number of AAs. An ideal choice would be to have only one AA. This would clearly resolve the above described privacy issue completely, as an attacker cannot distinguish vehicles based on their used AA anymore. To implement this, OEMs would have to cooperate and use a common AA. As they plan to establish a common root certificate authority (CA) for Europe, this seems to be a usable approach. In order to limit the number of PSCs signed by a single AA certificate, one could significantly limit its lifetime. New ones can be deployed together with PSC updates.

Additionally, one should coordinate the lifetime of an AA's certificate with the lifetime of its issued PSCs. Thereby, any possibility to distinguish PSCs based on their signing AA should be ruled out. Moreover, the number of AA certificates to be stored securely inside the vehicles is kept (very) low.

The privacy gain from using a single AA is evaluated in Sect. 5.2 in more detail.

Validity Restriction. The mandatory validity restriction of PSCs is a limited validity period. It is determined by a start and end time stamp. Both are used with an accuracy of one second. The PSC distribution scheme described in [3] and [1] defines that PSCs are delivered from an AA to an ITS-S upon request of the ITS-S. The remaining details are implementation specific, as they are not covered by the standard. However, a possible pitfall for privacy of pseudonym users exists which is caused by the mentioned time stamps.

This pseudonym usage privacy issue arises from the planned way of (re-)using PSCs in Europe. Thereby, each vehicle uses a pool of PSCs which are (re-)used until the full pool gets updated [11, 28]. The update period will probably be in the order of months.

A different approach is described in [20] for WAVE in the USA. Thereby, each PSC is only used once and the validity period is the order of minutes. However, this approach is not favored by manufacturers and maintainers of ITS-Ss, as it introduces significant overhead in the ITS system for PCS distribution. Either vehicles require frequent, reliable connections to the AA (or pseudonym certificate authority (PCA) [20]) or a huge buffer filled with PSCs for future use. Even if the initially proposed validity period of five minutes gets doubled, this would still require a maximum amount of 144 PSCs per day. To protect the buffered PSCs, these have to be stored in secure memory, e.g., inside a Hardware Security Module (HSM). However, adding more memory to an HSM significantly increases its price. Moreover, many issued PSCs will stay unused as their validity period elapses while the vehicle is not in use. One would have to know the usage times of each vehicle in advance to avoid that, which is hardly practicable. Thus, the approach from [20], while providing good privacy, probably bears too much overhead for large scale deployment.

An alternative approach for securing re-usage of PSCs is discussed in the following.

There are mainly two approaches for PSC generation inside the AA. Either the AA generates the PSCs upon request or the AA keeps track of the expiration of its users' PSCs to generate new ones in advance. In both cases a straight forward implementation would take the same time stamp (e.g., the current time at the AA) and use it as the common start validity time stamp of the signed PSCs. However, this means that all PSCs of a set delivered to an ITS-S have a very similar (or even the same) start validity time stamp. Thereby, making this information volatile constant data. Furthermore, this time stamp will be different with a very high probability for most cars as there is no timed synchronization of PSC requests.

The PSC users have no possibility to protect themselves against an attacker using validity time stamps for tracking them, as they cannot change the content of a PSC without invalidating its signature. Therefore, countermeasures have to be taken within AAs.

A straight forward solution would be to discretized the time stamps defining the validity period of PSCs. For example, all PSCs issued in one month could receive the start of this month as their start validity time stamp. The longer the discretization steps, the more vehicles will receive a set of PSCs with the same validity period. Consequently, the probability that multiple vehicles with common values in these data fields meet on the street increases removing the possibility to distinguish them.

Subject Attribute. The subject attribute field holds the subject type and public key of the PSC. This key is randomly generated and the subject type is fixed for all PSCs. Thus, there is no possibility to link PSCs based on this data set.

Subject Info. The subject info field holds a fixed value for all PSCs. Thus, it provides no possibility to track vehicles.

Generation Time. The generation time is individual for each message. However, the time difference between two sequential messages is clearly defined by the standard. Neither ETSI ITS nor WAVE define any change to the sending interval before or after a pseudonym change.

A common assumption is that clocks of ITS-S are well synchronized using GPS [29]. Thus, time intervals between message generation of individual cars should be quite stable. Additionally, inside a group of cars the generation times of messages should be randomly distributed leading to an even distribution of used time stamps. These time stamps are generated and transmitted with microsecond resolution [9]. Hence, collisions in this data field which could confuse an attacker are unlikely. Thus, an attacker can track vehicles just based on the generation time of their messages with high probability.

In case of BSMs the sending interval is fixed. For CAMs, it is determined by multiple parameters and can be in the range from 1 to 10 Hz. However, the current interval can be found in the transmitted CAM itself [7]. This allows the attacker to easily use this information to avoid being confused by the variable sending interval of CAMs.

Furthermore, the time step is set at the network layer. Hence, tracking capabilities of the attacker are not limited by the lower layer channel access mechanism. For example, the actual sending time being somehow randomized by the probabilistic lower layer CSMA-CA scheme, used within ITS-G5 and IEEE 802.11p, does not confuse the attacker.

We propose two solutions to overcome the described vulnerability. Both require the cooperating vehicles to use the same sending frequency before and after the pseudonym change for a minimum time span, e.g., one second. Firstly, one could reduce the accuracy of the generation time to the maximum transmission interval being 100 ms for BSMs and 1 s for CAMs. The security entity does not need to determine the sequence of received messages according to standards. Moreover, the validity time spans of PSCs are also given with full second resolution. Therefore, currently there is no need to use a high precision time stamp for the generation time of type *Time64* and it should be substituted by the lower resolution *Time32* type. A side effect would be a reduction in the size of the security envelope by four bytes [9].

For the second solution, immediately after the pseudonym change the next sending must be delayed by a random waiting time. The true random number generator required for ECDSA signatures could be used to obtain it.

The length of the random waiting time should be in the order of the normal time difference between two successive transmissions. For example, for BSMs it would be between zero and 100 ms. Consequently, the attacker cannot determine the next generation time and gets confused. The impact on higher level layers, e.g., applications, should be low. From their perspective a maximum delay looks just like one missed message from the other vehicle.

ITS Application Identifier. The content of the ITS Application Identifier (AID) field identifies target application as well as message type (e.g., CAM) and thereby also the security profile used for the given message. In case all vehicles monitored by an attacker only send the same type of message, e.g., CAMs, he cannot discriminate the sender based on this data. However, future extensions of VANET communication may lead to a multitude of different messages sent by ITS-Ss. In case these send differing sets of messages, e.g., due to differing available applications, an attacker can distinguish them and this information is volatile constant data.

A receiving ITS-S should use the ITS AID value to check whether the sender's PSC allows to sign this particular type of message. However, the security gain of this mechanism is very low. The reason for this is that the security entity cannot check if the real payload really corresponds to the received ITS AID value. Thus, an attacker who can assemble an arbitrary message can put unauthorized content, e.g., a DENM inside the network layer payload. Then, he can have it signed with the CAM security profile by the security entity with a PSC being only valid for CAMs. Thereby, the receiver's security entity will accept the incoming message as being properly signed.

Instead, the attack has to be detected at the application or facility layer. The receiving entities at these layers have to determine the actual ITS AID of the received message and need to check whether the sender's certificate holds the required privileges.

Furthermore, the attacker is not required to have direct control over the PSC to carry out the above described attack. It is sufficient to have control over the interface to the security entity, as it has no possibility to check the content of the payload it wraps into the security envelope. Thus, we consider the security gain of the presence of the ITS AID field as neglectable.

Moreover, the security entity does not need to distinguish different message types sharing the same security profile. Therefore, the ITS AID field should be removed from the security envelope, as it only adds overhead to it. Instead, one should limit the contained information to the used security profile, as done in the preceeding standard version [5].

Certificate Request List. An ITS-S requests up to six unknown certificates (PSCs or AACs) by using the least three bytes of their hash values. Standards are unclear about when to remove entries from the request list [3,9]. It should be flushed after a pseudonym change, as the current state of certificates required by an ITS-S can be expected to be highly discriminative between ITS-Ss.

Trailer Field. There is only one type of trailer field in the standards. It holds metadata for interpreting the digital signature as well as the signature itself. Most parts of the trailer are fixed and the signature of multiple messages can only be linked together with the help of the respective public key. Therefore, the signature does not carry any additional privacy related information compared to the public key in the corresponding PSC (see Sect. 3.1 above).

Moreover, the encoding of the used ECC (elliptic curve cryptography) point may vary in general, but is probably constant for a particular vehicle. There are four options for the ECC point type field in the standard, with the core difference being enabled or disabled ECC point compression. With both choices used, this information is volatile constant data. In the worst case, with only two cars in a group and both using a different ECC point type, this information is already enough to render any pseudonym change useless. Thus, the standard should only allow only one option to be used. For other reasons to do so see [23].

3.2   Data from Access and Network Layer

The identifiers of the access layer (i.e., MAC address) and the network layer (so called GeoNetworking address) are coupled to the hash value of the currently used PSC. Thus, their impact on privacy is the same as outlined in Sect. 3.1 for the signer identifier field inside the security envelope.

3.3   Data from Facility Layer

The CAM is defined as a deeply nested data structure holding mandatory and optional data sets [8]. Thereby, an *ItsPduHeader* and a *CoopAwareness* field are present on the top level. The simple *ItsPduHeader* only holds basic information like the protocol version, message id and station id. These fields hold the same information as their respective counterparts in the security envelope. Therefore, their impact on privacy aspects is the same as for those data sets already described in Sect. 3.1.

The *CoopAwareness* field has two parts being the current generation interval (usable by an attacker as described in Sect. 3.1) and the *CamParameters* field consisting of several different so called containers (i.e. dedicated data sets). These are described in detail in the following.

Basic Container. The always present basic container holds the components station type and reference position.

Station Type. The station type associates the vehicle to some generic class, e.g., passenger car or light truck. This unchanging information is clearly volatile constant data.

Reference Position. The current position of the ITS-S measured at the vehicle's reference point (see [4]) is available in each CAM. Prior work already showed that this information can be used to bypass simple pseudonym changes [17,29]. Therefore, the advanced pseudonym switching strategies suggested in these references should be used.

High Frequency Container. The high frequency container is part of every CAM. In case of an ITS-S being a vehicle the only used sub-part is a basic vehicle container. Parameters of the vehicle's current movement are given in this data set. These include heading, speed and driving direction. All these values can be used for advanced vehicle tracking [17,29]. However, the remaining data inside this container has not been regarded in prior work.

Dimensions. The vehicle's dimensions length and width are given. According to [7] the resolution is set to 0.1 m. This value stays constant during one journey of a vehicle and thus it has to be regarded as volatile constant data. It is possible that the length of a vehicle changes from one journey to another, e.g., by extending it with a trailer. However, this is rare in practice especially for passenger cars.

To evaluate privacy aspects of broadcasting a vehicle's dimensions, we determined the number of different currently sold vehicle models in Germany. Then, we assigned them to the individual discretization steps of vehicle length and width. We took publicly available data from the German Kraftfahrt-Bundesamt [21] to obtain the share of different vehicle types, separated into OEMs and their models, on the overall traffic in Germany caused by new cars. Foreign cars traveling on German roads are excluded from this data set. However, it should still give a reasonable estimate about the distribution of models' dimensions. Moreover, we used public information from the 45 different OEMs present in [21] to obtain the individual dimensions of models.

We find that 73 % of all vehicle models share a common combination of width and length with at least one other model. These cars have a market share of 75 %. Thus, for a share of 25 % one can determine the model directly given its discretized dimensions. Even the most populated set of vehicles with length 4.3 m and width 2.0 m includes only 17 % of all cars.

Thus, distribution of vehicle dimensions clearly decreases the probability to find proper (i.e., indistinguishable) partners for a cooperative pseudonym change. Further discretization of the values to, e.g., 0.3 m would significantly improve the situation for many vehicles but can still not help the ones with outstanding dimensions and/or low penetration rates.

Dynamics. The parameters longitudinal acceleration, curvature (consists of curvature value and confidence), curvature calculation mode and yaw rate are included in the high frequency container. Thereby, the curvature calculation mode is again a value which is unlikely to change for an individual vehicle and may differ for different vehicles. Therefore, it should be regarded as volatile constant data.

The remaining values model a vehicle's trajectory. Many approaches for modeling and predicting such trajectories exists, e.g., [10,19]. In case of pure tracking, i.e., no realtime interaction between attacker and vehicles, the attacker does not need to process the information in realtime. Thus, he can use computationally expensive but accurate and complex movement models. As we have seen above, the attacker can determine either the vehicle type directly or a group of possible vehicle types. This information can be used to tune the parameters of a movement model making it very accurate. Moreover, the prediction must only work well for a short time span as the CAM generation rate is at most one second.

To evaluate the impact of using an advanced movement model on the attackers ability to track vehicles one should use data obtained from real test drives instead of pure simulator output. This is because simulators like the well known SUMO use a predefined vehicle model. Therefore, tracking these simulated vehicles with a model which fits the one used to generate their movement will probably yield unrealistically high success rates. Further analysis of this issue is beyond the scope of this work and is a subject to future work.

Optional Data. Six more data sets may be optionally present in the container. Three of them (steering wheel angle, lateral, vertical acceleration) can be used to improve the movement model described above.

The remaining three values (acceleration control, lane position, performance class) each describe a vehicle's feature. These can be expected to change quite slowly, i.e., they should be regarded as volatile constant data. As all these fields are optional and can be added or removed individually, also the combination of sent data sets may differ between vehicles. Thus, usage of each extra value will increase the change that a particular vehicle uses a unique set of data inside its current vicinity. Thereby, it will strip itself from finding proper partners for a secure pseudonym change.

Optional Containers. In addition to the basic and high frequency container, the low frequency container is distributed cyclically, but not in every single CAM. It contains the vehicle role, exterior lights and path history fields. See [8] for details about inclusion rules.

In case of an uncommon vehicle role, e.g., rescue vehicle, the corresponding additional container is present in the CAM. The density of such vehicles in ordinary traffic is usually low. Thus, an attacker can easily track them just based on the presence of their dedicated containers in their CAMs.

Typically, the status of exterior lights changes slowly. Thus, this data set is volatile constant data.

The path history field should obviously be erased when a pseudonym change occurs or the inclusion rate of the container has to be such low that sequentially sent values of this field cannot be linked. Otherwise the attacker can simply link the pseudonyms based on this data. However, the current standards do not specify such behavior, but it is recommended in [6].

4   Vehicle Uniqueness

Secure pseudonym switching schemes from prior work are based on the assumption that broadcast data cannot be mapped to an individual vehicle except of the changed identifiers. We have shown in Sect. 3 that this is clearly not the case due to the presence of volatile constant data. To evaluate the impact of our findings on vehicle privacy we introduce the metric of *vehicle uniqueness (VU)*. It measures how much a particular vehicle differs from its vehicular environment regarding data observable by an attacker.

Prior work showed that tracking of vehicles becomes more difficult along-side with higher traffic density and longer distances traveled during a cooperative pseudonym switching maneuver [28]. However, this only holds in case the attacker has no extra information for re-identification of vehicles after a pseudonym change. VU is a metric for the availability of such extra information. In case a vehicle is unique inside the area of pseudonym switching the attacker can always track it, independently of the used pseudonym switching algorithm.

To calculate VU an exposed feature vector e_i holding all available volatile constant data is assigned to each vehicle. Thereby, $i \in \boldsymbol{I}$ relates to a particular vehicle within a group of vehicles $\boldsymbol{I}$ ($|\boldsymbol{I}| \geq 1$) cooperating during a pseudonym change. VU is defined by

$$VU = \mathbf{Pr}\{|\{x|e_x = e_y; x \neq y; x, y \in \boldsymbol{I}\}| = 0\}.$$

This means that $VU \in [0; 1]$ is the probability that there is just one car within $\boldsymbol{I}$ having one particular exposed feature vector. Such vehicles are indistinguishable for an attacker in regard to volatile constant data. Thus, these vehicles are proper candidates for performing a cooperative pseudonym change.

In the following, we take three different pseudonym switching schemes into regard. These are

1. uncoordinated pseudonym switching (ETSI ITS and WAVE) with $|\boldsymbol{I}| = 1$ with high probability,
2. mix zones with $|\boldsymbol{I}|$ depending on traffic flow and size of the mix zone and
3. silent periods with $|\boldsymbol{I}|$ depending on traffic flow and length of silent periods.

Within current standards pseudonym changes are uncoordinated, as every ITS-S decides on its own when to perform the change without including information from other ITS-Ss in its decision process. Results of an evaluation using the proposed VU metric are given in Sect. 5.

5 Evaluation

In the following we take three different system parametrizations into consideration. At first, a system using a multitude of AAs is studied. This resembles the currently planed way of realizing VANETs based on ETSI ITS and WAVE. Secondly, the approach from Sect. 3.1 for usage of a single AA is studied to show its significant improvement potential on privacy of ITS-Ss. Afterwards, privacy impact of further discretization of vehicle dimensions as suggested in Sect. 3.3 is studied. Lastly, a summary about results achieved in the given evaluation is provided in Sect. 5.4.

5.1 Multiple Authorization Authorities

In this section we include the following data into e_i:

- AA of PSCs, we assume one AA per OEM and
- Vehicle dimensions (see Sect. 3.3).

We assume that all cars from the same OEM use the same encoding of ECC points (see Sect. 3.1). Thus, this data does not influence VU in our case and is not regarded further. The rest of the volatile constant data sets from Sect. 3 are assumed to be identical for all cars. This leads to a best case assumption for privacy of vehicles, i.e., a worst case assumption for the attacker. Moreover, we assume that the probability of two cars within I sharing a common value of e_i ($|e_i| = 3$) only depends on the share of their particular model within the set of all vehicles.

We use the vehicle distribution from [21] to estimate VU. Moreover, an analysis of vehicle dimensions for the models of different OEMs (see also Sect. 3.3) shows that the data included in e_i allows to uniquely identify the model of a vehicle, e.g., as VW Golf VII, from a single CAM including the PSC. Thus, one can calculate the probability to encounter a vehicle with a particular e_i from the mentioned vehicle distribution data set.

The number of vehicles encountered during a pseudonym switching maneuver $|I|$ is varied by varying the traffic flow (given in $\frac{vehicles}{kilometer}$) and size of mix zones or length of silent periods, respectively. The traffic density is varied from 16 to 45 $\frac{vehicles}{kilometer}$ per lane following [17] to represent low volume traffic as well as a jammed setup. We use the parameter set from [28] for the size of mix zones (25 m – 400 m), length of silent periods (1250 ms –20 s) and velocity range (0 – 250 $\frac{km}{h}$). The obtained results are given in Fig. 1.

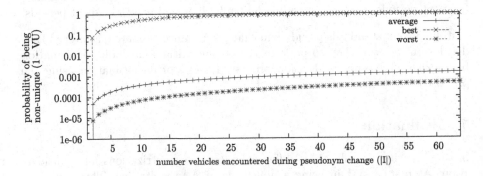

Fig. 1. Vehicle uniqueness during pseudonym change with $|e_i| = 3$.

Thereby, the *best* case relates to the most common car model. It is obviously the least unique one within the set of all vehicles. However, only about 7.7 % of all vehicles can profit from the good results for this model having a high chance to find indistinguishable partners for a cooperative pseudonym change. Moreover, the *worst* case relates to the least common car.

One can see from Fig. 1 that the value of $1 - VU$ increases alongside with $|\boldsymbol{I}|$. However, for an *average* vehicle it is very low for all regarded values of $|\boldsymbol{I}|$. However, combinations of high velocity and high traffic flow, leading to high values of $|\boldsymbol{I}|$, rarely occur in practice. Thus, VU will exceed 99.9 % in most real world scenarios with moderate traffic flow.

This means that the attacker can track those ITS-Ss even after a performed PSC change with more than 99.9 % probability. In combination with other techniques from prior work, such as trajectory based tracking, hardly any privacy of vehicles can be expected to remain.

Higher values of $|\boldsymbol{I}|$ than the ones used above would relate to unrealistically high traffic flow or extending the size of mix zones and length of silent periods to values rendering higher level ITS-applications unusable [28]. One should note that, even medium size mix zones have been shown to lead to significant performance degradation of VANET based driver assistance systems [22]. Calculation of VU is independent of the pseudonym switching strategy, but the achievable size of $|\boldsymbol{I}|$ differs. While cooperative PSC switching strategies can adjust it, uncoordinated ones, e.g., from ETSI ITS or WAVE, cannot do so.

The obtained data on vehicle uniqueness shows that the presence of volatile constant data is able to render PSC changes during driving almost useless. An attacker can almost always re-identify vehicles based on this data after the pseudonym change.

5.2   Common Authorization Authority

In order to reduce vehicle uniqueness the usage of a single AA for all ITS-Ss, as proposed in Sect. 3.1, is considered in the following. Thus, in contrast to Sect. 5.1 the exposed feature vector $\boldsymbol{e}_i$ only holds vehicle dimensions, i.e., $|\boldsymbol{e}_i| = 2$. The AA identity is no longer present in $\boldsymbol{e}_i$ as it is identical for all ITS-Ss.

The same vehicle distributions and traffic scenarios as in Sect. 5.1 are used for evaluating the proposed privacy improvement technique. Thereby, well comparability of both systems is ensured.

Obtained results for the system using $|\boldsymbol{e}_i| = 2$ are given in Fig. 2.

Comparing the results from Fig. 2 to the ones from Fig. 1, one can see that using a single AA reduces vehicle uniqueness (increasing $1 - VU$) by a factor of about 8. Thus, privacy of ITS-Ss is increased. The values for the least common vehicle are unchanged. However, for the most common and average vehicle an improvement of privacy is achieved, although uniqueness of an average vehicle is still quite small. The most common group of indistinguishable vehicle contains about 17.0 % of all vehicles.

5.3   Further Discretization of Vehicle Dimensions and Common Authorization Authority

A further mechanism to reduce vehicle uniqueness is to reduce the accuracy of vehicle dimensions included in CAMs, as suggested in Sect. 3.3. To evaluate its

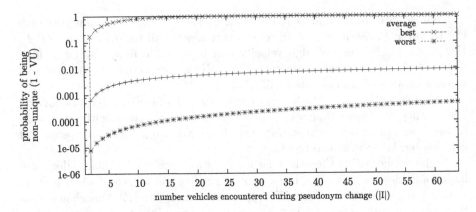

Fig. 2. Vehicle uniqueness during pseudonym change with $|e_i| = 2$ and standardized vehicle dimension's accuracy.

impact the setup described in Sect. 5.2 is used. Additionally, resolution of vehicle dimensions length and width are further discretized to resolutions of 0.2 m and 0.5 m. With decreasing resolution the data quality available for applications is lowered. However, no detailed requirements regarding this parameter set have been published so far. Thus, future work is required to obtain a tradeoff between privacy and application requirements.

Obtained results for the system using $|e_i| = 2$ together with lowered accuracy of vehicle dimensions are given in Fig. 3.

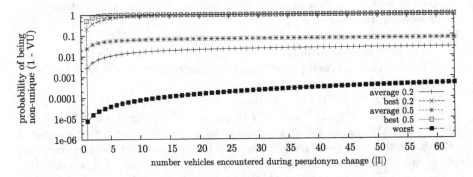

Fig. 3. Vehicle uniqueness during pseudonym change with $|e_i| = 2$ and lowered vehicle dimension's accuracy.

One can see from the comparison of Figs. 2 and 3 that lowering the resolution of vehicle dimensions, as given in CAMs, significantly decreases vehicle uniqueness. Thus, privacy of vehicles is well increased. The most common group of vehicles holds about 20.8 % and 50.8 % of all vehicles for resolutions of 0.2 m and 0.5 m, respectively.

Usage of lowered vehicle dimension's resolution without a common AA would be possible. However, we find that the increase in vehicle privacy is quite low even when using a 0.5 m resolution. The reason for this is that, within the fleet of a single vehicle manufacturer, there is a far smaller set of vehicles with whom a vehicle can be identical regarding its dimensions in comparison to the set of all vehicles from all manufacturers. Thus, we do not recommend to use only the discretization approach.

5.4 Summary of Evaluation

The obtained results show that, even without other tracking mechanisms, an attacker can track a vehicle with high probability using just a small set of constant volatile data, even though the vehicle performed a pseudonym change. This shows that the presence of volatile constant data is able to render PSC changes useless, as an attacker can re-identify vehicles using this data after the pseudonym change. Combining this attack with further tracking mechanisms, e.g., from [28], promises to achieve even higher tracking probabilities. Thus, the mechanisms for avoiding volatile constant data in VANET messages suggested in Sect. 3 should be used to limit the trackability of vehicles.

6 Conclusion and Future Work

With upcoming deployment privacy aspects of VANETs have gained increased attention, especially in Europe. Therefore, we studied the influence of information currently present in ETSI ITS and WAVE standard messages on various protocol layers on proposed privacy protecting pseudonym usage strategies.

We find that the main requirement of pseudonym change strategies, the cooperation of multiple indistinguishable vehicles, is unlikely to be found in practice with current standards being in use. This is caused by massive presence of individualizing content, which we call volatile constant data, within current VANET messages. It can be used by an attacker to easily distinguish vehicles independently of changing vehicle identities. Multiple suggestions have been made to improve this situation, which require to adjust corresponding standards within ETSI ITS and WAVE frameworks.

A metric called vehicle uniqueness is introduced to measure the chance of a vehicle to find proper cooperation partners for a secure, i.e., privacy ensuring, pseudonym change. Our evaluation shows that the currently standardized uncoordinated pseudonym switching yields very low probabilities for secure pseudonym changes. Limiting the amount of volatile constant data significantly increases the level of vehicular privacy within VANETs by decreasing vehicle uniqueness.

Future work can study the influence of the suggested privacy enhancement mechanisms on VANET applications, e.g., driver assistance systems. Such systems will probably need adjusted parameters to work based on more discretized, i.e. less accurate, input data sets.

References

1. Intelligent Transport Systems (ITS); Security; Security Services and Architecture, v1.1.1, September 2010
2. Memorandum of Understanding for OEMs within the CAR 2 CAR Communication Consortium on Deployment Strategy for cooperative ITS in Europe, v 4.0102, June 2011
3. IEEE Standard for Wireless Access in Vehicular Environments - Security Services for Applications and Management Messages, 1609.2-2013, April 2013
4. Intelligent Transport Systems (ITS); Facilities layer function; Facility Position and time management, v0.0.2 (2013)
5. Intelligent Transport Systems (ITS); Security; Security header and certificate formats, v1.1.1, April 2013
6. C2C-CC Basic System Standards Profile, January 2014
7. Intelligent Transport Systems (ITS); Users and applications requirements; Part 2: Applications and facilities layer common data dictionary, v1.2.1, September 2014
8. Intelligent Transport Systems (ITS); Vehicular Communications; Basic Set of Applications; Part 2: Specification of Cooperative Awareness Basic Service, v1.3.2, November 2014
9. Intelligent Transport Systems (ITS); Security; Security header and certificate formats, v1.2.1, June 2015
10. Ammoun, S., Nashashibi, F.: Real time trajectory prediction for collision risk estimation between vehicles. In: IEEE 5th International Conference on Intelligent Computer Communication and Processing (2009)
11. Bissmeyer, N., Stubing, H., Schoch, E., Gotz, S., Stotz, J.P., Lonc, B.: A generic public key infrastructure for securing car-to-X communication. In: 18th ITS World Congress (2011)
12. Bittl, S., Gonzalez, A.A.: Privacy issues and pitfalls in VANET standards. In: 1st International Conference on Vehicular Intelligent Transport Systems, pp. 144–151, May 2015
13. Bittl, S., Gonzalez, A.A., Heidrich, W.: Performance comparision of encoding schemes for ETSI ITS C2X communication systems. In: Third International Conference on Advances in Vehicular Systems, Technologies and Applications, pp. 58–63, June 2014
14. Burmester, M., Magkos, E., Chrissikopoulos, V.: Strengthening privacy protection in vanets. In: Proceedings of 8th IEEE International Conference on Wireless and Mobile Computing, Networking and Communications, pp. 508–513 (2008)
15. Buttyan, L., Holczer, T., Weimerskirch, A., Whyte, W.: Slow: a practical pseudonym changing scheme for location privacy in VANETs. In: IEEE Vehicular Networking Conference, pp. 1–8, October 2009
16. Eichler, S.: Strategies for pseudonym changes in vehicular Ad hoc networks depending on node mobility. In: IEEE Intelligent Vehicles Symposium, June 2007
17. Gerlach, M., Güttler, F.: Privacy in VANETs using changing pseudonyms - ideal and real. In: 65th IEEE Vehicular Technology Conference, pp. 2521–2525, April 2007
18. Hoh, B., Gruteser, M., Xiong, H., Alrabady, A.: Achieving guaranteed anonymity in gps traces via uncertainty-aware path cloaking. IEEE Trans. Mob. Comput. 9(8), 1089–1107 (2010)
19. Houenou, A., Bonnifait, P., Cherfaoui, V., Yao, W.: Vehicle trajectory prediction based on motion model and maneuver recognition. In: IEEE International Conference on Intelligent Robots and Systems, pp. 4363–4369, November 2013

20. Harding, J., et al.: Vehicle-to-vehicle communications: readiness of V2V technology for application. Technical report DOT HS 812 014, Washington, DC: National Highway Traffic Safety Administration, August 2014

21. Kraftfahrt-Bundesamt: Neuzulassungen von Personenkraftwagen im August 2014 nach Marken und Modellreihen (2014). http://www.kba.de/DE/Statistik/Fahrzeuge/Neuzulassungen/MonatlicheNeuzulassungen/monatl_neuzulassungen_n ode.html

22. Lefévre, S., Petit, J., Bajcsy, R., Laugier, C., Kargl, F.: Impact of V2X privacy strategies on intersection collision avoidance systems. In: IEEE Vehicular Networking Conference, pp. 71–78, December 2013

23. Nowdehi, N., Olovsson, T.: Experiences from implementing the ETSI ITS securedmessage service. In: IEEE Intelligent Vehicles Symposium, pp. 1055–1060 (2014)

24. Petit, J., Schaub, F., Feiri, M., Kargl, F.: Pseudonym schemes in vehicular networks: a survey. IEEE Commun. Surv. Tutorials 17(1), 228–255 (2015)

25. Scheuer, F., Plößl, K., Federrath, H.: Preventing profile generation in vehicular networks. In: IEEE WiMob, pp. 520–525 (2008)

26. Schütze, T.: Automotive security: cryptography for Car2X communication. In: Embedded World Conference, pp. 1–16, March 2011

27. Stübing, H.: Multilayered Security and Privacy Protection in Car-to-X Networks, 1st edn. Springer, Wiesbaden (2013)

28. Tomandl, A., Scheuer, F., Federrath, H.: Simulation-based evaluation of techniques for privacy protection in VANETs. In: IEEE 8th International Conference on Wireless and Mobile Computing, Networking and Communications, pp. 165–172 (2012)

29. Wiedersheim, B., Ma, Z., Kargl, F., Papadimitratos, P.: Privacy in inter-vehicular networks: why simple pseudonym change is not enough. In: Seventh International Conference on Wireless On-demand Network Systems and Services, pp. 176–183, February 2010

Author Index

Printed in the United States
By Bookmasters